The War on Poverty

The War on Poverty

A Retrospective

Edited by Kyle Farmbry

LEXINGTON BOOKS
Lanham • Boulder • New York • London

Published by Lexington Books
An imprint of The Rowman & Littlefield Publishing Group, Inc.
4501 Forbes Boulevard, Suite 200, Lanham, Maryland 20706
www.rowman.com

16 Carlisle Street, London W1D 3BT, United Kingdom

British Library Cataloguing in Publication Information Available

Library of Congress Cataloging-in-Publication Data

The war on poverty : a retrospective / edited by Kyle Farmbry.
pages cm.
Includes bibliographical references and index.
ISBN 978-0-7391-9078-4 (cloth : alk. paper) — ISBN 978-0-7391-9079-1 (electronic)
1. Poverty—United States. 2. Poverty—Government policy—United States--History. 3. Poor—United States—History. 4. Economic assistance, Domestic—United States. 5. Public welfare—United States. I. Farmbry, Kyle, 1970–
HC110.P63W373 2014
362.5'560973—dc23
2014020215

∞ ™ The paper used in this publication meets the minimum requirements of American National Standard for Information Sciences Permanence of Paper for Printed Library Materials, ANSI/NISO Z39.48-1992.

Printed in the United States of America

Contents

Preface

In December of 1984, several of my friends and I organized a fundraiser for poverty alleviation. The impetus that led to our project was a famine that at the time was impacting the Horn of Africa. Images we viewed on the nightly news, aired from thousands of miles away, consisted of children with bloated stomachs, flies buzzing around them, and countless tears from parents who had witnessed their children pass away from what were diseases and conditions of poverty. For some of us discussing the images during our ninth grade social studies classes, the unfairness of the world's conditions seemed striking. "It was," as one of our teachers reminded us, "the luck of birth" that permitted us learn about such conditions on television, versus having to learn about them by living them. As some of us attempted to make sense of the dual realities—the comforts of our home environments versus the extreme poverty we saw each night—we decided to do what we could, albeit in our own small way, about the situations others faced.

In hindsight, if measured in terms of dollars raised, our resulting fundraising effort made little direct impact. However, if measured by our awakening to the disparity in conditions that can exist between people, then I think the impact may have been a bit more substantial. In time, some of my immediate peers and others of my generation were drawn to other civic initiatives that aimed to address issues of poverty and inequality in the United States and abroad. In some cases, we volunteered our time for various nonprofits working on issues of education, health, or areas where social inequities were important components of the broader situation. Some people ended up organizing local grassroots efforts addressing various social issues, and in the long term making social advocacy the core of their careers. Some joined the Peace Corps, others advocated for what became AmeriCorps. Ultimately, many found ways to integrate service and advocacy at the local, national, or international levels into our careers.

Twenty years prior to what for me, and I believe many of my generational peers, were triggering images that developed our interests in issues of poverty and inequality, much of the nation was also introduced to its own generational images of poverty. This time, the images for those coming of age in the 1960s were frequently cast from rural communities in Appalachia, the poverty-stricken areas of the nation's cities, and southern communities disproportionately impacted by years of segregation. For some, lived disparities that were part of a nation that was just in the early stages of wrestling with post *Brown v. Board* notions of equality shaped their passions for social justice. For others their youthful idealism was shaken by their own unique awakenings to the fact that not everyone in this nation shared the comforts that many had been told was the norm of American society. The presidents of this generation, John Kennedy and Lyndon Johnson, committed in their own ways to work on the issues of economic and social inequality. For Kennedy, it was largely through a call to service. For Johnson, it was through a declaration of a war on poverty.

Now, three decades after sitting in my mid-1980s high school classroom and five decades after the foot soldiers of the War on Poverty embarked to work in many of the nation's most economically marginalized communities, my undergraduate and graduate students and I discuss the domestic and international inequities noted in today's headlines. I often find myself drawn to some of the same questions I considered two decades ago. Why does poverty exist in the United States and abroad? How can we make sense of our various inequities? What can be done about the issues of social and economic marginalization that serve as foundations for so many of our other challenges? My students and I know, as do many veterans of the anti-poverty efforts of the 1960s, that the answers to these questions are not so easy.

This book explores questions of poverty. The authors are people who study issues of inequality and social justice, as well as being engaged as practitioners trying to address these issues. The task I placed before the authors was to identify an issue in the broad poverty discourse and write about it. I hope now, as I did when I started this project, that a blend of voices, perspectives, and areas of expertise around poverty might lead to conversation that will help find a solution to challenges facing people in our most economically marginalized communities.

Several years ago, I came to realize that writing a book is a process that can be extremely taxing on the people around the author. My experiences with this project have taught me that for people around editors of books, the process can be taxing as well. Now, as I come out of the isolation that this project has required, I owe several people my gratitude. In my case, my appreciation begins with my parents, Deidre and Larry Farmbry. As two people who had a child at very young ages, I recognize that it is their sense of purpose and their strength that helped me avoid many challenges that I otherwise would have encountered. Stacie Reis, despite our meeting well into my work on this project, provided tremendous support and encouragement, which helped me to get through the completion of this book. Thank you for your patience.

Numerous people worked behind the scenes to bring this effort to completion. Al Passarella, Rosie Uyola, Portia Allen-Kyle, and Joanna Maulbeck jumped into the project with an incredible amount of enthusiasm. Graduate students Mariam Rashid, Catherine Mwai, Chris Primiano, Mateus Baptista, Erica Tom, and Apoorva Chandra assisted with research. Christen Madrazo and Garnet Henderson took red pens to paper and helped provide all of the authors critical editorial feedback.

My colleagues in the Graduate School at Rutgers–Newark, Adriana Afonso, Sandy Reyes, Chengbo Yin, and Diane Filippone, helped ensure that my schedule permitted my being able to work on completing this project. They were extremely patient with closed doors and my days working out of the office, and they found numerous ways to protect much of my time.

Various friends helped in their own ways to ensure that I kept some sort of balance while working on various stages of this book. I particularly want to thank Steve Levy, Daryl Nann, Termeh Rassi, Lisa Lin, Dawson Tyson, Priscilla Monico, Danny Maurin, Mike and Heather Libonati, Abigail Moore, and Malcolm Hoover.

Finally, I want to thank the authors of the various chapters. They dealt with my constant e-mails, calls, and cajoling. Among those who are the practitioners, I know there was some discomfort, as the writing stretched you from the one-page memos or policy briefs that comprise much of your daily writing. Among the academics, I know I challenged some of the assumptions that had been reinforced by dissertation committees, students, colleagues, and others within circles that at times provide safe places to develop ideas. For both sets of writers, I hope the final product proves to be worth any pressure I may have placed on you. More importantly, I hope that our writing can make an impact for others.

Introduction

The War on Poverty—Some Initial Thoughts

Kyle Farmbry

Much of the political process in this nation is grounded in framing discourse to develop and advance social initiatives. The rhetorical tools used in such a process often send clear signals about the importance of various initiatives to the developers of policy. The latter half of the twentieth century witnessed the emergence of such discourse and the resulting initiatives as the nation began to acknowledge some of the domestic challenges in areas of economic well-being for many of the nation's citizens.

In his 1964 State of the Union address, President Lyndon Johnson used the power of rhetoric to frame what would ultimately become approaches to addressing some of the most pressing concerns of the era. It was during this speech that he challenged Congress to declare "an all out war on human poverty and unemployment in these United States" (Johnson 1964). Johnson's declaration signaled an acknowledgment at the highest level of the Executive Branch of one of the most pressing challenges in the United States. It also signified an important stage in what became a critical period of reflection on poverty issues. At the beginning of the period we understood little about poverty, why it existed, and what strategies might be implemented to address its existence and impact in society.

Now, fifty years following this declaration, hindsight allows us to reflect upon the development of a science around poverty issues, strategic processes in the public sector to attempt to address the issue of poverty, and means of building a discourse grounded at times in deep moralism and at other times in disengaged rationalism to explore what might be done to address poverty in America.

Johnson's declaration was made in the context of a major shift in the role of government during the 1960s. A mix of determinism by those at the various levels of the federal government, as well as a degree of optimism in the ability of government to meet society's needs were underlying components of the shift. For Lyndon Johnson, addressing poverty was a way that his presidency could make a critical mark on the domestic challenges that the nation faced. It was also a way that he could distinguish his presidency from that of John Kennedy. While Kennedy had been viewed as assuming a tepid approach to poverty, Johnson could make a bold effort (as he would also aim to do with civil rights) to address the area as one of major domestic importance. For many of the idealistic policy professionals who staffed his administration, largely as holdovers from the Kennedy years, engaging in a major domestic policy agenda around poverty would present an opportunity to address many of the goals that initially brought them to Washington.

The years since Johnson's declaration have provided time to reflect on the lessons of the era. For some, the ideas of the era helped to shape a framework for an expansive government role in shaping programs and policies for the nation's economically marginalized. For others, the ideals of this era represented an overexpansion of government roles. In some cases, the War on Poverty was a success, largely because it focused attention on some of the pressing social issues that the nation encountered. In other cases, the War on Poverty represented the worst in planning and government engagement, and set in place processes of spending that would take years to reverse.

Underscoring this era and many of its lessons were also critical conversations about how groups of people would be contextualized in the broader national discourse related to poverty. We came to have numerous conversations about the poor. We developed descriptions, crafted by some of our deepest thinkers in fields such as sociology and anthropology, of who the poor were and how they lived their lives. New economic models emerged to help us measure the impact of programs for the poor. We debated what resources and services they were entitled to receive. Some of the conversations focused on articulating differences between the deserving and the non-deserving poor. Other conversations would draw immediate linkages between race, gender, immigrant status, and any one of dozens of other variables and poverty. With linkages drawn between these variables, those individuals living in conditions of urban and rural poverty, and the developers of emergent policies, the conversations about poverty that stemmed from and followed this era would frequently have undertones that would impact how domestic policy would be developed and implemented for decades to come.

As conversations around the poor ultimately integrated into historical conversational trends around poverty in the nation, we would find ourselves exploring appropriate policy responses to addressing poverty in this nation. Such responses spanned a wide range of sectors—including housing, labor, education, and many other areas. Depending on where one sat on the political spectrum, impressions of the success of each policy varied. Each, however, provided more points of reflection around several questions. What should be done about poverty? Why should it be done? And, by whom should it be done?

This book is an attempt to reflect on some of the lessons and discourse related to poverty that have emerged in the years following the announcement of the War on Poverty. The authors are scholars and practitioners examining a wide range of social concerns that intersect with matters of poverty. Some are engaged in studying poverty-related issues through the lens of various academic disciplines. Others are actively working as practitioners implementing policies and programs that address people's economic and social well-being.

THE EMERGENCE OF THE POVERTY POLICY DISCOURSE

While the policy discourse on poverty in the United States has roots that extend to the earliest days of the nation's founding, the latter half of the twentieth century and the early twenty-first century are grounded largely in a postwar awareness of an emergent middle class that began to rise in the years following the war. A strong postwar economy and opportunities for large segments of the population to obtain a college degree, or a home, as a result of numerous new policies that were in place helped the broader U.S. society to applaud the level of economic achievement that the nation seemed to be attaining. It also masked some of the challenges that the nation was undergoing at the time.

In 1958, Harvard Professor John Kenneth Galbraith published *The Affluent Society*. In the book, Galbraith presented a history of the evolution of economic thought leading to postwar America. While most of the book points to much of the economic opportunity that had come to represent postwar America, the last chapter in Galbraith's book touched on the issue of poverty in the nation. A critical conversation introduced by Galbraith focused on types of poverty that existed. On the one hand was something known as case poverty, which exists at the individual level. As he noted:

> Case poverty is commonly and properly related to some characteristic of the individuals so afflicted. Nearly everyone else has mastered his or her environment; this proves that it is not intractable. But some quality peculiar to the individual or family involved—mental deficiency, bad health, inability to adapt to the discipline of industrial life, uncontrollable procreation, alcohol, discrimination involving a very limited minority, some educational handicap related to community shortcoming, or perhaps a combination of several of

> these handicaps—has kept these individuals from participating in the well-being. (Galbraith 1998, 236)

On the other hand was what was referred to as insular poverty. Galbraith compared this geographic isolation to an island, noting:

> In the island, everyone or nearly everyone is poor. Here, evidently, it is not easy to explain matters by individual inadequacy. We may mark individuals down as intrinsically deficient in social performance; it is not proper or even wise so to characterize an entire community. The people of the island have been frustrated by some factor common to their environment. (Ibid.)

While Galbraith noted the existence of these forms of poverty, he also claimed that the poor in America were transitioning from a "majority to a relative minority position" in U.S. society (Ibid., 238).

Galbraith's conclusion of a shrinking population of the poor differed greatly from that of Michael Harrington, whose 1962 book *The Other America* sought to introduce the poor within American society to a nation concerned with the splendors of its move into an increasingly middle-class nation. Harrington argued that one-fifth of the population—or at least 40 million people in the United States—were poor. He suggested that most of this population was invisible to those who could develop policies to help address their overall condition and improve their status in society.

For Harrington, much of the task in what was viewed by some as an age of relative affluence was to ensure that the conditions of the poor in American society were acknowledged. As he noted:

> There is, in short, a language of the poor, a psychology of the poor, a world view of the poor. To be impoverished is to be an internal alien, to grow up in a culture that is radically different from the one that dominates the society. The poor can be described statistically; they can be analyzed as a group. But they need a novelist as well as a sociologist if we are to see them. They need an American Dickens to record the smell and texture and quality of their lives. The cycles and trends, the massive forces, must be seen as affecting persons who talk and think differently. (Harrington 1962, 19)

His book served as an attempt to serve in such a role and illustrated for the broader American public some of the conditions that this largely invisible segment of the population encountered.

KENNEDY, JOHNSON, AND POVERTY

John Kennedy's life of privilege helped protect him from knowing—even from a distance—the poverty that Harrington presented. During the 1960 presidential race, while traveling in rural Appalachia, he came to encounter rural poverty. He was noted during the tour to be shocked by "the hungry children I saw in West Virginia; the old people who cannot pay their doctor bills, the families forced to give up their farms" (Kennedy 1960).

Despite his mention of these challenges, it was not until 1963 that Kennedy's administration began to seriously weigh policy agendas on poverty. In 1963, journalist Dwight MacDonald's review of Harrington's book brought to President Kennedy's attention matters of poverty as an area of domestic importance. In the spring of 1963, Walter Heller, chairman of President Kennedy's Council of Economic Advisors, drafted a memorandum to the president concluding that certain large segments of the poor (families headed by women, the aged, and the disabled) would remain poor even if full employment in the economy were reached. In response to this memorandum President Kennedy instructed his executive agency heads to develop a case for a major policy effort to confront poverty that would be introduced as part of the legislative program of 1964.

The president's assassination in Dallas in November of 1963 cut short the opportunity of Kennedy's being able to address some of these emerging concerns around poverty. Some of the underlying goals that had begun to emerge however would be adopted by Lyndon Johnson as he would shape the domestic agenda of his administration.

Unlike Kennedy, Johnson had been exposed to poverty in his youth and as he was building his early career. An important stage in his development of his notions on poverty stemmed from his work in rural Texas communities with the National Youth Administration, a New Deal–era program launched by President Roosevelt. As a result, he saw poverty as an issue that he could relate to and deal with in a very different way than Kennedy could.

1964 ECONOMIC OPPORTUNITY ACT

In his 1964 State of the Union Address, Lyndon Johnson formally articulated the notion of a War on Poverty by noting:

> Let this session of Congress be known as the session which did more for civil rights than the last hundred sessions combined; as the session which enacted the most far-reaching tax cut of our time; as the session which declared all-out war on human poverty and unemployment in these United States; as the session which finally recognized the health needs of all our older citizens; as the session which reformed our tangled transportation and transit policies; as the session which achieved the most effective, efficient foreign aid program ever; and as the session which helped to build more homes, more schools, more libraries, and more hospitals than any single session of Congress in the history of our Republic. (Johnson 1964)

In March of 1964, the Johnson administration sent Congress what would become the central piece of legislation associated with the War on Poverty, the 1964 Economic Opportunity Act. The construction of this piece of legislation has been described as a cobbling together of distinct agendas, instead of a comprehensive strategy aimed at identifying and implementing strategies for addressing poverty or a collection of various policies—each advocated by various entities (Moynihan 1969).

Comprised of seven titles, the Economic Opportunity Act was ultimately the result of specific interests related to the development of numerous policy initiatives addressing poverty. Input from the Council of Economic Advisors, the Bureau of the Budget, the Department of Labor, and the Department of Justice supported the inclusion of initiatives on youth engagement that make up Title I of the act. Much of the Economic Opportunity Act was shaped by work that had been developed by the President's Council on Juvenile Delinquency to develop approaches to youth justice and economic inclusion issues. Specific sections created programs such as the job corps and workforce training programs, as well as the college work-study program. In sum, the section recognizes that one of the ways that the nation could help address the potential problem of youth delinquency, identified in the early years of the Kennedy administration as an area of concern, would be to find means of investing in the educational or employment prospects of youth.

Title II of the act deals with the development of urban and rural community action programs. A central component of these efforts was aimed at developing measures to facilitate community organizing and community development initiatives. At the core of these efforts was a critical definition related to community action, which focused on the "maximum feasible participation of residents of areas and members of the groups served." This notion of maximum feasible participation ultimately came to represent a strategy of wide-scale community engagement and community mobilization that was critical in how the programs were developed—it also became a point of major controversy.

Title III specifically dealt with programs related to addressing rural poverty. At the time, rural poverty was a concern—largely because it had played a central role during the 1960 presidential campaign. In 1963 President Kennedy launched the President's Appalachian Regional Commission as a strategy for addressing some of the challenges of rural poverty in Appalachia. The inclusion of Title II was viewed as an expansion on this initiative and as a means of responding to needs articulated by a particular constituency.

Titles IV and V addressed issues of work and employment as they related to poverty concerns. Title IV addressed matters of employment and investment incentives and encouraged the development of various loan guarantees and financing partnerships with Small Business Administration revolving loan programs. Title V addressed various work experience programs through the expansion of workforce training initiatives such as the Manpower Development and Training Act of 1962 and the Vocational Educational Act of 1963.

Finally, Titles VI and VII addressed various strategies for the development of the administrative systems to help address some of these areas of poverty alleviation. Title VI established the Office of Economic Opportunity (OEO), which served as the primary coordination mechanism for efforts that came from the Economic Opportunity Act. Title VII established various income thresholds for participation in programs in the act.

HOW TO CONCEPTUALIZE THE POOR

As the notions that underlay the War on Poverty advanced, there were critical factors related to the constructed notions of who the poor were in the eyes of the policy makers developing strategies to deal with them. Clearly, the work of Galbraith and Harrington helped to bring images of who the poor were to a broader public, as did the widely circulating images of the rural poor who Kennedy had encountered in his visits to rural Appalachia. However as the decade of the 1960s progressed, other voices began to surface to help policy makers conceptualize who made up the poor. In 1966 anthropologist Oscar Lewis attempted to build a working definition of a term he referred to as the "culture of poverty." According to him, the culture of poverty:

> can come into being in a variety of historical contexts. However it tends to grow and flourish in societies with the following set of conditions: (1) a cash economy, wage labor, and production for profit; (2) a persistently high rate of unemployment and underemployment for unskilled labor; (3) low wages; (4) the failure to provide social, political, and economic organization, either on a voluntary basis or by government imposition, for the low income population; (5) the existence of a bilateral kinship system rather than a unilateral one; and finally, (6) the existence in the dominant class of a set of values that stresses the accumulation of wealth and property, the possibility of upward mobility, and thrift and that explains low economic status as the result of personal inadequacy or inferiority. (Lewis 1968, xliii)

Furthermore, he suggests that the culture of poverty tends to be:

> both an adaptation and a reaction of the poor to their marginal position in a class-stratified, highly individuated, capitalistic society. It represents an effort to cope with feelings of hopelessness and despair that develop from the realization of the improbability of achieving success in terms of the values and goals of the larger society. Indeed, many of the traits of the culture of poverty can be viewed as attempts at local solutions for problems not met by existing institutions and agencies because the people are not eligible for them, cannot afford them, or are ignorant or suspicious of them. . . . The culture of poverty,

> however is not only an adaptation to a set of objective conditions of the larger society. Once it comes into existence, it tends to perpetrate itself from generation to generation because of its effect on the children. (Ibid., 188)

Policy analysts and researchers who attempted to develop conceptualizations of groups who were targeted in some ways in the antipoverty programs of the era often did so at the risk of immense criticism, as Daniel Patrick Moynihan learned following the printing of his 1965 "The Negro Family: The Case for National Action," in which he argued that many of the challenges that were faced in urban settings stemmed from issues of family dissolution within the African American community (U.S. Department of Labor 1965). The response to Moynihan's report served as a signal to others who would attempt to articulate positions that aimed to frame some of the pressing positions of the poor. One of Moynihan's most vocal critics was sociologist William Ryan (1971), who argued that Moynihan's perspective was common to that of others who often blame the victims of social policies before developing solutions to fix those individuals.

Imagery of who the poor were developed further in the summer of 1965, when urban riots broke out and resulted in the broadcast of imagery of primarily African American urban rioters. The urban riots throughout the latter part of the 1960s spoke to the fact that there were numerous unresolved issues pertaining to poverty in urban settings in the United States. They also served as an awakening to some of the correlations between race and poverty in urban settings.

In trying to understand some of the conditions that led to the riots, the National Advisory Commission on Civil Disorders, which was formed by President Johnson in the aftermath of the riots, drew critical linkages between poverty and racial disparities in the nation. "Our nation is moving toward two societies, one black, one white—separate and unequal," noted the report in its introductory pages. As the report continued, "What white Americans have never fully understood—but what the Negro can never forget—is that white society is deeply implicated in the ghetto. White institutions created it, white institutions maintain it, and white society condones it" (Report of the National Advisory Commission on Civil Disorders 1968, 2).

EMERGENT CRITICISM OF THE WAR ON POVERTY

The late 1960s witnessed critical conversations evolve on the success and failures of poverty initiatives. Daniel Patrick Moynihan's *Maximum Feasible Misunderstanding* (1969), for example challenged many of the notions of community action that emerged during the era. To him, the implementers of community action initiatives were individuals who were involved with designing programs, with initially the pressures of demonstrating programs weighing heavily upon processes of developing and designing the initiatives. Others also shared some of the concerns that were in existence and related to the development of strategies for addressing some of the challenges around achieving success in addressing poverty.

Richard Nixon's success in the 1968 presidential race provided an opportunity for several critical policy shifts in how factors of poverty would be considered. First, almost as soon as Nixon assumed office, he began dismantling the Office of Economic Opportunity, which had been clouded in his opinion by many of the challenges introduced by the community action initiatives of the era.

However in August of 1969, Nixon introduced a proposed Family Assistance Plan, an antipoverty measure that, had it succeeded, would have provided every family in the United States with a guaranteed minimum income. While this initiative did not receive adequate Congressional support to lead to its implementation, it did raise questions about the type of initiatives that might receive support from a Republican administration for addressing some of the challenges of poverty that existed in the United States.

1980S AND 1990S: DISMANTLING AND EMERGENCE OF NEW APPROACHES TO POVERTY

By the early 1980s, broad federal approaches to addressing poverty found themselves in reversal. Instead of an agenda that focused on government's providing a wide range of resources related to addressing social challenges, such as poverty, much of the focus during the era was instead on identifying ways that government could minimize its approaches to dealing with these issues. Ronald Reagan's claim that "we declared a war on poverty and poverty won," signaled a changing tone in how the executive branch would view many of the changes in how it would address issues of poverty. In the 1981 budget act, Reagan was able to incorporate initial changes that would ultimately set a course for even greater decreases in funding in areas of employment and training programs while simultaneously initiating a series of large-scale demonstration programs that soon began to show some success in promoting work.

Supporting much of the framework advocated within the Reagan White House was the work of social scientists such as Charles Murray, who in his book *Losing Ground* (1984) interrogated some of the major shifts, as he saw them, in welfare policy in the United States since the 1960s. Murray was proving to be a critic of policies related to welfare, arguing in some cases that welfare should be completely eliminated. While Murray's research was viewed as a means of articulating some of the challenges of conceptualizing poverty, others, such as William Julius Wilson, suggested that changing social and spatial dynamics helped to frame some of the challenges related to poverty. In his *Declining Significance of Race* (1980), he noted that the challenges that the African American poor were facing were decreasingly solely about race and more about class stratification. As he noted, "the modern, industrial, post-World War II era, which really began to crystallize during the 1960s and 1970s . . . may be characterized as the period of progressive transition from racial inequalities to class inequalities" (Wilson 1980, 3).

Wilson also argued that much of the intellectual agenda around poverty had been taken over by members of the conservative think tanks and policy organizations. To Wilson, much of this was due to the criticism that Moynihan had received in the 1960s as he attempted to write about issues of poverty. As he noted, liberal social scientists and authors had been reluctant to face the fact that many of the problems of urban life in America were also the problems of racial inequality. Ultimately, he suggested that some of the liberal thinkers who considered many of the structural challenges related to poverty be reengaged in the policy discourse.

In 1985, Mary Jo Bane and David Ellwood published an article in *The Journal of Human Resources* noting that many of the individuals who at the time were receiving AFDC benefits had been receiving such benefits for an extended period of time (Bane and Ellwood 1994). Their findings would later be used in a broad-scale attack on welfare and other policies assisting the poor.

By the early 1990s, the policy discourse linking poverty policies to welfare were at their apex. The 1992 election of Bill Clinton into the presidency witnessed the rise of a Democrat in the role of the president who claimed that a part of his agenda would be to "end welfare as we know it." The 1994 Congressional elections brought into office a cohort of Republican members of Congress who would implement a broad agenda that would include a push to dramatically reform welfare strategies.

In 1996 The Personal Responsibility and Work Opportunity Reconciliation Act (PRWORA), was enacted, and eliminated Aid for Families with Dependent Children, the New Deal Era program that had provided assistance to millions of poor families across the nation. AFDC had been under attack at the time for an assumption that a disproportionate number of its participants were having children out of wedlock and were staying on this form of welfare for long periods of time. As a result of PRWORA, AFDC was replaced with a new program, Temporary Assistance for Needy Families (TANF) that required work, penalized states that did not require welfare recipients to work and individuals who refused to work, and set a lifetime limit on the duration individuals could receive welfare.

EMERGENCE OF ASSET-BASED APPROACHES FOR ADDRESSING POVERTY

The 1990s also witnessed the emergence of initiatives aimed at enhancing wealth creation among individuals who might be positioned to help increase the asset base for individuals. In his 1991 book *Assets and the Poor*, Michael Sherraden argued that poor people will save if they are given the opportunity to do so. He identified many of the benefits of assets in reducing poverty, noting that they improve the stability of low-income households, create an orientation toward the future, and usually make it possible to acquire more assets. He also introduced the idea of a special kind of savings account for the poor in which savings would be matched by public or private funds. Known as individual development accounts (IDAs), these instruments would be restricted to specific uses: the purchase of a home, investment in education or job training, or ownership of a small business—in short, the acquisition of assets.

Sherraden's concept caught the attention of federal policy makers, who instituted notions of these individual development accounts in their considerations of strategies for enhancing the assets of the poor. As a result, in 1996 individual development accounts were introduced as a means of building approaches for shaping considerations.

TWENTY-FIRST-CENTURY RECOGNITION OF THE INCOME GAP

At the very beginning of the twenty-first century, the general outlook for antipoverty efforts in the United States was positive. In 2000, the poverty rate fell to its lowest level in nearly thirty years. Unemployment was also at a near record thirty-year low. Despite the broad indicators of economic improvement, gaps in wealth were beginning to become acknowledged. As Michelle Miller-Adams notes, the economic expansion "had actually exacerbated one of the starkest divisions in American society: the distribution of assets, or family wealth" (2002, 1). She observes that between 1983 and 1998, the wealthiest 1 percent of households saw their average wealth rise by 42 percent. At the same time, the average wealth of the poorest 40 percent of households fell by 76 percent (Ibid.).

This increasingly recognized economic divide between the wealthy and the poor was exacerbated by an increase in challenges brought about by the economic crisis of 2008. The impact on those individuals on the economic margins was tremendous. As economist Joseph Stiglitz argued, a drop of housing values and a major decline in wealth among most Americans correlated with an increase in CEO compensation to the point where by 2010 the ratio of CEO compensation to the pay of the typical American worker was at

243 to 1 (Stiglitz 2010, 3). The impact had tremendous racial correlations, with the average African American household losing 53 percent of its wealth and the average Hispanic household losing 66 percent of its wealth between 2005 and 2009. The average white American household lost 16 percent of its wealth during the same time period (Ibid., 13). The correlations between race and economic inequity continued.

Ultimately, the conversation around these issues of domestic economics had by this era undergone a shift to a point where factors of poverty had been largely replaced by a conversation around factors of broad inequities in U.S. society and a search for ways that the widening gaps between various economic classes could be minimized.

THIS BOOK

Now, fifty years following the launch of Johnson's War on Poverty, we find ourselves still wrestling with matters of conceptualization and the development of strategies related to poverty. While our discourse on poverty has changed in many ways since Michael Harrington and John Kenneth Galbraith revealed to the nation many of the pressing economic conditions confronting millions of our citizens, there are still numerous challenges that we find ourselves facing as we frame our modern conceptualization of poverty and our strategies for dealing with its prevalence in our nation.

The chapters of this book have been grouped in an attempt to provide some thematic perspectives for considering some of these issues. This introductory chapter and the chapter by Sebawit Bishu and Mohamad Alkadry provide opening contexts for considering poverty challenges. I have attempted to provide a historic context for some of the background policy discussions from the mid-1960s to the present related to matters of poverty. Bishu and Alkadry explore three different issues related to poverty: education, housing, and transportation. They draw heavily upon the literature in the field of public administration to wrestle with some of the administrative frameworks that have shaped how policies in these three areas as well as other critical areas have evolved to further distance the economically marginalized.

The next two chapters examine poverty in relation to two groups that we often see in policy discourse related to poverty. Regina Malveaux and Rachel Dolezal explore the issue of low-income female households and poverty. They interweave the policy narrative with the human narrative that has shaped the lives of women and children—particularly those who are struggling with economic conditions on a day-to-day basis. Portia Dinoso Campos examines issues of immigration and poverty. Her work is driven partially by the fact that a year following the passage of the Economic Opportunity Act the 1965 Immigration and Nationality Act was signed into law. Over the past fifty years, as we have seen numerous policy initiatives related to poverty, we have also witnessed the emergence of numerous initiatives related to immigration. Many of the policies that have emerged related to immigration and poverty have impacted one another in the development of strategies for ensuring that new arrivals to the nation are able to fully engage in the broad economic opportunities of the nation.

Rural geography plays a linking theme in the next two chapters. Jennifer Stollman and Susan Glisson examine poverty in Mississippi—a state that played a prominent role in the broader war on poverty and in the various initiatives of the Great Society. Their chapter explores some of the challenges that Mississippi faces in areas of poverty today. Joanna Maulbeck looks at poverty in Appalachia, a region critical to the poverty discourse—for it featured largely in President Kennedy's and President Johnson's later policy initiatives related to rural development, as well as current conversations as we think about poverty today.

Keesha Middlemass and Al Passarella examine poverty as related to facets of the criminal justice system. Middlemass examines poverty as it relates to the war on drugs and incarceration. She observes that the convergence of the War on Poverty and the War on Drugs has resulted in a disproportionate number of poor people incarcerated or under the control of the justice system. Passarella considers poverty as it relates to juvenile justice and notes that while juvenile justice was not a direct consideration of the War on Poverty, issues of justice in relation to youth have shared policy background and policy impacts that influence the economic well-being of youth in the justice system.

For Rosie Uyola and Portia Allen-Kyle, issues of housing are the intertwining factors examined. Uyola examines the housing foreclosure crisis of the early twenty-first century and its impact on urban residents. Allen-Kyle examines questions of suburban poverty, suburban gentrification, and NIMBYism that have framed local redevelopment policies—and ultimately led to an increased concentration of the economically marginalized.

Socioeconomic status as related to health care and education provides the linking themes to the next chapters. Venessa Perry's examination of poverty and health care provides a history of the push for wider coverage and access to health care, as well as an overview of pressing challenges today. Franklin Dickerson Turner's chapter on education examines the development of Title I of the Elementary and Secondary Education Act (ESEA) and Head Start. These two outcomes of the War on Poverty have driven some of the educational initiatives aimed at achieving equity in the latter decades of the twentieth century and the first decade and a half of the twenty-first century. However, as Turner notes, there remain numerous challenges in ensuring members of economically marginalized communities are able to navigate the obstacles in place to ensure that they receive a high quality of education.

The last section examines challenges and opportunities related to economics of poverty. Michael Vorgetts examines workforce development issues. Vorgetts observes that in an era when the number of available jobs is shrinking, the challenge of creating the work that might impact the level of poverty becomes increasingly difficult. As a result, individuals engaged in workforce training strategies must think about workforce development and poverty in a much different context than they may have before. Daphne Berry examines worker cooperatives as potential instruments in poverty alleviation. By providing examples of the work of such cooperatives, she illustrates how these entities might assist in engaging communities at the economic margins in creating economic opportunities for their members. David Madland, Karla Walter, and Alex Ingrahams examine the concept of inclusive capitalism—a notion that encourages more democratic ownership as a strategy for increasing wealth.

I conclude the book with a final chapter in which I aim to integrate some of the findings pointed out by authors throughout the book. I provide a brief overview of three areas that I believe are critical in addressing issues of poverty: innovation for poverty alleviation; addressing wealth gaps; and building ongoing learning systems related to poverty alleviation. I present these three under a broad framework of mutuality consideration that I suggest might serve as a foundation for developing further strategies for addressing challenges related to poverty.

It is my hope, as it is for many of the authors of chapters in this book, that our work will keep critical issues related to poverty and inequity in the eyes of policy makers and others who might be able to address some of these issues in years to come. More importantly, we hope that as further reflection is done by people trying to make sense of poverty, that our work included in these pages will be of use in ensuring that effective strategies for addressing poverty, inequality, and their resulting condition for the nation might be addressed.

Chapter One

The Poverty-Policy Link

Three Examples

Sebawit G. Bishu and Mohamad G. Alkadry

American cities have undergone several physical, economic, and social transformations over the last six decades. This chapter argues that each aspect of the nation's urban transformation was impacted by public policies introduced in both federal and state legislatures and enacted by urban or metro-level administrations. Policy implementers and local executives played a significant role in the implementation of the housing, transportation, and education policy issues that guided or accompanied these transformations.

In the twentieth century, industrialization led to the emergence and expansion of industrial and commercial cities. In turn, cities began to replace and outstrip agrarian communities. A second transformation in the twentieth century took place when the nation's economy shifted its economic base from industrial (manufacturing) to service-based economy. This shift had a significant impact on almost all American cities, causing the out-migration of manufacturing industries from urban centers to suburbs and—in the past few decades—to other countries, where labor cost is much lower and labor laws are more lax.

Another significant factor that shifted the economic landscape of American cities is the evolution of technology. Labor-intensive manufacturing industries are now being replaced by technology-intensive and high-skill jobs that require less labor. Although this transformation increases the efficiency and quality of the production process, it tends to create a huge gap in the labor market: highly skilled professionals grab high-end employment opportunities, while the traditional blue-collar workforce is left behind (Moss and Tilly 1991).

This chapter first explores six of the structural factors that were initially explored by Teitz and Chapple (1998) as "Causes of Inner-City Poverty": structural economic shift, human capital gap, gender and ethnic based discrimination, spatial mismatch, demographic changes and "unintended" consequences of government policies. Each factor has greatly contributed to the economic and social transformation of urban inner cities in the United States. The chapter then focuses more attention on the "unintended" consequences of public policies and how they affect the urban landscape of American cities. This section discusses the three major policies that are believed to have defined the socioeconomic and physical landscape of American cities. Finally, the last section of the chapter proposes links among the three policies discussed in the chapter.

STRUCTURAL FACTORS DETERMINING URBAN POVERTY

Poverty is a complex phenomenon intimately related to political, social, and economic environments. In this chapter, we look briefly at six factors that were initially discussed by Teitz and Chapple (1998) as "Causes of Inner-City Poverty" since the late nineteenth century. The first is structural economic shifts that have been observed over the past century. The second is the increased human capital gap between the haves and the have-nots. The third is gender and ethnic based discrimination that results in further impoverishing the poor. The fourth factor is spatial mismatch, specifically the mismatch between labor and employment opportunities. The fifth factor involves demographic changes, specifically the continuous demographic change in urban inner cities. The sixth factor is the "unintended" consequences of government policies.

STRUCTURAL ECONOMIC SHIFT

The structural economic shift argument presents that urban poverty is a product of the evolving nature of the United States economy in the twentieth and twenty-first centuries. It is argued that the changing landscape of the American economy from an industrial base to a service-based economy has put a large section of the American working class out of work (Wilson 1996; Wilson 1987). Scholars such as Wilson (1987) argue that three factors have contributed to the creation of the structural economic shift: 1) the influence of technology and the development of the manufacturing industry; 2) the growing global economic competition; and 3) the expansion of the service sector and decline in the manufacturing industry.

Until the 1970s, the manufacturing industry supported a thriving labor force; it provided job opportunities to most inner city residents and blue-collar employees. Stressing the critical role of the manufacturing industry, Teitz and Chappel argue that a few manufacturing industries, "such as automobiles, steel, electrical equipment, chemicals, and heavy machinery," capitalized on the labor market (1998, 37). While the evolution of the manufacturing industry into highly technological-based industry has contributed to the positive growth of productivity in the manufacturing sector, it has also left behind a significant part of the manual workforce.

In the 1980s the decline in the manufacturing industry was further exacerbated by global economic competition. Global economic competition led to the out-migration of industry production, which in turn resulted in the loss of many manufacturing jobs in the United States. Bluestone and Harrison (1982) also argue that global economic competition of the early 1980s resulted in the decline in manufacturing industries that were a major source of employment for inner city residents. Besides expansion of the service sector, globalization has fostered easy access to cheap labor in developing countries, leading to the relocation of manufacturing industries to places in developing countries while eliminating jobs from the labor market in the United States. Sassen (1991) argues that the upside of global open market competition is the re-creation of what she calls "a world city;" the downside, she argues, is exacerbated poverty in our cities, leading to a widening income gap between the "have's" and "have not's."

HUMAN CAPITAL GAP

The value of a productive workforce in a society is a function of physical and human capital (Teitz and Chapple 1998). According to Becker, human capital incorporates the "skills, trainings, education and abilities" an individual earns (1962, 49). Other scholars also argue that having the skills and physical ability to perform jobs increases the productivity of an individual (Becker 1975; Hungerford and Solon 1987; Tilak 2002). Teitz and Chapple also argue that employment opportunities and productivity gaps in the workforce are functions of "education, job skills, and work experience—in addition to an individual's innate ability" (1998, 41). Hence, investment in human capital whether in the form of formal education and/or skill trainings increases an individual's chance of being marketable and productive in the job market. In the context of urban poverty, urban inner city populations tend to have less education and fewer skills to meet the needs of the job market (Kasarda 1993). This is often a result of historical, and sometimes even unjust, practices.

There appears to be a vicious cycle that includes poverty, human capital, and education factors. Discussing the link between poverty and student performance, Nyhan and Alkadry (1999) argue that poverty tends to be the most important factor in determining student performance on achievement scores. Particularly in poor inner city communities, they argue that when there is a high concentration of poverty coupled with poor student test performance, low school performance results(Nyhan and Alkadry 1999). In an era of "No Child Left Behind" and charter schools, the lower performing schools suffer further from the distress about the quality of education in poor communities.

President Lyndon Johnson's War on Poverty was one of the first major initiatives in American history to address urban poverty issues, particularly through improving education. The argument behind this policy is that better education leads to improved human capital, which in turn helps the poor achieve increased productivity and better employment opportunities. Human capital improvements, largely triggered by improving education opportunities, will likely enhance employment potential of individuals. Better employment potential is key to moving individuals out of poverty and from situations of economic dependence to situations of economic independence (Teitz and Chapple 1998).

RACE/ETHNICITY AND GENDER-BASED DISCRIMINATION

The gender and racial discrimination perspective explains inner city poverty beyond structural and economic arguments by contending that urban poverty is a dynamic and complex process (Hanson and Pratt 1995). This perspective of understanding urban inner city poverty helps explain why particular groups of society are more prone to be affected by poverty than others. Women tend to be disproportionately impacted by poverty compared to men. African Americans tend to be disproportionately impacted by poverty compared to white Americans. Many researchers have attempted to study the link between gender, race, and poverty. Although this link is complex and, causal relationships are hard to draw, Teitz and Chapple argue,

> Research on discrimination frequently focuses on the poor, but it is difficult to demonstrate the specific ways in which discrimination affects income levels. The most common model suggests that discrimination causes poverty by hindering the movement of qualified workers into employment and preventing the exodus of inner-city residents into suburban neighborhoods that have the schools and quality of life to promote upward mobility. But discrimination also plays an indirect role in causing poverty because it creates segregation and its attendant concentration effects on poverty; because it lowers wages for women, exacerbating the problems incumbent in female-headed households. (1998, 43)

Hence, scholars who support this approach to understanding poverty argue that unless one looks at, and addresses, gender and racial/ethnic-based discrimination in inner cities, it is practically impossible to alleviate the causes and consequences of the injustice that comes with poverty (Rodgers 2006; Iceland 2006). To focus on the consequences would be similar to a health care provider focusing on treating the symptoms and not the source of disease.

One scholar argues that gender-based discrimination prohibits women from "gaining access to material and social resources (ownership of productive capital, paid labor, education and training), and to participate in decision-making in the main political, economic and social policies" (Bravo 2003, 63). The same can be said about racial/ethnic-based discrimination in cities. Gender and ethnic/racial based discrimination tends to be more prevalent in cities with large immigrant populations. Another researcher reports that "poverty rates among African Americans and Hispanic minorities in the U.S., 24.3% and 20.8% respectively, were between 2.5 and 3 times higher than among whites (8.3%) in 2006" (Gradin 2008, 5).

Beyond socioeconomic factors such as race/ethnicity, income, gender, or household structures, an important attribute of the gender and ethnic/based divide in U.S. inner cities is the fact that female-headed, single-parent families are common among minority populations (MacLanahan 2007). This household structure especially puts women in a more vulnerable socioeconomic position than white and minority men. Women and particularly single mothers, who tend to be the primary care providers to their families, also find it much harder to break the poverty barrier.

Employment patterns in urban inner cities manifest themselves in the high concentration of blue-collar jobs and minimum wage jobs as well as a high level of unemployment. Poverty-stricken inner-city areas also manifest in high concentrations of the poor; high concentrations of unemployment, below-standard housing conditions; as well as high concentrations of minority groups.

SPATIAL MISMATCH

The concept of spatial mismatch in the inner city refers to the mismatch between available labor and employment opportunities (Wilson 1996; Kain 1992). The out-migration of labor-intensive manufacturing industries from metropolitan areas out to the suburbs coupled with limited public transportation opportunities available to inner city residents contributes to poor inner city spatial mismatch conditions. Therefore, inner cities with higher concentrations of unemployment indicate a mismatch between the relative locations of jobs and inner city residents. In an explanation of spatial mismatch, Teitz and Chapple note that:

> the theory of spatial mismatch argues that while firms offering low-skill jobs, particularly in manufacturing, have left the inner city for the suburbs, their

> minority work forces have not followed, because both discrimination in housing markets precludes their residential mobility and the costs of commuting and acquiring job search information inhibit access to job opportunities. (1998, 48)

Wilson (1996) in particular attributes increased spatial mismatch to three principal factors. The first is the migration of manufacturing jobs out of the reach of the urban poor. The second is a human capital deficit of inner city residents for example to engage in jobs that require special skills. The third factor is the out-sourcing of low-skilled manufacturing jobs to countries where the labor costs are cheaper and labor laws are more favorable to business.

As argued by Wilson (1996), the issue of spatial mismatch may also be partially explained by the human capital gap and the structural economic shift arguments previously discussed in this chapter. Inner city residents with limited education and skills are at a disadvantage when marketing themselves in a competitive job market. The dynamics of structural economic change which contribute to the shift from manufacturing economy to service economy has also led to the mismatch of skills and jobs for inner city residents who are predominantly engaged in labor intensive jobs.

DEMOGRAPHIC CHANGE AND SOCIAL CAPITAL GAP

Inner cities are places of continuous demographic change. Poor residents and those seeking to take economic advantage of them flow in, while those seeking a better quality of life flow out to the suburbs. Although such constant in- and outflow by itself is not a problem, what becomes a matter of concern is the lack of social stability for the population that stays behind in inner city communities. Wacquant and Wilson (1989) also argue that an important characteristic of the "under class" is its spatial concentration, as well as the concentration of people of similar socioeconomic characteristics and with high rates of unemployment. As a result, spatial concentration of the poor affects the potential for increased social capital in inner cities. In the same line of argument Teitz and Chapple claim that:

> the depletion of social capital in the inner city occurs when the middle class departs for suburbs, leaving behind few residents who can offer social resources, such as providing role models to the neighborhood youth and access to social networks that transmit job information and create mutual trust between potential employer and employee. (1998, 51)

Housing segregation contributes to the concentration of low-income groups together, which affects social capital. Housing segregation also acts to keep the poor inside the inner city. Social capital can be manifested in two forms:

social dimension and institutional dimension. According to Norris and Inglehart (2004) elderly the social dimension analyzes race/ethnic, gender and other differences in accumulated "social aspects" of social capital. They argue that the social aspect of social capital is related to "social class, age, and ethnicity and are closely related to the unequal distribution of the civic resources of time, money, knowledge, and skills" (Norris and Inglehart 2004, 78). A second dimension of social capital is where "structured institutional" affiliations provide support and identity to inner city residents. The "structured institutional" aspect of social capital comes in the form of support for educational mentorship, day care or elder care facilities, skill training facilities, or even other educational and recreational facilities such as parks, churches, community organizations, and recreational centers (Norris and Inglehart 2005). Particularly, the "structured institutional" aspect of social capital plays a significant role in providing institutional support to women with children or individuals who are primary caregivers.

"UNINTENDED" CONSEQUENCES OF PUBLIC POLICIES

A host of "misguided" public policy interventions have worsened the poverty conditions of inner city residents with respect to each of the structural factors outlined above, such as structural economic shift, human capital gap, demographic change, spatial mismatch, and race/ethnicity and gender-based discrimination. Some argue that economic and trade policies have been the root cause of structural economic changes. Human capital deficit in inner cities has been exacerbated by budget cuts in public spending on education and job skill trainings (Teitz and Chapple 1998). Mandatory school district boundaries present a good example of social capital deficit. Families living in inner cities within certain school attendance boundaries, are often forced to send their kids to poorly graded/rated schools.

Jackson (1985) also argues that another good example of a policy's "unintended" consequences is the outcome of the Federal Government Aid for Homebuyers (FGAH). This policy has led to the outmigration of middle-income families to suburbs, which left low-income families concentrated in inner cities. This particular housing policy has consequently fostered social capital deficit in inner cities. Housing policies that placed housing projects in established inner city communities resulted in the injection of transient residents into long-standing communities (Mohl 1995). This led to many of the problems that inner cities face today, such as crime, drugs and poverty. Accordingly, Teitz and Chapple (1998) argue that the spatial distribution of poverty across American cities translate into a high concentration of poverty in urban inner cities as compared to suburbs.

Three major policies of the last century serve as model case studies for illustrating the unintended consequences of government policies: the Housing Acts of 1937 and 1949; the Interstate Highway System Act of 1956; and the No Child Left Behind Act of 2002. The first two policies have been claimed as significant public policy initiatives that have had major impacts on the urban socioeconomic landscape of American cities. The third, the No Child Left Behind Act of the early twenty-first century, addresses issues of education quality at both the elementary and secondary levels. Each of these policies attempted to address urban poverty issues through the provision of decent and affordable housing, the improvement of deteriorated commercial and inner city infrastructure conditions, an increase in urban mobility and connectivity, and the improvement of education quality.

POLICIES IMPACTED: HOUSING, TRANSPORTATION, AND EDUCATION

On their face the three policies discussed here just look like policies aimed at making society better for everyone. The Housing Acts of 1937 and 1949, the Interstate Highway System Act of 1956, and the No Child Left Behind Act of 2001 are examples of policies with negative "unintended" outcomes. The three policies have largely contributed to defining the socioeconomic and physical landscape of our cities in the United States. Although positive policy outcomes have been recorded, these policies have also caused significant destruction of the socioeconomic and physical landscape of American cities. The following section of the chapter will present the historic development of each of these three policies, their intended purpose, and a discussion of the policy outcomes. The following discussion provides a review of the Housing Act of 1937, also known as the Wagner-Steagall Housing Act, and the Housing Act of 1949.

HOUSING POLICIES

Housing Act of 1937: Wagner-Steagall Housing Act

The primary goal of the Housing Act of 1937 was to provide decent and affordable housing for low-income and working-class population (Edson 2011). Besides addressing issues of housing shortage, the details of the Housing Act of 1937 claimed to assist states across the United States to address the dilapidated and unhealthy housing conditions of the urban poor. The Housing Act of 1937 declares the following as its goals:

> 1) To promote the general welfare of the Nation by employing the funds and credit of the Nation, as provided in this Act—
>
> (A) To assist States and political subdivisions of States to remedy the unsafe housing conditions and the acute shortage of decent and safe dwellings for low-income families;
>
> (B) To assist States and political subdivisions of States to address the shortage of housing affordable to low-income families; and
>
> (C) Consistent with the objectives of this title, to vest in public housing agencies that perform well, the maximum amount of responsibility and flexibility in program administration, with appropriate accountability to public housing residents, localities, and the general public. (United States Housing Act of 1937)

The Wagner Act required that for every public housing unit constructed, matching substandard housing would be removed. This aspect of the Housing Act of 1937 was set to ensure that dilapidated housing units were replaced by decent and affordable public housing units (Edson 2011). The policy also left it to local-level administrators to determine the details of its implementation. The operationalization of this policy followed that when the federal government provides funding, the local public housing authority administers the implementation of the policy (von Hoffman 2009). The discretional administrative authority given to local level administrators ensured that they could determine both where new upcoming public housing units were constructed as well as who would benefit from the projects. Von Hoffman (2000) also argues that to avoid competition with the private housing market, this particular housing policy put a limit to the income groups that could participate in the program. Hence, this aspect of the policy ensured that only individuals with certain income levels could participate in the public housing program and will not compete with the private sector. This policy was therefore highly criticized for its destruction of tight urban neighborhoods, its disproportionate impact on urban inner city residents, and the over exercised power over eminent domain (Jacobs 1961; Anderson 1964; Wilson 1966).

The Housing Act of 1949

The aftermath of the Great Depression era and the Second World War increased the deteriorated housing conditions of American inner cities, thus resulting in the need for policy intervention. Title I of the Housing Act of 1949 was known for its ambitious provision to address the poor housing conditions of American cities and revitalize American inner cities. It stated:

> This title authorizes the Housing and Home Finance Administrator to make loan and grants to localities to assist locally initiated, locally planned, and locally managed slum-clearance and urban redevelopment undertakings. . . .

> The Act authorizes $ 1,000,000,000 in loans over a 5-year period. Advances of funds would be available to finance the planning of local projects, and temporary loans for the acquisition and clearance of land, and the preparation of the land for reuse; these loans would be repayable when the land is sold or leased for redevelopment. . . . As a further condition to federal aid there must be a feasible method for the temporary reallocation of families displaced from the project area and the permanent provision of decent, safe, and sanitary dwellings at prices and rents within the financial means of families. (United States Housing Act of 1949)

This particular policy made federal loans and grants available to those who qualify to take part in urban slum clearance and redevelopment projects at the time. The Act also bestowed eminent domain authority on local administrators to make decisions on the slum clearance process.

Aside from its vision to serve as an economic boost to American inner cities in a time of economic distress, the Act also had four stated goals (von Hoffman 2000). First, the Act aimed to provide decent affordable housing that would replace unhealthy and poor housing conditions. Second, the Act aimed to mitigate crime rates in inner cities. Third, the Act was intended to trigger economic development and redevelopment of inner cities. Finally, the Act sought to improve the rate of private investment and to increase the tax base.

The initial focus of the Housing Act of 1949 was on slum clearance, and the building and provision of public housing projects. However, the policy later evolved to focus on inner city renewal and redevelopment. This shift of focus emphasized high-end redevelopment projects that would serve as economic engines to urban inner cities, leaving much less concern for its initial intent, which was to provide affordable and decent housing to the urban poor. Like the Housing Act of 1937, the Housing Act of 1949 also empowered local administrators to exercise eminent domain over inner city residents. As the Housing Act of 1949 evolved, it primarily focused on urban renewal projects fostering inner city prime land for businesses and development projects (Roback 1982). Although this policy was well supported in its initial implementation, it was later highly criticized for taking much longer than anticipated (Jacobs 1961; Anderson 1964; von Hoffman 2000; Wilson 1966).

"Unintended" Consequences of Housing Acts of 1937 and 1949

Although the housing acts of 1937 and 1949 addressed some of the inner city housing issues, they were not able to address inner city housing issues to the level initially anticipated. During implementation, both housing policies evolved focusing more on slum clearance than on providing decent and affordable housing to the urban poor. Furthermore, in both instances, the Acts inserted much discretion in the hands of local administrators to make decisions that defined the final output of the housing development projects. Local decision making also resulted in local lobbying and the so-called "not in my backyard" behaviors, which were largely exhibited by affluent and more politically powerful communities (von Hoffman 2000). These communities ensured that the undesirable public housing projects were confined to inner cities and to areas that were predominantly poor and often minority (Wilson 1966). During the later years of the implementation of the Housing Act of 1949, urban renewal projects redefined the initial intentions of the housing policies thus serving businesses as well as middle- and high-income communities at the cost of the livelihood of the urban poor. Particularly, the Housing Act of 1949 was criticized for its negative impact on the urban poor for two reasons: first, it displaced the urban poor using eminent domain, leaving the poor with very few options for alternative housing options, and second, the Act interrupted intact neighborhoods and their social infrastructures such as schools, churches or community organization with the injection of transient and less community-vested residents who inhabited the public housing projects (Jacobs 1961; Wilson 1987; von Hoffman 2000).

At the time of the implementation of both housing policies, most American inner cities were ridden with high rates of poverty along with dilapidated housing conditions. Inner city lands were also underutilized and local organized advocacy groups were rare or poorly supported. These characteristics made inner-city poor populations prone and vulnerable to the negative effects of public policy choices overseen by local administrators. Administrators and policy implementers also found it "reasonable" and practical to implement urban renewal approaches to address the problems of dilapidated and poor urban inner city neighborhoods.

TRANSPORTATION POLICIES

The Interstate Highway System Act of 1956

The Interstate Highways System Act of 1956 (IHSA), also initially named by President Eisenhower as "the national defense highway system," was signed into legislation by President Eisenhower in 1956 (Gutfreund 2004). The interstate highway system was envisioned to stretch 41,000 miles across the United States. Besides responding to national defense needs, this particular policy envisioned that the highway construction would help to clear dilapidated sections of urban areas. Research conducted by the Transportation Research Board's National Cooperative Highway Research Program (NCHRP) indicates that the original inception of the interstate highway system act envisioned that the policy would respond to the growing urban demands for:

The need for roads for national defense and a growing peacetime need for longer trips;
Cities at a critical point, needed to serve massive entering traffic to the centers;
Early action to support the acquisition by government of slum areas for renewal;
Sporadic development could hobble the logical projection of new arterials: and
The decline of business districts in city centers, had to rank first in needs. (2006, 20)

The intent of the IHSA can be summarized into three main purposes: defense, increased accessibility, and declining conditions of urban inner cities. The implementation of this particular Act required communities to be relocated to create space for the highway construction. However, this policy did not provide guidance on how to address housing demolition and relocation of inner city residents affected by the interstate highway construction (Gutfreund 2004).

"Unintended" Consequences of the Interstate Highway System Act of 1956

The IHSA was one of the major catalysts for dramatic change in the physical landscape of American cities. A significant limitation of this particular policy was the fact that it overlooked the social and economic consequences of the highway construction on communities being affected. Highway engineers who were involved in the design and construction process of the interstate highways across the nation, determined the highway routes and, as a result, determined which communities would be impacted by the construction. Mohl argues that:

> When policy makers and highway engineers determined that the new interstate highway system should penetrate to the heart of the central cities, they made a fateful decision, but also a purposeful one. . . . In retrospect, it now seems apparent that public officials and policy makers, especially at the state and local level, used expressway construction to destroy low-income and especially black neighborhoods in an effort to reshape the physical and racial landscapes of the postwar American city. (2002, 1)

Mohl's argument is that destruction caused by construction under the IHSA was not random but rather a well-thought-through scheme to clear urban inner city slums to make way for high urban renewal projects. In the 1950s and 1960s, the implementation of the Interstate Highway policy was a critical component of the era's urban policy. The Interstate Highway Act implementation was not only focused on increasing connectivity and resolving mobility issues but was also focused on clearing poorly maintained and undervalued prime urban land for economic development. Mohl's discussion on the implications of the Interstate Highway System Act also lays out the argument that administrative discretion, with the intention of efficiency and getting things done, can have a negative ripple effect on the lives of people and communities, particularly the poor. This policy action left a lasting mark on the physical as well as the socioeconomic landscape of American cities. It also appears that a majority of the population affected by the construction of the highway in the mid-1950s included folks with less political and economic power: poor and minority communities. This particular policy action promoted reconstruction, revitalization, and economic development of urban centers without fostering alternative opportunities for the urban poor affected by the policy action (Claire 1959).

A living example of the effect of the Interstate highway Act of 1956 is documented in the development of Overtown, a city in Miami-Dade County. According to Mohl (1995), the construction of the Miami expressway in the 1950s and 1960s provided administrators, political leaders, and business owners the opportunity to claim prime inner city properties, which were predominantly held by the African American urban poor. Mohl (1995) also argues that the policy facilitated the ability of administrators to push Overtown residents away from inner city territories and toward the northwestern part of Miami-Dade County. He documents:

> As early as 1956, the Florida State Road Department, in conjunction with local officials and business people, routed Interstate 95 directly through Overtown and into downtown Miami. Alternative plans using an abandoned railroad corridor for the downtown expressway were rejected in order, as the planners stated, to provide ample room for the future expansion of the central business district in a westerly direction. When the downtown leg of the Interstate 95 expressway was completed in the mid-1960s, it ripped through the center of Overtown, wiping out extensive housing as well as the black business district. One massive expressway interchange alone took up twenty square blocks of densely settled land and destroyed the housing of about 10,000 people. Some 40,000 African Americans made Overtown home before the interstate came, but less than 8,000 now remain in an urban wasteland dominated by the expressway. By the end of the expressway building era, little remains of Overtown to recall its days as a thriving center of African American community life. (Mohl 1995, 401)

The city landscape in Miami-Dade County today demonstrates the physical divide between poor and affluent communities, which was primarily created by the construction of the interstate highway in the mid 1950s. Hence, Mohl's argument of the negative effect of the Interstate Highway Act of 1956 on the communities of Miami-Dade County recognizes how a lack of administrative accountability and poor administrative discretion can have adverse effects on less powerful communities.

In fact, the impacts of policies on these communities can be devastating. In a comparative critique of administrative actions in the United States and British Imperial functionaries at the turn of the twentieth century, Alkadry and Blessett (2010) provide a scathing assessment:

> Is it aloofness or dirty hands? American administrators and British imperial functionaries were not mere observers to the destruction of African American and African ways of life. . . . They were active players in that destruction. In the case of African Americans, housing, transportation, and urban renewal policies implemented by administrators were the major tools to achieve the objectives of the mob and capital alliance. Overtown, introduced earlier in this article, would not have been spliced into four quadrants, its businesses would not have vanished, and its community would not have been destroyed if it was not for the active role that administrators played. It is hard to overlook dirty hands in this situation. (553–54)

To this day, implementation of the Interstate Highway Act (ISHA) continues to be one of the major urban development policies executed in the United States. At the beginning of the discussion of this section we stated the three main agendas of the ISHA, which were defense, increased accessibility and to clear deteriorated urban inner city slums. At face value one can argue that the policy has indeed achieved its goals to a great extent. However, it is not the purpose of this discussion to argue how much of its goals it has achieved. But what we find interesting is the unintended implications of the policy action which brought destruction to the lives of many households and individuals living in inner cities. From that perspective, the ISHA largely failed to foresee its implications for the social, economic, and physical space of those who had no power to challenge its implementation.

EDUCATION POLICIES

No Child Left Behind (NCLB) Act of 2002

In 2002, President George W. Bush signed the No Child Left Behind Act, which elaborated on the implementation of a new policy that defined the educational landscape of elementary and secondary education in the United States. This policy, which is the reauthorization of the Elementary and Secondary Education Act (ESEA), demanded both state-level testing as well as the requirement for schools to report their Adequate Yearly Progress (AYP). The policy aimed at improving the nation's overall education quality as well as ensuring assistance to less-advantaged children. According to the Executive Summary on the No Child Left Behind Policy the premises of this policy had seven main areas, which address:

> 1- Improving the academic performance of disadvantaged students, 2- Boosting teacher quality, 3- Moving limited English proficient students to English fluency, 4- Promoting informed parental choice and innovative programs, 5- Encouraging safe schools for the 21st Century, 6- Increasing funding for Impact Aid, 7- Encouraging freedom and accountability. (2001, 2)

The NCLB Act was initially formed by legislators with a strong conviction that public education reform would significantly improve the state of elementary and secondary public education in the United States. At the very core of NCLB were several standard measures that keep track of student performance and encourage student performance improvement. An important piece of this policy is also its call for holding schools accountable on the basis of student performance on standardized tests. In a sense, NCLB was even more shortsighted in estimating its implications on increased disparity, than that of the other two (housing and transportation) policies discussed in this chapter. The following discussion presents how this policy fell short of standing for the purposes to which it initially came to place.

The Adequate Yearly Progress system ensures that an accountability system is put in place to follow up on the progress of schools at the state level. It was established as a statewide accountability system to follow up on the yearly progress of each school. The policy envisioned that, by 2014, all schools would achieve proficient scores in both reading and math (Neill, Guisbond, and Schaeffer 2004). According to Neill, Guisbond, and Schaeffer (2004), the policy was initially set to "assess every student in reading and math at least once in grades 3–5, 6–9 and 10–12. By the 2005–06 academic year, states must assess each child every year in grades 3–8 and once in grades 10–12 in math and reading. By 2007–08, states must add an annual science assessment in the three grade spans" (7).

A noteworthy assumption of the NCLB policy is that standardized test assessment scores determine the progress of each school, hence should determine the bases on which schools are graded and sanctioned through the Adequate Yearly Progress (AYP) system. When schools fail to perform to the required level demanded by the AYP system, the system puts sanction on their entitlement for Title I funds. Unfortunately, most schools that highly depend on this funding source are also inner city schools that serve children from low-income households. Having discussed the major premises of this policy, the following section presents how the policy failed to achieve its stated goal of enhancing education quality across the United States and ensuring that every child, especially less advantaged children, is given the opportunity for quality education.

The Missed Steps of No Child Left Behind Act of 2002

The No Child Left Behind education policy was highly criticized for its failure to achieve its primary goal, which was to ensure that every child receives quality education. A key component of the NCLB policy is its strong ground for "accountability for results." The high standard and demand for high yearly progress results pushed administrators to shift their focus from quality education to ways to secure high student performance scores. This is primarily because of the sanction put in place by the AYP system. Therefore, to secure the level of required yearly progress report, a minority of teachers and administrators are reported to push weaker students out of the system, or even go as far as helping poorly performing students cheat in their assessment examinations (Neill, Guisbond, and Schaeffer 2004).

NCLB is primarily criticized for its assumptions that schools can be held accountable for student performance based on standardized assessment tests (Neill, Guisbond, and Schaeffer 2004). The standardized testing system is criticized for its assumption that one system fits all as well as for its failure to recognize that students at different levels require different educational assistance and testing measures. The second criticism, which is also most relevant to our discussion, is the pressure put on schools to perform to the expected level by the AYP based on students' performance. This has left teachers and school administrators with the challenge of finding ways to maintain the expected level scores at the expense of delivering quality education. The flawed assumption of the NCLB Act that putting pressure on schools to perform to the required level by the AYP will result in improving education quality has been highly challenged. The criticism was even more significant because of its adverse effect on the same group of people that it had initially assumed to assist, children from disadvantaged communities.

COMMON THREADS AMONG ALL THREE POLICIES: "THE ROLE OF THE ADMINISTRATOR"

Policy is made by legislators to correct existing problems and to improve people's lives. Both intended and unintended policy outcomes define the livelihoods of individuals and communities. The outcomes can be positive or negative, or a mix of both positive and negative outcomes. For instance, the baby bonus policy that aimed to increase the population in Canada had a positive externality of economically empowering women who received these checks. Similarly, a policy that is aimed at creating better housing conditions in inner-city communities can result in negatively affecting the same communities it intended to help. A common thread across all three policies discussed in the previous section is that administrators who implement policies play a significant role in determining policy outcomes. Policy makers and legislators make policies that are implemented by desk administrators and street-level administrators who implement policies. The three cases in this chapter's discussion show that policy outcome may significantly differ from its original intent by policy makers when touching the ground.

In the case of both the Housing Acts of 1937 and 1949, legislators empowered local administrators with the tools they needed to plan projects that would help communities. These administrators were empowered by transferred federal dollars to determine locations and beneficiaries of the public housing projects. The two cases that were presented in this chapter (both housing and interstate highway system policies) showed that local administrators had a significant role to play in defining policy outcomes. This was primarily significant when local administrators were empowered to decide and impose eminent domain over individuals and communities, which were being affected by the housing and highway construction projects. In this scenario local administrators made decisions about what location decisions were more economically and politically feasible, paying less attention to the impact of these decisions on communities around the nation (Alkadry and Blessett 2010).

The "adequate yearly progress" demand of the No Child Left Behind policy also put pressure on school administrators and teachers who eventually worked on ways to acquire the results required by the Act. This was done to maintain federal funding as well as for teachers to maintain the required performance level by the AYP. The policy ignores the deafening research that suggests that poverty is responsible for most of the variance in student achievement. Nyhan and Alkadry (1999) argue that 85 percent of the variance in student achievement is driven by whether or not kids are on reduced or free lunch programs. This fact challenges the oblivious response of legislators and administrators to the correlation between poverty and achievement on test scores.

Having discussed the process and outcomes of the three policies—The Housing Acts of 1937 and 1949, The Interstate Highway Act of 1956, and The No Child Left Behind Act of 2002—we conclude with a discussion of how administrative decisions in the context of the three policies over the years have made compromises on the administrative value of social equity. The discussion of each policy will reflect on how the sole focus on the ethic of "getting things done" has had a detrimental impact on engendering social justice through each of the policy outcomes discussed in this chapter.

SOCIAL EQUITY AND THE HOUSING ACTS OF 1937 AND 1947

Each of the three policy areas discussed in this chapter has contributed to the structural factors related to urban poverty discussed in the first part of the chapter. The concentration of low-income African American populations in urban public housing projects led to a compromised quality of life. The neglect of social equity issues was prominent when the economically and politically affluent parts of the society were able to lobby and determine where public housing projects were built, leaving the poor with not much chance to react to the policy decisions that affected their lives. The negative effect of administrative decisions reinforces racial segregation, concentrating low-income families in high-rise public housing projects. The concentration and segregation of low-income families in urban areas led to the depletion of social capital. The other significantly compromised structural factors affecting urban poverty through the Housing Acts were in spatial mismatch. When public housing projects concentrated low-income families together either in inner cities, or away from where the jobs were, already disadvantaged families were left with fewer employment opportunities. Historical records also indicate that affluent families were able to lobby and influence administrative decisions on where public housing projects were to be built. This determined which and where communities were to be displaced for urban redevelopment projects (von Hoffman 2000). In conclusion, either through the exercise of eminent domain or other compromised administrative decisions, both Housing Acts of 1937 and 1949 had significant effects on engendering social equity among the urban population in the United States.

SOCIAL EQUITY AND THE INTERSTATE HIGHWAY ACT OF 1956

Along with the Housing Acts of 1937 and 1949, the Interstate Highway Act of 1956 played a monumental role in increasing the gap in social equity within American cities. The Interstate Highway Act of 1956 contributed to the displacement of low-income communities from inner cities, thus increasing economic and social inequalities in these communities. It was often the case that displaced communities resettled away from where they had built their livelihoods for generations, thus increasing spatial mismatch and social capital deficit. During the implementation of the Interstate Highway Act, local administrators and transportation engineers at local levels were empowered with eminent domain authority (Mohl 2002). This scenario opened opportunities for local administraters to determine which communities were likely to be affected by the highway construction. The interstate highway construction left communities disintegrated; many had only few options as to where they could settle or pursue employment opportunities. Historical records also indicate that affluent communities along with city administration institutions took advantage of the Interstate Highway Act implementation to clear urban inner cities where most low-income families reside (Mohl 2002). Hence, implementation of the Interstate Highway Act since 1956 has negatively influenced social capital; increased spatial mismatch; and reinforced social disintegration through increased racial and economic disparities.

SOCIAL EQUITY AND THE NO CHILD LEFT BEHIND EDUCATION ACT OF 2001

Similar to the previously discussed housing and transportation policy areas, No Child Left Behind Education policy outcomes bring to light how social equity can be compromised by government policies. The NCLB policy has been criticized for compromising elementary and secondary education quality, and thus increasing human capital deficit among elementary and secondary school children. As was the case in the last two policy areas, NCLB education policy implementation left school administrators and educators with the discretion authority on how schools, students, and teachers performances are determined.

The two assumptions made by the NCLB policy, that enhanced standardized test scores and imposing sanctions on schools and educators to be the best approach to improving education quality in schools, provide a skewed perception into improving education quality (Neill, Guisbond, and Schaeffer 2004). The criteria assumed by the NCLB policy to test students only in reading and math subjects has also left schools directing their focus on the two subject areas. An important and critical component of the NCLB policy, Adequate Yearly Progress evaluation report, determines if schools are eligible for federal funding, leaving schools that highly depend on federal funding in a difficult position. The bottom line is that when an education policy of this magnitude determines national level education policy outcomes its implication can have irreversible impact that can be difficult to make amend to.

CONCLUSIONS

Legislation is very important as a statement of policy direction, but we cannot ignore the impact of administrative policy making through rule making and more importantly through implementation. While legislation stays in effect until changed through the legislative process, administrative policy making evolves and is more subjected to the whims of time and geography than legislation. Time and geography tuned the three policies discussed in this chapter in ways that were largely unintended by federal policy makers at the time.

In terms of time, as societal values shifted over the past five decades, so did administrative values. Administrative values play a defining role in determining how policies are being operationalized and implemented, hence determining policy outcomes. Administrative values have evolved over the years from a focus on efficiency and accountability during the early days of the twentieth century. Scientific management scholars like Fredrick Taylor and the architect of modern bureaucracy Max Weber have championed these two administrative values. Administrative values, like societal values, evolved in the 1960s to engage social equity as an administrative value. Since the 1980s, administrative values seemed to have realigned in the direction of efficiency and effectiveness of policies.

What implications does time have on the three policies discussed in this Chapter? War on poverty policies, housing policies, and transportation policies were conceptualized during an era of heightened national sensitivity to issues of social equity. They were however implemented in decades that placed greater significance on values of efficiency. This is true of many of the policies that were conceptualized in the 1950s and 1960s, and that went through many implementation phases. While the legislation stayed constant, the administrative values governing implementation changed considerably in five decades.

In terms of geography, the three policies, housing, transportation, and education, rest on the principle that state and local officials will be responsible for planning and implementation. Administrative values change not only from decade to decade, but also from one state and region to another. The above discussion indicates that the outcomes of all three policies—those pertaining to housing, transportation, and education—were significantly subjected to the discretion of state and local administrators. Values, especially as they relate to poverty and race relations, varied and so did the implementation of policies. We argue that administrators should look beyond political and economic factors when taking policy implementation actions.

Regardless of the dominant administrative values at the time or place, administrative and policy decisions that influence the livelihoods of individuals should stand the tests of high ethical grounds with emphasis on social equity (Frederickson 2010). Although aware that there is no 'one best way" to execute administrative duties, administrative decisions with limited resources must minimize the negative effects of the decisions on the public, especially vulnerable communities who cannot adequately advocate for themselves.

Chapter Two

Women and Children First?

How Low-Income Female-Headed Families Have Fared since the War on Poverty

Regina Malveaux and Rachel Dolezal

At our emergency shelter and job readiness center at the YWCA of Spokane, we often hear the stories of women and children who have encountered a number of struggles. "Janet," one mother, recently lost a job as a result of ongoing problems with reliable child care. "Karen's" story is a little different. She had a great position with the state but was ultimately forced to leave it when she and her children needed confidential safe shelter from an abusive, gun toting spouse. For "Tawana," the story is of working hard to complete the Career Path program (the state's "Welfare to Work" initiative), only to find both her aid and her placement jeopardized as a result of a recent illness leaving her unable to complete her mandated placement hours in a reliable fashion.

The stories of these women are reflective of thousands of stories of women and their children across the country—and have been similar to stories of women for many generations. The narrative surrounding women and children has changed dramatically over the past century. In the early twentieth century they were framed from the perspectives of those who were to be assisted—when assistance was to be provided by the state and localities. In the years following the World War I, questions began to arise regarding the support of these women from the perspective of the roles of mothers and war widows. By the 1930s, further shifts were witnessed as part of the broader income support mechanisms of the New Deal Era. After World War II, the conversation related to many of these policies began to undergo a significant political shift. The perception of females in these households as members of the undeserving poor began to change as early as the middle of the 1950s and continued through much of the century. By the 1960s, the perception of single, low-income mothers as members of the undeserving poor coupled with an increase in the number of women eligible for income support helped diminish the appetite for supporting female-specific antipoverty initiatives.

Over the decades since the War on Poverty began, the nation has experienced a dramatic shift in how it has perceived single mothers and their children; from the experiences of a struggling minority group deserving need to being viewed as an integral part of the breakdown of the nuclear familial narrative often heard in conservative arguments against safety net support funding. Interwoven in conversations about women and children in poverty at the precipice of the declaration of the War on Poverty are two competing themes of discourse. The first theme examines the role of state and local governments versus federal programs to address income support initiatives for mothers and children in poverty; whether the government has a responsibility to support mothers and children and the extent of this responsibility has been a persistent issue in U.S. society for much of the nation's recent history (Gordon 2012). The second theme focuses on discourse related to the deserving versus the undeserving poor; the idea that the impoverished are broken into two categories: those who deserve a helping hand versus those who are using the system as a means to skirt responsibility

This chapter explores the challenges facing low-income, female-headed households and examines the historical perspectives of women and children in poverty. Drawing upon initiatives launched during the years of the War on Poverty, this section will cover critical issues that emerged after declaration of the War on Poverty including the feminization of poverty and the increase in the number of female welfare recipients. Following this, we will analyze the changes brought about as a result of the 1996 Personal Responsibility and Work Opportunity Act and their long-lasting impacts on the experiences of low-income working mothers today. Finally, we will discuss the narratives of women currently struggling to support their families and how to best address their needs.

MOTHERS, CHILDREN, AND POVERTY: A HISTORICAL FRAMEWORK

Prior to the New Deal era, the issue of support for low-income women and their children was often left to states, local governments, and local charities. In the years immediately following World War I, with concerns related to families left fatherless and husbandless due to the war, a number of efforts were established to help ensure that some of these initiatives assisted women in need. During the 1920s, mothers' pensions emerged in many states and localities as a result of efforts aimed at supporting mothers and their children who had lost a husband or father during World War I. Language in these programs was specific: covering issues such as morality, as well as who was deserving and undeserving of these quasi-antipoverty initiatives. Over the years, the concepts of the deserving poor versus an undeserving poor among women and single mothers would shift. The second wave of New Deal reforms brought the passage of the 1935 Social Security Act, and specifically, Title IV, creating the Aid for Dependent Children (ADC) program. Although Federal authorization for the programs led to increased funding and standardized eligibility, requirements allowing for expansion of the programs were administered and implemented at the state level. By 1941, renamed Aid for Families with Dependent Children (AFDC), support for mothers and children increased substantially, reaching approximately 925,000 children each month, almost quadrupling monthly program participation in eight years since its inception.

With the passage of the amendments to the Social Security Act in 1956 came the incorporation of rehabilitative principles at the federal level. These amendments reflected the change in thinking about public welfare that began in the previous decade and reformed the nature of the AFDC program. According to the law, the goal of the rehabilitative AFDC program was to "encourage self-care and self-support" (Mittelstadt 2005, 12) among recipients, who were now referred to as clients. Thus, AFDC was expanded to include federal funds for the provision of key social services aimed at reducing welfare dependency while supporting mothers and children.

POVERTY AND MORALITY

As the concept of reducing poverty began to take hold nationally, states, especially those in more conservative parts of the country, began to look at poverty not just in an economic sense, but in a moral sense. Poverty, some began to argue, was rampant due to the lack of morality and breakdown of traditional societal roles. Single-parent households, primarily led by women, became a favorite target of states and lawmakers looking to earn conservative credentials, with one of the most notable incidents of discriminatory policy occurring in Louisiana in the early 1960s.

Following the passage of the ADC, states, especially conservative southern states, contested the idea of providing dollars for programming and services for single mothers; arguing, loosely, that the payments would essentially reward immorality. In July 1960, the Louisiana state legislature passed a suitable home law that forbade providing ADC payments to women who had children out of wedlock. The law condemned the homes of such women as morally unsuitable. Louisiana Governor Jimmie Davis referred to the targeted ADC clients as "a bunch of prostitutes" who did not deserve public funds. Although other southern states had passed restrictive welfare laws, none were as restrictive as Louisiana's. Some 6,000 mothers, caring for more than 23,000 children, were stricken from Louisiana's rolls in the next two months. The Louisiana legislature argued that it was within its rights to interpret the suitable home provision as including unwed mothers; their out-of-wedlock births, the legislature states, rendered their homes "morally unsuitable" for their children. Based on this act of defiance, the Eisenhower administration forced states to provide either support or foster care for children. In 1961, the Social Security Administration adopted the Flemming Rule, named after Eisenhower's HEW Secretary Arthur Flemming, to create the foster care component of the ADA (Yarrow 2009).

1960S: ACTIVITIES OF THE OEO AND MOBILIZATION

Despite incidents like the one that occurred in Louisiana, the 1960s witnessed an increased mobilization of the poor and disenfranchised, particularly women and African Americans. One such movement, driven by the National Welfare Rights Organization (NWRO) engaged scores of organizers from a wide range of entities to advocate on behalf of broader scale access for mothers and children to AFDC benefits and other income support. Founded in June of 1966, the NWRO had an impact in terms of mobilizing and organizing individuals around the issue of welfare rights. Of the 20,000–25,000 individuals who joined the NWRO in the late 1960s, 95 percent were women receiving AFDC, and the vast majority of them were African American. These two groups had been disenfranchised for decades with regards to income equality and access to social service resources.

In addition to the NWRO and its focus on mobilizing on the issue of income inequality, the Federal Welfare Act of 1967 and amendments to the Social Security Act implemented a number of essential programs that helped mothers receiving welfare in gaining social supports and employable skills. These changes allowed for the creation of the Work Incentive Program (WIN), which allowed AFDC clients to register to participate in workforce training or apprenticeship programs, but exempting mothers with children under the age of six years old. Other such programs and initiatives included the JOBS program, daycare centers to help care for children while mothers worked, and provisions allowing welfare recipients to keep a portion of their earnings. States attempted to circumvent offering services to women via the changes to the SSA and AFCD, most notably the state of Alabama, which imposed a "substitute father" regulation on women cohabitating with men who may not be the father of their child or children. However, this rule was struck down in *King v. Smith* (1968), which declared that the efforts to exclude mothers who cohabitate with men other than the father of the child was inconsistent with the SSA amendment's declarations and equal protections afforded those women.

ERA OF WELFARE TRANSFORMATION

The 1970s saw increases in the number of people who were recipients of some form of income support through AFDC—many of which were headed by single women. The general public was also beginning to recognize that much of this increase was largely paralleled with an increase in the number of women of color on income support. Governments at the local, state, and federal level also began weighing the various costs of providing increased levels of support to a growing number of single mothers and children receiving AFDC support. A strategy implemented was to begin to identify means for limiting the access to various services. By 1981, Congress passed the Omnibus Budget Reconciliation Act, which required some welfare clients to work in return for receiving welfare. Under this act, exemptions from such workfare requirements were only available to mothers of infants and toddlers. Similarly, The Family Support Act of 1988 was enacted with the goal of aiding recipients of AFDC benefits into work by expanding child care subsidies, hardening penalties for recipients who were not compliant with work requirements, and offering transitional health care benefits for recipients moving from welfare dependency into work.

PERSONAL RESPONSIBILITY AND WORK OPPORTUNITY RECONCILIATION ACT OF 1996

By the mid 1990s the debate around welfare in the United States reached a tipping point regarding the reshaping of support to families through AFDC. The Congressional elections of 1994, which brought into office a cadre of House Republicans set on reforming the various income support measures provided by the federal government, shaped much of the conversation around program alteration. Some of the provisions proposed by the newly elected members of the House included denying benefits to children born out of wedlock to mothers currently on the welfare roll and denial of benefits to unmarried mothers under the age of 18, both of which were disproportionately African American mothers. In addition to the goal of reducing welfare rolls, legislation also sought to promote employment and marriage, decrease single parenthood and teen pregnancy, discourage substance abuse through specified penalties, and restrict welfare benefits to citizens (Banerjee 2003). With the passage of the Personal Responsibility and Work Opportunity Reconciliation Act of 1996 AFDC was replaced with Temporary Assistance for

Needy Families (TANF), and set into motion a mechanism to help ensure that a lifetime limit of five years of support and work requirements were set into place with these various initiatives.

The impact of PRWOA passage was evident on several levels. Overall, PRWOA decreased the number of welfare caseloads from 5.5 percent in 1994 to 2.1 percent by 2001. There was also however an increase that correlated with the number of low-paying jobs in a number of low-skill fields, with most of the former welfare recipients being placed in part-time work with salary ranges of $6 to $8 per hour. In the five years after its enactment, welfare rolls decreased from 12.2 million to 5.3 million recipients (Hays 2004). Of primary concern to many researchers in the years after welfare reform was the role of the time limitations and the role of the work requirements in the context of the decline of the national welfare caseload. One study found that while time limits had a significant and substantial negative effect on the use of welfare and positive effect on the engagement in employment activities, the effect of these time limits on household earnings was insignificant (Grogger 2003).

Additionally, new requirements led to concerns with regards to both welfare programs and recipients alike. Factors such as the ability of mothers to provide for their families and the relationship between parental behaviors and children's social, behavioral, and emotional outcomes were being examined (Brooks-Gunn and Duncan 1997). Most of the women being removed from the welfare rolls were being placed in low-wage jobs with few benefits or opportunities for growth. Work-related costs such as child care, transportation, meals, and uniforms serve as an additional source of strain for these mothers, who will be unable to meet their financial obligation even with employment prospects (Edin and Lein 1997). These jobs are highly routinized, require little autonomous decision making, and often require nonfixed schedules with nonstandard hours; this can lead to complications in mothers' ability to secure adequate child care (Hays 2004; Scott et al. 2004). As a result of these employment patterns, many low-income mothers experience extreme tiredness and stress (Scott et al. 2004). This exhaustion and role overload has led to mothers losing benefits as a result of being able to fulfil eligibility requirements to maintain benefits, such as visiting a caseworker during office hours (Clampet-Lundquist et al. 2003).

Given the time limitations on the receipt of welfare benefits and mandatory work requirements to maintain eligibility, the interactions of recipients and agencies has become more superficial in nature (Scott et al. 2004). Evidence also suggests that recipients who have transitioned off welfare often do not access critical services and work supports for which they qualify (Clampet-Lundquist et al. 2003). Connecting mothers and their families to these supports and services can help to ease the burden of low-wage work by ensuring that their incomes are higher than what they would receive from welfare. Practitioners play a critical role in this, as the information that they are tasked to provide can create a safety net for mothers and their families (Banerjee 2003).

REALITIES TODAY

The nearly two decades since the passage of PROWRA have resulted in a number of challenges facing single mothers today. These include a number of shifting economic realities that ultimately not only affect many single mothers, but also indicate that there are more single mothers in our nation. In 2009, a joint Shriver Report/Center for American Progress report entitled *A Woman's Nation Changes* Everything observed that women had become half of the workforce in America and that mothers were two-thirds of the primary and co-breadwinners in American families. Furthermore, in early 2014, the Shriver Report's *A Woman's Nation Pushes Back from the Brink* noted that of the 100 million people who lived at the brink of poverty (roughly 133 percent of the federal poverty level), nearly 70 percent were women and the children who depended on them. This equals nearly 24 million women and 28 million children.

Today's realities reflect an increase in the number of minimum-wage workers in the nation; with women being nearly two-thirds of minimum-wage workers in this country. Additionally, more than 70 percent of low-wage workers get no paid sick time. Forty percent of all households with children under the age of 18 include mothers who are either the sole or primary sources of income. American women are approximately half of all workers in this country, but the average woman earns only 77 percent of what the average man makes, and women of color earn even less. At a time when women constitute nearly half the nation's workforce, earn a majority of college and advanced degrees, and are the majority of the country's breadwinners, why do women and the children who depend on them constitute roughly 70 percent of the more than 100 million Americans living in poverty, near poverty, or going in and out of poverty? The numbers are staggering: nearly one-third (33.9 percent) of people in single-mother families in the United States are poor. Six in ten (60.4 percent) live below 200 percent of the poverty threshold. Sixty-four percent of those polled believe that the government should set a goal of helping society adapt to the reality of single-parent families and use its resources to help children and mothers succeed regardless of their family status. Also, a majority—51 percent—believe that the government should set a goal of reducing the number of children born to single parents and use its resources to encourage marriage and two-parent families.

STRATEGIES FOR ADDRESSING SOME OF THE CHANGING REALITIES

Recognizing that the population of families led by single mothers is a common reality in many situations, one of the challenges is how to adjust to this reality. Two critical themes underscore much of the consideration here. First, the reality is that women as a whole make up a significant percentage of the workforce. The second consideration is that with this shift, there is a need to recognize that the makeup of families is different from the traditional nuclear family. The image of a mother and father standing beside their children and family pets in the suburbs is generally regarded as an archaic model of happiness and success. This vision of the traditional nuclear family is becoming less relevant in addressing the most crucial needs of a population that is in constant flux. As a result, there is a need to question our notions of the meaning of "family" and what we expect an American household to look like. Somewhere along this transition, we should also be examining and shifting our expectations of the mechanisms of support for low-income female-headed households.

Understanding the Realities of Childcare

For many mothers, the challenge of finding quality, affordable childcare is one of the factors that frame many of the emotional and economic realities they confront. For some women, the notion of relying on daycare centers to raise their children while they work is unacceptable. Some women dream of having a child and taking time off work, or maybe being a stay-at-home mother while their partner provides. For others, the image of a high-profile career is their greatest motivation into the future, and the only disruption along the rising staircase is the unexpected baby on the way.

The great equalizer for all working mothers is the hunt for quality, affordable childcare. Searching for just the right fit in a caregiver for your child while doing the emotional math of how much time you can feel good about being absent from your child's life is a tenuous balance. What if she cuts her first tooth and you are not there to see? While you are at work, will he take his first step? Say his first word? Will your child love and bond with Miss Jenny at daycare more than with you? These are some of the tearful questions that run through a first-time mother's mind, and even after a second or third child, we still have to overcome a great mountain of maternal instinct to feel OK being separated from our children full-time. If, however, it feels at all like a relief to drop off your child or children and head to the office, the motherly conscience reminds us that we are teetering dangerously close to becoming an absentee parent and the perils of raising a child without the guidance and nurturing they need. As one of us recalls:

> I was raised to see mothering as the greatest accomplishment in life. Nothing greater, my parents said, for a woman, than to become an honorable wife and nurturing mother. Although I was an independent little girl with a strong will, I believed the hype. I drew pictures of my eventual family, relishing the thought of my happily ever after. Little bouncing babies appeared in my journals, along with a strong husband, a large plot of land out in the country, a spacious garden and even an apple tree in the back yard. Five years of an abusive marriage ended my storybook adventure. But, it wasn't the abuse that made me leave; it was child protective services showing up to our house and threatening to take my son away if I didn't escape to a safe place, away from our abuser. Two months later, in a mold-ridden efficiency apartment, I clipped out job ads as the bills continued to climb. I realized that I would not—could not—be the primary caregiver of my child. I had to take on a second low-wage job to cover the court fees and other expenses to ensure our safety. I will never forget the load of guilt I felt as I walked away from "Bumble Bee Preschool," turning my back on the screams of my three-year-old with his arms outstretched, "Mommy, don't go!! . . . Mommy! . . . Mommy! . . ." His cries were silenced with the shut of my car door as I turned away and drove to work.

Many mothers become accustomed to this routine, and we learn that the quicker you walk away and hop in your car, the faster the child stops crying and settles in. The lingering memory of their pleas and outstretched arms haunts us at the office, and sometimes we might wonder if this separation anxiety is our fault. Maybe it's our fault for meeting that wrong man, maybe we did "ask for it" when that guy raped us, or maybe we should have tried to stick it out through a few more slapping sessions with the husband. Guilt sets in. What if we had made better choices or insisted on a condom that one night? What if we would have waited to have children until the money was stacked up, allowing us to stay home with them? What if our children develop reactive attachment disorder or become substance abusers or even criminals because they aren't bonding with their own mother in their first years of life? These and other questions plague us as mothers, during the workday and at night before we fall asleep.

In addition to facing the psychological hurdles of our single parenthood and navigating the moments of guilt we feel for utilizing daycare centers, mothers in the workforce are confronted with the brick wall of child care costs. For full-time care, it costs about the same amount each year as it does to send a student to college. That's about $8,000–$10,000 per child, depending on where you live. While some care centers offer a marginal sibling discount (5–10 percent savings per additional child), there is no way around the reality that as much as 30–50 percent of the mother's wages will sometimes be sopped up by child care alone. Let's not forget while we are talking expense scenarios that working moms make about 7 percent less income than their childless peers. (Budig and England 2001).

Some moms find that by cutting back on the hours they work and shortening the number of childcare hours, they actually have a net savings for monthly income; but oftentimes such cutbacks will eliminate their ability to compete for a job promotion and, in some cases, will be a cause for job loss. The 2012 Child Care Resource and Referral Network found that infant childcare in New Jersey absorbs about 36 percent of the income made by a single mother versus 10 percent of the income of two-parent households. In addition to care costs taking a smaller bite out of the income pie, two-parent households have the option of staggering shifts to eliminate childcare altogether. For single moms, resourceful alternatives are in short supply. Some might turn to family or friends if they are lucky enough to live in proximity to someone who doesn't have a day job and can volunteer to babysit. Often times, the reality is resorting to the cheapest care centers with open availability.

One of the scariest realities that single mothers face is the risk that their child will be neglected, injured, or sexually assaulted outside the home. The U.S. Department of Health and Human Services reports that 5,321 child daycare providers across 39 states in 2006 were found to be perpetrators of abuse or neglect. The type of abuse that these providers were found guilty of ranged from physical abuse (14 percent), to neglect (53.8 percent), to sexual abuse (21.9 percent), and psychological maltreatment or multiple types of abuse (10.3 percent). While ongoing evaluations and revisions of care regulations are necessary to minimize the risk of maltreatment in child care programs, there is also a need for more education about how to define and locate high-quality child care centers.

Support services in the form of subsidized best-practice facilities or other assistance for mothers who seek but can't afford quality child care are among the potential solutions to this quality versus cost dilemma. Certainly, one of the most devastating situations is when a woman escapes an abusive domestic situation and forges a new life with her children, only to have her babies subjected to the same abuse in the care facility she works so hard to pay for.

Support with Dignity

Where support mechanisms are being developed, one of the biggest obstacles is ensuring that such aid comes with a level of dignity for mothers. Many single mothers have been shamed by family, friends, and others for their social circumstances. Assumptions about promiscuity, undereducation, poor judgment, or general incompetence are among the mix of conclusions commonly levied toward single mothers. For married women with children, seeking support also comes with social stigmas such as a lazy partner, mutual lack of effort, or for procreating amid poor economic circumstances. In *Reclaiming a Spoiled Maternal Identity: Young Mothers' Experiences and Re-*

jection with Stigma, Fessler (2011) discusses how support that lacks dignity leads to a stigmatized identity, particularly for young mothers. She states that:

> In addition to individual level effects, stigma may contribute to poor outcomes in more structural ways. Community agreement about what "deserves" stigma justifies discrimination against stigmatized individuals thereby lending support to social structures and policies that may be detrimental to the well-being of young women and their children. Through these policies, stigma may further cause poor outcomes for young mothers. Finally, stigma may affect the ability of young women to access services that are available. Fear of negative social interactions may discourage young mothers from seeking potential sources of social or economic support. (2011, 14)

Providing dignity within service delivery can oftentimes be the missing element for successful initiative outreach efforts.

Workforce Development

Poverty is an endemic problem in the United States, especially with regards to families with young children headed by single mothers. Of particular relevance to family policy and the ongoing debate about poverty and welfare reform is the difference between the effects of maternal employment without income gain and the effects of maternal employment with income gain. Over the past thirty years, public programs for the poor have moved away from cash assistance toward a workforce training and employment model with regards to individuals with dependent children. Improving the experiences of children has been a goal expressed by those lobbying for this change; however, the results have been reduced welfare costs while increasing the rate of maternal employment. Although we can see the welfare roll shrinking and employment rising, what effect does this workforce development actually have on poverty and children?

In recent studies (Morris et al. 2002), preschool children's performance and learning improved when maternal employment produced an income gain but remained static when maternal employment did not result in income increase. For adolescents, achievement worsened and delinquency rose when their mothers entered the workforce, whether there was an increase in income or not. Oftentimes, sibling care is a factor when a single mother transitions into full-time work, which often reduces the amount of time spent on homework and cuts down on social enjoyment and extracurricular activities. Furthermore, mothers who took on less complex jobs, worked for longer hours, or were employed in the child's first year of life often were associated with unfavorable outcomes.

Additional research on the effects of income has consistently reported that poverty has a negative association with children's cognitive development, and that those who live in chronic poverty have lower academic achievement than those who are in transitory poverty (McLoyd, Aikens, and Burton 2006).

The impact of employed mothers who gained income through workforce development presents a very different picture. About a $1,000 increase in annual income sustained on average across two to five years was shown to boost child achievement by at least 6 percent. For annual increases of up to $2,200 per year, there was up to 12 percent higher achievement (Duncan, Morris, and Rodrigues 2011). Although these figures would suggest that nothing would help child achievement more than increasing family income, this seems to be far from the truth. Families who took part in only a labor force program, aiming to get the mother a job as quickly as possible, showed very little improvement in child achievement. However, in programs that emphasized maternal education through a more comprehensive human capital development model, improvement in child performance was seen, with some cases seeing performance improvement as high as 25 percent.

Further studies suggested that other factors such as reducing the mother's stress and depression improved parenting behavior and thus led to higher achievement rates for children. Although maternal employment which leads to increased income does seem to have positive effects on children's development, maternal education and overall happiness had even greater immediate and long-term benefits for children. Scholars agree that there is little evidence to suggest that increases in employment or reductions in welfare, by themselves, produce positive impacts on the academic and social achievement of children. Evidence suggests that programs targeting development, education, and empowerment of the mother over a prolonged period of time (human capital development programs) produce the greatest gains for mothers and children (Fox et al. 1995).

CONCLUSIONS

This chapter has presented an overview of some of the dynamics related to single, female-headed households with children and the challenges they face. Poverty and societal stigma offer two of the larger hurdles women must face when attempting to raise their and their family's standard of living if they do not follow the archaic societal norms set before them. While strides have been made to assist women and mothers struggling with the effects of poverty, considerable work needs to be done before women achieve equal footing with their male counterparts.

Removing perceptions and stereotypes of single mothers and women in the workforce would be a huge victory for the movement toward gender equality. Women are often thrust into dual roles that are neither appreciated nor respected with the same gratitude that males and single fathers receive. A single father who works two jobs to provide for his child is often viewed as doing his duty while a single mother is shamed for not being attentive to her child's needs. These perceptions, although diminishing, still exist and still present a significant barrier for single mothers to overcome. Additionally, removing barriers and expanding resources to keep mothers and women out of poverty are key and essential elements toward reducing the burden. It is easier for a career-oriented single mother to achieve greater professional success if she is able to access quality and affordable childcare. Eliminating barriers and diminishing the notions of women and single mothers as lesser will help to bring us closer to the goal of gender equality within society.

Chapter Three

Immigration and Poverty

Portia Diñoso Campos

On October 3, 1965, a year and a half after declaring a War on Poverty, President Johnson stood at the foot of the Statue of Liberty and signed the Immigration and Nationality Act of 1965. In the years since the signing of the Act, the debates and issues related to both poverty and immigration have become intertwined as the changing demographics of the nation have led to better comprehension of some of the challenges related to the intersection of these issues. The messages of immigration and poverty often run counter to one another. On one hand, immigrants are viewed as the people who add to the economy. On the other hand, they can be viewed as an economic drain.

This chapter examines the plight of the immigrant poor through various perspectives. First, this chapter will begin by addressing the question, "Who are the immigrant poor?" This section will briefly identify the different groups of foreign-born citizens who migrate to the United States and the motivations driving their immigration. Next, this chapter will briefly examine key pieces of legislation that have affected the relationship between poverty and immigration and shaped the composition of the U.S. immigrant population, including the 1965 Immigration Act; the 1980 Refugee Act; the 1990 Immigration Act (IMMACT); the 1996 Illegal Immigration Reform and Immigration Responsibility Act (IIRIRA); the 2013 Comprehensive Immigration Reform (CIR) bill; and the 1996 Personal Responsibility and Work Opportunity Reconciliation Act (PRWORA). Next, this section will further examine the key policy implications related to central issues of immigration and poverty. This will be followed by proposed solutions as to how we can address the plight of the immigrant poor. Through a discussion of discrimination, welfare and poverty, and human rights, this chapter will conclude with an analysis of the policy implications associated with these key pieces of legislation.

WHO ARE THE IMMIGRANT POOR?

In 2004, the Robert Wood Johnson Foundation conducted a focus group study of immigrant and refugee communities that helped to identify who might be considered the immigrant poor. The report pinpointed several characteristics belonging to this population. The immigrant poor are foreign-born immigrants who lack skills from all perspectives: social, economic, political, and cultural. For one, the majority lack proficiency in the English language and are therefore deficient in basic communication skills for daily survival, such as seeking directions and asking questions at the grocery store, hospital, public library, and so on. They also earn low pay, work long hours, do not advance in their jobs, and worry about financial matters. As a result, they want for affordable and safe housing. Families tend to live in cramped quarters and households are often comprised of two working parents where the children are left home alone after school. In addition, many families lack transportation and must rely on family and friends. Due to their deficiency in the English language, many are unable to pass the driver's exam and therefore cannot legally drive a car. For some, public transportation is not always available or convenient. They rarely have health insurance or access to basic preventive health care. In regards to education, some believe that their lack of American schooling prevents them from moving up the ladder (Garrett 2006).

Hence, the immigrant poor are those who have a difficult time escaping poverty. According to Steven and Smolensky (2009), the composition of the immigrant population can influence the poverty rate. For one, if the poverty rate among a pool of immigrants is high, they will have less effect on the poverty rate over time if they improve their labor skills and status. Diverse levels of education and labor market skills among immigrants can also influence the poverty rate. For instance, an incoming stream of immigrant labor that includes a high number of uneducated foreign-born citizens negatively affects the poverty rate.

But while immigration has been cited as a cause of poverty, its significance in this matter has been overinflated and does not solely explain the poverty trend. For instance, Chapman and Bernstein's (2003) analysis of U.S. Census data from the 1990s revealed that if the number of immigrants had increased, then the poverty rate would have fallen in California and in New York. They point out that, essentially, an increase in inequality led to the rich getting richer and the poor getting poorer, regardless of native- or foreign-born status.

KEY LEGISLATION REGARDING U.S. IMMIGRATION

A series of important pieces of legislation since the early 1960s have influenced the demographic landscape of immigration and have had an effect on the relationship between immigration and poverty. They include the 1980 Refugee Act, the 1990 Immigration Act (IMMACT), and the 2013 Comprehensive Immigration Reform (CIR) bill (which is still being debated in Congress as of this writing). And although the 1996 Personal Responsibility and Work Opportunity Reconciliation Act (PRWORA) is not an immigration bill, it also impacts immigrants, especially the immigrant poor.

1965 IMMIGRATION ACT

The 1965 Immigration Act, also known as the Hart-Cellar Act, forever changed U.S. immigration policy and, until this day, is considered the foundation for modern immigration law. Prior to the passing of this law, the Quota Acts of 1921 established a system to control immigration into the United States. These Quota Acts were significant in that they were the first laws to quantify immigration by basing the admittance of immigrants on their country of birth and by limiting the number of immigrants (regardless of nationality) entering the United States. The number of immigrants from a particular country was not to exceed 3 percent of the number of foreign-born persons of that respective nationality who already resided in the United States in 1910. When the 1965 Immigration Act was passed, it did away with the national origins quota system by centering on family reunification and employment preference (Center for Immigration Studies 1995; Keely 1971).

However, the passing of the 1965 Immigration Act did more than refocus the basis upon which immigrants were allowed to enter the country. During this time period, the sentiment of the nation led Congress to hold hearings and debates on two main issues surrounding immigration as well as the nation's image: humanitarian values and the preservation of the American culture. In regards to humanitarian values, the Quota Acts were not exemplary. For instance, they created a "barred zone," also known as the Asia-Pacific Triangle, which specifically restricted Asian immigration. Proponents of the 1965 Immigration Act denounced the Asia-Pacific Triangle as being racist and discriminatory, and instead, emphasized the need for family reunification. Many organizations and legislators, including ethnic societies, labor groups, and religious and nonsectarian groups, supported the push to allow an increased number of immigrants from countries outside of Northern Europe. Legislators who sponsored and championed this notion were not only bipartisan but were also from districts that included large ethnic voting groups.

With regards to cultural preservation, those who favored the preservation and maintenance of American society did not oppose termination of the Asia-Pacific Triangle policy. Their primary desire was to maintain the national origins quota system, immigration quota advantages, and historical and familiar ties with Northern and Western European nations in order to preclude any threats to the economy and citizen access to jobs (Keely 1971). However, the 1965 Immigration Act defined employment clearances and requirements for certain prospective immigrants. Thus, the use of immigrant labor was allowed when there were not enough able and qualified workers in the United States and as long as this did not have an adverse affect on wages and working conditions (Center for Immigration Studies 1995; Keely 1971). Overall, the 1965 Immigration Act was a compromise between those who supported the two main immigration propositions.

The 1965 Immigration Act was a symbolic undertaking in that it expressed the notion of civil rights beyond geographic borders by allowing people of all nations equal opportunity to immigrate to the United States (Center for Immigration Studies 1995; Keely 1971). The designers of the law did not foresee the great impact that it would have on immigration—the result was a massive increase in the number of immigrants—or that it would "become a vehicle for globalizing immigration" (Center for Immigration Studies 1995, 11). Nor did they anticipate an increase in the use of nonquota admissions—which did not have a numerical limit—such as the reinforced requirements for family reunification. Policymakers did not expect that these new, equal quotas would be fully utilized by European, Asian, and Middle Eastern nations.

Despite the belief held by many policymakers that the increase in immigration would be limited following the passage of the 1965 Immigration Act, there was in fact a dramatic rise in the number of immigrants to the United States over the years. In 1970, approximately 4.8 percent of the total U.S. population (9.7 million people) was foreign born. As of 2008, the foreign-born population increased to about 12.5 percent (38 million people) (Kandel 2011). In 2010, the foreign born comprised about 13 percent of the total population, nearly 40 million individuals (Grieco et al. 2012). By 2013, the United Nations reported that the United States hosted the largest number of international migrants in the world: 45.8 million. Between 1990 and 2013, the United States gained the largest number of international migrants, about 23 million. That equates to approximately 1 million additional migrants per year (United Nations, High Level Dialogue on International Migration and Development 2013).

1980 REFUGEE ACT

One of the most significant pieces of legislation that ultimately led to an increase in the number of immigrants entering the United States was the 1980 Refugee Act. This act established the Federal Refugee Resettlement Program, designed to facilitate "the effective resettlement of refugees and to assist them to achieve economic self-sufficiency as quickly as possible after arrival in the United States" (U.S. Department of Health and Human Services 2012, 1). The Act eliminated geographical and ideological criteria and it defined "refugee" according to standards set forth by the United Nations (Center for Immigration Studies 1995; Martin and Yankay 2012, 2). It also created separate admission guidelines for refugees. The granting of refugee or asylee status is dependent upon legal guidelines, political expediency, the relationship between the United States and the individual's country of origin, and the geopolitical context in the respective time period (Portes and Rumbaut 2006). Prior to the beginning of each fiscal year, the President consults with Congress to establish "an overall refugee admissions ceiling as well as regional allocations" (Martin and Yankay 2012, 2). In 2011, the total refugee admission ceiling was 80,000 and approximately 56,384 individuals were permitted to enter the United States as refugees.

The main purpose of the Act, which was initiated by Senator Edward Kennedy, was to establish an organized and permanent set of administrative procedures that would address the admission of refugees and recognize their unique circumstances, especially since the United States was already admitting a large number of refugees annually and using a "patchwork" (Kennedy 1981, 145) of various procedures in response to various crises.

Since 1975, more than 3 million refugees have resettled in the United States. Since the enactment of the Refugee Act of 1980, the annual refugee admission rate has fluctuated to as high as 207,116 in 1980 to as low as 27,100 in 2002 (Office of Refugee Resettlement, n.d.). In 2012, approximately 58,238 refugees and nearly 29,184 asylees were admitted into the United States (Office of Refugee Resettlement 2013). And in 2014, President Obama released a Presidential Memorandum allowing the admission of up to 70,000 refugees into the United States for that coming year.

But while the United States endeavors to extend its humanitarian efforts to those across geographical boundaries, the nation must also continue to strengthen these efforts within its borders. For instance, Koyama (2014) pointed out that there are millions of refugees in the United States who possess limited English language proficiency, which restricts their employment options and opportunities. And while the Office of Refugee Resettlement is responsible for providing English language education, these programs receive little funding and often see budget cuts in favor of vocational training. As a result, many refugees lack the resources to become economically self-sufficient, forcing them into poverty.

1990 IMMIGRATION ACT

The 1990 Immigration Act expanded the original 1965 Immigration Act by increasing the number of available visas by 40 percent, thereby raising the annual limit of legal immigrants to 700,000. In addition to retaining family reunification as a major criterion for entry into the United States, it also more than doubled employment-based immigration (from 54,000 to 140,000, comprising about 21 percent of the total) and diversified the immigrant population by admitting immigrants from "underrepresented countries" (Bush 1990; Center for Immigration Studies 1995; Waters and Ueda 2007; Zolberg 2007).

Overall, the Act divided the preference category into two groups: family based and employment based. In addition, the employment-based categories increased from two to three classifications; the three classifications were further subcategorized into three different groups of immigrant workers. Hence, five categories of employment-based immigrant visas were created: priority workers; advanced degree; skilled workers; other workers; special immigrants; and employment creation. In essence, the 1990 Immigration Act was a major piece of "housekeeping" legislation that reserved the majority of visas for professionals and skilled laborers, making available only about 10,000 visas for unskilled laborers (Espenshade et al. 1996).

1996 ILLEGAL IMMIGRATION REFORM AND IMMIGRATION RESPONSIBILITY ACT

While the main purpose of the 1996 Illegal Immigration Reform and Immigration Responsibility Act was to address illegal immigration issues and strengthen the enforcement of existing U.S. immigration laws, this Act put into place employment eligibility verification guidelines for employers and imposed sanctions on those who engage in unfair immigration-related employment practices, including the improper disbursement of government aid to aliens (Legal Information Institute n.d.).

The nation was also experiencing an economic recession during this time period, which heightened anti-immigrant sentiment, especially among lower-income Americans. In response, the 1996 Illegal Immigration Reform and Immigration Responsibility Act also monitored the use of social programs by shifting the financial responsibility for immigrants to their respective sponsors, who were required to sign an enforceable affidavit promising to provide financial support to the immigrants until they become naturalized and/or economically self-sufficient. If these immigrants utilized public benefits, then sponsors were liable for reimbursing those costs (Fix, Capps and Kaushal 2011; U.S. Immigration Since 1965 n.d.).

1996 PERSONAL RESPONSIBILITY AND WORK OPPORTUNITY ACT

The 1996 Personal Responsibility and Work Opportunity Act (PRWORA) had a dramatic impact on the immigration debate. The Act reduced or eliminated federal aid eligibility for legal immigrants during their first five years of U.S. residence (Singer 2004, 21). For instance, the eligibility criteria and funding structure for food stamps, Medicaid, TANF, and other federal means-tested benefits as well as state/local public benefits were altered (Hanson et al. 2002).

Ken and Bruen (2013) illustrate how eligibility for welfare benefits is determined in the case of an immigrant family. In their study, they examined the use of benefits and public services at the individual level. They noted that state policies, the unit of assistance (at the individual or family level), and an individual's immigration status (such as citizenship status, refugee and asylee status, lawful permanent residence status, temporary/provisional immigration status, and undocumented citizen status) all play a role in whether immigrants are eligible for public benefits or programs. More specifically, they point out that in order for recipients to receive Medicaid, CHIP, and SSI benefits, eligibility must be determined on an individual basis. As a result, many American-born children of immigrant families are beneficiaries of Medicaid or CHIP health insurance while their noncitizen parents are not. At the household level, benefits may be provided through SNAP and cash assistance. But since many immigrant families include ineligible noncitizen immigrants, the household SNAP allotment or cash assistance amount is reduced (Ken and Bruen 2013). For example, if a very poor, three-person family consists of parents who have been lawful permanent residents for two years and they have an American-born child, then the computation of the benefit level is based only on the child and not the ineligible parents.

Hence, the financial cost of providing benefits to noncitizen immigrants and most naturalized citizens is lower than for native-born citizens. Furthermore, the average value of benefits utilized for each immigrant recipient is almost always lower than their native-born counterpart; as a result, they actually receive fewer government benefits, and they tend to use public benefits at a lower rate than native-born citizens. Moreover, highly skilled immigrants tend to provide more contribution to government resources while consuming fewer government services. They are also more likely to generate more efficiencies for the local economy as compared to low-skilled immigrants who bring a lower amount of human capital. This is why a highly skilled immigrant work force is generally preferred over low-skilled immigrant labor (Hainmueller and Hiscox 2010).

Although the poverty rate among children is higher than that of any other age group and children of immigrant families have an even higher poverty rate (at about 23 percent) than children of native-born citizens (roughly 18 percent), many immigrant children and their families do not qualify for welfare benefit programs "because eligibility is determined by legal status and, more importantly, citizenship" (Passel 2011, 33). Since many parents of immigrant children are ineligible for these programs and some parents are not legally authorized to reside in the United States, outreach efforts to encourage child participation in welfare programs is further complicated.

2013 COMPREHENSIVE IMMIGRATION REFORM BILL

The 2013 Comprehensive Immigration Reform (CIR; S.744) bill, also known as the Gang of Eight[1] immigration bill, is still being debated in Congress as of this writing. The main pillars of the CIR bill include creating a path for unauthorized immigrants to become citizens, reforming the current legal immigration system, developing an effective employment verification system aimed at preventing identity theft and barring the hiring of unauthorized workers, and improving the process for admitting authorized workers while also protecting workers' rights (Bipartisan Framework for Comprehensive Immigration Reform 2013).

KEY POLICY IMPLICATIONS

While the main purpose of the 1965 Immigration Act was to restrict the flow of immigrants into the United States through social (family reunification), economic (fulfilling labor shortages with skilled workers), political (upholding and respecting human rights), and cultural (increasing diversity) means, it also led to the unintended consequence of opening the door to a larger and more diverse pool of potential immigrants, especially those who are from much poorer areas of the world and whose potential income gains would far outweigh the compensation that can be earned in the source country.

Social and Economic Perspectives

From a social and economic perspective, the 1965 Immigration Act favored family reunification (or kinship ties) over skills and education, which decreased the costs of migration for consecutive cohorts of immigrants from "new" source countries to the United States (Center for Immigration Studies 1995; Hatton and Williamson 2002; Kothari 2011; Rector 2006). Hatton and

Williamson (2002) point out that "as a result of their lower skill levels, the new immigrants were located further down the US income distribution level than were previous immigrants" (p. 14). For example, data from the U.S. Census Bureau in 2012 shows that many foreign-born citizens have attained less education, possess a lower income, and live below the poverty line. About 31.5 percent of foreign-born citizens 25 years of age and older possess less education than a high school diploma (as compared to about 10.9 percent of native-born citizens) while approximately 22.1 percent are high school graduates (as compared to 29.5 percent of native-born citizens).

While there are more foreign-born citizens in the labor force (about 67.8 percent) as compared to native-born citizens (approximately 64.1 percent), data also show that median earnings are much lower for the foreign-born (males, $37,113; females, $32,162) than for their native counterparts (males, $50,935; females, $38,778). More specifically, about 49.5 percent of foreign-born citizens earned less than $35,000 in 2012 (as compared to 35.2 percent of the native population). On the other hand, Suro, Wilson, and Singer (2011) observed that while many foreign-born citizens experience "low pay, temporary employment, and [are] twice more likely to leave high school [they] are more likely to be employed" (p. 11).

The median age of the foreign-born population in 2012 was about 41.5 years, roughly 6.9 percent are below 18 years of age, and nearly 24.8 percent are 55 years or older. Moreover, approximately 18.6 percent of foreign-born citizens rely upon Social Security income (as compared to about 29.9 percent of the native-born population), about 4.6 percent have supplemental security income (as compared to about 4.6 percent of the native-born population), roughly 3.1 percent have cash public assistance income (as compared to about 2.7 percent of the native-born population), nearly 8.10 percent have retirement income (as compared to about 19.1 percent of the native-born population), and almost 13.4 percent rely upon food stamps/SNAP benefits (as compared to about 11.1 percent of the native-born population). When it comes to poverty levels, about 18.2 percent of the foreign-born are below the poverty level as compared to 14.4 percent of native-born citizens. But while it seems that poor immigrants are utilizing more public assistance and welfare programs, this is not the case. Foreign-born citizens comprise about 13 percent of the total U.S. population, which equates to an estimated 41 million. Therefore, only about 7.5 million of the foreign-born rely on these public assistance and welfare programs as compared to roughly 35 million of the native-born population.[2]

According to Rector (2006), this inflow of poorly educated immigrants is the result of the 1965 Immigration Act's inclination toward kinship ties over skills and education as well as lax border enforcement and nonenforcement of laws against illegal immigration. He states,

> In recent years, these factors have produced an inflow of some ten and a half million immigrants who lack a high school education. In terms of increased poverty and expanded government expenditure, this importation of poorly educated immigrants has had roughly the same effect as the addition of ten and a half million native-born high school drop-outs. (Rector 2006, 1)

But blame should not be placed on family reunification efforts completely; rather, proponents of employment-based immigration indicate that the nation must be more attuned to the economic needs of the country by placing a balance between family-based immigration and employment-based immigration. For instance, Enchautegui (2013) found that "family and immediate relative immigrants produce a higher share of service, farm, construction, and maintenance workers than the U.S. population as a whole" (p. 6). In addition, she found that preference toward family immigration has declined since 2002, which could be attributed to the passage of the 1996 Illegal Immigration Reform and Immigration Responsibility Act and its preference toward a highly skilled and professional immigrant labor pool. And in his research, Peri (n.d.) found that immigration essentially did not affect the poverty rate for native-born families within the last twenty years. Moreover, during the 2000s, U.S. native-born workers who lacked a college degree were able to find higher wages within the twenty highest-immigration metropolitan areas due to the presence of a large, highly skilled, and educated immigrant labor force. His study also points to the fact that highly educated immigrants more than offset the competition from less educated immigrants by creating an increased demand for low-wage jobs.

Political Perspective

Prior to the passage of the 1996 Personal Responsibility and Work Opportunity Act, several federal court rulings established that "local authorities could not discriminate against legal immigrants in public welfare programs" (Hanson et al. 2002, 237), thus limiting the number of federal policies targeted at immigrants. For instance, in *Graham v. Richardson* (1971),[3] Justice Harry Blackmun, on behalf of the majority, reemphasized that the Fourteenth Amendment entitles all persons—including foreign-born citizens—equal protection under the laws. In *Foley v. Connelie* (1978),[4] the courts extended the right for foreign-born citizens to receive education and public welfare, along with the ability to earn a living and hold a licensed profession, while the right to govern is reserved for citizens. In *Plyler v. Doe* (1982),[5] Justice William J. Brennan reiterated the need to grant minors, including undocumented citizens, equal protection of the laws (Dinnerstein 1985). Thus, legal immigrants were allowed access to the same welfare programs as their native-born counterparts. Just prior to the passing of the PRWORA, states were left with the responsibility to choose whether federal funding for TANF and

Medicaid would continue to be allocated to eligible legal immigrants and whether a state-funded program should be created for immigrants who no longer qualified for the federally funded benefits (Hanson et al. 2002; Singer 2004).

But legislation like the 1996 PRWORA not only breaches the Human Rights Declaration, it also contradicts the original intent of 1965 Immigration Act to uphold and promote civil rights. Although states were responsible for deciding whether to continue providing legal immigrants with welfare services, the Welfare Reform Act also limited the authority of state and local governments to provide any benefits to undocumented immigrants. If state and local governments wanted to provide welfare services to illegal immigrants, then they had to enact a state law after August 22, 1996, affirming that they would provide services to eligible recipients. Hence, state and local governments that took such action sent a public message "that they are making a choice to provide benefits to undocumented immigrants" (Singer 2004, 28).

President Clinton acknowledged that PRWORA was unfair to immigrants. As a result, the Balanced Budget Act of 1997 (BBA) and the Agricultural Research, Extension, and Education Act of 1998 restored benefits to immigrants. With the BBA, Social Security Income (SSI) payments were reinstituted to most legal immigrants who were residing in the United States prior to August 1996, and the Act stipulated that an individual remained eligible for Medicaid so long as he or she continued to receive SSI. On the other end, the Agricultural Research, Extension, and Education Act of 1998:

> restored eligibility for food stamps to immigrant children, elderly immigrants, and disabled immigrants who resided in the United States prior to the date of the passage of the 1996 act. The law also extended the refugee exemption from the food stamp bar from five to seven years. (Singer 2004, 28)

Later, the Bush administration enacted the Farm Security and Rural Investment Act of 2002, which restored refugees' eligibility to receive food stamps and reinstated food stamp eligibility to legal immigrants who had resided in the United States for at least five years, as well as for immigrant children without residency criteria.

Several issues exist in regards to intergenerational conflict for welfare benefits among the immigrant population. For one, older workers and retirees are more likely to be citizens with voting power. Children and young workers are more likely to be immigrants and/or children of immigrants and they, along with their parents, are less likely to have the ability to vote. The reliance of the elderly on Social Security and Medicare will most likely continue as these programs are spared from budget cuts. While state and local governments are able to provide programs and benefits for children, there are limited financial resources to distribute; therefore, government must sometimes resort to conservative spending and budget cuts and unfortunately children's programs, such as education and other benefits, usually receive the brunt of the cuts (Passel 2011).

Overall, welfare reform has led to the broad dichotomization of the immigrant population into qualified immigrants and unqualified immigrants, and the distinguishment between immigrants who have obtained government consent to reside in the United States legally and those who have not. Broadening this distinction and then creating several subclassifications of immigrants has actually resulted in distorting the differences between immigrants who have government consent to reside in the United States and those who do not. While giving states greater responsibility in the distribution of welfare and public service resources is more efficient, it also results in limiting those resources so that states can make more cost-effective choices when it comes to allocating insufficient finances (Fix and Tumlin 1997).

Cultural Perspective

Anti-immigrant sentiment in the United States has been brewing—heightened by a very weak economy, increasing demand for the nation to be fiscally conservative, labor market competition, demographic changes in localities, and media attention—and it has contributed to budget cuts aimed at immigrants (Chapman and Bernstein 2003; Hainmueller and Hiscox 2010; Hopkins 2010; Shields 2004). To illustrate, a Roper poll administered in the 1990s revealed that the majority of Americans felt that both legal and illegal immigration displaced American workers, placed stress on social welfare programs, and endangered the American culture.

Although the type of anti-immigrant sentiment present today is similar to sentiments expressed in the past, its undertones are different. Briefly, inequality between native unskilled workers and immigrants competing for jobs has persisted throughout American history. For instance, some research reveals that anti-immigrant sentiment based on demographic changes and certain conditions is more evident at the local level. According to Hopkins (2010), towns that have considered passing anti-immigrant ordinances tend to be "wealthier, larger, and more transient, with fewer residents living in the same house in 1995 and 2000" (p. 53), and have more than three times as many immigrants in proportion to their population, approximately 7 percent as compared to 2 percent of their population. Fix (1997) pointed out that in California—a state that is accustomed to addressing immigrant issues, particularly in farm communities—they found that a structural economic rift occurs when persistent poverty and insecurity results in:

> a disconnect between a flourishing agricultural industry and the overburdened towns and cities that provide the services needed by growing migrant populations. These communities are ill-equipped to assimilate sudden waves of newcomers, since their tax bases are limited and since the working poor have little to spend and initially pay little in taxes. (9)

Essentially, citizens who reside near larger proportions of immigrants do not necessarily possess negative attitudes toward them; rather, anti-immigrant sentiment is fueled when there is a sudden, threatening change in a community's demographic condition alongside salient national rhetoric that fuels anger, fear, and suspicion. In response, a local municipality is likely to consider passing a local anti-immigrant ordinance. While the federal government has the responsibility to oversee immigration levels, localities have reacted on their own by taking a unilateral stance on various immigration-related concerns, ranging from schooling to zoning issues (Hopkins 2010).

Because quota laws did not apply to all immigrants, they left the door open for the mass migration of Latin American immigrants, especially those from Mexico, which supplied a cheap labor force for industries and businesses located in the northern United States (Massey 1995). Therefore, if immigrants are a substitute for native labor—rather than a complement of economic production—then immigration has a negative impact.

Another fear that holds true today is American citizens' concern about the "quality" of immigrants that America allows to enter into the nation.[6] For instance, levels of inequality are fostered by recent immigrant groups expressing increased signs of social exclusion, especially among immigrant groups with high rates of unemployment and underemployment, increasing poverty rates, growing pockets of ethnic and racial segregation, and polarization of income levels (Shields 2004). As a result, current policies, such as the 1990 Immigration Act and the 1996 Illegal Immigration Reform and Immigration Responsibility Act, focus on improving the skill levels of immigrants and restricting the number of unskilled laborers entering the United States in order to improve immigrant assimilation into society (Shields 2004). Furthermore, "rich natives oppose low-skilled immigration more than do poor natives" (Hainmueller and Hiscox 2010, 79), and both rich and poor native citizens equally oppose low-skilled immigration labor—evidence that anti-immigrant sentiment is primarily fueled by market and nonmarket pressures and labor market competition rather than by issues of racism or xenophobia (Hainmueller and Hiscox 2010; Timmer and Williamson 1998).

Moreover, the employment categories and restrictions established by the 1990 Immigration Act and the 1996 Illegal Immigration Reform and Immigration Responsibility Act shifted the focus from promoting the ideas of civil rights (as expressed by the 1965 Immigration Act) to economic gains and incentives as well as contributing to xenophobic fears. As a result, current policy issues focus more on improving the skill levels of immigrants, restricting the number of unskilled laborers entering the United States in order to improve immigrant assimilation into society, and lessening the reliance on welfare programs and public services (Bush 1990; Center for Immigration Studies 1995; Legal Information Institute n.d.; Nwokocha 2008; Shields 2004; Waters and Ueda 2007; Zolberg 2007).

SOLUTIONS: HOW DO WE TAKE CARE OF THE IMMIGRANT POOR?

Policy makers and the public should be aware of the issues that arise among welfare, poverty, and immigration for a number of reasons. First, income level can directly affect the ability of households to access health care and maintain a positive health status. At the local level, steps can be taken to improve the lives and mobility of immigrant citizens by developing and/or restructuring programs that serve this community, such as providing or continuing English as a Second Language programs, providing more information to foreign-born citizens, and targeting public services toward the needs of immigrants and refugees. Ultimately, almost all immigrants share the goal of becoming legal American citizens or green card holders and to be contributing members of society (Garrett 2006). Another solution is to look at the efforts that the U.S. government has made in assimilating refugees into the country. Studies have shown that, as a result of these efforts, many refugees have attained economic success and are contributing members of the nation's economy (Haines 2007).

It was also found that, within California communities, the combination of immigration control and immigration policy "could intensify this new rural poverty" (Fix 1997, 10). To illustrate, researchers found that increasing border control restrictions, the difficulty of undocumented aliens in obtaining a green card, and the struggle of legal immigrants to qualify for social programs and public assistance "could lock migrant workers and their families into an easy-to-exploit underclass" (Ibid., 10). Therefore, a number of solutions should be employed to address this situation, such as ensuring that legal immigrants continue to receive food stamps and other public benefits, maintaining and providing health, education, and job training programs to migrant and seasonal farm workers as well as most transient workers, disbursing impact aid to rural school districts in order to educate migrant students, and imposing employer sanctions alongside border enforcement while also reducing regulations disputes and minimizing discrimination against those who look like or are assumed to be foreigners. Although administrative costs are high and eliminating these programs could save the federal government approximately one-quarter of the cost of providing welfare reform, doing nothing and/or not maintaining these programs would produce "a kind of dead-end poverty" (Ibid., 20) resulting in the creation of a new class of immigrants who lack rights and who "would be likely to end up serving as a new magnet for illegal migration" (Ibid., 19).

Moreover, political rhetoric generated by the media has heightened citizen concerns over immigrants' dependence on welfare services. For instance, the controversy surrounding the Comprehensive Immigration Reform bill has led opponents to worry that public charge[7] laws will not be enforced. Foreign-born aliens who are regarded as public charges are barred from entering the United States and an immigrant who is found to be a public charge faces possible deportation (Edwards 2001).

Although the 1996 Illegal Immigration Reform and Immigrant Responsibility Act strengthened immigration policy by raising the qualifications and increasing the obligations of individuals who "sponsor" an immigrant (by signing an affidavit of support and assuming financial responsibility), there is no certainty that the Charge Doctrine will continue to be upheld because it is not written into law (Edwards 2001).

For the most part, policymakers have the difficult task of addressing and balancing the issues surrounding welfare, poverty, and immigration. According to the Universal Declaration of Human Rights, an international document that provides a possible framework for considering issues related to immigration, it is a direct violation to exclude legally abiding noncitizens from social benefits. The Declaration states that an individual who is "lawfully present within a particular jurisdiction" is also "entitled to the same fundamental social welfare benefits as anyone else [and] governments must not distinguish between the human rights of citizens and those of noncitizens lawfully present within that jurisdiction (Reichert and McCormick 1998, 18).

CONCLUSION

Even if immigrants who arrive in the United States are economically independent, the dynamic state of the economy coupled with other effects cannot always guarantee that immigrants will always be economically self-sufficient. They face the same problems that the general American citizens face. For instance, the foreign-born population is diverse in age, education, economic mobility, etc. and will always face issues of health, the elderly, etc. The only difference is that they are foreign-born citizens.

In retrospect, the U.S. government and American citizens should not only be aware of such complexities but also strive to create an environment attuned to those needs—the needs of the immigrant poor as well as the needs of the nation. Review of the 1965 Immigration Act, the 1990 Immigration Act, the 1996 Illegal Immigration Reform and Immigration Responsibility

Act, 1996 Personal Responsibility and Work Opportunity Reconciliation Act, and the 2013 Comprehensive Immigration Reform bill show that the nation has always been at odds in balancing social issues (namely family-based immigration) and economic concerns (more specifically, employment-based immigration) that would benefit everyone. Unfortunately, fears in trying to achieve some level of equilibrium between social and economic concerns has fueled xenophobia, where the American public is led to believe that foreign-born citizens are consuming noticeable amounts of public services. The reality is that research reveals that they consume a small amount of public services. In addition, they also contribute more than they take out and, as set forth in the 1996 Personal Responsibility and Work Opportunity Reconciliation Act, they are not allowed to utilize public services during their first five years in establishing residency.

While addressing the immigration debate is an ongoing battle, it cannot be neglected that the issue of how we take care of the immigrant poor is at hand. The immigrant poor face issues of assimilation and isolation in communities, limited English language proficiency, and low job skills and education levels. By addressing these social needs, creating a public agenda or continuing English as a Second Language programs, American society would be playing a part in initiating and upholding humanitarianism and, in turn, investing in these individuals will lead to them to being contributing members of society. Otherwise, if the American public does nothing then the endless cycle of poverty will continue.

NOTES

1. The CIR bill was introduced by Senators Charles E. Schumer of New York, John McCain of Arizona, Richard J. Durbin of Illinois, Lindsey Graham of South Carolina, Robert Menendez of New Jersey, Marco Rubio of Florida, Michael Bennet of Colorado, and Jeff Flake of Arizona, also known as the "Gang of Eight" ("Bipartisan Framework for Comprehensive Immigration Reform," 2013).

2. According to the U.S. Census, an estimated 269 million of the total population is native born. Source: U.S. Census Bureau, 2008–2012 American Community Survey.

3. In *Graham v. Richardson* (1971), Carmen Richardson, a resident alien of Arizona, met all the requirements to receive welfare benefits with the exception of meeting the residency requirement in the State of Arizona. He challenged the constitutionality of this requirement by filing a class action lawsuit against the commissioner of the State's Department of Public Welfare. The District of Arizona's three-judge court ruled in favor of Richardson.

4. In *Foley v. Connelie* (1978), although Edmund Foley was a legally resident alien, his application for a position as a New York State Trooper was denied. In a 6–3 decision, the Court held that the function of policing is a basic government function and therefore reserved for citizens.

5. In *Plyler v. Doe* (1982), 1975 education laws in the State of Texas disallowed the use of local district state funds to educate children of illegal aliens. The Court cited that the Equal Protection Clause of the Fourteenth Amendment was violated.

6. The "quality" of immigrants refers to whether or not immigrants are skilled. For example, an immigrant who possesses a college degree may be considered highly skilled or of a high "quality" (Shields 2004).

7. Essentially, a public charge is someone who is considered a "charge" or responsibility of the public because he cannot provide for himself, hence relying on public assistance for daily survival. The Charge Doctrine is one of the conditions of the social contract and is based on the notion that the immigrant should not only be self-sufficient but should also be a contributing member of society and not a societal burden—this is also one of the reasons why the United States has a selective immigration process (Edwards 2001).

Chapter Four

"The Movement's Broadway"

Race, Poverty, Education, and Health Care in the State of Mississippi

Jennifer A. Stollman and Susan M. Glisson

Mississippi often occupies mythic territory for many Americans. Writer William Faulkner's fictional outsider Quentin Compson's musings: "What's it like there? Why do they live there? Why do they live at all?" effectively sum up most people's assumptions about Mississippi. With all due respect to Quentin Compson, most (out of the state) people's conceptions of Mississippi are based on myths and stale stereotypes perpetuated by both literary and Hollywood depictions. Within the state, defensiveness and political demagoguery contribute to wild speculation and outright lies in policy debates. Plagued by this veneer of untruth, it is difficult to have honest, fact-based conversations as well as informed advocacy and policy within the state, much less within the nation at large. Called the "Broadway of the Civil Rights Movement" by the activists of the Student Nonviolent Coordinating Committee, Mississippi has the potential to serve as a laboratory for progressive policies and community building whose interventions could transform the state and ripple out to the nation at large. Through the critical analysis of statistics and community-based research, this chapter will rethink the relationship between Mississippi, poverty, and race, specifically how those intersections play out in education and health care in the state.

This chapter argues that an honest examination of the state's educational and public health systems reveals deep and problematic links to vulnerable communities. With no intention to be comprehensive in nature and in order to continue productive conversations about the state and its peculiar relationship to poverty and race, this chapter examines prevailing myths, stark realities, and possible solutions to existing problems. The authors believe that examining the myths and realities of both education and health care will provide insight into why the state continues to occupy the lowest rungs in national averages. Education is consistently underresourced and populations are neglected, which has led to a historic, deliberate denial of equal educational opportunities. As a result, there exists a dual educational system that produces a cycle of disparities in knowledge gained and skills acquired that rivals the outcomes under Jim Crow. Regardless of race or class, neither the public nor the private systems in the state are turning out significant numbers of prepared students ready to pursue meaningful, sustainable careers or to become effective community leaders. Furthermore, because of poor educational systems, many of our youth are being tracked into low-wage, low-skilled jobs with little room for advancement. Many of the state's most promising youth exit the state for higher paying jobs and greater professional prospects. Consequently, the state experiences "brain drain." Corporations cannot find suitable applicant pools and therefore refuse to locate their businesses here. Poor education creates employment inequity. Like education, health care inequities also cripple Mississippi's productivity, citizen cohesion, and confidence.

This chapter argues that past and continuing inattention to just and accessible health care has enabled economic, social, and political racism to thrive. Myths that suggest that the state's citizens choose to live unhealthy lifestyles, that all citizens have equal access to medical attention, and that abuse of welfare is rampant each allow others to block health care legislation and create insurmountable obstacles to medical care. In short, two of the mainstays of an active and engaged citizenry, quality education and affordable and accessible health care, are often deliberately underfunded or targeted for deep budget cuts, thus ensuring this cycle will continue for years to come.

The chapter's purpose is twofold. First, this chapter demonstrates that inequities are not solely based on race. Accepting the intersectionality of identities, educational and health care inequities exist along both racial and class lines, creating a long-called-for-but-as-yet-unrealized potential powerful interracial coalition between marginalized populations. Second, health care and educational myths and problems impact not just obvious low-income and nonwhite individuals; they also negatively affect the entire state's citizenry, undermining the ultimate well-being of all of the state's residents.

EDUCATIONAL MYTHS

Beginning in the early 1960s, the War on Poverty has enabled a few seriously damaging myths to proliferate in the state of Mississippi regarding race, class, and education. First and foremost, there is a myth that only African Americans are poor. In the state of Mississippi race and class intersect to create serious poverty. In 1967 when Bobby Kennedy arrived in the state of Mississippi, he was shocked to not only have his ideas about blacks and poverty confirmed, he was stunned when he encountered poor whites (Edelman 2012). Fast-forward forty-seven years and the myth of colorblindness (much like the myth that America's election of the first black president indicates that we are living in a postracial society) imposes new threats to progress. Such myths hamper racial and class progress, because they reinforce the false notion that people are responsible for their own poverty. Such ideas mask the reality that educational racism and classism continue to exist at all primary and secondary educational levels. Additionally, the myth of colorblindness allows state legislators and politicians to underfund, under resource, and defund educational programs thus leading to sustained educational inequality. Colorblind and postracial notions permit educational achievement gaps as well as the classist and racist notions that education is "best bestowed on certain capable populations."

Because of their tremendous discomfort with the state's legacy of racism and inequality, many Mississippi citizens rely on the myth of colorblindness and the idea that we are living in a postracial society. In fact, many state and national public commentators insist that with the reelection of President Obama, that those who still "harp" on race are actually sustaining and manufacturing race problems where none exist. Continued belief in these myths is dangerous, because it reifies the myth of equality, equal access to education opportunities, and ideas about racial inferiority. These myths not only cause damage to the psyches of all in Mississippi who rely on false notions of either inferiority or equality, the myths allow, enable, and even encourage individuals to ignore and sustain institutional racism.

Additionally, the myth of voluntary segregation is especially problematic as it relates to education. Mississippi citizens cling to the notion that racial, class, and ethnic groups voluntarily separate themselves with respect to residence, employment, and recreation. In fact, residential racism continues to not only be sustained but thrives in the state. Despite the illegality of formal racist or classist covenants, most new subdivisions in Mississippi's urban and suburban areas are developed and exist almost exclusively along race and class lines. Since educational districts follow residential patterns, educational segregation is fortified. Myths about voluntary segregation, successful national educational legislation, and colorblindness not only mask the reality of Mississippi educational inequities; they prevent the development of effective programs and obscure possible solutions and strategies needed to deal with these very real inequities.

REALITIES

Mississippi's public school education is in dire straits. Despite the fact that over 90 percent of Mississippi's children attend public schools, educational race and class segregation is still the reality. Far from the prevailing stereotype that whites are rich and nonwhites are poor, the majority of white children who are in Mississippi public schools are, in fact, low-income students. Sustained disparities in wealth demonstrate a direct link between race, class, poverty, and educational inequality. Mississippi's deeply stratified educational system comprised of public schools and private academies is a dismal failure with serious repercussions impacting the future and progress of the state and opportunities for its citizens. Colorblindness has helped to continue the patterns of education and opportunity created by the policies of Jim and Jane Crow. Most people unfamiliar with the state's educational system would be surprised to learn that our primary and secondary schools are, for the most part, racially and/or class segregated. The existing costly, dual, and substandard public educational system is fortified by the continued presence of private academies—created largely to avoid school integration. While many outside of the state believe that these 1960s and 1970s educational systems are on the verge of extinction, this is far from the case.

Another myth causing substantial harm to Mississippi students is the success of the "No Child Left Behind" program. Initially intended to ensure educational equity, this program has hog-tied educational innovation, buried teachers in endless paperwork and empty forced assessment measures, and forced educators to leave the profession. Far from ensuring educational equity, the No Child Left Behind program has failed miserably. Instead of concentrating on comprehensive and tangible student success, the program, adopted in Mississippi in 2003, focuses on useless and endless paperwork, which de-emphasizes excellent teaching, rewards teaching to tests, and enforces draconian measures if schools fail to achieve. Test scores underscore this point. According to the state's "NCLB Report Card" issued in 2011/12 assessment revealed that for third graders, 42 percent of black students were proficient; 65 percent of whites were proficient; and females scored 58 percent and males scored 49 percent. Math scores for third graders indicated that 56 percent of black children are proficient and 77 percent of white students are proficient, 65 percent male and 69 percent female. These scores do not markedly improve for upper grades. College ACT scores in 2010 averaged 18.8 out of a possible score of 36. Additionally, in 2012, the State Department requested and was given a waiver from key provisions of NCLB. According to Liz Willen from the Hechinger Report, "Only [61 percent] of Mississippi students graduate on time—more than ten percentage points below the national average" (Willen 2012).

Private academies and charter schools proliferate throughout Mississippi, where there are approximately 250 private academies. The gap for low-income students in private schools, including charter schools, from 2003–2011 appears nearly as large as or larger than the gaps in public schools (Southern Education Foundation 2013). Minority enrollment in those schools is only 21 percent. With a 40 percent nonwhite population, this statistic demonstrates economic and educational inequality (World Population Statistics 2014). Designed to prevent "overwhelming" class or racial integration, these schools are costly and offer substandard educations (the average cost for private elementary school is over $4,000 and for high school, the cost is over $7,000). Racial anxiety among white parents clouds their ability to make informed choices about education. Many of the private academies are staffed by non- or poorly trained professionals, offer curricula that ill-prepares students for college or employment and, since accreditation is voluntary, important educational standards may not be achieved. Opportunity and excellence in a student's academic career have been associated with better social and economic outcomes later in life. Mississippi's wealthiest families place their much-needed resources into frightfully substandard private academies. These educational statistics have serious ramifications for the success of Mississippians and the state's economic, social, and political progress. Higher educational attainment is linked to higher earnings. In comparison, poor student performance is linked to a higher risk of high school dropout, risky health behaviors, delinquent or criminal behavior, and limited economic success (Evans et al. 2012).

Mississippi's educational concerns extend to early childhood education settings. Mississippi remains the only state in the South—and just one of eleven in the country—that does not fund any preK programs. Failure to prepare children for kindergarten or first grade costs the state a lot of money. One of every fourteen kindergarteners and one of every fifteen first graders in Mississippi repeated the school year in 2008, the most recent year for which statistics are available. Despite students' lack of preparation for kindergarten and schooling, legislators have held firm to the belief that the economically depressed state cannot afford preK. Fewer than half of the state's four-year-olds attend any type of preK program as compared to the national average of 75 percent (Willen 2012).

Within the next few years, it is likely that low-income students will become the majority of all public school children in the United States. With huge stubbornly unchanging gaps in learning, schools in the South and across the nation face the real danger of becoming entrenched, inadequately funded educational systems that enlarge the division in America between "haves and have nots" which will then be "prologue for a nation not at risk but a nation in decline" (Southern Education Foundation 2013). Already frequently scoring at the bottom—or near bottom—of national educational surveys and without serious intervention, Mississippi's educational system is beyond the risk of failure; its defeat is ensured.

Underfunding is central to the state's educational challenges. In 1997, the state legislature passed the Mississippi Adequate Education Program. This law provides a formula designed to ensure an adequate education for every Mississippi child whether that child lives in a wealthy community or a poor community. Since 1997 however the Act has been woefully underfunded by over one billion dollars. The obvious ramifications are that the majority of Mississippi's children continue to be poorly educated. Additionally, a stunning lack of healthy learning environments, books, and other supplies hampers student access to even an adequate education. Some teachers seeking to ensure their students have the proper supplies are forced to seek funding elsewhere. Some of the students are forced to learn in spaces that lack heat or air conditioning. Others are forced to learn in facilities with poor plumbing systems (Mader 2013).

In addition to substandard conditions and the lack of supplies necessary to do their job properly, poor salaries also discourage talented teachers from coming to or staying in the state. During the 2012–2013 academic year Mississippi pay rates ranked among the lowest in the nation. The average teacher salaries in the state were $41,646, with starting salaries as low as $31,000 (National Education Association 2012). Through threatening the loss of tenure, robbing pensions, and limiting promotion, the state's educators are exhausted, overwhelmed, and feeling defeated. Despite the fact that in 1998 the Mississippi legislature adopted the Critical Teacher Shortage Act, hiring increases have barely occurred.

Another reality hampering educational opportunity in the state is the forceful reappearance of tract education. Most often targeting low-income racial and class populations, tract education encourages certain students to focus on narrow employment goals and opportunities. Reified by racial and class stereotypes, expectations are lower for low-income and nonwhite students. A quick survey of the elementary, secondary, and college preparatory curricula indicates that certain vocational programs with limited economic potential are directed at certain populations. A survey of the private academies and charter schools reveals a decided lack of vocational education in wealthier districts leads those students and citizens to presume that professional expectations and educational opportunities are expected of them. While vocational education is to be applauded, the question of equity with regard to opportunity arises when it's clear that certain students, based on their class and racial identities, are pushed into predetermined education tracks.

Tract training and underfunded and underresourced educational initiatives negatively affect low-income and nonwhite student populations. Psychologically, Mississippi's youth learn that they are not worth the investment, that the state does not view them as important resources, and that they are not capable. This causes enormous defeatism among Mississippi's students. Conversations with these students across the state reveal feelings of defeat and disempowerment. Higher education and higher paid professional jobs are not seen as viable opportunities for poor black and white students. These students are quite cognizant that they possess neither the skills nor knowledge needed for professional advancement. Higher expectations and nurturing potential are just not realities for these populations. In many ways, the concept of "disposable populations" freely exists. Certain racialized and classed student populations are viewed as having little or no potential, special gifts, or insights. As students mature through the educational system, they feel left behind.

Some students suffer from internalized racism and classism. Too often, poor black and white students have adopted notions about their inferiority. For example, during an informal conversation with one of the authors of this chapter, one student wondered why she needed to study literature or higher mathematics at all. She explained that she did not need this education; rather she called for more "practical" education like "changing the oil in her car." Further comments revealed that she did not hold high expectations for herself or understand her unique abilities. She failed to understand how such "unnecessary" subjects teach her to think analytically and critically—skills needed to gain entrance into the state's higher education institutions or to gain professional employment.

The legacies of Jim and Jane Crow, the concept of disposable populations, educational tracking, under resourced educational systems, and internalized racism all enable social, economic, and political racism to thrive. According to John Sutter in a recent CNN article:

> Huge income gaps also are associated with gaps in empathy and trust, and that eventually morphs into hopelessness. Surprising links have emerged between income inequality and a host of social problems, including mental illness, substance abuse, incarceration, educational failure, teenage pregnancy, lower life expectancy, violence and infant mortality. Such links don't exist when you look just at average income. The inequality itself is to blame. (Sutter 2013)

While the author is referring to Louisiana, since circumstances are similar, the same might be said for Mississippi.

CURRENT AND FUTURE IMPACT ON THE STATE

Clearly, and to echo historian James Silver's pivotal observations in his seminal work *The Closed Society*, Mississippi suffers from terrible inertia. Most Mississippians will never leave the state and understand that the state will most likely not progress. Many citizens do not see a need for change. The educational system's false foundations regarding who has potential and who does not, who should hold power and who should not, creates tremendous anxiety for its citizens. We see people not only afraid of change, but because they have not been educated for change, they are ill-equipped with the intellectual and physical skills to improve their state. The inertia does not just create stasis for low-income people or populations of color, it holds the entire state down.

Across the state's historical landscape, there has not been substantial faith in state productivity and potential. As agricultural jobs became more mechanized, beginning in the 1940s, job opportunities in the former plantation South declined. Whites were able to shift to more urban areas and into manufacturing jobs. African Americans, blocked by racism and inadequate skills development opportunities, were not. In addition, residential segregation increased during this period, due to "white flight" and the increased concentration of black dwellers in federally subsidized housing. These factors reinforced the creation of high-concentration areas of poverty that are predominantly black. Thus, while many in Mississippi like to boast that the state has had more elected black officials than any other state as evidence of a tremendous improvement in race relations within the state, many African American elected officials preside over areas of deeply entrenched, generational poverty and have few resources to address the inequalities.

A perhaps surprising by-product of such new geographic concentrations means that white elites in poorer areas find themselves aligning with black political leaders in order to access power. Take, for example, the bankrolling of two mayoral candidates for the capital city of Jackson. In the early 2000s, white business leaders successfully supported a black candidate, Frank Melton, for mayor. But Melton's antics as mayor made the business leaders' second choice in the 2013 election less viable, and a solid voting block of the predominantly black city's residents lifted the community organizing candidate into the mayor's office, over the business community's preference. While political alliances are always shifting in the state, they have one common consequence, which is that poor or working-class whites are left out of the political power dynamic (Adams and Gorton 2006).

Additionally, new businesses are less likely to move to Mississippi for two reasons: first, the staff needed to create a new business does not want to relocate to the state, because they do not want their children to go to inadequate schools. Second, because of the inadequate schools, businesses fear that they cannot achieve a solid applicant pool. In 2003, when the Nissan Corporation opened a plant in Canton, they hoped for an applicant pool of 30,000; they received an applicant pool of 3,000. There is a direct correlation between low investment in our schools and therefore our children, and inadequate job creation and job opportunities that offer increased economic growth. Further underscoring a deep lack of confidence in the state, in a 2011 survey of business leaders across the state, 62 percent said that their children would have to leave the state in order to get a good-paying job (Southern Education Foundation 2013). The children of the state's business leaders recognize that there is little to no opportunity for job growth or advancement and either choose to go to college outside of the state or graduate with the intention of moving out of the state to begin their professional careers. So, in effect, Mississippi exhibits serious "brain drain" among our best qualified and prepared students.

EDUCATION SOLUTIONS

Solutions begin at the earliest stages of education. Education must be fully funded from preK through high school. Jake McGraw, editor of Rethink Mississippi, argues that universal preK funding for the state's children is a necessity. He argues "that one in three children live below the poverty line and without high-quality early education integrated with health and social services, childhood poverty will likely become a lifelong affliction" (McGraw 2014). McGraw writes that while the legislature has been "parsimonious," other private groups' programming and the federally funded Head Start program help to cover the lapses in financial costs and programming (Ibid.). The legislature needs to properly fund preK students so that Mississippi's most vulnerable populations receive a proper early education, nutrition, and health services to ensure that they are ready for formal schooling.

Older pieces of legislation, such as the Mississippi Adequate Education Act, which have never been fully funded, must be supported. As stated earlier, the very name of the act conveys the state legislature's attitude about education. The authors see the most promise for full funding of the Mississippi Adequate Education Act in a statewide grassroots effort perhaps through a referendum for a constitutional amendment. Barring such success there are opportunities through the legal system to compel the state legislature to fully support the unfunded mandate. Additionally, we would propose some specifics about fund allocation. Specifically, monies must be allocated for professional development for educators and teacher pay raises. Also, funding would need to be earmarked for after-school activities, especially in civic engagement, the arts, and wellness. Studies show that successful after-school programs increase retention rates and improve the likelihood of graduation. Legislative action focused on education is mandatory, already happening in the state, and needs to continue.

If we turn to Mississippi's history of successful grassroots community activism, there is hope in citizens of the state coalescing around the issue of full education funding. In particular, the Parents' Campaign and Southern

Echo represent two grassroots efforts that have been effective in securing progressive education reforms. The goal of the Parents' Campaign is provide excellent public schools for children throughout the state. The Parents' Campaign seeks to develop strong partnerships with other parents, educate Mississippi parents on the state of public education and specific schools, link parents to legislators, and push for legislation that advances public education in the state. Southern Echo understands that racism is not only prevalent but the leading barrier in the state. To end racism, Southern Echo assumes a multipronged approach. This organization promotes a model of community organizing that focuses on leadership development, education, and training organizations working to develop effective leadership at the grassroots level. Understanding that the political leadership in the state is often ineffective, Southern Echo focuses on empowering individuals and communities and utilizes a training and technical assistance approach to build a network of grassroots organizations. Focusing on truth-telling, Southern Echo encourages Mississippi's African Americans to confront the state's past and present in order to effectively devise effective strategies to advance the interests of families. Among other issues, Southern Echo focuses on education and models for how Mississippi's citizens need to harness their communities' political power to impact change in educational funding and practices. Honest and productive conversations about the legacy of racism begin the process of community and subsequent educational transformation.

A central reason for the poor state of Mississippi's educational system is that while many parents and students experience firsthand the devastating state of education, they may not be aware of past or proposed educational policies and legislation. They may be working to effect change locally but are stymied in their efforts because of existing state mandates and programs. In the summer of 2013, The Winter Institute funded and staffed Rethink Mississippi, an Internet policy blog. Rethink Mississippi focuses on information delivery educating the state and beyond about Mississippi's political, social, and economic issues and suggesting policy changes and group initiatives designed to advance the state. This blog serves as an essential informational and grassroots organizing tool. More easy access educational forums are required to encourage local and state collaborative efforts around education.

Related to educational deficits is the staggering mass incarceration problem in Mississippi. The state's educational professionals must recognize that "zero tolerance" policies are creating and sustaining a school-to-prison population. Schools must examine how race and class are determining how they deal with the problematic behaviors of children. They must seek out less punitive measures for minor infractions and consider the context that the state's children live and learn in. Behavioral infraction policies must be reexamined and reformed for their excessively punitive approach. Education professionals must consider how poverty, race, and class impede student chances at gaining an effective education that will equip them with the skills and knowledge needed to get jobs that will support them instead of sending them through the school-to-prison pipeline. More adequate resources must be funneled to the schools to ensure that students are learning in educationally friendly environments and that they are given the proper tools for learning and the support services needed to be successful during their K–12 education. Additionally, students and young adults who find themselves in the juvenile and criminal justice systems must be given educational opportunities while incarcerated. They must also be able to acquire knowledge and skills and gain credits toward their high school diplomas, better GED programs, and finally higher education preparation so that when they exit the criminal justice system they can effectively continue their education. Such programs are currently being developed. For example, the University of Mississippi, under the direction of Professors Patrick Alexander and Otis Pickett, has developed credit-bearing educational programs at Parchman, the state's major penal colony, that allow those who are incarcerated to work toward their higher education degrees.

Recent advocacy by Mississippi civil rights veterans like Bob Moses has argued that education exists as a civic and civil right. Responsible citizens require good educations, and since our nation is among the wealthiest in the world, education should be affordable to all. In order to fulfill the fundamental tenets of life, liberty, and the pursuit of happiness, many public commentators and important education scholars have argued that a solid education is required. Studies show that while a college degree made the most difference in terms of increasing the income earning potential for black women, those same women still earn less than white males who do not possess a high school diploma. For Mississippi to combat racial and class inequities, attention to the fundamental problems in the state's educational system must be addressed. Local to legislative initiatives must be considered and properly funded and implemented to make the state more productive and to retain political, social, and economic equality for its citizens.

HEALTH CARE MYTHS AND REALITIES

As in education, Mississippi's health care system suffers from and is stagnated by several myths. There is a perception that too many of its citizens prefer to make unhealthy food choices, that they are too lazy to exercise, and that they only consider their health when in crisis. Also, many Mississippians incorrectly assume that race and class have no bearing on health care, specifically in access to medical personnel, diagnoses, and treatment. Finally, there is the long-standing national myth of welfare abuse, specifically the belief that the health care entitlement system is plagued with low-income white and black abusers. According to the state's former governor and onetime Republican presidential candidate Haley Barbour, "One of the great problems in the conversation is the misimpression that if you don't have insurance, you don't get health care" (Stein 2011).

Contrary to Mr. Barbour's assertion that everyone who wants health care receives health care, the actual numbers simply do not add up. According to the Mississippi Office of Public Affairs "Of Mississippi's [eighty-nine] counties, [thirty-nine] do not have a pediatrician serving the area and, [forty-nine] have a designated shortage of primary care health care workers." As of 2012, 57 percent of the population lives in a dental health care shortage area. And 60 percent of Mississippi counties (fifty counties in all) do not have a practicing obstetrics/gynecological practitioner (Office of Public Affairs).

In addition to critical gaps in availability and access of qualified health professionals in underserved and especially rural and poor regions of the state, there are far too many Mississippians who do not have health insurance, so they cannot access health care that may be available. Public health advocates note that the income of Mississippians is among the lowest in the nation, and residents have the least amount of access to health care services. Before the current economic crisis and rising unemployment rates, 23 percent of adults age 18–64 in Mississippi reported having no health care coverage. As noted by health care policymakers, "One of the most promising opportunities to address the high rate of uninsured residents includes Medicaid Expansion. Medicaid Expansion remains an incredibly good deal for the state of Mississippi. It will bring billions of dollars into the state and will create jobs while increasing access to health insurance" (Shappley 2012). The state's political leadership has simply chosen to deprioritize the health of the majority of its citizens and, instead of paying less in the form of preventive health care measures, they have chosen to bear the costlier burden of health care costs when Mississippi's bodies are in health crises. Where they have options to improve the health outcomes of Mississippians, they most often choose political expediency and agendas over well-being. Observers in the recent national push to expand Medicaid as part of the larger implementation of health care have noted the consequences of the state's leadership in failing to take advantage of programs that could help its residents.

> Most of the states that are rejecting or noncommittal on Medicaid expansion also rank near the bottom in population health in an annual survey. Conversely, the residents in many of the states that have embraced the expansion are among the nation's healthiest. For more than 20 years, America's Health Rankings has ranked state population health on measures that include diabetes, obesity, smoking, and physical activity. States at the bottom of the list include Mississippi at number fifty. (Commins 2013)

"It is amazing." says Sara R. Collins, vice president, health care coverage and access, at the Commonwealth Fund: "States that are not expanding have among the highest rates of diabetes and obesity among lower income families. These are people earning less than $25,000 a year. These are families, many of them are uninsured, who would significantly benefit from the insurance coverage provided by the Medicaid expansion if those states were to expand."

In addition to denying the structural inequities that block access to affordable health care, political leaders often attack the very Mississippians who are the least served by their policies. Meanwhile, Haley Barbour continues to shame impoverished citizens. "Most of the health disparities in Mississippi are not because of the inability to get access or afford health care," he recently noted. "They are because of diet, alcohol, because of drugs, the very high incidence of illegitimacy that leads to high incidence of low-birth weight children" (Stein 2011).

But what is the real picture? Many of the counties in Mississippi are considered food deserts. In the Mississippi Delta alone, in one region, there were only two grocery stores located within an approximately 840-square-mile area. The lack of available healthy food is multiplied by the lack of privately owned vehicles and access to public transportation; many are not able to travel to a space where one could even begin to make healthy choices. If one has a car, most often the closest available food comes from the local gas station—fried chicken on a stick, fried potato wedges, and, a favorite in the Mississippi Delta, Kool-aid pickles. Dr. Aaron Shirley, a heroic civil rights figure in the state who was the first black resident at the University of Mississippi Medical Center in 1960, notes the irony that in the 1960s, Mississippi's black population starved; now it is dying from a preponderance of unhealthy food (Hansen 2012). And it is not just a matter of getting healthy food to residents. Recent examinations of the market-driven solutions that create fresh fruit and vegetable programs in "food desert" areas, as touted by Michelle Obama, show that these programs do not actually improve health outcomes in substantive ways. Instead, the stress of living in poverty and concomitant deleterious health effects that such stress causes do not change under such individual approaches (Gilligan 2014).

In case it is not clear, there is a direct correlation between healthy outcomes and wealth and unhealthy outcomes and poverty—all of which are mediated by race. The inequities are stark; the life expectancy of a black man in Mississippi compares to that of the average American in 1960 (Gilligan 2014). According to the Place Matters initiative of the Joint Center for Political and Economic Studies, in 2013 the five healthiest counties in Mississippi, starting with most healthy, are DeSoto, Lamar, Lafayette, Rankin, and Madison. Notably, each of these counties are ranked wealthier and whiter than the remaining counties in the state. The five counties in the poorest health, starting with the least healthy, are Quitman, Coahoma, Wilkinson, Holmes, and Claiborne—counties considerably poorer and that have higher proportions of black residents. Finally, the Delta in particular has higher rates of physically inactive adults and a lack of recreational facilities. These factors result in pretty devastating life expectancy rates. For example, between 1990 and 2008, life expectancy at birth varied by more than ten years between counties within the Mississippi Delta. Life expectancy in the region is lower than that of the Dominican Republic, Estonia, or Sri Lanka. Beyond these physical and emotional costs of obesity and poor health, there are great financial costs. These figures belie the state's repeated assertions that it cannot afford to invest in healthy outcomes.

There is some good news to report. In 2007, the state legislature passed the Healthy Students Act, which was specifically designed to address high rates of childhood obesity. Largely because of this initiative, the Mississippi Department of Health reports a statistically significant decline in obesity in elementary students and the overall percentage of children's weight is declining. However, these declines fall along racial lines; white students are losing more weight than nonwhite students. The reason for this inequity is that the Healthy Students Acts was another unfunded mandate; thus, the only schools able to take full advantage of its impacts are those schools that already possessed adequate resources.

Mississippi's political leadership is exploring new strategies in its health care economy. Recently the state enacted the Health Care Industry Zone Act to spur health care development. Under the act, businesses such as laboratory testing facilities, medical supply distributors, and biotechnology research facilities that either make an investment of at least $10 million or create a minimum of twenty-five full-time, permanent jobs within the health care zone are eligible for certain tax incentives. In 2013, the act was expanded to include health care investment in communities that developed a certified health care master plan in lieu of meeting the original law's acute care bed count. Twelve zones have been approved based on the certification of community master plans (Mississippi Economic Council).

SOLUTIONS

There is still much work to do. First and foremost, the state must participate fully in the implementation of the Affordable Health Care Act. Mississippi Health Care Access, a state nonprofit coalition of organizations formed to advocate for the expansion of Mississippi's Medicaid program, noted that 300,000 citizens in the state would fall into a coverage gap without health care expansion. Most of these people are members of vulnerable working families, because they would earn too much to receive Medicaid yet not enough to afford to participate in the new health care exchange. In addition to providing much needed support for health insurance for the working poor, the new Medicaid expansion would also create 9,000 new health care related jobs, economic opportunity the state desperately needs.

Additionally, the state legislature must fully fund the Healthy Students Act. Given its success in those school districts that already had resources to implement it, with the appropriate funding and support, it can also produce healthy outcomes in underresourced school districts. With a local health council, new funding for nurses in each school, and training for cafeteria employees, districts whose students have the lowest health outcomes could begin to thrive by eating better food, having access to health care at school, and by living in a community whose adults are creating a culture that promotes wellbeing. Additionally, state and private resources should be used to continue and expand support to nonprofits like the Mississippi Roadmap to Health Equity, which sells produce from local small farmers and offers cooking classes focused on foods that might be unfamiliar. It also provides recreational space for exercise and play and seeds and technical assistance for school gardens throughout the state. Other efforts that deserve support include Diversity Diner, which is a faith-based nonprofit effort modeled on Café Reconcile in New Orleans to train at-risk youth in the developing restaurant industry in Mississippi.

In addition to physical health, Mississippi officials must look much more closely at the links between poverty and poor mental health as well. In her 2003 study centered on families in North Carolina and provided stipends, Professor Jane Costello concluded that long-term poverty encourages psychiatric, behavioral, and emotional problems in children. When certain rural families were given stipends, child psychiatric problems and crime declined. Her study also demonstrated that early intervention with financial aid was crucial; teenagers who were given stipends did not reveal any marked psychiatric improvement. Those families who did receive supplements felt that such monies helped ease the "feast-or-famine existence" (Velasquez-Manoff 2014). Another study conducted by the University of North Carolina at Chapel Hill revealed that the stressors of poverty impact parenting (Velasquez-Manoff 2014). While these studies were conducted in North Carolina, it is important to understand what they determine with regard to the problematic link between poverty and mental health everywhere. Given these studies' findings, Mississippi should make a long-term investment in low-income and nonwhite families who find themselves in poverty. Lifting these families out of abject poverty and providing them with safety nets in the form of stipends would hopefully have similar effects on Mississippi's at-risk children and parents. Early intervention can disrupt the generational consequences of poverty.

In the 1990s, aid to families shifted from community-based block grants to more direct aid to families. One successful model that is showing great promise in Mississippi is HealthConnect. Using local community health professionals, the program provides in-home preventive care door-to-door. It has already shown great success in the capital city of Jackson, where it operates in an abandoned inner city mall and offers health care services as well as supporting health providers in Jackson schools. Shirley hopes to expand the program into Mississippi Community Health House Network, an initiative that would link community-based health providers to district health houses and, for more serious illness, to regional hospitals. For a $20 million investment, this program, sponsored by Jackson State University, will be able to create fifteen health houses in the Mississippi Delta alone (Hansen 2012).

There is also a need for racial healing as evidenced by the presence of two professional medical associations segregated by race. Because of the history of Jim and Jane Crow segregation in the medical profession in Mississippi and the discrimination experienced by black doctors, there is a lingering mistrust and suspicion between black patients and white doctors. Moreover, there is tension between black doctors and the largely white-dominated state medical profession. One highlight in response to this dynamic is the developing University of Mississippi Medical School (UMMC) requirement that all medical students are trained in social disparities.

Mississippi could lead the way forward in a number of areas. Historian John Dittmer asserts that sixty years ago, Mississippi was "the standard by which this nation's commitment to social justice would be measured" (Hansen 2012). Mississippi's current state of affairs, as it relates to education and health care, suggests that much more work needs to be accomplished. Inequities and disparities in education and health care exist and continue to grow. Evidence of classism and racism is quite present when examining how Mississippi's legislature and chief executives both understand and approach the state's health and education problems. Legislative acts have been poorly thought out or have gone unfunded. Crucial to the success of Mississippi is an understanding that health care and educational initiatives that poorly serve low-income or nonwhite populations affect not only those populations but all state populations. Failure to create, implement, and properly fund important education and health care initiatives hampers the state's economic, social, and political advancement as well as the state's ability to compete both nationally and internationally. More importantly, though, in neglecting the state's most at-risk populations, governors and legislators fail in their responsibility to uphold basic human rights of all Mississippians. The need is great and the opportunity ripe for a new movement for human rights in the state, one that finally moves beyond the white supremacist politics of the past in order to secure a more equitable future for all of the state's residents. As "the

Movement's Broadway," Mississippi's next great performance waits in the wings.

Chapter Five

Poverty in Appalachia

Joanna Maulbeck

"How can you frighten a man whose hunger is not only in his own cramped stomach but in the wretched bellies of his children? You can't scare him—he has known a fear beyond every other," wrote John Steinbeck in *The Grapes of Wrath* (1939). The classic novel, set during the Great Depression, tells the story of tenant farmers from Oklahoma who travel to California in an effort to escape economic hardship. Contemporarily considered as one of the most influential books of the twentieth century, the novel largely contributed to the "discovery" of poverty in rural America in the 1940s. About twenty years after Steinbeck completed *The Grapes of Wrath*, Harry M. Caudill, a member of the Kentucky Legislature, wrote *Night Comes to the Cumberlands*, another account of rural poverty, this time specific to Appalachia. As a descendent of migrants who came to Appalachia before 1800, Caudill wrote of the Cumberland Plateau's transformation from a land of rich soil and timber to a distressed terrain, exploited for its natural resources: "The present crisis is compounded of many elements, human and material," he observed. He continued:

> They have produced what is probably the most seriously depressed region in the nation—and the adjective applies in much more than an economic sense. They have brought economic depression, to be sure, and it lies like a gray pall over the whole land. But a deeper depression lies in depression of the spirit which has fallen upon so many of the people, making them, for the moment at least, listless, hopeless, and without ambition. (Caudill 1963, 325)

These accounts are somewhat reflective of their era's sentiments toward rural poverty, with Steinbeck writing during Franklin D. Roosevelt's New Deal program, and Caudill writing after John F. Kennedy's promise to alleviate rural poverty. Under the leadership of Kennedy and his successor, Lyndon B.

Johnson, increased awareness of poverty in Appalachia helped lead to the War on Poverty's efforts to alleviate rural poverty After declaring the War on Poverty in his 1964 State of the Union address, Johnson traveled to an Appalachian home in Inez, Kentucky, to generate support for his antipoverty initiative. Various photographs feature Johnson discussing the region's struggles with families in Appalachia.

This chapter examines the story of Appalachian poverty in four sections. I begin by providing an overview of Appalachia and its role in the narrative leading to and from the War on Poverty. Next, I examine the legacies of the Appalachian Regional Commission (ARC) and the Economic Opportunity Act (EOA) as both were used as primary means to combat poverty in Appalachia. I continue with an examination of some of the lessons from the Appalachian experience related to poverty issues. I conclude with an analysis of the War on Poverty in Appalachia.

DEFINING APPALACHIA

Variants of the name "Appalachia" date back to the sixteenth century; while the term first refers to a Native American village, it later came to mean the mountain range north of the village itself. In the late nineteenth century, Appalachia was described as a specific cultural region by William Goodell Frost of Berea College. He wrote about "mountain people" that lived quaint lives in log cabins, preserving early American handicrafts, music, and folkways. He wrote of their isolation, stating that it's a "longer journey from Ohio to eastern Kentucky than America from Europe" (Frost 1976, 494). Since then, accounts of Appalachia have emphasized its rural landscapes and isolated communities, at times romanticizing Appalachian frontiersmen for self-sufficiency, and at others disdaining them for backwardness and ignorance. All of Appalachia has been described using similar rhetoric, although the area stretches over 200,000 square miles, and includes a variety of counties in thirteen states.

Although endowed with natural resources, including rich soil, timber, and coal, Appalachia has been associated with poverty. As Caudill argues in *Night Comes to the Cumberlands,* poverty in the region can be attributed to exploitation of natural resources by corporations from northern cities, such as Philadelphia and New York, starting at the end of the nineteenth century. Corporations bought timber from the region for as little as 76 cents each. "At an ever-rising tempo this valuable portion of the mountaineer's legacy was transferred to men who lived far away," writes Caudill (1963, 63). In addition to buying timber, corporations purchased underlying minerals. Coal operators erected towns and employed residents for cheap labor while reaping great profit. This subjected Appalachia to grow dependent on coal production. When coal production dwindled after World War II, as companies began using more efficient technology instead of manpower and large national industries began using natural gas and fuel oil, Appalachia's economy faltered.

KENNEDY, JOHNSON, AND POVERTY IN APPALACHIA

In 1960, John F. Kennedy visited West Virginia as part of his presidential campaign. Kennedy, a Catholic, delivered a speech to the Greater Houston Ministerial Association, a group of Protestant ministers, urging them not to allow religious differences to dictate the course of the election. Instead, he asked them to focus on more critical issues, emphasizing "the hungry children [he] saw in West Virginia; the old people who cannot pay their doctor bills; the families forced to give up their farms; an America with too many slums, with too few schools."[1] A few months later, on the eve of the primary, he promised the people of West Virginia that he would introduce a program to Congress for aid, alleviating such critical issues, if elected president (Eller 2008, 54).

Keeping the promise that he had made during the campaign, Kennedy created the Area Redevelopment Act (ARA) in 1961. ARA was created based on the recommendations of the West Virginia Task Force, a committee that he designated as responsible for recommendations in assisting areas in poverty. The committee suggested that ARA focus on funding low-interest industrial loans as well as providing grants to local governments and worker training programs in an effort to alleviate poverty in economically depressed urban and rural areas. These exact initiatives were executed not only in West Virginia, but also in other mining areas with high unemployment in the states of Kentucky, Michigan, Minnesota, and Pennsylvania (Dillon 1963).

The Conference of Appalachian Governors, an organization formed in 1960 by governors of ten Appalachian states, agreed with one of President Kennedy's representatives, to establish a small group within ARA to focus on Appalachia. Despite the focus, ARA's impact on the region was limited. As Sundquist (1968) points out, entrepreneurs were hesitant to partake in the government's loan program and invest in Appalachia, a mountainous, remote area subject to flooding.

In 1963, Kennedy created the President's Appalachian-Regional Commission (PARC). PARC collaborated with the Council of Appalachian Governors, consisting of representatives from West Virginia, Alabama, Georgia, Kentucky, Maryland, North Carolina, Tennessee, and Virginia (PARC 1964). PARC was a federal-state committee that gathered ideas regarding poverty alleviation in Appalachia. Recommendations focused on development of transportation, human resources, and water in Appalachia, as well as encouraged the creation of a permanent commission to address Appalachia's struggles. Unfortunately, President Kennedy was assassinated before the recommendations were actualized, temporarily interrupting the initiative (Eller 2008).

Although Kennedy initiated an effort to alleviate poverty in Appalachia, he never publicly announced a crusade against poverty. When Lyndon B. Johnson became president and announced that he would "carry forward the plans of John Fitzgerald Kennedy," he then proceeded to declare "unconditional war on poverty in America." When describing the War on Poverty, the first initiative that he elaborated upon was the "launch of a special effort in the chronically distressed areas of Appalachia" (Miller Center 1984).

Johnson's interest in making rural poverty a component of his antipoverty efforts brought hope to those who would ultimately advocate for continued support in Appalachia. PARC seized upon the opportunity to urge Johnson to distinguish poverty in Appalachia from the broader context of the War on Poverty. They included their recommendations for confronting poverty in their region in *Appalachia: A Report by the President's Appalachian Regional Commission 1964*, which suggested the creation of development programs for the Appalachian region and its people, along with a regional organization that would oversee such efforts (PARC 1964).

In response to the report, the Appalachian Regional Development Act (ARDA) was passed in 1965. ARDA stated that it "recognizes the comprehensive report of the President's Appalachian Regional Commission" and "concludes that region-wide development is feasible, desirable, and urgently needed" (ARDA 1965). The Act attempted to facilitate development in Appalachia by building infrastructure, regional industry, and entrepreneurial communities, as well as diversifying and improving the regional economy. It also attempted to provide a framework for coordinating federal, state, and local initiatives to respond to Appalachia's challenges.

Most notably, ARDA created the Appalachian Regional Commission (ARC) to organize multifaceted efforts involving federal, state, and local actors in order to alleviate poverty within the region. The Commission was delegated to consist of a federal member that is appointed by the president and the governor of each participating Appalachian state. It was formed to focus specifically on four aspects of development: highway construction, resource development, flood control and water tower projects, and improvement in human services (Edwards, Asbury, and Cox 2006).

Some legislation, such as ARDA, focused on Appalachia specifically. However, issues of rural poverty in Appalachia were also targeted in other federal poverty legislation of the 1960s. The Economic Opportunity Act (EOA) brought the Office of Economic Opportunity, Volunteers in Service to America (VISTA) Job Corps, and Head Start to Appalachia. They provided, and continue to provide, services to the region through various pathways, including but not limited to educational and vocational training, development of health care services, and encouragement of civic participation and leadership.

When President Johnson declared the War on Poverty, he continued to confront poverty in Appalachia with special attention. Special attention was given through the Appalachian Regional Commission (ARC). Poverty was also confronted through organizations that emerged under the Economic Opportunity Act (EOA), such as Job Corps, Youth Corps, Head Start, and Community Action Agencies.

THE LEGACY OF THE APPALACHIAN REGIONAL COMMISSION

The ARC continues to provide funding to projects that coincide with the organization's four major goals. The goals include: building the Appalachian Development Highway System to reduce Appalachia's isolation; developing and improving Appalachia's infrastructure to make the region economically competitive; increasing job opportunities and per capita income in Appalachia in order to reach parity with the nation; and strengthening the capacity of the people of Appalachia to compete in the global economy (ARC n.d.). ARC targets these goals in an effort to assist Appalachia in achieving socioeconomic parity with the rest of the nation (ARC 2010).

MINIMIZING ISOLATION AND ENHANCING ECONOMIC DEVELOPMENT

The goal to construct the Appalachian Development Highway System (ADHS) originated within the Appalachian Regional Development Act of 1965. Construction of the highway system was authorized within ARDA in an effort to connect Appalachia to the interstate system and generate economic development in the area. The 3,571–mile highway system is still under construction, with 81 percent of it completed in 2012. The remaining and "most expensive" parts are yet to be constructed (ARC n.d.). ARC oversees and promotes its construction, predicting that its construction will elevate economic growth.

While persisting with initiatives that emerged in the 1960s, the Appalachian Regional Commission has also pursued economic development through recently established initiatives. In part, these initiatives focus on creating economic opportunity by expanding access to capital and credit, investing in entrepreneurial projects, and investing in new industries. In addition to creating new economic opportunities, ARC has also prioritized serving already established businesses through organizations such as the Export Trade Advisory Council.

Expanding access to capital and credit is a contemporary focus partially because of ongoing consolidation of banks in urban settings. Such practices decrease the number of community banks in rural Appalachia, limiting access to capital and credit in the region. This further leads to low business lending, ultimately limiting business creation, expansion, and growth. During the 2007 recession, when lending in the whole country decreased, it particularly did so in Appalachia. With ARC's support, a network of Community Development Financial Institutions (CDFI) has created capital in Appalachia (ARC 2012).

Basic types of CDFIs include credit unions, development venture capital funds, and loan funds (NCRC 2007). Loan funds have been most prevalent in Appalachia. They have focused on microenterprise, small business development, and housing finance sectors (NCRC 2007). In addition to relying on credit unions, venture capital funds, and loan funds, a central bank for development leaders—Appalachian Community Capital—was established in 2013. According to ARC, the bank is expected to leverage $223 million in bank capital and create 2,200 jobs (ARC 2013).

Along with creating CDFI opportunities, ARC has pursued the creation of economic opportunities by investing in projects designed to build entrepreneurial economies and new industries, including entrepreneurial projects, tourism, and infrastructure development. From 1997 to 2007, ARC invested almost $43 million in various entrepreneurial projects and $10.2 million to form an advisory council to increase tourism (ARC n.d.).

New industries focusing on infrastructure development were also created. They primarily targeted the development of a water system, since more than 25 percent of residents do not have access to a community water system and rely on private well water for drinking needs, and almost 50 percent of Appalachian homes rely on on-site water disposal (ARC n.d.). By funding infrastructure projects that target water services, jobs were created while serving residents with new or improved water and waste-water services.

While ARC has pursued the creation of economic opportunities through efforts such as expansion of capital and credit as well as investment in entrepreneurial economies and new industries, the organization also focuses on serving already established industries. The Export Trade Advisory Council (ETAC), for example, was designed to serve as an advocate for the region within the global business community and identify ways to expand their outreach to external markets. The ETAC is to advocate for Appalachia's already established industries, which focus on production of auto parts, electronic components, wooden household furniture, upholstered household furniture, food processing machinery, and packaging machinery, bringing in $5 billion annually to Appalachian manufacturers. Auto parts and electronic components are leading exports, with the former contributing to 65 percent of exports and the latter to 30 percent.

As described above, efforts to create economic opportunities and serve already established industries have produced results. However, their significance is somewhat limited. On one hand, ARC invested in 340 entrepreneurship initiative projects, creating over 1,700 new businesses between 1997–2007 (ARC n.d.). Tourism projects generated 2,588 jobs in the region (ARC n.d.) as well as revenue. In 2011, tourists to Great Smoky National Park have contributed $818 million into local economies (Harbison 2013). However, on the other hand, Appalachia faces structural barriers in development. While CDFI creates an option for capital and credit, its lending is small compared to conventional bank lending (NCRC n.d.). Financing gaps are likely to remain or widen between regions unless there is equal access to credit and capital. Along similar lines, despite Export Trade Advisory Council's advocacy, it will become increasingly difficult for Appalachia's manufacturing to compete with low-wage, labor-intensive industries overseas (Bernard, Bradford, and Schott 2005). Regional furniture and lumber industries have especially been impacted by globalization, with companies such as Stanley Furniture relocating production from Virginia to Southeast Asia in 2010 (Roberts 2010). Job opportunities are limited, with only 35 of 420 Appalachian counties experiencing positive job growth between 2007 and 2010 (ARC n.d.).

EDUCATION AND HEALTH CARE

In addition to focusing on economic development, ARC has also focused on social services in the region, such as education and health care. Organizations such as Appalachian Higher Education and Appalachian Health Policy Advisory Council were created for such social service needs at the end of the twentieth century.

The Appalachian Higher Education (AHE) Network was developed in 1998 to increase college attendance in the region. Postsecondary education attainment is lower in Appalachia than the rest of the nation. Between 2007 and 2011, 7.5 percent of Appalachian residents earned associate degrees and 21 percent earned bachelor's degrees. This is below the national average of 7.6 percent and 28.2 percent (Pollard and Jacobsen). Although 50 percent of Appalachian high school students enroll in postsecondary education or the military, this figure drops to 20 percent–40 percent in most economically distressed areas of Appalachia. To work toward ameliorating such discrepancies, AHE was founded in nine states: Alabama, Georgia, Kentucky, Mississippi, North Carolina, Ohio, Tennessee, Virginia, and West Virginia. The Network provides grants of $2,000–$10,000 to fund high school campus visits, information sessions, and other activities to increase college attendance (AHE n.d.).

A year after the AHE Network was founded, the Appalachian Health Policy Advisory Council was formed. Its members are diverse, including rural health directors, academics, local health care practitioners, and economic development officials. They are to advise the Commission on the region's health issues. Advice has constituted of propositions for research on health disparities between the region and the rest of the nation, which has resulted in the Commission undertaking such research studies.

In addition to collaborating with the Appalachian Health Policy Advisory Council, ARC has provided various grants within the health industry. Grants have assisted in acquiring equipment in local hospitals and clinics, training for health professionals, and support for community-based health education activities. Finally, in the area of health care, collaboration with organizations such as the Centers for Disease Control and Prevention has addressed life-threatening diseases, including diabetes and cancer (ARC n.d.).

Despite these efforts, Appalachia continues to struggle with college attendance and medical care. In the 1990s, although the number of adults who are college graduates increased in Appalachia, the gap between college graduates in Appalachia and the rest of the nation grew from 6.1 percent to 6.6 percent. The gap between the rest of the U.S. and Appalachia was most pronounced in distressed regions. Central Appalachia, for example, had less than half the national proportion of college graduates (Haaga 2004).

In terms of medical care, Appalachia has lower preventable mortality rates when compared to the rest of the country (PDA 2012) as well as 36 percent fewer dentists per 100,000 population than the U.S. average (Krause et al. 2012). Residents from distressed areas of Central and Southern Appalachia particularly lack access to quality care. Compounding the problem is retention of providers in Appalachia, who struggle with higher caseloads and a higher proportion of nonpaying patients.

It is evident that Appalachia continues to struggle with college attendance and medical care. Particularly problematic is the emergence of inequity within the region. Residents from most distressed areas are most limited in accessing education and health services. Although the poverty rate in the region has decreased, as has the number of counties in distress, development has not been constant throughout the region. ARC has described some Appalachian economies as "successfully diversified," while noting that other Appalachian communities "still require basic infrastructure such as roads and water and sewer systems." In essence, ARC recognizes that Appalachia has transformed. It has transformed from an area of "widespread poverty" to an area of "economic contrasts" (ARC n.d.).

THE LEGACY OF THE ECONOMIC OPPORTUNITY ACT

Some of the most influential legacies established under the Economic Opportunity Act included the Office of Economic Opportunity (OEO), and Volunteers in Service to America (VISTA). Although these programs were implemented on a national level, their legacy was unique and pronounced in Appalachia.

Community Action Programs (CAP), which were established under the Office of Economic Opportunity, fostered efforts for citizens to tackle poverty in the region. By incorporating locals into the poverty alleviation effort, federal funds were predicted to quickly and efficiently serve their purpose. Unfortunately, policy makers and communities did not reach consensus in defining "community action," and the concept came to represent varying ideas to various stakeholders (Eller 2008). Some community action programs were "designed to confront local bureaucracies and power structures in the interest of the poor, while others were little more than transformed economic development commissions, controlled by local elites" (Eller 2008). Most community action agencies (CAAs) resembling the former were led by directors from outside of the area, who were limited in altering institutional structures and political alignments.

As issues surfaced within community action agencies, Appalachian citizens voiced their concerns, often through protests. Some protests served as catalysts in dismantling CAAs. In Knott County, Kentucky, for example, a protest dismantled a CAA that catered to eight counties and replaced it with a county-level program that locals thought would be more responsive to the needs of the poor. Similarly, in Raleigh County, West Virginia, Appalachian Volunteers (AVs) encouraged citizens to elect one of their own as a chair of the county CAA, replacing the director of the agency, who was a former school superintendent (Eller 2008).

Thus, while CAP may not have transformed Appalachia's economy, it contributed in mobilizing community members. CAP encouraged local involvement and advocacy, eventually cultivating grassroots protests. As Richard Straw stated: "While the overall success of the War on Poverty was limited, there were some unexpected results in the mountains. In many communities, there emerged the belief that change and improvement would come only through organizing at the grass-root level" (Edwards, Asbury, and Cox 2006).

As mentioned above, AVs encouraged protests in Appalachia. AVs were VISTA volunteers working in the region. As such, they were free to live and work among the poor, determining how to best fight poverty. They operated outside government structures, and were more willing to take risks. In turn, they became strong advocates of confrontation and civic action. The VISTA workers who joined the Appalachian Volunteers were more "radical" in their views. They attributed poverty to "colonization" rooted in corporate and elite interests. They questioned projects associated with the War on Poverty, criticizing poverty alleviation methods for their shortsightedness and their lack of acknowledgment of social, political, and economic contexts within which poverty developed (Kiffmeyer 2008). Some even questioned the VISTA program itself. "The very fact that a volunteer goes into a community to assist degrades, threatens, and sometimes angers the mountain people. The college outsider is viewed from the start as having superior education and wider background," a volunteer wrote (Kiffmeyer 2008).

Locals collaborated with VISTAs and AVs at times, and at others orchestrated their own protests. They mobilized to address various grievances, including issues related to the environment and worker rights. For example, a campaign was developed to eradicate strip mining. Although strip mining continues today (primarily in Kentucky, West Virginia, Virginia, and Tennessee) the anti-strip-mining movement of the 1960s and 1970s was a salient effort in eradicating the practice. Citizens rallied to sit-in on strip mine sites, destroy mining equipment, and lobby to influence law (Fisher 1993). In addition to focusing on strip mining, grassroots organizations also invested their efforts in expanding workers' rights. In 1969, more than 40,000 miners across three Appalachian states—West Virginia, Ohio, and Pennsylvania—launched an extensive strike that shut down the mine industry in its advocacy for reform in state workers' compensation and mine safety law. This time, they proved successful in instituting concrete change. The strike ended when health benefits were granted to victims of black lung disease, and new safety standards for underground mines were established (Mulchaly 2000).

Although the initiatives established under EOA did not significantly reduce poverty, community action and VISTA programs inspired grassroots activists, which mobilized communities. In doing so, grievances surfaced. Environmental issues pertaining to strip mining as well as human rights issues pertaining to mining, were addressed. Through this process, a sense of pride and identity in the region developed. Even the word "Appalachia" became accepted within the region. The need to express a positive image of Appalachia developed (Edwards, Asbury, and Cox 2006). Grassroots activists challenged the media, which often described the region as "a vast junkyard," a landscape of "man-made desolation of corrugated hills and hollows laced with polluted streams," and its people as "disease-ridden," "unschooled," and "without hope" (Life 1964). Activists strived to create a well-rounded account of the region, challenging the sensational rhetoric of the past.

REFLECTING ON THE PAST, ENVISIONING A BETTER FUTURE

In 1969, 17.8 percent of the population of Appalachia was in poverty, 4.1 percent higher than the national average of 13.7 percent. Since the beginning of the War on Poverty, poverty rates have slightly declined and have come to mirror the national average (Black, Mather, and Sanders 2007). Between 2007–2011, 16.1 percent of residents of the Appalachia region lived below the poverty level, 1.8 percent higher than the national average of 17.9 percent (Pollard and Jacobsen 2014). In addition to poverty in Appalachia being closer to the national average than it was in 1969, certain living conditions have also improved. In 1960, for example, less than 50 percent of homes in Central Appalachia had plumbing facilities, and by 2000 nearly all Central Appalachian homes had plumbing (Black, Mather, and Sanders 2007).

While the general situation in Appalachia has improved in terms of poverty, certain areas in Appalachia remain distressed. Poverty rates in Appalachian Kentucky were 24.8 percent between 2007 and 2008 (ARC n.d.). Due to some counties' progress and not others', wealth inequality within the region is more pronounced than ever. Communities located along the highway are mainly the ones that have benefited from development initiatives. Educational and health facilities, along with shopping centers, have been constructed in certain counties closer to the Appalachian corridor highway. Hazard, Kentucky, for example, a former coal mining community, now hosts a Wal-mart, retail outlets, modern housing developments, and several job prospects. However, miles from Hazard, Kentucky, lay communities that remain rural and "distressed." As of October 2013, 93 of 420 counties continue to be "distressed" in the region (ARC n.d.).

THE COMPLEXITIES OF RURAL POVERTY: DRAWING FROM THE APPALACHIAN EXPERIENCE

Significant investments in Appalachia through the War on Poverty and subsequent initiatives have provided some opportunities for addressing poverty; however, they have led to limited regional impact. The reason for such limited impact is a complex question, encouraging exploration as to why ARDA and EOA's efforts have had only limited impact on the region. It leads to the deciphering and examining of ARDA and EOA's initiatives

With the origins of the War on Poverty rooted in Kennedy's presidential campaign in Appalachia, the Conference of Appalachian Governors, and the President's Appalachian-Regional Commission, rural poverty has come to be associated with the region. Perhaps due to this association, poverty in Appalachia has been battled through efforts that attempt to develop the region and its people. ARC plays a large role in regional development through investments (in projects that focus on capital, credit and entrepreneurial development, as well as highway and water system development) and support of various organizations (such as the Export Trade Advisory Council). Social services were provided through OEO's community empowerment initiatives and continue to be the focus of organizations such as the Appalachian Higher Education (AHE) Network.

By attempting to develop Appalachia through focus on regional and social transformation, the complexity of poverty has been somewhat simplified. Poverty alleviation initiatives have been simple in that they have failed to "confront realities of injustice and economic exploitation that continue to marginalize poor people" (Eller 2008). In other words, poverty alleviation initiatives neglect the region's history, which provides an account of exploitation of the land and its people as wealth has been sparingly distributed between several corporations and local, politically powerful elites. In addition to neglecting Appalachia's historical narrative, poverty alleviation initiatives have overlooked systemic inequalities that serve as barriers to prosperity. The potential of ARC initiatives remains unfulfilled partially because as the organization promotes the use of CDFIs to create credit and capital, banks continue to consolidate in urban areas, allowing inequity across regions to remain pronounced. Similarly, while the Export Trade Advisory Council advocates for interests of Appalachian industries, international trade agreements limit Appalachia's competitiveness to low-wage, labor-intensive industries overseas. In essence, poverty alleviation techniques have attempted to alter the region and its people, disregarding the systems that have created poverty in the region in the first place. The complexity of the issue has been underplayed and the root of the problem misdiagnosed.

Simplification of poverty has had ramifications for Appalachia, as well as for the rest of rural America. Over the years, Appalachia has come to represent rural poverty. However, rural poverty is not a phenomenon unique to Appalachia. It is vast, encompassing various regions across America, including Native American tribal lands, the Mississippi Delta, borderlands between the United States and Mexico, and other areas. While poverty in Appalachia continues to be researched, the expansiveness and variations of rural poverty must be studied, as well.

In conclusion, ARDA's and EOA's initiatives during and since the War on Poverty have been limiting to Appalachia and rural areas in general. While ARDA and EOA's efforts have attempted to alleviate poverty through initiatives that focus on development of the region and its people, such attempts neglect historical contexts and systemic inequity. The rhetoric also associates rural poverty with Appalachia, ultimately undermining the vastness of rural poverty in the nation.

CONCLUSION

Fifty years after the War on Poverty, poverty persists, especially in rural areas. According to the U.S. Department of Agriculture (USDA) Economic Research Service, we have learned that U.S. counties that have had 20 percent or more of their population living in poverty over the last 30 years are defined as "persistently poor." Using this definition, 353 counties are "persistently poor" within the United States, 301 of which are located in nonmetro areas, particularly in the South (USDA 2013).

While traveling through persistently impoverished areas of Appalachia, Kevin Williamson, a *National Review* journalist, recently shared his experience: "It's a classic economic death spiral: The quality of the available jobs is not enough to keep good workers, and the quality of the available workers is not enough to attract good jobs," he wrote (2014). Instead of participating in black-minded introspection, he observed citizens going about their day-to-day lives. In observing some of their lives, he saw—"pills, dope, morning beers, endless scratch-off lotto cards, the federally funded ritual of trading cases of food-stamp Pepsi for packs of Kentucky's Best cigarettes and good old hard currency, tall piles of gas-station nachos, the occasional blast of meth, Narcotics Anonymous meetings, and petty crime" (Ibid.).

Williamson's article, entitled *The White Ghetto*, is similar to accounts written about Appalachia fifty years ago. Recognizing that the article is certainly not reflective of Appalachia as a whole, it is important to include in this chapter. It is important because it is telling of the legacy of the War on Poverty. Fifty years after the War on Poverty, Williamson's words parallel the words of Harry Caudill in *Night Comes to the Cumberlands*: "They have produced what is probably the most seriously depressed region in the nation—and the adjective applies in much more than an economic sense. They have brought economic depression, to be sure, and it lies like a gray pall over the whole land. But a deeper tragedy lies in the depression of the spirit which has fallen upon so many of the people" (Caudill 1963).

NOTE

1. NPR. *Transcript: JFK's Speech on His Religion*. Retrieved from http://www.npr.org/templates/story/story.php?storyId=16920600.

Chapter Six

War as Metaphor

The Convergence of the War on Poverty and the War on Drugs

Keesha M. Middlemass

Poverty is not a crime. Yet, the War on Poverty, which in particular included the transformation of the state's apparatus through neoliberal policies that call for economic deregulation, welfare devolution and retraction, the cultural trope of individual responsibility, and an expansive penal apparatus has morphed with the War on Drugs, an initiative associated with crime (Wacquant 2009; Soss et al. 2011; Alfred and Chlup 2009). Over the last thirty years, elected officials have merged poverty to become tantamount to criminality and supported criminal justice policies that have disproportionately incarcerated poor people (Hedges 2013). The power of the state and its disapproval of poor people and criminals are visible through the erection and implementation of similar policy aims in both "wars" that focus on the management of bodies, pushing them to the margins of society. The respective populations are marginalized and punished simultaneously in the belief that poor people engage in the "culture of poverty," which spawns the "culture of criminality" (Kohler-Hausmann 2007; Soss et al. 2011). Excepting Wacquant (2009), existing research on the criminal justice system and the welfare system offers little insight into questions about how the transformation of the social fabric, including race politics, media rhetoric, and popular discourse, has and will continue to affect individuals and communities captured by both "wars."

By examining the genesis of the "welfare queen" and the War on Drugs, this chapter examines the social construction of poor people as criminal and the "war's" imposition on poor criminals. Drawing from an ethnographic study in Newark, New Jersey, I rely on firsthand narratives about poverty and prisoner reentry to demonstrate how the two "wars" have merged. Personal accounts communicate how drug felony convictions in particular (but all felony convictions in reality) result in a denial of public benefits, which makes reentry challenging for many former prisoners.

The creation and implementation of punitive policies is largely due to legislators' response to the public's fear of crime; the political response to public fear enshrined popular myths about race and criminality into the minds of average Americans (Gilens 1999). Fear of crime led the way for massive changes in federal law in the 1980s and 1990s, including new surveillance techniques and "tough on crime" policies. The specific policies embraced mandatory minimum sentences, "truth in sentencing," and "three strike" statutes, all of which restrict early prison release, rely heavily on long prison terms to incapacitate, and are designed to punish those who offend society's sensibilities. Other policy changes incorporated social discipline through regulations that pushed heteronormative paternalistic ideals onto welfare recipients (Richie 2012; Jacobson 2005; Scott and Gerbasi 2005; Middlemass forthcoming). The punitive rules of both "wars" bled into each other, and the use of incarceration was deemed a corrective measure for poverty. The lived experiences of individuals caught by both "wars" point to politicians' racialized discourse offering policy "solutions" to manage "the problem," all the while maligning welfare recipients and former prisoners as incapable of fulfilling acceptable societal roles (Best 2010; Gilens 1999).

WAR AS METAPHOR

As a metaphor and the government's response to poverty and criminality, "war" is apt. As an allegory, "war" is a powerful word that immediately brings to mind armed combat, physical confrontation, and hostilities. War is also a powerful symbol that represents aggressive competition and rivalry between two opposing sides that are in conflict over a set of values, morals, principles, or tenets. In terms of the War on Poverty and the War on Drugs, the phrases represent the notion that the federal government's resources will be utilized and employed to defeat the "enemy"—poverty and drugs—and that the "wars" will continue and not cease. As a result, the policies had no boundary and operated as an extension of the state's power through other means, such as political rhetoric, administrative strategy, and legal directives.

In his State of the Union Address on January 8, 1964, President Lyndon Baines Johnson declared, "an unconditional war on poverty in America." In policy terms, this meant a number of related laws and strategies to reduce poverty, which included housing, education, food stamps, economic opportunity zones in local communities, the expanded role of the federal government in health care (e.g., Medicare and Medicaid), and Head Start (a federal program that provides comprehensive services to low-income families and their children). The full force of the federal government was directed at "destroying" poverty.

Starting in the 1970s, however, distinctive political discourses emerged about criminality and welfare recipients, and each time they were accompanied by distinct changes in policy. Studies of discursive politics are critical to understand welfare and criminal policy creation; researchers in the area of political discourse and public policies parse out the language of politicians to reveal the ways in which discourse trumps fact to create new policies (Hancock 2004; Lens and Cary 2010; Mendelberg 2001). An analysis of the public discourse around criminality and welfare demonstrates that the policy responses that followed—in many instances, the lived experiences of those managed by the state—were depicted as individual problems of those who lacked a moral code (Hancock 2004; Lieberman 1998).

For instance, under President Reagan, the primary support system for poor women and their children was challenged, and it was done so with little public outcry, because the political discourse was laced with the "language of morality and racial fear" (Nadasen 2007, 52). Poor black women, in particular, were vilified and demeaned as illiterate drug addicts who were sexually promiscuous and undeserving of public assistance (Nadasen 2007). Ronald Reagan's social construction of welfare recipients was assisted by his use of racialized discourse during his first bid for the presidency in 1976: Reagan's candidacy then, and again in 1980, focused on telling good stories. Levin (2013) argues that Reagan's stories and anecdotes converged on a single point: "the welfare state is broken, and I'm the man to fix it." The broken welfare state became part of Reagan's stump speech, and although Reagan often gets credit for the term "welfare queen," he is not its originator. The first time "welfare queen" was seen in print was October 12, 1974, in the *Chicago Tribune*, for whom investigative reporter, George Bliss, wrote an article entitled, "Welfare Queen Jailed in Tucson," describing Linda Taylor's jewelry, furs, and Cadillac. Linda Taylor may have been the original welfare queen first captured and socially constructed by the media, but the fascination with Linda Taylor resulted in the racialized and gendered construction of "the welfare queen" and dependency (Hancock 2004; Neubeck and Cazanave 2001; Fraser and Gordon 1994).

Reagan's assault on welfare recipients was continued under President Clinton, when political rhetoric resulted in the passage and implementation of landmark welfare reform legislation in 1996 (see Toft 2010). Temporary Aid for Needy Families (TANF) was designed to use time limits to deny social benefits, which was "one of the most aggressive reform efforts in the history of the American welfare state" (Brock 2009, 964). In addition to the use of stringent eligibility criteria and limited cash assistance, greater emphasis was placed on shaping welfare recipients as criminal rather than using empirical evidence to demonstrate need-based assistance (Hancock 2004). TANF's eligibility criteria stretched into new areas of government interest, including the promotion of marriage, surveillance, and DNA tests to identify absent fathers. The poor began to be policed and their welfare benefits sanctioned when elected officials deemed single mothers as criminal. Criminal procedures followed, and enshrined the racist gendered stereotypical and popular mythology into reality and made poor people criminal (Kohler-Hausmann 2007; Hancock 2004), transforming the welfare system. The political discourse turned into policy, and pushed recipients off welfare rolls and into low-wage jobs, which severely limited their ability to provide the necessities of life and prohibited the potential to supplement the little income they were able to earn (Brock 2009).

Political efforts to pass statutory measures that perpetuate the myth of the drug-using welfare queen persist and ensure that the poor become poorer while determining that welfare recipients are criminal. For instance, Florida and other states passed statutes mandating drug testing in order to receive welfare benefits in 2011 and 2012.[1] Although the Florida law was struck down as unconstitutional by the 11th Circuit Court on December 31, 2013, in *Lebron v. Wilkins*, the law required drug testing as a precondition to receive benefits, and welfare recipients had to pay for the drug test. Passed with overwhelming support by Republicans and signed into law by Governor Rick Scott in May of 2011, the argument was that drug testing was necessary under TANF to ensure that welfare recipients were job-ready, achieving family stability, and using public funds appropriately. The 11th Circuit Court argued that the drug tests were instead "suspicionless," and that there was no special need for suspicionless drug testing. The position of the state was to advance a patriarchal form of social control over welfare recipients and to be "tough on crime" simultaneously (Brown 2013; Brock 2009).

THE SOCIAL CONSTRUCTION OF RACIALIZED DRUGS BEGAN THE WAR

Despite the government's response to drug use, including Nancy Reagan imploring a generation of kids to "Just Say No," the creation of "Drug Free Zones," and public service announcements designed to discourage drug use, America has a remarkable excess of drug users. Paradoxically, Americans also have a disdainful attitude toward drugs while they are consuming all kinds of drugs with abandon (Gahlinger 2001). For instance, there are a multitude of mind-altering and pleasure-inducing prescription drugs prescribed to treat various disorders (e.g., bipolar disorder, ADD/ADHD, anxiety syndrome, general nervousness, pain management, etc.), and the American public has a large appetite for these drugs in all their legal and illegal forms (Ives and Ghelani 2006). This contradiction is found in the historical, political, and social construction of drug users, abusers, and the drugs themselves.

Historically, drug use in the United States became problematic only when drugs were distinctly associated with minority racial and ethnic groups and/or the counterculture, who were unpopular and feared as "other" by the dominant mainstream (Musto 1991). Propaganda was conflated with factual accounts, which merged with racist and xenophobic beliefs, in order to present "facts" about patterns of drug use among different racial groups. The societal-historical and political reactions to drug use, drug-related activity, and drug addiction were the motivating principles to sustain and encourage drug prohibition. Dominant religious and cultural traditions collided with changing social mores, and the use of particular drugs was associated with certain subcultures, (hated) minority groups and foreigners (Musto 1991). An "us" versus "them" mentality framed the policy debate to ensure that unpopular social groups, particularly minorities, were funneled into a separate system that categorized and disciplined them apart from other drug users in order to maintain a racially segregated drug policy. Drug laws maintain the boundaries of whiteness and require an ongoing political framework to enforce and buttress white ideology.

At the turn of the twentieth century, racist attitudes toward Chinese immigrants were bound up with the economic depression of the 1870s. For instance, smoking opium was viewed as a Chinese practice. Because of the collision of racist ideology and economic depression, exclusionary laws were passed to prevent Chinese from buying land and living in certain neighborhoods,[2] while special laws were passed to prohibit smoking opium. Yet, pharmacists and doctors continued to dispense opium in its other forms, such as morphine, in order to treat various ailments and diseases, and the government continued to dispense purveyors of patent medicines (Houck and Siegel 2010).

Almost 100 years after Chinese opium users were targeted, legislators targeted cocaine users as two distinct classes of drug users in the 1980s. Crack and powder cocaine are derived from the same coca plant, have no pharmacological differences, and offer similar physiological and psychoactive effects regardless if the form of cocaine is smoked, injected, or snorted (Hatsukami and Fischman 1996). The major differences are in its appearance, production, and use. Powder cocaine is a crystalline-like powder that is "cut" with sugar, flour, or cornstarch. Crack cocaine is powder cocaine that has been dissolved in liquid, cooked, cooled, and cut into "rocks." Users can liquefy and inject both powder and crack cocaine; powder cocaine can also be snorted while crack cocaine can be smoked or "freebased" (Hatsukami and Fischman 1996). Users of powder cocaine and crack cocaine differ; whites are more likely to use cocaine in all its forms, but white drug deals tend to take place in private homes, businesses, and nightclubs making it harder to police while crack cocaine is much cheaper, and is distributed and used in open-air drug markets in poor neighborhoods (Coyle 2003).

Violence associated with crack cocaine, its distribution, and the open-air drug markets where it is consumed took place principally in urban communities (Coyle 2003). The crack epidemic and its related images were splashed across major news outlets, and the resulting violence and media's attention to the crack epidemic of the 1980s led to a strong response from politicians who criminalized the behaviors related to using crack cocaine but not powder cocaine. Elected officials used these differences to create diverse policy responses to the two distinct subgroups of drug users by framing crack cocaine and powder cocaine as two different types of cocaine needing separate criminal justice responses. This resulted in a disproportionate number of first-time black crack cocaine users being demonized, disproportionately arrested, and harshly incarcerated for long periods under mandatory drug sentencing laws.[3] Corresponding laws, however, were not created for white powder cocaine addicts; by creating two different classes of drug offenses for two different groups of people who used powder cocaine (whites) and crack cocaine (blacks), blacks were incarcerated and whites were sent for drug treatment (Auerhahn 1999; Chin 2002; Musto 1999).

Another example of the racialization of drug use is related to the abuse of prescription drugs like OxyContin, which is primarily a drug of choice of white people. In order to feed their fix, "oxy" users often take higher doses than prescribed, seek prescriptions from multiple doctors, "lose" prescriptions so more prescriptions must be written, steal and forge prescriptions, and then turn to heroin when they are unable to secure "oxy" (Leger 2013). Typically, "oxy" abusers are offered drug treatment, which means their addiction is remedied from a medical approach despite clear evidence of illegal abuse. White drug addiction has been framed as a neurochemical imbalance that should be treated in a clinical setting rather than a failure of willpower or character. The belief is that white drug addicts are not criminal and therefore are not deserving of a prison sentence; rather, they merit health interventions and medical attention because their drug addiction is not their fault as their drugs are "prescribed" by a doctor.

NIXON'S WAR ON DRUGS

Under the direction of Harry J. Anslinger, the first director of the Federal Bureau of Narcotics (1930–1962), drug use was increasingly criminalized as he established a punitive federal drug policy that focused on law enforcement efforts instead of education and prevention (see Sirin 2011).[4] Anslinger relied on propaganda, myth making, and horror stories to dissuade people from doing drugs and convinced them that drugs were evil. For instance, Anslinger reported that marijuana caused people "to fly into a delirious rage" and even claimed that some went on to commit violent criminal acts (McWilliams 1990, 70) after taking it. In some instances, the propaganda was so farfetched that people stopped listening to the Federal Bureau of Narcotics and ignored its warnings about the evilness of drugs. In opposition and near the end of Anslinger's term, the counterculture surged and made smoking marijuana fashionable among college students. Alongside marijuana, LSD and heroin use surged. In response, President Johnson's administration passed the Narcotics Addict Rehabilitation Act of 1966, and declared that addiction to narcotics was a mental illness and a disease similar to alcoholism.

This skyrocketing demand for drugs in the late 1960s set the stage for President Nixon's "War on Drugs." In 1969, in a special message to Congress, Nixon branded drug abuse as a "serious national threat." Two years later, in June 1971, President Nixon had a "drug problem" on his hands. Marijuana was increasingly being used openly by white middle-class university students and others in mainstream society, resulting in what Nixon believed was a "straight society" becoming a "drug society" that was inclined toward radicalism: "these radical demonstrators that were here the last two weeks. They're all on drugs and raising hell."[5] In response to the increased use of marijuana, President Nixon created the Special Action Office for Drug Abuse Prevention and commissioned a national report on marijuana usage, the Shafer Commission. The Shafer Commission concluded that marijuana was not a danger to public safety. Nixon ignored his Commission's report, declaring drug use as "public enemy number one," and immediately began the "War on Drugs" (see Schmidt 1971).[6] Nixon launched interdiction efforts in Mexico, oversaw the creation of the Drug Enforcement Agency in 1973, slashed funding for social programs and drug addiction, and criminalized drug users for tearing apart the moral fiber of the nation. Some argue that Nixon's efforts produced the exact opposite of the desired effects; instead of decreasing drug use and drug imports, his efforts increased the international drug trade and created markets that previously did not exist (e.g., marijuana grown in Colombia to replace the interdiction efforts that were successful in Mexico). By shifting blame and calling drug users a danger to society and a threat to public safety, Nixon criminalized drug addiction and quickly learned the first lesson in the iron law of drug economics: "the harder the police crackdown on a substance, the more concentrated the substance will become" (see also Gabbidon 2010).[7]

President Nixon's response to drug use did not differ considerably from past responses to drugs; significant factors in American society support the moralistic views about drug use and the beliefs that using drugs are dangerous and immoral. These views have held steady while drug use has peaked and declined. The difference between now and then is that, despite the federal government's position that marijuana has no medical benefits, (and therefore deserving of its Schedule I rating) more and more people believe the opposite: that marijuana has medicinal properties.[8] Many people have shown that there are tangible and concrete health benefits and medical properties related to using marijuana and, in the last decade, there has been increased cultural, political, and social support for marijuana use, which is reflected in the number of recent referendum and changes in state laws decriminalizing marijuana for medical and personal usage. Additionally, legal experts, legislators, and frontline law enforcement officers are beginning to openly question why society is sending thousands upon thousands of nonviolent drug offenders to prison, which wastes public funds, destroys lives, and diverts limited police resources from investigating violent criminal acts, organized crime, and terrorism.

With Nixon's declaration of a "War on Drugs," presidents of both political parties have directed billions of dollars toward their own approach to this war, except President Carter, who, in 1978, wanted Congress to revisit criminal laws. President Carter argued that any criminal "penalties against the use of a drug should not be more damaging to the individual than the use of the drug itself; and where they are [more punitive] they should be changed. Nowhere is this clearer than in the law against the possession of marijuana" (Wodak et al. 2002, 105). President Carter wanted marijuana decriminalized. However, Congress ignored President Carter's suggestion, because cocaine use increased sharply in the late 1970s, and marijuana was widely viewed as a feeder drug at the time; therefore, decriminalization efforts were stopped before they began (Collett 1989).

The urgency of the drug crises escalated in the 1980s, and the use of punitive policies focused on drug use became the norm. Such a change supported a political agenda that remade the U.S. criminal justice system. King (2008) argues that the dramatic increase in drug arrests, particularly of black Americans, stems directly from policy decisions about drugs. The type and number of drug felony offenses dramatically surged in the 1980s and 1990s and, in turn, the number of people serving long prison sentences for nonviolent drug-related crimes escalated substantially (Brownstein 1996; U.S. Sentencing Commission 1995). Although blacks have never been the major users of drugs, they have become the primary law enforcement target in the "War on Drugs" (Cose 2002). According to Mauer (2009), the "War on Drugs" has led to the dramatic escalation in the prison population, and this escalation is accompanied by profound racial and ethnic disparities. Mauer demonstrates that two-thirds of the incarcerated population are black or Latino Americans charged with drug offenses, which is out of proportion to the degree that these two groups use or sell illegal drugs.

Fighting crime related to the "War on Drugs" became an urgent political problem for Nixon, and passing legislation was paramount for many elected officials (see Chambliss 2001). Official responses included the diversion of public resources, originally designated to address social problems like the lack of housing and poverty, funneled to fight the "War on Drugs." Politicians and public officials, along with the media, convinced the public that all black men were violent and the "War on Drugs" was necessary to keep public streets safe (Brownstein 1996; Chin 2002; Chambliss 2001).[9] Under President Reagan, "tough on crime" policies became "zero tolerance" programs; the 1986 Anti-Drug Abuse Act criminalized the act of possessing drugs, and demand-side drug fighting efforts were paramount over decreasing supply-side demands.

President Clinton continued Reagan/Bush's approach, and increased the "War on Drugs" budget, though it took on a new dimension when it became a political necessity for Clinton to win reelection; he championed for more cops on the streets and punitive penalties for drug convictions.[10] President Clinton cemented his "tough on crime" stance when he earmarked an extra $1 billion to fight the "War on Drugs" in his 1995 budget. The 1995 federal budget set aside $13.2 billion for the implementation of a wide array of drug policies: $7.8 billion was spent on supply side efforts to combat the importation of drugs at their source while only $5.4 billion was spent on decreasing the demand for drugs through education and prevention programs (Rosenberger 1996). Since the election of President Barack Obama in 2008, drug policy has stayed remarkably consistent at the federal level, while some states have "gone up in smoke" by dramatically changing their laws legalizing or decriminalizing marijuana for personal or medical use and, in some states, both.

THE TWO "WARS"

The war metaphor becomes a form of justification for a type of governance that is contradictory to the goal of decreasing poverty and class inequality and undermines prisoner reentry efforts. The prison population, which is predominantly male, is disproportionately drawn from low-income and poverty-stricken communities (Western and Pettit 2010), and when prisoners become former prisoners, they are excluded from most welfare programs due to their felony conviction. Incarceration is "a significant institutional influence on life chances" that reinforces and increases inequality; "the inequality is cumulative, deepening the disadvantage of the most marginal men in society" (Western and Pettit 2010, 11, 12). The marginality is the combination of both "wars" attacking the same subpopulation within the larger society.

Parallel transformation of the criminal justice system and the welfare system took place in the 1990s under President Clinton and in the 2000s under President G. W. Bush. Fundamental changes included: sentencing laws; restructuring of police powers following 9/11; increased use of electronic surveillance technologies, such as ankle bracelets, to monitor and track defendants and parolees; and amassing public and private databases used to both limit eligibility for government programs and allow law enforcement to identify and pursue (i.e., stalk) potential defendants. Social engineering through the criminal justice system became the state's response to promoting societal norms and discouraging criminal elements through exclusionary and disciplinary tactics. An assortment of social control mechanisms designed to "correct" behavior and uphold moralistic values were created, and the main tool became the modern prison (Foucault 1977). The criminal justice system regards individuals and entire communities as disreputable and in need of systematic police tactics which are paternalistic and authoritarian in nature. This suggests that policies are strategically targeting a narrowly defined population and socially constructing the group as criminal (Foucault 1977). 95 percent of prisoners are released back to the community (Travis 2005), which leads to the challenge of remaining out of prison. Former prisoners reentering society are predominantly poor (Alfred and Chlup 2009; Hedges 2013).

The hurdles to reenter society are many, and "secret sentences" that are implemented postincarceration due to a felony conviction hamper efforts by restricting access to government benefits (Chin and Holmes 2002). The invisible punishments, also known as the collateral consequences of a felony conviction, deprive individuals of a wide variety of rights, benefits, and social privileges (Travis 2005; Middlemass forthcoming). Recidivism, the inability to stay out of prison, can also be framed as the "success" of the modern war's ability to extend its surveillance apparatus and burdensome requirements across geographical and political jurisdictions and institutional databases. In the case of patriarchal control mechanisms, the state relies on a felony conviction to enforce structural inequalities between felons and nonfelons.

The policies implemented under the "war" refrain have led to a punitive welfare apparatus and hyperpunitive criminal justice system that incarcerates the poor at disproportionate rates (Hedges 2013). A new social group and entire subpopulation of "others" has been created through the shared experience of poverty and incarceration, among other factors, and this subpopulation is disconnected from the economy and the broader social order (Western and Pettit 2010; Middlemass forthcoming). This new social group has few economic and financial resources and tends to have low levels of educational achievement, which negatively affects their social mobility; the social and economic disadvantages are sustained over the life course (Western and Pettit 2010). Distinctions as a "felon" or as a "welfare recipient" are socially constructed "other" labels, which guarantee that the resulting stigma contributes to government surveillance and the denial of public benefits. The unintended consequences of social engineering poverty programs to control welfare recipients has spilled over to other policy areas connected to the criminal justice system's use of a felony conviction.

The criminal justice system is now a coherent set of retributive bureaucratic agencies that use a felony conviction to restrict access to programs designed to help, and potentially reduce, recidivism. Various state institutions and their political rhetoric work to produce a "monster" to target in order to shape their social interactions (Ingebretsen 1998). In the power struggle, white patriarchy is imposed on a largely black and brown prison population. The felony project becomes complete when they are denied access to poverty programs, and the social control strategies "swarm" outward and "move beyond their ostensible target to contiguous spaces, thereby expanding their grip over larger fields of social relations" (Smith 2007, 47).

As the state aggressively cuts poverty programs, including housing, food stamps, and cash assistance, more than 730,000 men and women are released from prison every year with few resources and return to communities experiencing concentrated poverty (Clear 2009; Thompson 2008). For the vast majority of former prisoners, a felony conviction is on their public record as a result of their criminal past, and upon returning home, many want to shed the past and create a new life, one that is free of crime. However, with few economic resources, low educational achievement, and few job prospects, many are in need of public assistance; without assistance, they are often rendered homeless. This is the result of the "wars" on former prisoners, who are poor.

POVERTY AND CRIME RHETORIC

The United States is overreliant on the criminal justice system to address societal challenges related to poverty and crime (Demleitner 2000; Wacquant 2000; Alexander 2010; Middlemass forthcoming), and poverty continues when former prisoners attempt to restart their lives. The felony conviction socially disables former prisoners and, although there has been no public announcement, the state has created a set of policies in response to the perceived threat of crime (Middlemass forthcoming; Gottschalk 2006). Under the guise of welfare reform, policies are having a significant impact on poor former offenders' lives as they are exposed to the coercive powers of the regulatory state (Smith 2007).

Silverglate (2011) argues that no economic classes are safe from the troubling forms of social control executed by the state; seemingly innocuous behavior is regulated by a vast number of vague, yet complex, prohibitions.

These regulations are the "war" inflicted upon the socioeconomically disadvantaged, who are locked out of the workforce due to their felony conviction as employers have strong negative perceptions about individuals with a felony conviction (Pager 2007). The state now operates as a social control mechanism that criminalizes behavior which then socially handicaps those who have served time in prison. The "wars" are now similar in that the state withdraws social benefits and is scaling back redistributive policies through exclusion of former offenders while policing the poor for criminal behavior.

Feminist historians and policy analysts argue that welfare programs are an important vehicle the state uses to control poor families, promote racial division, and intervene in gender roles (see Smith 2007, 33–34). Eligibility rules are constantly changed, former offenders are degraded, and the state's message to former offenders is one that they are unworthy. Piven and Cloward (1993) argue that degrading and punishing the poor through an endless array of harsh treatments sanctioned by the state is demoralizing and discouraging. The denial of assistance is reinforced through politicians' rhetoric and the media, which socially construct the poor as unworthy delinquents (Hancock 2004; Toft 2010). The demonizing portrayals create a narrative in which the state can "restage the work ethic fable for the audience of the day" (Smith 2007, 18).

The state systematically operates as a "father figure" who knows what is best for society, and by problematizing the poor as morally suspect, criminal, and monstrous, the state can reinforce negative stereotypes and create punitive laws. Ingebretsen asks the question: "How does one create a monster? What are the uses of the monstrous?" (1998, 99); he argues that the monstrous image is a useful political and social strategy used to erase the presence of those deemed a "monster" from civic life. The creation of a "monster" lurking in the halls of public housing, which is reinforced via the local news and official rhetoric, becomes a potent political tool (Stuntz 2001; Toft 2010), the combination of which is used to exclude and repudiate poor former criminals and constrain their limited alternatives (see Carey 2005). Politicians cater to voters' fear of the monster criminal felon (Middlemass forthcoming). Demonization, discipline, and punishment strategies become the norm in formulating policies directed at disciplining poor former offenders through the reduction or denial of public assistance or public housing.

PERSONAL NARRATIVES ABOUT THE DUAL "WARS"

The War on Poverty merges and extends the War on Drugs, and the resulting state policy vehicles broaden social control mechanisms that extend the state's power via databases and data collection focused on the intersection of a felony conviction and poverty. The paternalistic approach to manage and control former offenders prevents them from accessing programs designed to alleviate poverty and reduce recidivism. The state, in adopting paternalistic policies that shame, degrade, and demean, broadcasts the message that anyone who has broken the social contract is to be governed and continually punished through the embedded disciplinary mechanisms found in the technologies of control. The regime of punishment creates contradictory outcomes; by restricting admittance, slashing budgets, and blocking access to social benefits, the state imposes financial sanctions on those who have limited employment opportunities and few legal financial resources. By limiting and restricting access, the impact of the regulatory state leads to continued stigma, forcing many to live on the margins of the larger hegemonic authority.

The state enjoys an unusual level of authority that drives convicted felons underground, which exacerbates racial divisions and economic disparity, and tacitly reinforces the idea that they are unworthy and undeserving of public assistance. Below, I draw from an eighteen–month ethnographic study in Newark, New Jersey, and rely on firsthand accounts and personal interviews to describe what it is like to be poor and reenter society as a convicted felon. Firsthand narratives communicate how a felony conviction translates to a denial of public benefits, which makes reentry difficult and recidivism a potential certainty for many former prisoners attempting to reenter society. The participants were reentering society in Newark, New Jersey, and according to the State of New Jersey Department of Corrections: Office of Transitional Services, the returning population is mostly male (91 percent), single (83 percent), and black (63 percent). The average age of individuals leaving state prison is 34 years old, and at least half of them have a minor child. The average reading level of the returning offender population is 6th grade, and the average math level is 5th grade. Two thirds of former prisoners do not have a high school diploma or its equivalent, the General Educational Development (GED) diploma. They have spent an average of 2.5 years behind bars and have a history of criminal activity. As a result, the returning prison population has a myriad of complex issues that must be addressed simultaneously, including drug and alcohol addictions, mental illness, poor employment skills, low education levels, chronic and/or communicable physical ailments, and mental health conditions.

As one exchange between former prisoners details, they struggle to get on their feet:[11]

"If you ain't got family support, you done or gotta do it all on your own, and that's not really possible, you know."

"Yeah, I don't have family I can rely on—just me and my kids. I'm struggling to just get by and do the daily things without slipping back into the life."[12]

"Got to have a plan, and I'm talking about a plan for every single day. What are you going to do today, tomorrow, the next? Without a plan, you can get all messed up and go back."[13]

Another exchange describes how far "behind" some former prisoners are and what that means for their reentry efforts:[14]

"Everything is hard right now."

"Yeah, things have changed a lot, and you have to catch up to what has changed. It's like everything is different. Everything. Cell phones didn't exist when I went in. All this stuff people got now, I don't even know."

"Right, I have a Walkman, and its old school. I'm getting batteries and the kids are plugging their stuff into the wall. When did that happen?"

Not knowing the latest technology or having much experience in the outside world drastically affects one's success in reentering society and being able to "fit in" and normalize to the current fast-paced world of the twenty-first century. Although the above instances relate to incarceration and being away from the community for long stretches of time, the challenge, after surviving prison, is to restart one's life *without* public benefits. One policy area that negatively impacts all convicted felons are federal laws that deny public housing. Due to the extensive use of background checks, individuals are denied access to public housing, even if they have been crime free and "doing good" for years.

Under President Clinton, the culture of public housing underwent drastic changes with the introduction of tenant screenings, evictions based on criminal activities or a single arrest (a conviction is not required for housing authorities to begin eviction proceedings), and the use of a criminal conviction to reject applicants (Holzman 1996; Hellegers 1999; Renzetti 2001). Commonly known as "One Strike and You're Out," which was codified in the Housing Opportunity Program Extension Act of 1996, the law made clear that all forms of past and present criminal activity on or near public housing premises was forbidden. *Yet*, federal public housing policies declare that individuals with a felony conviction are eligible for public housing after a set time period following their date of conviction. For instance, drug possession charges make an individual ineligible for any and all federal benefits for up to one year after the first conviction and five years after the second conviction. This means that after a time limit, and no new convictions, a previously convicted drug felon is eligible for public housing; however, in practice, local public housing authorities in Newark prevent all convicted felons from accessing public housing, despite evidence of rehabilitation, stable low-wage employment, and completion of state-sponsored programs.

For example, Eric and Mark, whose experiences are the norm, describe how their search for housing was a real struggle. Eric explains:

> But it's impossible to do what you need to do, when you going to the shelters, trying to find a place to sleep each night. You get released, and you go to the shelter, and that's really the only option, or I mean, I could sleep in the park, train station and just be homeless, well, I am actually homeless. We all homeless.

Mark reinforced this struggle and how he dealt with his homelessness: "I slept in my car and in vacant buildings. They all over Newark, so I just move from abandoned spot to the next."[15]

Others were denied public housing numerous times, so they made the "best" decision from a set of bad options. Yolanda, a mother who was convicted of a felony assault charge nine years prior to sitting down and speaking with me, demonstrates the challenges she faces in making the "best" decision:

> I was denied [housing] and given the run around, told to keep on applying, and all the time nothing. I'm denied Section 8 because of my charge, and it means that I have to make hard decisions, stay with my baby's daddy, which ain't a good situation. Hell, my poor choices didn't help me, and that is why I am here, and I know I am making poor decisions, but I got to have a place to sleep, my kid needs a place to sleep. It's so hard, and it's been 9 years.[16]

During the same time period of "tough on crime" politics in the 1990s, Congress passed the Violent Crime Control and Law Enforcement Act of 1994 that implemented punitive education laws denying prisoners and convicted felons who wanted to go to school from accessing Pell Grants. The political response toward prison inmates and convicted felons taking college courses and pursuing educational programs was uncompromising, as politicians removed funding sources for educational programs inside prison (Middlemass forthcoming).

In conjunction with the War on Drugs, President Clinton and other politicians made political points to earn favor with voters. Senator Kaye Bailey Hutchinson, former senator from Texas, argued in 1993 that Pell Grants for prisoners removed money from the hands of hardworking families who had to pay for college. Her premise, however, was erroneous. Pell Grants are funded based on financial need, up to a maximum amount determined by the federal government. Applicants do not compete against each other for a limited number of Pell Grants; rather, *anyone* who qualifies based on federal eligibility standards is approved the grant (Middlemass forthcoming). Pell Grants are "non-competitive needs-based federal college funds available to all qualifying low-income students" (Fine et al. 2001, 5). The negative impact of this policy was that many incarcerated men and women leave prison without a high school diploma or other educational credits. The larger impact of denying Pell Grants is the connection between education and legal employment.

During one focus group, the participants spoke about the negative effect not having a formal education on finding legal employment as they reenter society:[17]

"It's hard, without an education, I mean, I hope this all works out, because if I can't figure out how to get a job, I'm going back, you know."

"All I want to do is get a job, my own place, because I am tired of living with a bunch of men, pay my bills, and you know, that's about it."

"Crazy, right? Here we spent all this time running from normal, and now all I want is to live a real boring and normal life."

"But without help, I can't do normal. All these restrictions, I mean I know I messed up, but I served my time, I'm doing good, but all they do is make it harder to get ahead and do right."

After spending decades incarcerated, many of the participants are reentering society without earning a GED, which puts them at a disadvantage for finding and securing legal employment. Without legal employment, former offenders risk being sent back to prison by their parole officer and, if no longer on parole or probation, they are unable to secure housing on the private market, which increases their risk of "going back" due to their inability to secure a legal source of income.

As discussed in another group session, the lack of public benefits makes staying out of prison more difficult. Here, several men discuss their time inside prison in relationship to how hard it is to reenter society without public benefits:[18]

"Even if I do everything right [according to parole], be a better person, make my way forward, I might not make it."

"Me, too. I got time behind me and I try to disassociate from all that's behind me, but it's a struggle to exist, and that becomes a way of life. It's better to be out [of prison] than in, but struggling is becoming a way of life, and it's so hard."

"We can do good and not get into any trouble, keep on task, go to meetings, but all people see is my felony. To everyone I meet, I am a felon, and all my hard work means nothing. I am a criminal, and will always be treated as a criminal, so why be good?"

"We all here because there ain't no rehabilitation going on inside or outside. We go in and come out. We on our own. People on the outside all they want is their own justice, and for prison to be hard, and it is, no doubt; it's hard in ways you can't even know, but we out, so now what?"

"Inside is all agony, pain and hardness, and you come out and have to overcome all that when you back, but you do that on your own. Ain't no one looking out."

"All that's inside, the rules of how you live life, the tricks and trades of prison, always being aware, can't trust no one, can't run your mouth, can't talk about your life, can't be open, can't communicate, can't ask for help. Easy to get locked back up when you not asking for help."

I continued to attend weekly sessions at a nonprofit organization in Newark, to learn more about the reentry process, and found that the same theme would emerge from week to week. For instance, the theme of "going back" was a lived reality for many visiting the nonprofit organization:[19]

"What we doing now, coming home, it ain't no way to live, can't do anything, and we broke. That constant fear of getting sent back, with a record, you always guilty, even if you did nothing. I'm a felon, will always be, and it changes everything and makes me nothing."

"It is so hard because you ain't get nothing. You know that you don't have an income. And then when you go to welfare, emergency housing doesn't give you a place, even though I'm in treatment, they will deny me so I'm still like out on the streets."

"Everything is negative. It's always hurdles, doors shut all the time. It's hard to get basic stuff done."

Trying to get help from welfare, even when eligible for benefits, is challenging. "Like, they got metal detectors and everything now in all these [welfare] places because they know what they doing to these people. They don't work to help you; one day one of those people are not going to be able to handle it [the negative response] and they are going in there and shoot up the place, this is the welfare department, the place of last resort for help. Ain't no damn help."[20]

"I think welfare wants you to run around, like a chicken with your head cut off. They want you to run here, there, go there, do this, and do that, then your food stamps are not on your card, so now you trying to run to these places but you don't have the money to get on the bus to these places, you know, and you ain't got food in your stomach to run to these places. Real easy to give up when you got nothing."[21]

"I went to welfare, and I tried to get the benefits through that program. They crazy, but they gave me food stamps. No place to live or eat my food, but I got the stamps. I tried to get the other stuff, like TRA [Temporary Rental Assistance], but they wouldn't give it to me. Nah, they going to tell me because I owe child support I can't get TRA. Child support is like the IRS. They will hunt you down and get you. I been locked up, ain't got a place to sleep, and I sure as hell ain't got no child support to give. If you don't give the child support people they money each month, they block you from getting an ID, and without an ID you can't get a job, and then I can't pay up. Welfare told me that this was the last [food] stamps I get because I owe child support, and until I pay, no more welfare."[22]

A felony conviction and the resulting denial of public benefits are a result of the War on Poverty merging with the War on Drugs. Many politicians are not interested in fighting poverty and most are not interested in rehabilitating prisoners. As such, returning prisoners who are poor struggle to stay out of prison, because they are denied public housing, denied Pell Grants to gain vocational or educational credits, and struggle to get a job due to their unstable living conditions and lack of educational achievement. It is a vicious cycle, and the state, through an uncoordinated set of secret penalties and invisible punishments, socially constructs felons as outlaws. The state effectively creates marginalized "others" who are socially disabled (Middlemass, forthcoming). Regulations use a felony conviction as a permanent stigma that leads to social disability via a set of "loosely coupled institutions" that work together to ostracize individuals from the public square (Hagan et al. 1979). A felony conviction has become its own petit penal institution that is embedded in government processes (Middlemass 2007), and allows society to continue marking felons as fraudulent criminal noncitizens (Pager 2007).

The denial of public benefits to former offenders contributes to a new form of social disorder and, in some instances, leads to deviant behavior, which is required in order to eat and live because legal means of housing and public assistance are blocked. The tentacles of the states' institutions that create social boundaries echo Foucault's (1977) theory of institutional mechanisms that swarm and reach beyond the original target population is correct (see Smith 2007); former offenders' families and children come under surveillance, as well as the neighborhood. Thus, the War on Poverty combined with the War on Drugs is now a system of constant surveillance by the authorities. Contemporary poverty policies reach into other areas, such as access to education, employment opportunities, and achieving the "American dream," capturing a larger and larger population of poor people, and the prison population mostly consists of people from this sector of society. The paternalistic nature of the state creates disempowered poor people disconnected from the larger community, from the economy, and from the broader social order to remain a substantial social group that has few economic and financial resources (Western and Pettit 2010).

Within society, it has been hard for the community to become comfortable with modes of thinking that deconstruct dualistic notions of good/bad, citizen/noncitizen, or nonfelon/felon. A result of the community's resistance to avoiding a system rooted in socially constructed binaries is that felons are treated as noncitizens because they are "bad." Though uneven, as progress *has* occurred in limited areas, a disproportionate number of poor felons remain socially disabled and endure as marginal citizens (Middlemass forthcoming), while persistent rhetoric marking criminals as permanently malformed, perverted, and corrupt continues. In such a context, felons will remain poor, and the policies that support the "wars" on both poverty and drugs will create a new generation of disadvantaged people based on poverty and past criminal behavior, which is often rooted in poverty.

NOTES

1. In 2012, legislators in Georgia, Oklahoma, Tennessee, and Utah passed similar laws, and the National Conference of State Legislatures estimated that twenty-nine additional states introduced similar proposals.

2. As a result, for instance, opium dens flourished in Chinatown in San Francisco as the Progressive Era pushed its anti-Chinese sentiment into law.

3. In June 2011, the U.S. Sentencing Commission declared that individuals presently convicted and incarcerated for nonviolent crack cocaine possession under federal law would be eligible to have their sentences reduced by a federal judge *if* Congress did not block the action. Individuals currently convicted and incarcerated under state crack cocaine laws, like the Rockefeller Drug Laws in New York State, are not eligible for a reduction in sentencing.

4. For example, the Boggs Act of 1951 increased criminal penalties for marijuana use; the Narcotics Control Act of 1956 created "the most punitive and repressive anti-narcotics legislation. . . . All discretion to suspend sentences or permit probation were eliminated. Parole was allowed only for first time offenders convicted of possession, and the death penalty could be invoked for anyone who sold heroin to a minor" (McWilliams 1990, 116).

5. May 18, 1971, 12:16 pm–12:35 pm, Oval Office Conversation No. 500–17. President Nixon is meeting with Arthur (Art) G. Linkletter and DeVan L. Shumway. Conversation edited by author for lucidity.

6. *Timeline: America's War on Drugs*, NPR Special Series, "The Forgotten War on Drugs" http://www.npr.org/templates/story/story.php?storyId=9252490 (April 2, 2007).

7. Milton Friedman is known for creating the "Iron Law of Prohibition," and offered a devastating critique of the "War on Drugs." He argued that the solution was to take drugs away from the criminals and allow doctors and pharmacists to distribute them. In other words, legalize drugs and you will eliminate a vast layer of criminality, instead of spending billions of dollars enforcing prohibition, and should use the money for rehabilitation facilities and educational programs.

8. This shift is occurring across different sectors of society. Most prominently, Dr. Sanjay Gupta, an internationally known medical correspondent for CNN, issued a mea culpa concerning his previous position on marijuana. In a new documentary called *Weed*, he traveled the world seeking answers about marijuana from medical experts, growers, and patients. His motivation was based on his review of the scientific literature on medical marijuana in the United States, which he found "unimpressive." After his investigation, he came forward to apologize for his previous position (articulated in a 2009 *Time* article, "Why I Would Vote No on Pot"). Dr. Gupta criticizes his own approach, stating he did not look hard enough at the research and dismissed the voices of legitimate patients and health care providers. He, like many, lumped them together as drug users who were defying the federal government's Schedule I categorization of marijuana. Dr. Gupta previously believed the government's claim that marijuana had no medicinal value, yet his own research demonstrates that the government did not rely on science to base their claim; rather, it used politics and moral values to determine its lack of medicinal value. Further, research conducted outside of the United States indicates that marijuana has a low potential for abuse and many legitimate applications for medical use. Dr. Gupta believes that the federal government has systematically misled the public (CNN, August 8, 2013. "Gupta: Why I Changed My Mind on Weed").

9. Recent reports indicate a growing realization that the "War on Drugs" is a complete failure, at best (see the report, "Ending the Drug War: A Dream Deferred," published by *Law Enforcement Against Prohibition*, June 2011, found at: http://www.leap.cc/wp-content/uploads/2011/06/Ending-the-Drug-War-A-Dream-Deferred.pdf; Cardoso, Bavaria, and Zedillo 2009; Cronkite 2006).

10. Incarceration rates and crime data show that under President Clinton, who consolidated and embraced the Republicans' message of "tough on crime" in a series of political maneuvers called triangulation, which resulted in the largest documented increase in prison inmates. The resulting increase in state and federal inmates was due to campaign promises and presidential support of harsh imprisonment sentences for drug convictions and prison construction (Feldman et al. 2001).

11. Middlemass Field Notes, July 11, 2012.

12. "The life" refers to the drug-dealing lifestyle of large cash transactions; in some cases more than $20,000 a day.

13. "Going back" refers to going back to prison for any reason, such as violating parole or "messing up" and committing a new crime.

14. Middlemass Field Notes, May 9, 2012.

15. Personal interview with Eric on April 11, 2011 and with Mark on April 25, 2011.

16. Personal interview with Yolanda on April 19, 2011.

17. Middlemass Field Notes, May 9, 2012.

18. Middlemass Field Notes, June 20, 2012.

19. Middlemass Field Notes, June 27, 2012.

20. Interview with Wilson on April 25, 2011.

21. Interview with Wilson on April 25, 2011.

22. Interview with Charles on April 18, 2011. See Martin (2011) for a perspective about asset poverty and prisoner reentry.

Chapter Seven

Poverty and Juvenile Justice

Exploring the Intersections, Identifying the Solutions

Al Passarella

While juvenile justice was not specifically a target of the War on Poverty, its policy, including programmatic and bureaucratic changes, directly affected the vulnerable youth populations who are disproportionately represented in the juvenile justice system. The issue of addressing poverty as a "national disgrace" (Brauer 1982) translated into substantive efforts to reduce the negative consequences of the ailment that poverty had become. While juvenile justice exists within the context of poverty, did the War on Poverty shift how the United States views and treats social problems such as juvenile delinquency?

To answer this question requires an examination of the framework of juvenile delinquency prevention efforts that existed prior to the declaration of war, and how these measures intersect with the efforts toward poverty elimination. The War on Poverty constituted a significant moment in the evolution of the United States' philosophy in addressing the growing concern of poverty. During this time period, the dominance of solutions rooted in progressive principles moved through a decisive, often racially charged political environment to create some of the most potent legislation ever aimed at reducing poverty (Brauer 1982). Treating poverty with a rehabilitative model showed that it is best addressed as an ailment, not as a defect.

Poverty and juvenile justice intersect at the crossroads of insufficient resources and adolescent development. Research has shown striking correlations between poverty, social exclusion, and positive youth development (Kramer 2000), often showing that the most deprived of children face the greatest risk of engaging in delinquent behavior (Werner and Smith 1992), with special attention paid to the effects of poverty, social exclusion, and youth violence (Currie 1998). Additional research demonstrates that "the socially defined position of youth, the impact of market relations and poverty and inequality" all contribute significantly to shaping youth delinquency in the United States (Minor 1993). Further work shows that youths are more likely to engage in delinquent behavior in communities that suffer from capital and social disinvestment (Kramer 2000), as many of the poor communities in the United States do.

Even with the measurable success of the War on Poverty, an American child under 18 years of age is only half as likely to be poor as they were thirty years ago, with more children living in concentrated poverty and spending longer stretches of their childhood at or below the poverty line (Annie E. Casey Foundation 2012). This "sharp deterioration" in the societal conditions of the communities these children live in coincides with the poor in America becoming increasingly isolated, both by space and economics, creating chaotic environments ripe for violent crime (Currie 1998). Within the context of these environments, Kramer (2000) points out that the evidence and research suggests more than just a casual relationship between poverty, economic inequality, and social exclusion, with these factors acting as agents in the production of crime and violence by young people in the United States. To even the casual observer, the link between poverty and juvenile justice is evident.

This chapter examines the intersection of issues related to juvenile justice and poverty. I begin the chapter with an examination of the evolution of the juvenile justice system in the latter half of the twentieth century and the first decades of the twenty-first century. The latter half of the twentieth century is the starting point because this is where the beginnings of the modern juvenile justice system begin to take shape in terms of processes, policies, and functions. This is also the time period in which we begin to see the rise in disproportionality that exists within the system with regards to demographics and income status.

Next, I examine some of the critical issues that youth, affected by their economic vulnerability, might encounter that in turn may lead them to confront the juvenile justice system. Lastly, I present evidence of what is being done to address the issues arising from this intersection between poverty and youth delinquency prevention. I conclude with some projections regarding how future issues related to this intersection might be addressed.

HISTORIC FRAMEWORK

The concept of youth delinquency in the United States has an interesting ideological history that, pre-1960s, was primarily rooted in the desire to utilize and promote rehabilitative models as a way to reduce youth crime.

Youth crime was often regarded not as a precursor to a crime-filled adulthood, but more as an issue of wayward and rebellious youth going astray. Rehabilitative models for youth delinquency prevention were widely regarded as the most effective way of dealing with youth crime at the time. This was the foundation of juvenile court and shaped its operation through the late 1960s.

Rooted in the Progressive Era's ethos of building institutions aimed at promoting the safety and welfare of youth involved in crimes, these models operated based on the premise that criminality had no place in juvenile justice case law; that treatment and rehabilitation, not punishment and detainment, were the goals of juvenile courts and the juvenile justice system (Lindsey and O'Higgins 1970). Under these models, judges remedied delinquent behavior with treatments and services tailored to fit a variety of factors: the youth's circumstance, the crime in question, and the level at which treatment was needed to "correct" the delinquent behavior. Dispositions were usually set for an indeterminate amount of time, based on the general principle that the services were needed until positive modification of the behaviors that brought the youth before the court were achieved (National Research Council 2013).

While benevolent in nature, these rehabilitative models for youth justice proved to be subject to much criticism. Researchers and critics on both sides began to question the validity and effectiveness of the courts (Mennel 1983) and to what level the rehabilitative mission of the juvenile system was being accomplished (National Research Council 2013). "Child advocates argued that the juvenile court harmed the youth whose interests it claimed to serve, and conservative critics emphasized its failure to protected the public from young criminals" (Bonnie et al. 2013, p. 34). In addition to the disapproval of both advocates and critics, the promotion of punitive models aimed at dealing with these "teenage brigands" (*New York Times* 1960) began to take hold. Highly publicized reports by the FBI during this time period revealed a marked rise in arrests of individuals under eighteen. One of the more damning FBI reports of the era detailed a 220 percent increase in juvenile court cases from 1941 to 1959 (Barnosky 2006). While history has come to show that FBI statistics from this time period are notoriously unreliable, in the context of the time, the numbers, at least on the surface, showed the presence of increased activity in juvenile arrests and court cases.[1]

Within this context, a rather simplistic view of youth delinquency as the by-product of core American values gone wayward was beginning to take hold. As William F. Buckley put it, "until we destroy the deadly germ from which the poison growth of delinquency has sprung, it is a hopeless challenge that we face" (Barnosky 2006). Writings and lectures by noted psychiatrist Frederic Wertham and others began to beat a subtle drum of the nation drowning in a deluge of youth crime, fanning the flames of parents and teachers already worried by the firestorm of related news and statistics (Binder and Polan 1992). Additionally, theories delineating a spike in delinquency were being examined in the sociological context of being a product of low-income areas and households and their perceived lack of normative, middle-class values; in other words, poor and low-income communities produce delinquent youth because they lack morals and ethics (Gilbert 1986). Polls conducted on the subject and severity of youth crime during this time period showed considerable uneasiness about the issue (Gilbert 1986). Everything from depictions of violence on television to comics of poverty and substandard housing and their impacts on youth delinquency were blamed for the rise in negative attitudes toward rehabilitative models of youth delinquency prevention (Barnosky 2006).[2]

Federal attention to the issue of youth crime and delinquency began to emerge in the early 1950s when Senator Estes Kefauver (D-TN) placed a special focus on youth delinquency through the Senate Judiciary Subcommittee to Investigate Juvenile Delinquency. In his 1955 State of the Union address, President Eisenhower acknowledged the growing and persistent fear of youth crime and delinquency by proposing legislation that would allow states greater latitude to deal with the perceived issue of youth crime (Binder and Polan 1985). Despite all of the hysteria surrounding youth delinquency in this era, federal legislation introduced in both 1956 and 1957 died in either committee actions or congressional adjournment (Binder and Polan 1985).

As the decade changed from the 1950s to the 1960s, the skepticism toward the system and its ability to prevent delinquency and fulfill its previous promises was deafening (Dawson 1990). In his work *Juvenile Justice Reform: A Historical Perspective*, Sanford J. Fox (1970) summarized the issues, challenges, and ultimately the failures of the rehabilitative model:

> The greatest functional loss the juvenile court has suffered in the twentieth century, however, is its role in the predelinquency system of crime prevention. The predelinquency concept rested on the belief that society could recognize, and the law could describe, the conditions of childhood that would give rise to adult criminals, and that techniques were available—institutions, foster homes, probation, psychiatry—that could arrest the conditions and prevent crime. Loss of any of the elements of this belief would undermine the fundamental function of the juvenile court; the twentieth century has eroded all of them. . . . The call for family relations within institutions was nothing more than wishful thinking. Without ready access to family life for the children coming before it, the juvenile court lost much of its *raison d'etre*. (1233)

The two primary challenges to the system—the potential danger to those it aimed to protect versus the desire to deter delinquent behavior by more rigorous means—were at the front of the charge for new, systemic measures aimed at addressing these issues (National Research Council 2013). Federal legislation was introduced and enacted in 1961 in the form of the Juvenile Delinquency and Youth Offenses Control Act, which authorized federal monies to be supplied to states ($10M overall) over three years geared toward the prevention and control of youth crime. While the federal expansion into youth delinquency and prevention was a perceived as favorable by youth advocates, this increased role often led to continued acts deemed detrimental toward youth and youth advocates (Barnosky 2006).

The movement toward more punitive measures in the 1950s led to more conservative policy that picked apart many of the agencies that had been and would be vital in keeping the response to youth crime and delinquency prevention rooted in progressive policies (Ibid.). As a result, any of the advantages that progressive policy makers would have had access to through the passage of the Juvenile Delinquency and Youth Offenses Control Act were rendered impotent.

GERRY GAULT, DUE PROCESS, AND THE DEFINITION OF REHABILITATION

The early part of the 1960s saw practitioners and law enforcement administrators become increasingly concerned about how best to address acts of youth delinquency and how to step up prevention efforts to curb further delinquency. During this time period the federal response, which had been building since the mid-1950s, was beginning to take shape. The Kennedy and later the Johnson administrations began expanding federal presence in the area of juvenile delinquency greatly, creating special presidential task forces through both the President's Committee on Juvenile Delinquency and Youth Crime and the Committee on Law Enforcement and Administration (Bechard et al. 2011). The federal government, Kennedy stated when signing the bill into law, was going to be an active partner with states and localities in controlling and preventing delinquency (Binder and Polan 1992). This, along with emphasis on rehabilitation of welfare clients, manpower development, and training legislation, were part of a series of discrete responses by the Kennedy administration to identify social and economic issues that were influenced by poverty (Brauer 1982).

From 1961 through 1963, tens of millions of dollars in grants and aid flowed from the federal government to states and localities to build prevention programs and control the delinquency issue. Delinquency control and prevention was a key theme in the Kennedy administration's domestic policy, along with subtle yet measured efforts to reduce poverty. While Kennedy never got to see the effects of his plans materialize due to his assassination, the Johnson administration continued Kennedy's efforts, most notably discarding the subtlety with which the Kennedy administration operated. In an effort to establish his own presidential credentials and win reelection against Barry Goldwater, President Johnson vowed to make crime prevention, and specifically youth crime prevention, a front-and-center issue in his 1964 reelection campaign. Johnson's vow brought youth delinquency prevention firmly into the national conversation.

To ease voter anxiety on crime and social issues, the administration introduced the Law Enforcement Assistance Act of 1965, which authorized the attorney general to make small grants to aid local law enforcement and included the issuance of an executive order that established the President's Commission on Law Enforcement and Administration of Justice (PCLEAJ) in July 1965. These actions by the Johnson administration simultaneously laid the foundation for a national task force aimed at giving special attention to youth delinquency, while paying heed to the political pressures crime and other social issues were exerting both nationally and inside the administration (Binder and Polan 1991).

As the nation's policy makers began to focus on how best to remedy youth delinquency, youth advocates began to challenge the assertion that youths were receiving proper treatment within the current framework of the juvenile justice system. The framework during this time consisted of nothing more than informal processes, in which many of the judges that presided over juvenile court hearings lacked formal legal training, and youth were not afforded the due process that adults in the criminal system were given under the Fifth and Fourteenth Amendments.

The informality of juvenile court proceedings was commonplace, given the philosophy of minimal legal control and the casual, nonadversarial manner of the proceedings (Bonnie et al. 2013). This was evident in the notion that "the driving legal philosophy of the juvenile justice system was to entrust maximum discretion to the court and treatment staff with the absolute minimum of legal control" (Dawson 1990, p. 137). The variance in the structure and standards of the proceedings was vast. In some jurisdictions, "the judge would simply declare that the court is now sitting as a juvenile court," often without properly staffed probation officers or even separate detention facilities from adult offenders (Handler 1965).

Juvenile justice advocates argued that this was a blatant attempt to strip youth of procedural rights and protections afforded to adult offenders. In essence, children were not receiving the treatment the rehabilitative model had promised, and the proliferation of perceived treatment was being used to skirt basic legal practices offered to adults: evidentiary protections, due process, and procedural rights (Bonnie et al. 2013).

Though progressives saw the courts as avenues for welfare, where the state would offer rehabilitative services to youth, the reality was that the "services" offered were far more punitive in nature and practice than they were intended to be. Progressives had envisioned a juvenile court judge who was trained to protect the best interests of the child and therefore there was little need to limit the discretion of courts and their judges (Feld 1993). Unfortunately, the reality was a system that was unpredictable and inconsistent with regards to addressing youth delinquency. The tension between advocates for children and the state of delinquency prevention came to a head in 1967, when the Supreme Court case *In re Gault* set unprecedented standards as to what rights youths have in court and the responsibilities the courts have to these youth.

Gerald Gault was a 15-year-old youth from Arizona who, in 1964, was detained along with a friend for making lewd phone calls. On the morning of June 8, 1964, Gila County, Arizona, sheriffs arrested Mr. Gault and placed him into custody, without notifying his parents. Justification for custody, according to the court transcripts, was Mr. Gault being in violation of a six-month probation order from a prior charge in February of that year (*In re Gault section I 1967*).

Gault was brought before Judge McGhee on the obscenity charges without legal representation or notice of charges (Bonnie et al. 2013). Moreover, Mr. Gault and his parents never received counsel nor were they ever informed of their right to counsel (Stansby 1967 1204). Additionally the complainant, the neighbor Gault was alleged to have called, never appeared as a witness during his proceedings, with only the arresting officer who reported the alleged complaint being present (Adler 2007). After the proceedings were completed, Judge McGhee "committed Mr. Gault to the Arizona State Industrial School for up to six years—for a misdemeanor for which an adult would receive, at most, a $50 fine and a jail term of up to twelve months (Bonnie et al. 2013).

The *Gault* case was symbolic of the arbitrary nature of the juvenile justice system at the time. Irregularities were abundant in the *Gault* proceedings: Mrs. Cook, the person responsible for Mr. Gault's arrest, never made an appearance for either of the two hearings, and Mr. Gault incriminated himself during the hearings but was never informed of his right to remain silent. These irregularities, however, were not singular to *Gault*, but rather pervasive throughout the juvenile justice system. Prior to *Gault*, the privilege not to self-incriminate was not frequently recognized; the idea was that an admission of guilt helped children in the rehabilitation process. The plaintiff was not required to provide testimony under oath of their account. Within this context, the result was a guilty verdict without the due process guaranteed by the constitution.

Eventually, the *Gault* case made its way to the Supreme Court, where Mr. Gault and other juveniles were extended due process protections historically guaranteed to adults in a landmark decision in favor of the defendants. The raison d'être of the juvenile justice system differs philosophically from that of the criminal justice system, but the Supreme Court found that juveniles should still be extended the rights afforded to them by the constitution. In Arizona, where Mr. Gault was originally adjudicated, the court's philosophy on juvenile justice was as follows:

> Juvenile courts do not exist to punish children for their transgressions against society. The juvenile court stands in the position of a protective parent rather than a prosecutor. . . . The aim of the court is to provide individualized justice for children. (In re Gault, 181, 188)

This philosophical difference helped to justify the treatment of a minor vis-à-vis the criminal justice system. The legal doctrine of *parens patriae* had been invoked in juvenile justice cases. This doctrine claimed that the state should act as a parent rather than as a governor. The focus was on rehabilitation and therefore procedural formality should be disregarded if it impeded the possibility of rehabilitation. The state was seen as seeking to protect and help the child. With this principle in mind, a child had to answer all questions, like he or she would with his or her parent. It also followed that there was no need for counsel because the court had the child's best interest in mind and was not seeking to harm the child in any way (Stansby 1967). However, facilities were lacking and did not always meet the rehabilitative goals that courts hoped for. Furthermore, once rehabilitation became the goal of the criminal justice system writ large, there was little to differentiate it from the juvenile justice system. The Supreme Court reversed the lower court's ruling, arguing that Mr. Gault had not been afforded due process. Additionally, the decision effectively reversed the doctrine of *parens patriae* arguing *In re Gault* that the concept had been used to justify arbitrariness and irregularity rather than "enlightened procedures" (Lefstein 1967).

In their opinion the justices found that the juvenile justice system had not afforded youth entering the system due process guaranteed to them by the Fifth and Fourteenth Amendments. Basic tenets of the criminal justice system, such as attorney rights, right to avoid self-incrimination, and right to appeal, were not offered to youth in the juvenile proceedings, thus increasing the likelihood of unfair and unbalanced proceedings. On these grounds, the court ruled that the current process was unconstitutional and offered immediate remedies in the form of granting youth due process rights.

The *Gault* decision was critical in changing the status of children before courts, preventing them from being treated as second-class citizens. *Gault* extended the due process rights afforded to adults without challenging the need for a separate system for juveniles. The Supreme Court agreed that minors are not criminal but rather delinquent, and though this appears to be a question of semantics it points to the different legal paradigm used in cases involving minors. Though the penal system as a whole began moving toward more rehabilitative models, minors are seen as most in need of these services.

Despite the court's overturning of *parens patriae*, it maintained the belief that the goal for children is rehabilitation and not punishment.

ALIGNMENT OF FORCES

Two parallel forces, a national call for reducing delinquency and the rise of procedural and due process rights, met in the 1960s with both the decision and reverberations of *Gault* and the initiation of the Johnson administration's Great Society and War on Poverty efforts. Programs such as the Neighborhood Youth Corps, the Legal Services Corporation, and Head Start were aimed to create better opportunities for economically disadvantaged youth and children from underresourced communities. In addition to programs focused on opportunity creation, Johnson created two programs critical to the direction of national youth delinquency prevention efforts: the omnibus Crime Control and Safe Streets Act, which in turn spawned the Law Enforcement Assistance Administration to coordinate national anticrime efforts with states and localities using federal aid (Barnosky 2006).

The creation of these programs effectively placed youth delinquency efforts under the control of a federal agency with a law and order reputation. It also moved them away from the Children's Bureau and Health, Education, and Welfare (formerly HHS) agencies, the very agencies that created many of the rehabilitative templates for youth delinquency prevention. The money still flowed toward delinquency prevention but those equipped to best implement the programs became thoroughly detached from the process (Barnosky 2006). Those best equipped to deal with the programmatic processes of delinquency prevention were systemically being removed from the process just as the system as a whole was undergoing a massive overhaul in the wake of *Gault*. *Gault*, in providing youth with the standards and safeguards afforded by criminal law, undercut the courts and the system's reputation as a humanitarian agency; thus those best equipped to deal with the changes were removed from the process as part of the collateral damage that *Gault* unintentionally created (Mennel 1983). This turn toward a reactive approach to dealing with youth crime and delinquency seemed rooted in *Gault*, creating an adult-like judicial attitude more so than merely righting a constitutional wrong.

1970S

From all perspectives, the need for due process reforms in juvenile delinquency proceedings was clear, especially in the light of the large variance in types of punishments available to juvenile court judges. One issue with the overhaul, however, was that "the due process reforms did not constitute an explicit rejection of the juvenile system or even of rehabilitation as one of its goals (Bonnie et al. 2013). The crux of the matter lies within the due process reform itself: the reform challenged the characterization of youth offenders as innocent children, while supporting the notion that youth were different from adults and should receive different treatment within the system (Zimring 1998).

Within the fight over the direction of youth delinquency prevention, the system continued to grow, with little deviation from its original rehabilitative focus. For much of the 1970s, youth proceedings still existed in the separate juvenile system and were still focused, abstractly at least, on the task of youth rehabilitation as opposed to punitive measures (Bonnie et al. 2013). During the early to mid-1970s, data released by a presidential commission on juvenile justice presented conflicting figures about the seriousness of youth crime. From 1960 to 1974, the numbers of youth charged with violent crime increased by 216 percent; this coupled with increases in youth charged with property crimes made for an ominous forecast of the state of youth delinquency prevention (Raley 1995). However, on the other side of these statistics, 40 percent of youth incarcerated had committed no criminal act, and instead were being detained for low-level status offenses.

Within this convoluted framework, critics began to argue the merits of utilizing correction-based programs to reduce crime, primarily on account of the growing body of evidence that suggested the relative ineffectiveness of the rehabilitative model (Martinson 1974). In addition, the calls for reductions of status offenses, or minor charges such as curfew violations and truancy that are only illegal for those under 18, began to be questioned. "Critics found faults with the wide discretion granted to juvenile court judges with the limited procedural rights granted to children" (Branoksy 2006), even in the post-*Gault* era. Furthermore, evidence began to mount regarding the effectiveness of such deterrence, citing that the punishment meted out for such minor offenses was a counterproductive action: it encouraged status offenders to commit more crimes by placing them in detention with more serious offenders (Branosky 2006, Holden and Kapler 1995). Led by progressive Sen. Birch Bayh (D-IN), legislation aimed at correcting such ineffective deterrence was championed in the form of the Juvenile Justice and Delinquency Act (JJDA) of 1974.

The JJDA attempted to remedy the issue by putting a provision in the law requiring states to remove status offenders from detention and have juvenile offenders "sight and sound" away from adult offenders as a condition of the funding formula to receive aid for crime and delinquency prevention efforts. While this appeared to be an important shift toward sensible and fair sentencing standards for youth, the fight over who oversaw the funding and implementation doomed the legislation with regards to a progressive model of rehabilitation-focused youth delinquency prevention.

Congressional liberals wanted the program to be housed in the Health, Education and Welfare agency, where they saw a natural program manager for more rehabilitative programming. Conservative legislators, on the other hand, aimed to have oversight and program management based in the Department of Justice (DOJ), a favorite among conservative lawmakers because of its law and order reputation (Barnosky 2006). Ultimately, a compromise of sorts was struck between lawmakers; the DOJ was assigned oversight and delegation responsibilities for programing. From this compromise was born the Office of Juvenile Justice and Delinquency Prevention (OJJDP), a research and evidence-based division of the DOJ created to coordinate the anti-delinquency programs with a focus on rehabilitation and prevention.

Progressive lawmakers such as Sen. Bayh had hoped that OJJDP would be ground zero for youth delinquency and prevention efforts, with federal funds earmarked to divert youth from traditional court settings and into other programming, such as restitution projects, peer or neighborhood courts, and other community-based programs (Raley 1995). The office, however, struggled mightily to get out of the gate (Barnosky 2006; National Research Council 2013). The issues were twofold: one, the funding for OJJDP was paltry. Initially authorized with $125 million for funding, the Ford administration's 1975 federal budget requested $0 in funding for OJJDP efforts, with Congress and Ford settling on a modest $25 million for support (Barnosky 2006). The second issue was the lack of decriminalization of status offenses, which was a core recommendation for the act but was not adopted. Instead, the promotion of small, community-based facilities and removal of secure confinement for status offenses were adopted. While the issue of preventing status offenders from having system contact was still under debate, the funding issue soon became moot. In 1977, under the Carter administration, the Act saw an increase in funding of $50 million and by 1978, the budget for OJJDP had swelled to $100 million.

By 1980, the JJDPA had shown progress: juvenile courts saw a reduction in the number of cases referred, status offenses referred to the courts had dropped significantly, and detention for status offenses had dropped by half (Raley 1995). While progress was being made, a strategic movement by the National Council of Juvenile and Family Court Judges (NCJFCJ) to petition suppression of the provision to incarcerate status offenders in secure detention proved to be a critical turning point in how youth were viewed and treated by the courts and subsequently by the system as a whole.

Although the NCJFCJ wasn't entirely successful, a compromise was struck allowing for status offenders to be placed in secure facilities upon violation of a previous judicial order. Advocates found this to be troubling, as it was an obvious turn away from the intentions of the act and appeared to be moving closer to more punitive and criminal justice–focused measures (Raley 1995). A slight and subtle gesture to appease a key constituent, coupled with a return to conservative principles on youth crime, signaled a significant shift in the direction of youth justice.

1980S AND 1990S: CHANGING PERSPECTIVES ON YOUTH CRIME

Beginning in the late 1970s, a new era of conservatism toward youth crime began to emerge, with a number of states simultaneously lowering the age at which youths could be tried as adults and adding to the number of offenses for which youths could be charged as adults (Mennel 1983). With the election of Ronald Reagan in 1980 and reaffirmation of conservative norms and values in national politics, the juvenile justice system began to experience sweeping changes that created policies and measures for delinquency prevention that were markedly different from the rehabilitative models of the 1960s and 1970s (Bonnie et al. 2013).

Beginning in 1981 and lasting through to 1989, OJJDP began to see annual reductions in its budget, losing approximately $34 million over that eight-year period (Raley 1995). During the Reagan administration's attempts to shrink the size and scope of government, the OJJDP became a frequent target for cuts, and there were calls for outright elimination based on the notion that the office had become a haven for "soft on crime liberal experiments" and that the states would be best equipped to handle programming for delinquency prevention (Barnosky 2006). Meanwhile, states were becoming more punitive and less rehabilitative in their approach to youth delinquency prevention.

This was part of the administration's overall strategy to reduce the federal presence in social programming by providing block grants to states, which the administration claimed were the best practitioners when it came to dealing with social issues affecting their citizens. This strategy was founded partly in the Reagan administration's belief that state and local governments would fund the action-based services that their constituents demanded and fund fewer of the activities from what the administration termed the "advice-giving industry" (Mennel 1983).

Within this context, the 1980s brought increased federal attention to punitive juvenile justice models as opposed to delinquency prevention (Raley 1995). This included a stronger emphasis on prosecution of serious youth offenders, mandatory and harsher sentencing laws, and initiatives aimed at school violence prevention. Academics and advocates questioned this new approach because research and scholarship had shown that these punitive measures proved to be largely ineffective in reducing youth crime and preventing future episodes (Bechard et al. 2011; Barnosky 2006; Levitt 2004; Zimring 1998). Additionally, research examining arrest rates for serious violent and property crime showed that aggregate arrest rates had been declining since the late 1970s, with most youth offenses being of the nonviolent variety (Office of Technological Assessment 1991). Regardless of the evidence presented, the movement toward law and order approaches was starting to gain serious traction both inside and outside the D.C. Beltway.

The reactions were not without merit. The youth violent crime rate increased by 38 percent from 1988 to 1991 (Snyder and Sickmund 1995), with a specific increase in youth offenders involved in homicides. This increase came during what is now referred to as the crack epidemic from the late 1980s through the early 1990s, peaking in 1993. These increases, which are significant (and anomalous when viewed in a historical context), had followed a relatively stable period in youth violent crime. The transition from a period of relative stability to a jolting and significant increase in youth violent crime gained the attention of the media, especially in the most shocking crimes involving youth.

While the increase in crime and severity were to be taken seriously, the actuality of the situation was that those subjective cases were being blown entirely out of proportion by lawmakers wanting to appear tough on crime and a media that was eager to sell news. "Stories that played on readers' fears were common. Several popular magazines featured stories on the predicted crime wave, often depicted young black men as gang members, holding handguns" (Howell 2009). This propagandizing of youth crime created a feeling of hostility and fear toward young offenders based on anecdotal evidence.

The youth accused of these violent acts were being depicted by punitive-minded reformers as superpredators devoid of conscience and emotion, "not as the wayward youth whose welfare was the key concern of the system" as had previously been the case (Bonnie et al. 2013). In addition to the notion of the superpredator, researchers were offering predictions (which were later discredited) of tremendous increases in the numbers of these superpredator youth, with some estimations claiming that as many as 6 percent of the youth ages 14–17 in the coming decades would be repeat violent offenders (Howell 2009).

Such dire predictions spurred law and order reformers across the nation to take action. One of the most common punitive crime prevention measures involved making it easier to target youth crime with corrective remedies primarily found in the adult criminal justice system. States began to make judicial transfer of youth to the adult system easier by expanding the number of transfer-eligible offenses, thus giving prosecutors the leeway needed to pursue what was deemed "adult time for adult crime."

During this punitive era of youth delinquency prevention, every state expanded crimes eligible for adult transfer, with most states starting the eligible crimes list at age 10 and others having no transfer minimum at all (Synder and Sickmund 1995). Data from 1988 to 1992 shows a 71 percent increase in the number of males 15 or younger transferred to criminal court from juvenile court. With the expansion of charges now eligible for transfer to criminal court, 57 percent of the cases transferred involved property or drug charges, with only one third of cases involving person-to-person offenses (Ibid.). Additionally, the target of the law and order agenda for youth crime was increasingly becoming minority inner-city youth, especially with the fanning of the crack cocaine epidemic flames. In 1989, at the peak of the epidemic, 60 percent of youth inmates in correctional facilities were youth of color, with 40 percent of those being black youth (Mann 1994). Targeted laws dealing with the violence of the crack epidemic in inner cities, coupled with selective monitoring of communities impacted heavily by the epidemic, resulted in more minority youth, largely black youth, having formal contact with the tougher, stricter preventive measures. This was an obvious but largely ignored by-product of reactive law and order responses to the crack epidemic (Bonnie et al. 2013).

As the 1990s began to unfold, noticeable decreases in the overall amount of youth crime began to occur. Starting in 1993, arrests rates for violent crimes committed by youth offenders ages 13 to 17 began a downward trend that continued relatively unabated through 2012, with the rate reducing by 55 percent from its peak in 1993 and 1994 (Zimring 1998; OJJDP 2012). Violent and nonviolent arrest rates began to drop dramatically for white and black youth overall, yet growth in the arrest rate gap between black and white youth has remained stubbornly high, especially for violent crimes (Office of Juvenile Justice and Delinquency Prevention 2013).

INCOME INEQUALITY AND PUNITIVE MEASURES

Income inequality also began to play a larger role in the move away from youth delinquency prevention models and a renewed push toward punitive measures. Under the Reagan administration the budgets for Agriculture (–24.9 percent), Education (–18.6 percent), HUD (–40.1 percent), and Labor (–50.6 percent) were all cut either during the first term, second term or both (de Rugy 2004). Each of these agencies delivered services to poor or working-class communities, with a disproportionate amount of those being communities of color. The effects of these cuts proved to be devastating to these communities, many of which were suffering from the early stages of the deindustrialization of the American workforce. Analysis of the Luxemburg Income Study (Kramer 2000; Currie 1998) shows that American children during this period were far more likely to be poor than those in other industrialized nations, with poor American children more likely to experience extreme poverty than other poor children in comparable nations. Additionally,

Kramer (2000) notes the causal relationship between poverty, inequality, and violent crime by youth:

> The theory and research that have been reviewed make a compelling case for the thesis that poverty, economic inequality and social exclusion are causal agents in the productions of crime and violence by young people in America. Although these structural conditions do not often have a direct effect in producing violent crime, they are important because of the impact they have on social institutions like the family, the school and the community. . . . This violence by young people seems to generally take on one of three forms: predatory economic crimes, drug industry crimes or social relationship violence. (Kramer 2000, 133)

Work by the National Research Council (2013) notes some of the disproportionate contact of low-income and minority youth to the juvenile justice system. The first, differential offending, is a by-product of community factors that result in higher level of violence. Minorities, especially black youth, disproportionately live in communities that face greater stresses on structural social conditions: lack of education, resources, and negative public health indicators. These stressors create tremendous instability, resulting in youth being raised in environments that are severely compromised in terms of prosocial behaviors. This form of social exclusion leads to youth violence by the subsequent breakdown of social supports that affect youth.

Research by Fite et al (2009) illustrated that the differences in youth crime along race/ethnicity lines can be traced back to the level of stress and risk factors a youth grew up with in their community. As poor communities become more isolated, both spatially and economically, and social supports, such as job training, income benefits, and child protective services programing are further removed (Currie 1998), the connection between violent crime, particularly youth violent crime, and disproportionate income equality becomes more evident. Work by Werner and Smith (1992) shows that within a generally deprived population, it is the children within this population that are most likely to engage in crime and violent activity. Conversely, a review of evidence by Cullen (1994) shows that governmental assistance to the poor tends to decrease violent crime in lower-income areas.

When viewed in the context of lost social supports and exclusionary communities, the strategies of reactionary, punitive policies toward youth crime are seen to further exacerbate the issue. A variety of factors, such as patrolling strategies and patterns, police presence, and minority profiling can have a substantial effect on the overrepresentation of minorities in the juvenile system. This stems from decisions to patrol in high crime areas, in which impoverished and minority youth are usually overrepresented (National Research Council 2013), thus leading to higher levels of system contact.

When this set of approaches is put into place in spite of evidence that shows minority youth are overrepresented in the number of children living in poverty (Currie 1998), the result is a justice system that is disproportionately full of minority and poor offenders. At the same time, the system is experiencing a punitive overhaul and moving away from its rehabilitative roots. The product was a system that targeted economically disadvantaged, minority youth during a time when youth crime was noticeably decreasing. Policies and laws, in typical reactive fashion, were being enacted to further combat the net effects of what research was showing to be the cause of social disinvestment in poor, mostly minority communities. Money was being poured into these punitive measures in direct opposition to what research and scholarship were discovering to be cause of the youth crime and delinquency.

The 1990s and 2000s were a perfect storm of intensely focused law and order measures meeting higher rates of poverty, the effects of years of cuts to social safety programming being fully realized, and conservative reforming of the delivery of safety net programming.

RETURN TO REHABILITATION-BASED PREVENTION MODELS

As the 2000s began to unfold, a change in attitudes and norms related to youth crime began to emerge. Primarily born of a need to revisit costly punitive measures that were producing paltry results, lawmakers began to experiment with and revisit a rehabilitative model focused more on treatment and prevention and less on correction and punishment, a nod to criminal justice advocates who were calling for a more fair and balanced discipline system.

Research on reducing youth committed populations and creating rehabilitative models for delinquency prevention has increased significantly in recent years as states begin to reexamine crime and punishment policies to better allocate fiscal resources in trying economic times. While certain offenses do require a more punitive model and detention can serve a role in supervising the most at-risk youth, evidence has shown that depriving youth of their liberty has little to no effect on reducing overall rates of youth crime (Males et al. 2007) because upwards of 70 percent of confined youth are held for nonviolent or low-risk offenses (Holman and Ziedenberg 2006).

Additionally, work by Zimring (1998) goes as far as to assert that a pattern of increasing adolescent violence was never present and that there is no basis for making projections of youth violence based on current trends, while Lipsey (2009) shows a 10 to 13 percent reduction in recidivism when offending youth are treated with therapeutic interventions, even with those whose offenses were violent in nature. Furthermore, recent research has shown that confined youths are more likely to suffer from mental, physical, and emotional victimization, obtain less schooling, and face negative long-term employment and earnings consequences (Bonnie et al. 2013). Not only is this cost-ineffective for cash-strapped states and localities (Mendel 2011), but recent research even suggests that youth confinement increases the likelihood of adult incarceration and the associated costs (Aizer and Doyle 2013). Additional research suggests that youth tried and sentenced as adults have higher rates of recidivism and the severity of the subsequent offenses is greater than youth tried and treated in the youth system (Howell 2009).

This coincides with research by Lipsey (2009) in which a sample of youth offenders who were in rehabilitative programs focusing on counseling, skill building, or restorative interventions saw greater decreases in recidivism than those youth in sample groups whose programs focused solely on surveillance, deterrence, or discipline. Another study conducted by the Washington State Institute for Public Policy shows that the use of Multidimensional Treatment Foster Care, while slightly more expensive per youth than group homes, "ultimately saves an estimated $96,000 in lower costs to victims and the criminal justice system" (Mendel 2011).

Since 2000, youth confinement in state and county facilities has been reduced by over 40 percent (National Juvenile Justice Network and Texas Public Policy Foundation 2013). Of the states that are at the forefront of rethinking youth delinquency prevention, Connecticut offers one of the most promising and comprehensive models for juvenile justice reform. From 2001 to 2010, Connecticut was able to lower youth confinement by 50 percent (Ibid.), primarily through legislation aimed at promoting community-based detention models, enforcing limitations on confinement, and raising the age for automatic adult prosecution. Additionally, in 2001, legislation was passed to promote the use of mental health services in community-based programs in an effort to minimize youth involvement in the justice system (NJJN 2007). The year 2007 saw the passage of legislation prohibiting confinement of youth if less restrictive, offense appropriate alternatives were available and 2010 saw the elimination of mandatory adult sentencing laws for 16 and 17 year olds (Bradford 2013).

Similar to Connecticut, Illinois has made significant changes to its juvenile justice system. In 2011, the state legislature passed a requirement similar to Connecticut's that ensures confinement is used only as a last resort and absent a less restrictive, community-based alternative. In 2013, the legislature successfully amended the state's mandatory adult sentencing laws, which moved delinquent youth convicted of nonviolent offenses to juvenile court jurisdiction through age 17 (Schien 2013).

Louisiana reduced juvenile confinement by 52.7 percent overall from 2001 to 2010. The state also reduced confinement for drug offenses by 50 percent. This confinement reduction is attributed to a combined effort, following a settlement for chronic abuse allegations, to develop strong community-based interventions. Participation in both Juvenile Detention Alternatives (JDAI) and Models for Change initiatives and introduction of evidence-based therapeutic models to corrections at the Jetson Center for Youth combined to lower Louisiana's youth confinement rate (Bradford 2013).

In an effort to deincentivize juvenile confinement, Wisconsin's Youth Aids program provides localities with $100 million annually to cover juvenile programming, but they shift the entire cost of confinement for all but the most serious violent offenses back onto the localities for those youth in state-run facilities (Mendel 2011). Additionally, the state of Florida, which has had previous success with civil citations as a detention alternative in Miami-Dade County, enacted statewide legislation in 2011 requiring that other jurisdictions within Florida either replicate the civil citation program or develop similar diversion programs for nonviolent misdemeanors and status offenses.

These initiatives, research shows, save money. For youth on probation, $1,467 is spent to provide aggression replacement therapy which returns nearly $36,000 in benefits. For juvenile offenders in group or foster homes, multidimensional therapy returned $33,000 in benefits per youth (National Research Council 2013). This provides a clear fiscal message to encourage localities to invest in detention alternatives for nonviolent, low-level youth offenders.

CONCLUSION

This chapter detailed the progression of youth delinquency prevention efforts, moving from the early rehabilitative models toward an era of more punitive measures aimed at controlling perceived notions of law and order gone awry. At this point, the future of delinquency prevention appears to be a mix of fiscal conservatism coupled with rehabilitative-minded efforts rooted in research that suggests imprisonment and harsh sentencing may not be the best remedy fiscally or physically.

However, delinquency prevention is reaching a difficult point. The effects of the Great Recession have taken a toll on low-income and minority communities, two groups disproportionately represented in the system. In many ways, this need for fiscal reform has been a blessing as states and localities express a real desire to look for cost-effective, evidence-based means of reducing the number of youth who enter the system, with special consideration for reducing the number of poor and minority youth. Conversely, history has taught us two important lessons to heed: budgets bounce back and lawmakers never want to appear soft on crime.

While most legislative proposals aimed at social inclusion and rehabilitation of offenders are usually met with disparagement, recent movements toward restructuring sentencing guidelines for nonviolent and drug offenses show that perhaps the time is right to address the systemic issues producing youth delinquency and move back toward prevention over punishment. Only time will tell if this is a watershed moment in addressing inequality and disproportionality in delinquency prevention.

NOTES

1. Both the Children's Bureau and the FBI reported increased activity in juvenile courts but researchers insist it is impossible to tell if these figures are indeed accurate. Barnosky (2006) references work by Reitz and Ruth (2003) that challenges the validity of these statistics.
2. This is part of a larger pop culture panic as described by Barnosky in *Responses to juvenile crime in the 1950's* (324–326).

Chapter Eight

Home Sweet Home

Race, Housing, and the Foreclosure Crisis

Rosie Jayde Uyola

Alvornia Davis was eager to make much-needed repairs to her aging, multi-family home. She inherited the property in 1978, and it had been in her family for over sixty years. She and her husband Lamar, both in their seventies and now retired, had raised their children, their goddaughter, and their goddaughter's baby in the house; it was the only home they had ever owned. "We've been havin' real troubles renting lately," explained Mrs. Davis. "Nobody wants to rent a house fallin' apart, you know."

The young handyman who appeared on their doorstep one Sunday morning seemed like the answer to their prayers. "Excuse me, ma'am," he noted. "I was just walking by and noticed that your home is in need of repairs . . . judging by the slant in that roof and all. I'm a contractor and can help you with fixin' up your home. And don't worry about the cost—there's financing available."[1]

Located on Lehigh Avenue, the Davises' spacious, three-story home is part of the aging dilapidated housing stock in the historic neighborhood of Weequahic in Newark's South Ward. By 2006, the multiunit home had fallen to such disrepair that the couple was no longer able to attract tenants. Desperate to save her home, Alvornia took out an adjustable rate mortgage for renovations. Their subprime rate climbed into the double digits in less than six months, more in line with credit card rates than a home loan. After the introductory teaser rates expired, the Davises, like many other Americans, watched their monthly payment more than double, overnight. Soon, they were paying more than $3,000 per month. Alvornia and Lamar, already struggling to make ends meet on a fixed income of Social Security and state pension benefits, were unable to keep up with their bills. After a handful of late and missed mortgage payments, the Davises faced imminent foreclosure and homelessness.

The couple packed their belongings into boxes and were waiting for the sheriff to put a sign on their door, when a friend invited them to an outreach event sponsored by the Newark-Essex Foreclosure Taskforce. Created by Mayor Cory Booker and Essex County in 2007, the Taskforce is a collaborative effort by city stakeholders to address the impact of mortgage foreclosures on homeowners and tenants. The Taskforce's primary focus is to support housing security and neighborhood stability by providing legal resources, foreclosure counseling, and tenants' rights education. Members meet each month to discuss current foreclosure legislation, opportunities for advocacy, loss mitigation activities, and neighborhood impact. The Taskforce also coordinates events where homeowners in default or foreclosure are able to come and sit with a bank representative and receive information on their loan and possible home retention solutions.

Taskforce members took on the Davises' case with immediate results. City officials contacted executives at the couple's mortgage lending company and renegotiated their monthly payments to a manageable sum. Episcopal Community Development, a local community development corporation, brought in a team of construction professionals to make repairs. The Davises, along with hundreds of other Newark families, also completed credit and budget counseling in order to resolve delinquency, bring their mortgage payments current, and maintain ownership of their property.

The challenges faced by the Davises reflect the experiences of thousands of Americans. Homeowners in Newark, like homeowners in other communities who have historically lacked access to financial institutions, were vulnerable to aggressively marketed high-cost subprime mortgages and predatory lending. Once "redlined" from attaining access to credit, the urban neighborhoods of Essex County became inundated with high-risk subprime loans in the early twenty-first century. Foreclosures quickly followed these "greenlining" patterns in majority black and Latino lower income neighborhoods, where residents lacked alternative access to credit. Recognizing that many individuals and families, both homeowners and tenants, had been displaced as a result of the foreclosure crisis, cities responded by creating task forces to mitigate the impact of foreclosure on residents through prevention, intervention, and stabilization.

This chapter explores the rise of foreclosures in urban communities related to the subprime mortgage market crisis using Newark, New Jersey, as a case study. Examining foreclosure as a process, rather than an event, shows how a collaborative effort among researchers, government officials, nonprofits, and practitioners can produce useful data and responsive strategies by establishing and remaining in communication with one another. Using the financial crisis as an entry-point for this exploration, the complex relationships between urban geography, the subprime mortgage industry, and transnational capital circuits developed by global corporations come into focus. Understanding the impact of the foreclosure crisis is important because home ownership has been a key vehicle for wealth creation, increased education outcomes, and upward mobility in the United States since World War II. Subprime lending stripped equity from low-income and racially marginalized communities, creating instability for individuals, families, and municipal governments. Decades after President Lyndon B. Johnson declared a war on poverty, "free market" risk-based ideology of U.S. financial markets fueled subprime lending and displaced millions of Americans. To the extent that the war on poverty was also a fight against income inequality, that battle has been enervated by the foreclosure crisis.

FORECLOSURE CRISIS

The foreclosure crisis of 2005–2008 displaced millions of Americans, producing neighborhoods of boarded-up and vacant houses, plummeting tax revenues for municipalities, and a strain on social services, schools, and surrounding property values. Referred to as "the perfect storm" by scholar Kathe Newman, the recent foreclosure crisis in the United States is the result of predatory business practices of the subprime mortgage industry, the systematic deregulation of the financial markets, and the aggressive promotion of home ownership as national housing policy (Newman 2009). Whether lauded as a benevolent vehicle of upward mobility or attacked as predatory exploitation, the mortgage industrial complex has led to the commodification of real estate, thus connecting national and transnational capital markets to local urban communities of color.

The deregulation of mortgage markets encouraged usury as financial innovation. Historically "red-lined," low-income, and racially marginalized neighborhoods like the city of Newark were flooded with subprime mortgage originations that created a "green-lining" with the availability of high-risk credit in the 1990s. Over the past twenty years, the mortgage industry stealthily prospered through unscrupulous lending practices and deceptive credit ratings by appealing to the free market doctrine of risk-based pricing and the American ideology of consumer sovereignty. In economic terms, so long as consumers wanted to borrow and banks wanted to lend capital, the U.S. financial system existed in a state of supply-and-demand equilibrium. Documented cases of racial discrimination and predatory lending, disproportionately concentrated in low-income neighborhoods, were dismissed as anomalies in an otherwise benevolent and democratic access to capital.

The subprime mortgage market created inequitable geographies of foreclosure and home equity extraction, superimposed upon existing landscapes of discrimination and income and wealth disparities in urban centers like Newark, New Jersey (Engel and McCoy 2002; HUD-Treasury Joint Task Force 2000; Crump et al. 2008). As the lending boom reached its zenith and began to crumble between 2004 and 2006, the percentage of black Americans pushed into high-risk loans increased from 37 percent to 54 percent, and the share of Latinos and Latinas nearly doubled from 25 percent to 46 percent (Wyly et al. 2008). The housing crisis spiraled into global proportions after the mortgage industry bundled mortgages into complex, overleveraged, and unregulated financial vehicles, called derivatives, which it sold to pension funds, insurance companies, and banks across the country and around the world.

The predatory nature of the mortgage market is twofold: minorities are twice as likely as otherwise identical non-Hispanic whites to be targeted for a subprime loan, and a typical subprime borrower is not someone buying a house, but someone refinancing in an attempt to consolidate debt. Borrowers of such loans were charged double-digit interest rates (24 percent or higher) that were more in line with bad credit card rates than the prevailing prime mortgage rates (4–6 percent). According to Freddie Mac, about 10 percent of subprime borrowers could have qualified for a prime loan.

For over a decade before the housing bubble collapsed, community organizers and advocates for low-income families and communities of color documented abusive-yet-legal business practices and campaigned for regulation against a predatory industry. Prepayment penalties, penalty interest rates, yield-spread premium, adjustable-rate mortgages (ARMs), hyperadjustable-rate mortgages (aptly referred to as "HARMs"), balloon payments, teaser introductory rates, and the fantastically profitable mortgage instrument titled "NINJA," which required no verification of employment, assets, or credit history, are just some of the predatory practices that targeted racial minorities and distressed neighborhoods (Pearlstein 2007; Renuart 2004; Wyly 2008).

THE AMERICAN DREAM

Historically, Americans have lauded homeownership as the primary path to wealth. Faith in the potential of the housing market has been reflected by and created through federal policies often driven by bipartisan legislation. The purchase of a home is said to improve levels of social, psychological, emotional, and financial health. Supported by such claims that homeownership benefits both individuals and society as a whole, in 1995, the Clinton administration created new incentives and subsidies to increase homeownership. The introduction to the National Homeownership Strategy (1995) promoted homeownership as a strategy to strengthening families, communities, good citizenship, and even as an incentive for maintaining and improving public spaces.

Similarly, President George W. Bush made homeownership a pillar of his domestic agenda as well. In a speech given in May 2002 on the American dream, Bush stated, "Owning a home is a part of that dream, it just is. Right here in America, if you own your own home, you're realizing the American dream" (Bush 2002). The American Dream Down Payment Initiative (ADDI) aggressively sought to increase homeownership among low-income families by reducing down payment requirements for mortgages, promoting the production of single-family homes through tax credits for developers, and energizing the private sector to increase minority homeownership in a major nationwide effort. Soon after, the Obama administration established the American Recovery and Reinvestment Act of 2009, which expanded the first-time homebuyer tax credit to $8,000 for first-time homebuyers and the $6,500 tax credit for repeat homebuyers. When the rate of homeownership reached a high of 69 percent, it was celebrated as a moment of democratization of the "American Dream" for many citizens previously excluded from access to mainstream capital.

The ability to purchase a detached, single-family property is central to the American conception of a successful and stable life; in turn, it functions as a rite of passage that has historically excluded many low-income individuals and minority communities. According to Fannie Mae's 2011 National Housing Survey results, across all education levels, most Americans say owning makes more sense than renting, despite the recent housing crisis.[2] This belief is held consistently across all demographic groups.[3] Nearly two-thirds of current renters say that they will buy a house at some point in the future. Further, African Americans and Hispanics are more likely to cite various benefits, such as buying a home as a way to build wealth, homeownership as a symbol of success, and civic benefits. The survey data also indicated that while financial constraints and employment concerns may be keeping potential homebuyers on the sidelines in the short term, future improvements in employment and personal finances would result in an increase of homeownership rates in coming years. "In spite of the impact of the housing crisis on home values and homeownership rates across the country, Americans by and large still hope to become homeowners," said Doug Duncan, vice president and chief economist of Fannie Mae. "Some may not be financially positioned to own a home in the near future, but Americans may begin to revisit that aspiration as employment and household balance sheets improve over the coming years." Such enthusiastic responses are not surprising, considering that homeownership has been the cornerstone of national housing policy for decades during the Clinton, Bush, and Obama administrations.

HOMEOWNERSHIP, RACE, AND CLASS

Newark's journey from the epicenter of manufacturing a half century ago to a case study of urban crisis in the late 1960s has been mirrored by many other industrial cities across the United States. Rates of poverty among black Americans in postindustrial cities like Newark, Chicago's South and West Sides, Detroit, Cleveland, Pittsburg, Saint Louis, Camden, and Baltimore range from 25 to 45 percent (Sugrue 2005; Sugrue 2008). The residents of these central cities have struggled with tremendous loss of manufacturing jobs and the emergence of the low-wage service industry since the World War II period. In 1950, 35 percent of nonwhite and 57 percent of white heads of households were homeowners. Shockingly, a smaller fraction of black Americans owned homes in the 1990 than did whites in 1920 (U.S. Bureau of the Census 1993). Furthermore, houses owned by blacks are worth, on average, barely more than half of available housing owned by whites, and the value of the former, but not the latter, is currently declining (Hochschild 1996).

Fifty years later, that gap in racial inequality hasn't changed much. By some measures it has widened. In 2011, the median income for black households was about 59 percent of the median income for white households, up slightly from 55 percent in 1967, according to Census data analyzed by the Pew Research Center (King's Dream 2013). But if we consider "wealth"—in other words, everything a family owns including a home, retirement savings, and inheritance—the difference has grown. Pew found that the median black household had about 7 percent of the wealth of its white counterpart in 2011, down from 9 percent in 1984.

Much of this inequality can be traced to the distorted incentives for fraud and abuse, which undermined the mortgage insurance programs of the Federal Housing Administration (FHA) in the 1950s and 1960s. Newark, like many other urban black enclaves, was the scene of widespread and systemic economic exploitation, exacerbated by the FHA's practice of redlining predominantly black neighborhoods, which effectively eliminated mortgage insurance within their boundaries. Black Americans were barred from obtaining a mortgage loan to pay for properties in full, forcing them to buy "on contract" through an installment plan. Under the terms of most installment land contracts, the seller had the right to repossess the property by evicting the "homebuyer" for a single missed payment (Satter 2010). Contract selling attracted unscrupulous speculators who charged outlandishly inflated prices for property that often led to missed payments, subsequent evictions, and resale for additional profit.

The subprime mortgage crisis is the newest incarnation of contract selling, impoverishing those who do not have equitable access to credit. Alongside the older draconian regime of exclusionary redlining, the 1990s ushered in a new wave of highly profitable "greenlining" that made credit widely available to previously excluded borrowers but on vastly inequitable terms (Engel and McCoy 2002). "Greenlining," sometimes referred to as "reverse redlining," is intertwined with problems of racial, economic, and spatial segregation. The influx of available credit for disinvested communities presents a cruelly ironic turn of events. For generations, housing advocates fought to increase access to capital for low-income urban residents. On the eve of the twenty-first century, mutually reinforcing trends in macroeconomic growth, a deregulation of U.S. financial markets, and the promotion of homeownership as national housing policy coalesced to flood low-income and racially marginalized neighborhoods with high-risk, high-cost lending. This reversal in the contours of credit is responsible for instituting new geographies of debt, poverty, and equity extraction superimposed onto existing landscapes of racial and economic segregation.

SUBPRIME MORTGAGES AND GLOBAL MARKETS

In the United States, homeownership is not only a dream or an ideology; it is an integral factor of production in the postindustrial American economy (Newman 2009). In classical economics, factors of production are any commodities used to produce goods and services. Housing plays a major role in the growth of the United States economy, contributing to gross domestic product (GDP) through residential construction (residential fixed investment) and the services provided by existing houses (personal consumption expenditure) (Grist 2010). In 2005, housing-related expenditure accounted for 23 percent of the GDP (Grist 2010). Situating homeownership as a central factor of production in the postindustrial economy allows for critical analysis of the current foreclosure crisis. Since the early 1990s, the shift from commodity production to finance production in the U.S. economy has had a profound effect on urban centers. The flow of capital from neighborhoods through financial channels to investors and speculators all over the world fundamentally altered the nature of homeownership from a local to a global commodity (Newman 2009).

Emerging in the early 1990s, subprime loans dramatically increased their share of the overall mortgage market through technological advances and securitization. By 2007, there were between \$6.7 and \$9.1 trillion in outstanding financial instruments backed by American mortgages.[4] Trillions more were invested in third-party derivatives related to these instruments, the companies that held them, and over-the-counter trading indices that tracked them. By making capital available to previously untapped markets—20 percent of U.S. consumers have credit scores of 620 or below, on a 300–850 scale—the subprime industry entered an era of unregulated prosperity and growth. A new line of stratified, seemingly ubiquitous credit seeped into previously redlined American cities, which commodified the real estate market.

From 1997 to 2007, housing finance became an incredibly profitable enterprise at the center of the global economy through the process of securitization. Securitization is the financial practice of pooling various types of contractual debt (mortgages, auto loans, credit card obligations) and selling said debt as bonds, credit default swaps, securities, hedge funds, or collateralized mortgage obligation to various investors. Most mortgages in the United States are securitized at the moment of origination. Banks and mortgage companies create loans and almost immediately sell the servicing rights to investors in return for capital that is then used to make new loans. In the prime market, loans are sold to Government Sponsored Enterprises (GSEs)—privately held corporations with public purposes created by the U.S. Congress—to reduce the cost of capital for homeowners (U.S. Government Accountability Office 1989). In contrast, the subprime market is dominated by structured financial instruments and Special Purpose Vehicles (SPVs) that acquire loans and pool them into packages of Mortgage-Backed Securities (MBSs) that are underwritten by Wall Street and global financial markets (Wyly 2008).

The mid-1990s ushered in an era of unprecedented profitability for subprime mortgage lenders, investors, and bond rating analysts. Steadily rising home values and securitization enabled subprime originations to grow exponentially from 65 billion in 1995 to 332 billion in 2003 and then to 625 billion in 2006. The volatile securitization market seemed to be impervious. Individually risky loans that consistently scored the highest "AAA" scores from bond-rating agencies were bundled into MBSs (Dymski 2007; Engel and McCoy 2007; Peterson 2007). Once mortgages could be converted into securitized "tranches" and traded like a stocks or bonds, large institutional investors like pension funds created an inelastic demand, flooding mortgage lenders with capital. By 2008, home loans were so divided and spread over the financial spectrum, it was entirely possible that a given homeowner could have unwittingly owned shares in his or her own mortgage.

The booming housing market, falling interest rates, and national credit binge veiled predatory lending practices. Subprime lending, like contract selling, posed almost no risk to speculators, because borrowers who missed payments could be forced to refinance or enter into an immediate distress sale, bypassing foreclosure. Low-income and minority neighborhoods proved to be enormously profitable for brokers, lenders, and investors, perhaps even more so when homeowners fell behind: refinancing generated new upfront fees charged against the home's equity and forced sales protected investors from losses.

NEWARK: A CASE STUDY

Newark became a main target for subprime and predatory lending in the early 2000s. Following the collapse of the housing market in 2007, the city saw foreclosure rates skyrocket. Decades of racial discrimination in lending and housing markets made Newark residents, barred from traditional lines of credit, susceptible to exploitation.

In 2000, a combination of a loose monetary policy by the Federal Reserve, compensation plans that encouraged bank executives to take huge risks in the quest for short-term profits, and Congress's decision to legalize over-the-counter derivatives trading created a portal of commodified exchange between local neighborhoods and global markets. Lenders began bundling mortgages into financial instruments for investors, and mortgages that were not tied to the borrowers' ability to repay—or even to the value of the property—became aggressively marketed in underserved communities. First-time homebuyers, non-native English speakers, black and Latino families, women heads of household, and the elderly were all targeted for subprime loans. Many subprime borrowers qualified for loans at prime lending rates, but door-to-door brokers and home improvement contractors only offered adjustable rate or exotic mortgages, often with inflated points, double-digit interest rates, penalty ridden loan durations, and early repayment fees. Through community outreach campaigns, members of the Newark-Essex Foreclosure Taskforce learned of heartbreaking stories of seniors who had paid off their mortgages but still lost their homes, because they were talked into refinancing. Some predatory loans turned out to be cases of outright fraud in which lenders changed the terms of contracts after papers were signed. There were also cases in which homebuyers took out loans that they probably knew they could not afford, but they, like many Americans, saw homeownership as an avenue to wealth and stability.

Over a quarter of the subprime loans that were generated in Newark between 2005 and 2007 went into foreclosure by the last quarter of 2008.[5] The impact of these foreclosures must be understood in the context of the Newark housing market, where few residents are homeowners, and where many of the affected buildings are multiunit dwellings. Foreclosures have a devastating impact on tenants. The magnitude of this effect is often underrepresented in public data gathered from foreclosure court records, state legal files, and property auction lists, which only include information about homeowners, not tenants. In cities like Newark, the landlord is not a commercial real estate investor but a fellow member of the community who owns one or two additional homes in addition to a primary residence. When the housing market deteriorates, small-scale landlords are no longer able to maintain their property, pay taxes or utilities, or make needed repairs.

Although foreclosure cannot be cited as a reason for eviction in New Jersey, many residents move out after receiving letters from financial institutions, leaving behind vacant, boarded-up housing. The displacement of tenants can come when the landlord abandons the property and the tenants are now living in a property that is without utilities and is not being maintained. Some tenants are also displaced when they decide they do not want to live with the uncertainty of their landlord's foreclosure. In some neighborhoods, over half of the houses on whole city blocks are abandoned. These are often stripped of their metal fixtures, and become a public safety problem; they attract squatters and gang activity and are even prone to fires or gas explosions. These safety concerns largely impact families still living on the block and often encourage them to leave their homes. As a result, many urban neighborhoods that have experienced economic growth over the past few decades deteriorate.

THE NEWARK-ESSEX FORECLOSURE TASKFORCE

Few places represent the rise, fall, and revival of American cities more than Newark. At the turn of the twentieth century, the city was a bustling center of industry and a tapestry of multiethnic working-class communities. In the aftermath of the trauma of the 1960s, Newark not only epitomized the "urban crisis" transformations of America's industrial cities, it also had became a worst-case scenario of disinvestment, catastrophic planning, and abandonment.

Today, the city is on the road to a reawakening. In an effort to upgrade the city by revamping its waterfront, a boardwalk opened in August of 2013 to welcome residents and visitors to Riverfront Park along the Passaic River. In addition, the twenty-first century renewal strategy is creating more than three miles of greenway, a riverfront ribbon with bike and walking paths stretching all the way through downtown to residential neighborhoods in the Ironbound District. Commercial and multifamily development is also on the rise. In 2012, New Jersey had projects under construction totaling 3,306,551 square feet. Of that, Newark was responsible for projects totaling 1,168,793 square feet—or 35.3 percent of the state real estate development total—according to the data compiled by the New Jersey Department of Community Affairs.[6] The Newark Housing Authority increased the rate of affordable housing production by more than 100 percent with the construction of 1,600 new affordable units throughout the city. Yet, the city continues to struggle with foreclosure. Just eight miles from New York City, Newark had a foreclosure rate nearly twice that of the entire New York metro area in 2007. Between 2005 and 2008, roughly 6 percent of all homes were in foreclosure.[7] As of 2008, more than two billion in home equity and tax base was lost just from subprime loans originating between 2005 and 2006 in Newark and its surrounding urban suburbs (Center for Responsible Lending).[8] When it seemed that the situation could not get much worse, foreclosure filings in New Jersey increased 31.6 percent—to 31,603—in the first six months of 2009 compared to the first half of 2008 (RealtyTrac).[9]

The city of Newark enables us to better understand the processes of subprime mortgage lending and the impacts of national financial policy on urban residents. Like the Davises, many Newarkers did not seek to refinance their homes. Home improvement contractors offered direct financing, often before providing a quote for repairs. In contrast with media representations of black and Latino borrowers as irresponsible or ignorant, nearly all residents who came to the Newark-Essex Foreclosure Taskforce for help were financially literate. But, like homeowners in other battered cities that have historically been barred from access to credit, they lacked alternatives. As thousands of Newarkers lost their homes to foreclosure, city stakeholders came together in a regional effort.

Under the mandate of Mayor Cory Booker, the Task Force was formed in 2007, after Michael Meyer—director of the city's division of Housing and Real Estate within the department of Housing and Economic Development—sought suggestions from stakeholders around the greater Newark area as to how to best address foreclosures. Announcing the launch of the Taskforce, Meyer explained, "In Newark alone at the time, roughly 1,400 out of 20,000-plus properties of the city's housing stock were in foreclosure and there was no comprehensive, regional effort to do anything about it" (Hersh 2010). The Task Force is currently composed of representatives from over forty community development corporations, nonprofit housing counseling and legal service providers, government and community development officials, and advocacy organizations.

All members had been working on their own share of the foreclosure puzzle. Today, they share resources and data to present a united front against the crisis. Since its inception in 2007, the Taskforce has worked on a range of issues, from homebuyer counseling to foreclosure prevention. The Taskforce helps residents through a multifaceted approach of policy and advocacy. Members sponsor community outreach programs to support tenants' rights, provide legal resources to displaced families, and train housing counselors from local service providers and nonprofit organizations. The effectiveness of the Taskforce lies in its members' commitment to viewing the foreclosure crisis as a regional problem. Through interregional collaboration, urban and suburban responses to foreclosures present an opportunity to enhance both equity and efficiency.

CONCLUSION

By drawing the interconnections between race and foreclosure, we can critically examine the juridical and ethical underpinnings of racial and global subjugation in representations of the late-twentieth-century and early-twenty-first-century crises of global financial markets. Subprime mortgages and foreclosures are disproportionately concentrated among working-class families and communities of color. Not surprisingly, subprime lending shares of all loans are most concentrated in places that stand at the intersection of the two (Belsky 2008).

The deregulated mortgage market has created uneven geographies of debt, poverty, and insecurity, layered upon existing racialized landscapes of segregation and discrimination. While prevailing representations of the crisis focus on irresponsible borrowers who overextended themselves or on the greedy predatory lenders who cashed in on the American Dream, it is important that interdisciplinary scholarship contextualizes the mortgage industrial complex within a larger framework that includes the shift of the U.S. economy from commodity production to finance production. The state facilitated the expansion of financialization and the commodification of properties. The global financial crisis was not caused by ambitious borrowers; it was a by-product of the mortgage industrial complex, a fundamental restructuring of the postindustrial economy. City governments and community organizers, like the members of the Newark/Essex Foreclosure Task Force, are battling the social and economic hardships brought on by foreclosure with limited resources; however, their work is not a substitute for a federal change in regulation.

NOTES

1. Author's interview notes.
2. The fourth-quarter 2011 National Housing Survey focus on the state of homeownership aspiration is based on more than 3,000 interviews from October 3, 2011 to December 20, 2011 among homeowners and renters to assess their attitudes toward owning and renting a home, confidence in homeownership as an investment, the current state of their household finances, views on the U.S. housing finance system, and overall confidence in the economy. Data findings for this topic also are based on similar surveys conducted throughout 2011, 2010, and in December 2003.
3. The most detailed consumer attitudinal survey of its kind, the Fannie Mae National Housing Survey polled 1,000 Americans via live telephone interview to assess their attitudes toward owning and renting a home, home and rental price changes, homeownership distress, the economy, household finances, and overall consumer confidence. Homeowners and renters are asked more than 100 questions used to track attitudinal shifts (findings are compared to the same survey conducted monthly beginning June 2010). Fannie Mae conducts this survey and shares monthly and quarterly results so that we may help industry partners and market participants target our collective efforts to stabilize the housing market in the near term, and provide support in the future.

4. Inside Mortgage Finance. 2009. Mortgage Market Statistical Annual; SIFMA. 2010. Outstanding U.S. Bond Market Debt. http://www.sifma.org/uploadedFiles/Research/Statistics/SIFMA_USBondMarketOutstanding.xls. For an informed discussion of subprime mortgage securitization, see Neil Fligstein and Adam Goldstein, "Catalyst of Disaster: Subprime Mortgage Securitization and the Roots of the Great Recession," Department of Sociology University of California. Available online: http://www.tobinproject.org/sites/tobinproject.org/files/assets/Fligstein_Catalyst%20of%20Disaster_0.pdf.

5. For an in-depth analysis of the findings, see "Home Mortgage Foreclosure Essex County New Jersey" presentation by the Spring 2008 Community Development Studio Edward J. Bloustein School of Planning and Public Policy Rutgers University. Available online: http://policy.rutgers.edu/academics/projects/studios/essex08t.pdf.

6. According to PolitiFact and the *Star Ledger*, data from a real estate development firm, Jones Lang LaSalle, which used a database known as CoStar compiling statistics for Mayor Cory Booker's city administration showed that, in terms of square footage, Newark accounted for 35 percent—or a bit more than a third—of the residential and commercial real estate growth last year in New Jersey. But in terms of building permits and value of new construction, Newark can claim just 3 percent of that total. Available online: http://www.politifact.com/new-jersey/statements/2013/sep/15/cory-booker/cory-booker-claims-newark-represents-third-real-es/.

7. 2008 analysis conducted by the *New York Times*. Available online: http://www.nytimes.com/2009/05/17/nyregion/new-jersey/17mortnj.html.

8. Center for Responsible Lending. Impact of Subprime Foreclosures on Neighboring Homes and Tax Bases 2008. http://www.responsiblelending.org/issues/mortgage/research/subprime-spillover.html. The State of New Jersey experienced a $19.6 billion loss in property value and tax base, $99 million loss in tax revenue, and $6.3 billion loss in property value. For full report, see Center for Responsible Lending http://www.responsiblelending.org/pdfs/new-jersey-state-info-with-fc-starts.pdf, Federal Reserve Bank of New York Analysis of Loan Performance Data November 2007 http://www.ny.frb.org/regional/subprime.html, and JEC Majority Staff. October 2006. http://www.jec.senate.gov/Documents/Reports/10.25.07OctoberSubprimeReport.pdf. Visual data also available in "Foreclosure in Essex County, NJ. What We Know Now." presentation by the Community Development Studio to the Newark Essex Foreclosure Taskforce, February 26, 2008. Available online: http://policy.rutgers.edu/studios/foreclosureproject/CDStudioFeb26_08Progress1.pdf

9. In New Jersey, foreclosure filings increased by more than 30 percent during the first half of 2009 according to data released by the state judiciary. Nationwide, foreclosure activity increased 15 percent in the first six months of 2009 compared with the same period in 2008, according to RealtyTrac. Full dataset available online: http://www.nj.com/business/nj-real-estate/index.ssf/2009/08/nj_foreclosures_rise_dramatica.html.

Chapter Nine

Not in My Backyard

An Examination of Suburban Gentrification as a Tool for Combating Poverty

Portia Allen-Kyle

As demonstrated in many of the other chapters in this book, the War on Poverty had far-reaching effects on many aspects of American life. Government policies and programs such as urban renewal, the growth and location of public housing and integral social services, and the segregation and neglect of inner-city public schools have led to the development of inner-ring suburbs as safe havens that provide relief from chaotic inner-city life. In the years preceding the War on Poverty the suburban ideal embodied in the "American dream" was constructed in stark opposition to the desolate, deteriorating, crime-stricken image of cities. To address the alarming state of the nation's cities, many local, city, and state governments partnered with the federal government on initiatives to "clean up" urban areas and address issues such as crime, homelessness, and decay.

Urban renewal was one such initiative, which led to vast displacement, with only small proportions of the demolished land ever being developed into revitalized housing. Gentrification began to be examined by scholars during the period of urban renewal, since much of the housing that began to replace that which was demolished was aimed at drawing better-off suburbanites back into the inner cities. Failed policies such as urban renewal resulted in a number of unintended spillover effects on inner-ring suburbs; many suburbs either 1) experienced a decline as they took in greater numbers of poor residents who were either priced out of or displaced from inner cities, 2) grew and developed in a way that catered to low-income, minority, or ethnic populations, or 3) aggressively decided to react to the threat of poverty and decline by developing strategies to combat potential threat of poverty and exclude undesirable populations to avoid the outcomes of the previous two circumstances. In this first instance, the quality of life in the suburbs declined as the result of their eroding tax base, decreasing school quality, and the structural inadequacy of suburbs to provide essential social services to poor populations. In the second instance, suburbs often already comprised of lower-middle or working-class residents adapted to the influx of greater numbers of these low-income, minority, or ethnic populations that migrated into the town; these populations often became a defining characteristic of the suburb. This chapter will explore the latter of these strategies, with a focus on suburbs' use of suburban gentrification and revitalization as one aggressive and exclusionary strategy to address community concerns and combat the threat of poverty and decline.

This chapter examines some of these patterns of suburban change, with an emphasis on how suburban policy makers have responded to challenges of poverty. I begin by discussing the transformation of the suburbs since 1980. This section will focus on the fear of a poverty epidemic among residences and the complications of the public education system funding mechanisms. Next, I explore strategies currently available to communities to combat or redress the threat or presence of poverty, including a discussion of the shortcomings of these strategies. The strategy of suburban gentrification, which is an increasingly prevalent outcome of many of the approaches developed in suburban settings, will then be examined. Next, I discuss two affordable housing cases: *Southern Burlington County N.A.A.C.P v. Township of Mount Laurel* and *Mt. Holly v. Mt. Holly Garden Citizens in Action.* These cases, from the state of New Jersey, illustrate some of the dynamics related to suburban responses to poverty, including policies that risk leading to factors of suburban gentrification. I conclude with several considerations in the area of suburban poverty and some of the broad strategies that exist in this area.

THE TRANSFORMATION OF SUBURBS

Life in a single-family suburban home with a nice yard, dog, and a white picket fence has been the pinnacle image of the "American dream" since the mid-twentieth century. The growth of suburbs began post–World War II and was spurred by the GI Bill, which provided veterans with affordable loans to purchase homes. However, many blacks and other minorities (including minorities who were veterans) were denied access to these federal loans. Even when minorities were able to obtain loans, they were often prevented from purchasing in certain areas because of racial residential segregation and restrictive covenants. As a result, many of the inner-ring suburbs were usually monolithic in terms of both race and middle-class status.

Over the past thirty years, the suburbs have undergone significant demographic shifts. Beginning in the 1980s, the growth rate of suburban poor populations began to outpace that of cities (Kneebone and Berube 2013, 19). Throughout this time, cities were the target of state reinvestment strategies aimed at transforming high-poverty neighborhoods (Goetz 2011), leaving suburbs to largely fend for themselves in terms of growth strategies, maintenance, and resources. The changes to housing policy and urban development resulted in the gentrification of inner cities being characterized by class segregation, as well as racial discrimination and exclusion from these gentrifying neighborhoods (Wyly and Hammel 2004). Not surprisingly, suburbs experienced sharp increases in poverty rates, while cities saw long-term increases that were considerably less drastic (Murphy 2007). The tipping point in the distribution of poverty from being primarily characteristic of cities to that of suburbs occurred after the turn of the century, which saw rapid population growth in suburbs, particularly of poor populations (Berube and Kneebone 2008).

Though not all central cities experience poverty in the same manner (see Johnson 2007), suburban communities experience poverty in vastly different ways than do cities. In a study of the location of high-poverty neighborhoods within metropolitan areas, researchers attributed the cause of increases in such neighborhoods to a number of phenomena. The numerical increase of high-poverty neighborhoods in the urban core is correlated to the area's economic vitality, whereas growth of these high-poverty neighborhoods in inner-ring suburbs is linked to the rapid growth of the area's population (Cooke and Marchant 2006; Berube and Kneebone 2009). Suburban neighborhoods experiencing poverty tend to have higher median income, fewer welfare recipients, and fewer female-headed households when compared to inner cities; these areas also exhibit more residential crowding, lower English proficiency, fewer college graduates, and fewer professionals (Holliday and Dwyer 2000). While the federal poverty line, however inaccurate, gives a measure of "absolute" poverty, it is the relative poverty in terms of the other suburban residents that tends to matter most. Thus, a suburb's experience with and perception of "poverty" may be entirely dependent upon the level of community affluence, and the social distance between the community's most advantaged and disadvantaged residents.

While many later suburban migrants came from the inner cities, these patterns of migration cannot explain all of the growth of the suburban population or the growth of the poor population within these suburban areas. The varying origins of socioeconomically disadvantaged residents further complicate the understanding of the dynamics of poverty within suburbs. In an exploration of nonprofits serving poor suburban populations, Murphy (2010) developed a typology of suburbs and their experience with poverty. Her research contends that symbiotic suburbs are inner-ring suburbs that most resemble urban poverty, those with poverty rates over 20 percent prior to 1990; skeletal suburbs are those previously home to industry and manufacturing plants that have since left the metropolitan area (or even the country); overshadowed suburbs are those that have significantly poor populations but are very small in number and isolated geographically such that they are kept out of the everyday purview of other, more desirable, residents. Suburbs with this type of poverty appear affluent and insulated from poverty.

Given the different characteristics of suburban neighborhoods and the types of poverty that they experience, residents in each of these neighborhoods may develop varying fears about the implications of poverty on their communities. While poverty may be more tolerated, or normalized, in symbiotic suburbs (where poverty is long-standing) and in skeletal suburbs (where residents are homogenous in their experience of economic hardship) those residents in overshadowed suburbs may be less tolerant of poverty. Their lack of tolerance seems to be linked to their fear of poverty epidemics that have consumed suburbs and the cities around them.

THE FEAR OF A POVERTY EPIDEMIC

The fears held in suburbs are not readily identifiable to one explanation, due to the intricate relationship between race and class—and the popular narrative of this relationship in media, politics, and scholarship—within the United States. Though the focus of this chapter pertains to poverty, it would be remiss to overlook the role of race in this aversion to poor populations. Within the United States, there is commonly a conflation of race and poverty in both definition and media imagery, with the typical image of poverty being that of inner-city black and Latino residents (Gilens 1996). This is compounded by the expansive body of scholarly work that has highlighted the cultural deficiencies of low-income minorities and the poor (e.g., Lewis 1966; Anderson 1999), as well as those works that blame the demise of cities on the birth of suburbs (see Bruegmann 2005, 47). Since the Great Migration, scholars have examined the lives of inner-city black residents and come to conclusions about the decline of the family as a stable institution (Moynihan 1965), the lack of organization, and communal ties in black (and other minority) neighborhoods (McCord et al. 1969; Sampson 2012).

Suburban residents are not entirely unfounded in their fears regarding the potential effects of poverty on their beloved neighborhoods. In one study examining housing appreciation in inner-ring suburbs, those suburbs with greater than 30 percent minority populations had lower property values, higher population density per census tract, and lower median household incomes (Anacker 2012). Furthermore, fears of the threat of poverty can be further amplified by the anxiety of solving the impending poverty problem.

Public goods and services are all funded by local taxes and resources and, even aside from education, impoverished residents require more public resources that often must be met by the government given the overall dearth of nonprofits in suburbs capable of meeting the population in need. The general scarcity of funds to both maintain the "luxurious" amenities of many suburbs and provide essential services for low-income residents can lead these communities to develop an anxiety toward the settlement of low-income residents within their jurisdiction. This anxiety results in fear of poor populations, with much of the angst caused by increasing populations of children.

THE COMPLICATIONS OF PUBLIC EDUCATION

Historically, the quality of school districts is cited as a major reason middle-class families leave cities for inner-ring suburbs. The cost of a quality educational experience is intricately tied to the higher cost of living in suburbs through housing costs and property taxes. Given this interdependent structure and funding of public schools in the United States, any issue regarding housing choices and patterns of selection also becomes one of education. There are distinct differences in the decision to move to the suburbs between earlier white suburban migrants and later lower-income migrants from cities and rural areas. Early white suburban residents moved to the suburbs in order to pursue the American dream of owning a home and providing greater opportunities for later generations. Later low-income migrants into suburbs are more likely to have moved because they were priced out of the city, in search of safer environments, or following work that is no longer available in the cities.

The impact of poverty on the quality of the school district can serve as a major reason for established, affluent inner-ring suburbs to fear the influx of poor populations and racial minorities. In a national study encompassing school districts in which over 88 percent of the nation's school-age population are enrolled, it was found that districts with more than 20 percent black students had between 10.2 and 16.5 percent less adequate funding than districts where the student population was less than 20 percent black (Bifulco 2005). Thus, school districts with higher minority populations require more funding to provide the same educational opportunities, but the erosion of the tax base due to an influx of poorer populations, who are also often minorities, poses a real threat to the vitality of the quality school system that many white suburban residents pursued in their flight from the cities.

The influx of poorer students can also have a negative impact on the quality of the school system in terms of academic performance. The educational achievement gap between children of more affluent socioeconomic backgrounds and children of disadvantaged backgrounds is well documented. In the landmark *Brown* decision, the Supreme Court acknowledged the inferior nature of black schools segregated under Jim Crow and refuted the "separate but equal" doctrine. In the infamous 1964 Coleman Report, commissioned by Congress, it was concluded that school resources accounted little for the black-white achievement gap. Instead, the report found that such differences were due to differences in the socioeconomic conditions facing children and their families. One study found that inner-city students who move to suburbs suffer academically due to poor preparation for the newly encountered rigorous standards (Rubinowicz and Rosenbaum 2000). Thus, the conditions facing lower-income students prior to their moving to the suburbs can hamper their later educational outcomes. The lower academic outcomes of later, low-income migrants to suburbs can lead to the deterioration of school quality as their more affluent counterparts may withdraw their children from the schools for fear of a low-achieving contagion.

However, even within social classes, there are racial differences in student achievement (Rothstein 2004). In his seminal study of the academic performance of black students in the affluent suburb of Shaker Heights, Ohio, Ogbu (2003) set out to explain why black students performed at lower levels than white students at each level of schooling. These black students were found to disengage academically from school as a result of both cultural and structural forces (Ogbu 2003). As a result, this cycle of poor performance can perpetuate the fears and negative stereotypes of white suburban residents regarding the prospect of low-income or minority neighbors who will erode the quality of the school system or corrupt the educational values and achievement of white students by virtue of their being poor or minority.

As education is viewed as the key to success by many suburban, middle-class families, the threat of a poverty epidemic to the quality of schools may lead residents to take matters into their own hands. Whereas there are a number of strategies that local governments can employ to address poverty, the perceived imminence and severity of the effects of poverty on the community's quality of life can lead residents to view these strategies as inadequate. The next section will discuss the available strategies and policy options that suburbs may employ to fight poverty; an explanation for why these communities may forgo these options and opt for suburban gentrification will also be addressed.

STRATEGIES TO COMBAT POVERTY

As overall poverty in suburbs becomes more prolific, these communities are confronted with difficult decisions about how to deal with the problem. Deciding upon a strategy with which to combat poverty often boils down to questions of whose "job" it is to take care of the lowest rung of society.

While many believe that the government has some obligation to take care of those who are most disadvantaged and most in need, the counterproductive sentiments of rugged individualism create obstacles to their meeting these obligations. Government is further limited by its intimate relationship to market forces and the economic vitality of the nation; during economic downturns, there is often a contraction of fiscal spending, and social services provided by the government are often the first to go. Even during times when social safety net programs, such as Supplemental Nutrition Assistance Program (SNAP) and Unemployment Insurance (UI), expanded (such as after the Great Recession of 2008) these programs still often fall short of meeting the needs of low-income people (Allard and Roth 2010). This section will address policy options available to suburbs to address poverty, and illustrate the allure of suburban gentrification as a "better," more viable strategy to many suburban policymakers.

One approach for fighting suburban poverty relies upon regional strategies and intermunicipal collaboration. These strategies comprise an approach known as "new regionalism" which aims to address "contemporary, interrelated problems that transcend local government and state boundaries" (Alexander 2011, 632). The Department of Housing and Urban Development's (HUD) launch of the Sustainable Communities Regional Planning Grant Program is an example of the federal government promoting collaboration between local governments in order to solve complex issues such as housing and municipal resources (Alexander 2011). Salsich (1999) proposed another regional strategy aimed at addressing metropolitan growth concerns and promoting neighborhood revitalization. This strategy relies upon the use of regional land use policies: a model for sharing and redistribution of the tax base, region-conscious affordable housing planning, and an adequate regional governance structure.

Another example of such a regional strategy is the creation of a Race to the Top–like challenge for metropolitan areas (Kneebone and Berube 2013). Acknowledging that resources are scarce, a program like this would encourage the many municipal governments within a metropolitan area to come up with innovative and collaborative strategies for addressing poverty within the region. Other scholars have noted that a regional strategy would place significant limitations on the use of exclusionary zoning practices (Marcus 1970), which contribute to imbalance in the distribution of poverty across metropolitan areas. Implementing such a strategy includes increasing the strength and capacity of supporting organizations, redirecting mainstream funding toward tailored programs, and strategic use of data for evaluation of program effectiveness and success. While these programs are very comprehensive in their approach, it is the comprehensiveness of these strategies that bars their feasibility for many communities. Evidence of failed government-sponsored poverty policies and "solutions" may lead suburban communities to be wary of such options.

Another proposed strategy for addressing poverty is through unemployment benefits and relocation vouchers, thus acknowledging the relationships between place and opportunity. The distribution of suburban jobs is not uniform across suburbs in any given metropolitan region, making unemployment and the spatial mismatch between jobs and workers a large factor affecting the rising rates of poverty within suburbs. Skeletal suburbs, in particular, have extensive experiences with unemployment and poverty as these communities were entirely designed around industry that has since left the area (Murphy 2010). Moretti (2012) argues that an unemployment compensation policy that includes a relocation voucher can help recipients move to areas where there are greater employment opportunities, thus closing the gap between job availability and workers. However, while solutions such as these may help the workers involved and address problems of spatial mismatch, this does not address community sentiments that are hostile toward low-income (poor) populations, regardless of their employment status. The location of jobs is one that requires much strategy and planning, and solutions such as relocation vouchers and reforms to unemployment compensation often ignore the fact that communities that developed large office parks often purposefully refrained from building nearby affordable rental housing, or any rental housing at all.

While on a regional level, there is great incentive to address problems of spatial mismatch, many local governments do not collaborate with each other and often end up competing for desirable residents through the provision of resources and quality public goods and services such as parks and recreation. As such, a strategy to combat poverty that depends upon intermunicipal collaboration in a system of local control that is inherently designed to pit municipalities against each other in the funding schema based on property taxes is insufficient and unlikely. State or federal government intervention to provide incentives for intermunicipal cooperation will not likely be enough without being paired with other strategies such as mixed-income development to give low-income residents a place to live in certain suburbs in closer proximity to potential work. This approach also ignores other issues such as transportation and the importance of access to other essential social services.

Nonprofits have long been a safety net for the government, addressing social problems when government resources are limited. The demand for nonprofit services tends to increase when there is a severe need and a dearth of government social services, or where there is a spatial mismatch between the location of government services and the location of the population in need. Other scholars have found that demand heterogeneity is positively related to the growth of nonprofit sectors (Matsunaga and Yamauchi 2004), and thus it would be expected that the heterogeneous demands of newer poor residents would not align with those of the prior residents; thus, nonprofits within the area would increase.

However, leaving the problem of poverty to the nonprofit sector in suburbia is an inadequate solution. While nonprofits are largely reliable in inner cities because of the density of the target population, the spatial disaggregation of poor populations outside of urban areas makes the reliance on nonprofits a less viable solution. The dispersion of poor populations across different suburbs in the metropolitan area can make it difficult for nonprofits to deliver services. Suburban nonprofits fighting poverty are also at a disadvantage in terms of fundraising and resources, as many funders look to give to long-established organizations that typically fight long-standing poverty, that which tends to exist in inner cities (Murphy 2010). As such, suburban residents are more likely to look for a more direct and proactive strategy to combat the perceived threat of poverty within their communities.

Yet another option available to suburbs to combat poverty is the use of mixed-income development. The use of development to combat poverty has a number of logical, theoretical underpinnings. Mixed-income development, in particular, can have many potential benefits to low-income residents. These benefits can include improved outcomes due to higher quality social networks, extensive social interaction, and the availability of community role models (Joseph, Chaskin and Webber 2007). However, the use of mixed-income development is limited in its availability to many suburbs, especially those characterized by overall affluence. In order for a mixed-income development to succeed, it needs to be available to potential residents of all income brackets, which is often made possible through government subsidy of low-income residents. Without government intervention, in the form of the subsidy, there is no incentive for developers to rent properties at lower than market value, as their goal is to maximize profits. As such, communities that are affluent on a whole, and that do not qualify for federal funding, often cannot avail themselves of this strategy in practice.

THE ALLURE OF SUBURBAN GENTRIFICATION

The term "gentrification" is not clearly defined by scholars, despite the fact that its connotation is often regarded as negative. The process of gentrification in inner cities often begins with the influx of creative classes into previously undesirable, decaying urban neighborhoods (see Deutsche and Ryan 1984). Gentrification has both racial and economic implications for neighborhoods and their residents. Critical to understanding the dynamics of gentrification is acknowledging the importance of the need for residents (and scholars) to clarify the differences between the neighborhoods and their residents pre-, during, and postgentrification (see Brown-Saracino and Rumpf

2011). In a study of the geography of home equity by race, one scholar found that at the start of the gentrification process these areas had high concentrations of black and Latino homeowners, but these homeowners have high out-migration rates from the gentrifying neighborhoods and thus do not reap the financial gains from gentrification (Glick 2008). Race is an important factor in understanding the dynamics of gentrification, as many demolition programs have been found to target public housing developments with high proportions of minority residents (Goetz 2011).

"Suburban gentrification" is a topic only mildly covered by the research. However, the use of the word "gentrification" within the term is a bit of a misnomer. While gentrification is a term that is typically associated with transition of a blighted, inner-city neighborhood through redevelopment and attracting the professional class back into cities, the use of the term in the suburban context differs along a key axis. Whereas gentrification in inner cities typically involves neighborhoods that have lower median incomes, fewer residents, high proportions of minorities, and older, decaying infrastructures (Freeman 2005), suburban gentrification involves neighborhoods and areas that are either relatively affluent in their entirety *or* are characterized by vast disparities in socioeconomic status. The latter of these suburbs often have a significant proportion of the population that is affluent and a smaller—but significant—proportion of the population that is socioeconomically disadvantaged.

While these differences in population composition between these two types of neighborhoods may seem to make these suburbs different enough to warrant different strategies to combat poverty, this is not necessarily true. In this context, suburban gentrification is a strategy to combat poverty that involves the specific, planned redevelopment and revitalization of inner-ring suburbs. As such, this phenomenon both covers community strategies (e.g., the solicitation and approval of a new luxury apartment complex) and individual actions (e.g., the renovation and remodeling of residential properties with the purpose of increasing both individual and neighborhood value). As a community strategy, suburban gentrification involves municipal-level action taken by an entity such as the mayor, town council, or planning commission. As many inner-ring suburbs are dense in population, this action usually involves the redevelopment of already occupied land deemed as not meeting its optimal potential. Suburban gentrification can also be the result of individual actions, such as individual homeowners looking to maintain or increase the desirability of their property or neighborhood through beautification and renovation. As one scholar explains, "Gentrification represents one form of restructuring of the symbolic orders of time and space in class relations" (Bridge 2001). As suburbs were created as the spatial location of the American middle class, it is reasonable to believe that individuals may act upon their definition of their middle-class identity by redefining the icon central to their existence. Thus, renovating one's home, or building an addition to add square footage, is a rational step taken by homeowners wishing to maintain their personal (and communal) identity in the face of perceived neighborhood change.

Both the improved use and redevelopment of areas of land by a municipality and the improvement of private property result in increases to the cost of living within the community. In turn, such changes can aid in rendering certain communities out of financial reach for those who are socioeconomically disadvantaged. Blumer's (1958) theory of group threat and group position can help to explain the likely possibility of similar reactions of these two types of suburbs to actual and perceived threats of poverty. Blumer posited a theory of group interaction based on the perceived threat of the effect of the differences between the groups; in his postulation, much of group interaction is based on the size, position, and interaction of both groups in relation to each other, but particularly the majority group and its perceptions of threats posed by the minority groups. This theory can explain majority group reactions based on racial and religious differences, as well as ones based on socioeconomic status. In the context of suburbs and the potential influx of poor residents, the desire of current residents to exclude these populations from their communities could be based on the fear that proximity to and contact with such impoverished populations may decrease their quality of life and/or drag their property values down. As such, the reactions of these two different types of suburbs to both the experience with and stereotyped perceptions of socioeconomically disadvantaged populations can be partially explained by Blumer's theory of group interaction.

In the first instance, suburbs with very little socioeconomic variation or racial diversity were often purposefully designed to be this way (e.g., Levittown), and were developed based on the exclusion of groups outside of the monolith. Residents in monolithic suburbs may choose suburban gentrification based on the stereotype threat of poor populations in order to combat poverty. This is supported by findings that neighborhoods with higher property values are more likely to experience redevelopment (Charles 2011). In the second instance, suburbs that are overwhelmingly affluent yet still retain significant proportions of poor residents have something that monolithic suburbs do not have: experience with poor populations. Those in the second trope of suburb may choose suburban gentrification in order to contain and manage the growth of their already-existing poor population in order to prevent it from growing and negatively impacting the town.

The stereotypes underlying communities' aversion to tolerance of poor populations (and racial minorities) are not without merit, thus making suburban gentrification an enticing strategy to combat poverty. The uneven accumulation of capital between suburbs with high minority populations and those without creates the potential for racial and class conflicts, as those inner-ring suburbs with larger minority populations have the lower median household incomes, lower property values, and are more densely populated (Anacker 2012). As a result, many local homeowners may seek to claim their suburban space by redefining its exclusivity, which one scholar calls "suburban revanchism" (Niedt 2006). This reclamation process is brought to fruition in the exercise of suburban gentrification as both a community strategy employed to preserve the neighborhood, as well as an individual strategy employed to preserve home prices.

This differentiating characteristic of affluence between urban and suburban gentrification is in line with the research on residential redevelopment. One study found that median property value and school district ranking were positively and significantly related to the likelihood of residences to experience redevelopment; conversely, both the proportion as well as the change in the proportion of black residents were associated with significant decreases in the likelihood of experiencing redevelopment (Charles 2011). A further differentiating point is that suburban gentrification may not necessarily involve displacement, whereas residing in a gentrifying inner-city neighborhood is positively and significantly related to the likelihood of being displaced (Freeman 2005). Nonetheless, the differences distinct to suburbs that make suburban gentrification an attractive and viable strategy for combating poverty are problematic in their externalities and consequences.

THE PROBLEM OF SUBURBAN GENTRIFICATION

While suburban gentrification may be an attractive option to municipalities because of its ability to exclude undesirable populations in a politically correct and nonconfrontational way, it has the potential to create many harmful externalities in both the short and long term. The use of gentrification to exclude poorer populations from inner-ring suburbs may exacerbate spatial mismatch between jobs and low-wage workers. This is because this development strategy functions to exclude these populations from the municipality, thus pushing them farther away from cities. This strategy exacerbates the already prevalent problem of spatial mismatch of jobs, in that while, "more than 43 percent [of jobs] are [located] more than ten miles from downtown" areas of inner cities, the distribution of these jobs across suburban regions is not uniform (Kneebone and Berube 2013, 57–58).

Suburban gentrification also has the potential to perpetuate the decline of other inner-ring suburbs that already have disproportionately more than their fair share of the region's distribution of poor populations, and hence are more likely to take these populations in. Studies have found evidence of polarization of inner-ring suburbs with high proportions of minorities and those without, which corroborates theories of spatial organization and the uneven accumulation of capital (Anacker 2012). If local suburban municipalities decide to adopt a strategy of suburban gentrification, these towns will likely avoid housing their "fair share" of socioeconomically disadvantaged populations in the metropolitan area by excluding them from within their jurisdiction and forcing them into other areas of the region. This, in turn, places a burden on the resources and services of other municipalities in the metropolitan area that do absorb these populations. Thus, the spillover effects of a suburban gentrification policy in one suburb can potentially affect surrounding suburbs negatively, giving more support for a regional strategy and reasons why suburban gentrification should be discouraged by local town governments and their residents.

As with the gentrification of inner cities, racial considerations arise when adopting a strategy of suburban gentrification. As many metropolitan areas (i.e., both cities and their suburbs) are racially segregated, this could be perpetuated and exacerbated through the use of suburban gentrification to combat poverty, thereby also intensifying racial tension and discrimination. In moving to the suburbs, many black families often trade the inner-city stressors of crime and victimization, gangs, and failing schools for better opportunities. However, in their new residential locations these low-income black families are now subjected to racism and discrimination at a higher rate than their inner-city counterparts (Rubinowitz and Rosenbaum 2000). Like the presence of poor populations, the presence of minority populations makes suburban residents uneasy given that many communities, such as the Levittown developments, were founded with the goal of exclusion (see also Loewen 2005). The compounding of these fears and the conflation of race and poverty makes it hard for suburban residents to find a "solution" to one without directly relating to the other.

As the threat of poverty and decline is often perceived as accompanied by an influx of minorities, it is important to assess the potential impact of such a policy on the extent of segregation throughout the region. The strategy of suburban gentrification affords suburbs a seemingly race-neutral strategy to accomplish the exclusion of racial minorities (Niedt 2006). Whereas the maintenance of a homogenous population may be the goal, civil rights legislation strictly prohibits the achievement of this goal through racial residential covenants and outright exclusion. However, redevelopment that "prices out" minority residents (who are often low income)—in conjunction with the aversive (unconscious) racism (Dovidio and Gaertner 2002) of white suburban residents—accomplishes the goal of both combating poverty and maintaining racial homogeneity. Suburban gentrification is therefore the product of the fear of poor minorities and the desire to maintain their "suburban" identities through the preservation of middle-class to affluent white communities.

FROM MOUNT LAUREL TO MOUNT HOLLY: EXAMPLES IN PRACTICE

As discussed above, integral to the issue of suburban gentrification are the municipal regulations regarding land use and the community sentiments regarding poverty and affordable housing. In the state of New Jersey, two landmark cases regarding exclusionary zoning, land use, and affordable housing changed the dynamics between municipalities and their ability to deal with low-income populations: *Southern Burlington County N.A.A.C.P. v. Township of Mount Laurel* and *Mount Holly v. Mt. Holly Gardens Citizens in Action, Inc. Southern Burlington County N.A.A.C.P. v. Township of Mount Laurel* is a case involving the use of exclusionary zoning to preserve the tax base by blocking the construction of affordable housing within the town. *Mount Holly v. Mt. Holly Gardens Citizens in Action, Inc.* involved the planned redevelopment of an impoverished section of an otherwise wealthy suburb. The remainder of this chapter will examine these two cases and the characteristics of the suburbs that decided to redevelop, thereby highlighting and discussing the problem of suburban gentrification.

Exclusionary zoning refers to the use of zoning and land use ordinances executed in order to prevent certain populations (and businesses) from establishing themselves within the given municipality. These undesirable populations often include low-income people, minorities, and renters. In New Jersey, specifically, the use of the zoning ordinances "worked to encourage the movement of tax-generating businesses to the suburban areas and discourage the development of housing for the people who would be employed by these businesses" (Fox 1987, 538). These zoning practices allowed for the perpetuation of the concentration of the poor and minorities within inner cities, while allowing suburbs to develop as high-priced and exclusive. In support of exclusionary, single-lot zoning municipalities have cited purposes and justifications including the desire for "greenbelt open space, [the] inadequacy of community facilities to support denser development, sewerage limitations, [and] historic preservation" (Marcus 1970).

The experience of Mount Laurel illustrates one suburb's attempt to use exclusionary zoning to preserve the town's affluent profile. The Township of Mount Laurel, New Jersey, is a small suburb located approximately fifteen miles east of Camden with a population of approximately 40,000 residents, according to the 2000 census, a drastic increase from its 11,221 residents in 1970. The racial breakdown of the city in 2000 was 87.1 percent white, 6.9 percent black, 2.2 percent Hispanic, and 3.8 percent Asian. Less than 3 percent of families within the township lived in poverty, compared with over 6 percent of families within the state of New Jersey. The median family income in 2000 was over $76,000, exceeding New Jersey's $72,137. The town was growing increasingly expensive and, to help maintain this profile, a number of the township's building and zoning codes prohibited the development of multiunit rental housing. Through its zoning policies, the township aimed to maximize its tax base and price out low-income residents (who also happened to be minorities) by encouraging the construction of larger houses, which catered to high-income families. The township also constructed a number of shopping centers and office parks.

In the early 1970s, many urban residents were moving into suburbs and the township of Mount Laurel adopted a Master Plan that would direct the future growth of the community. At this time, the average house in the township was worth $32,000, and constantly rising. To maintain the increase in housing prices and to create housing stock aligned with these prices, the plan called for the development of the township's rural land into plots with minimum acreage requirements for single-family, detached housing. At the time of the plan's adoption, residents of the town expressed reservations with regard to allowing for multifamily dwellings because of the fear that such dwellings would attract poor populations and be prone to overcrowding. As such, the plan and its attendant zoning ordinances had limits on occupants and the number of children allowed in the town's sparse rental units. In 1971, faced with being priced out of the township, the very small group of low-income (and minority) residents of Mount Laurel filed a lawsuit against the township alleging the improper use of zoning codes to block the construction of affordable housing on the township's undeveloped land. The 1975 decision of the New Jersey Supreme Court was in favor of the plaintiffs, ruling that affordable housing was critical for the general welfare of the public, and the use of exclusionary zoning impinged upon the general welfare of the people in the state (Fox 1987). However, in the years following the decision, the township did little to address its lack of affordable housing other than rezoning twenty of its 14,700 acres for high-density residential use, as it decided that it had a very small "fair share" obligation to provide housing.

This case established the Mount Laurel Doctrine, prohibiting discrimination based on socioeconomic status by the state or its municipalities in the exercise of its zoning powers. Under this doctrine all New Jersey municipalities were required to take affirmative steps to provide adequate affordable housing accommodations for their "fair share" of the regional need. In response to the Mount Laurel decision, the state legislature enacted the Fair Housing Act in 1985, establishing the Council on Affordable Housing (COAH) to assess statewide need; allocate the need to municipalities based on their "fair share" basis; and to review and approve municipal plans to meet this obligation. However, the meager COAH requirement of municipal ordinances that provide a "realistic opportunity" for the approval and construction of affordable housing units—often multifamily rental units—did not adequately ensure or address that these units were ever built (Evans

2003). This is especially true of units constructed in the manner and for the purpose that the court intended.

It is critical to note that in the monumental ruling of *Mount Laurel I* the court acknowledged the incentives of townships to exclude individuals "not adding favorably to the tax base." The court also lamented the township's outward, explicit actions to exclude poor populations from residing within its boundaries. Nonetheless, the court refused to require municipalities to determine their precise fair share obligation for housing, nor did they require the use of zoning ordinances to accomplish the construction of units to meet their obligation. Instead, municipalities were merely required to ensure that zoning ordinances provided the opportunity for the possibility of the construction of affordable housing (Fox 1987). Further, the court's permissive attitude toward the use of zoning to protect a municipality's profile as one of only single-family residences is valid. In 1983, the Mount Laurel case again came before the court on rehearing, at which time the New Jersey Supreme Court again decided in favor of the plaintiffs, finding it unconstitutional for a municipality to use land use regulations to prevent affordable housing opportunities for low-income families.

Created to address the affordable housing obligation in the wake of *Mount Laurel II* was the birth of Regional Contribution Agreements (RCAs). Under RCAs, municipalities are able to circumvent the fulfillment of their fair share obligations by arranging for the construction of affordable housing in nearby municipalities. Through these agreements, made possible by a provision in the state's Fair Housing Act, townships could outsource as much as 50 percent of their obligations. In the years that followed *Mount Laurel I* and *II*, the majority of affordable housing was constructed in New Jersey's largest cities with already sizeable (and disproportionate) shares of the state's low-income population, thus perpetuating racial and economic segregation across the state. Municipalities remained able to exclude undesirable populations from settling within their borders by either maintaining single-family dwellings or constructing high-end luxury housing and commercial park developments. RCAs were legal until 2008, when New Jersey Governor Jon Corzine signed reforms to the Fair Housing Act into law, repealing the agreements' legality as a solution to affordable housing.

The lawsuit surrounding the redevelopment efforts of Mount Holly, New Jersey, is representative of a township with significant experiences with an impoverished population attempting to revamp itself by revitalizing the area where this population is housed. Mount Holly is a suburb of Philadelphia with a population of approximately 9,536 residents, according to the 2010 census. The racial breakdown of the city is 69.7 percent white, 26.7 percent black, 12.7 percent Hispanic, and 2.4 percent Asian. In 2003, the township proposed a "redevelopment" plan calling for the demolition of homes in a section of the town where the Mt. Holly Gardens development was located. It was also the location of the town's only predominantly African American and Hispanic neighborhood. In the proposed plan, the township would redevelop the blighted land to house significantly more expensive residences. While the town council and residents of other communities throughout Mount Holly greatly supported the plan, the residents of Mt. Holly Gardens did not. A significant proportion of the residents of Mt. Holly Gardens were homeowners and longtime residents but were classified as very low income according to federal guidelines. This redevelopment plan was proposed as a response to mounting concerns regarding the deterioration of the area and the dilapidation of the housing stock, as well as overcrowding, sewer and drainage issues, and a crime rate higher than the rest of the township. As a result, the residents, under the community group name Mt. Holly Gardens Citizens in Action, filed suit challenging the plan as a violation of Section 804(a) of the Fair Housing Act. Had the township proceeded on the redevelopment plan, many of these residents would have lost their homes and been forced to relocate to other areas, likely outside of Mt. Holly; the redevelopment plan did not allow for the renovation or revitalization of existing housing. In November of 2013—approximately ten years after the suit was filed and the early stages of the plan (demolishing houses) was carried out—the township settled the case with the residents. They agreed to compensate residents of Mt. Holly Gardens who wished to leave and provide new homes for those residents who wished to stay.

As demonstrated by the Mount Laurel and Mount Holly cases, the use of zoning and redevelopment by suburbs to exclude low-income and impoverished populations is not only an attractive strategy, but one that has been well utilized over the years. It is critical to note that while Mount Laurel dealt with the town's zoning of undeveloped land, Mount Holly involved the redevelopment of land already in use. Municipalities' adoption of such strategies has negative consequences for not only the immediate surrounding region, but also the state. At the time the Mt. Holly suit was filed, over 43 percent of the state's municipalities—or 246 municipalities—had no affordable housing units whatsoever, while another 34 percent had less than their fair (proportional) share of affordable housing units; twelve municipalities bear over 50 percent of the state's affordable housing burden (Evans 2003). This lack of affordable housing was considered to be in compliance with the Fair Housing Act through the RCA agreements. This unbalanced distribution of affordable housing contributes to spatial mismatch between jobs and housing for workers. Spatial mismatch is also problematic within the state, as municipalities that house large numbers of employment opportunities lack affordable housing, while the municipalities with wider availability of affordable housing experience negative job growth (Evans 2003).

CONCLUSION

The changing demographics of suburbs and the regional landscape and distribution of poverty have led to great fears within long-term suburban residents. Uneasy with the prospect of the government or nonprofits addressing poverty, many municipalities have long employed the strategy of suburban gentrification in order to preserve their tax base and community fabric. Historically, this has been done through the use of exclusionary zoning in town planning. At present, suburban gentrification occurs in suburbs that are now densely populated and strapped for land through both individual and community decisions designed to revitalize and redevelop the neighborhoods.

Suburban gentrification can lead to negative outcomes. One such outcome is a regional disconnect between jobs and workers. Another negative outcome is the hyperconcentration of poor populations in nearby cities and nearby suburbs that have less infrastructure than wealthier suburbs. The concentration of poor populations, as opposed to a "fair share" distribution among municipalities, leads to a strain on municipal resources and may contribute to further decline in the region. Overall, the state has made very little progress with regard to both the banning of exclusionary zoning practices and the construction of affordable housing. The inability of the state to address these problems leads suburbs to take matters such as "solving" or combating poverty into their own hands, which only exacerbates the problem. The state has also not taken active steps to prevent suburbs from adopting redevelopment strategies with the purpose of blocking poor people's settlement in more affluent towns. Given the intricate ties between property, ownership, and the "American dream," it will be hard for a governmental strategy that discourages the individual homeowners' redevelopment of housing stock. As such, policies at the local and state governmental levels are likely the best option for addressing suburban gentrification.

While this chapter focused on two suburban communities in New Jersey, the problem of suburban gentrification has widespread relevance across the country. Inner-ring suburbs in metropolitan areas across the country have experienced increases in poverty. Hence, it is very likely that suburban communities in these metropolitan areas are likely to employ proactive strategies to combat the threat and effects of poverty in their neighborhoods. Further research should involve the identification and examination of suburbs in metropolitan areas that have chosen to employ gentrification-like strategies. Such research should specifically examine the effects of the development and revitalization of higher-income suburbs on surrounding areas, including the specific mechanisms through which suburban gentrification takes place. The relationship between suburban and urban gentrification should also be explored to better understand the relationship between cities and their surrounding suburbs.

Chapter Ten

Poverty and Health Care

Venessa Perry

It is no secret that poverty and poor health are intimately related. Aside from inability to pay, the poor also face hurdles regarding access to care itself, transportation to health care facilities, information about free or discounted services, childcare needed while accessing health care, and sick leave or time off from work in order to do so (Ahmed 2001, 477). In addition to reduced access to preventive care and medical services, the poor also have less access to the safe housing, nutritious food, and other life factors that promote healthy lifestyles. Many of these public health issues can be solved by providing the public with more information about access to health care. However, simply providing information regarding access is not enough; other roadblocks prevent people from finding the care that they need.

The nexus between poverty and health care has been central to policy discourse for over a century. In the early 1900s, efforts to develop a national health policy were linked to progressive efforts to address a number of societal challenges linked to rapid urbanization, industrialization, and recognition of the ease of the spread of disease. This launched an exploration and discussion about the responsibility of the government to ensure access to medical care for all that has continued for over a century. It also led to the discussion of strategies for addressing the health care needs of the broader population, including the needs of the poor.

This chapter examines the intersections between health care and poverty. I begin with a historical overview of some of the policy issues related to the provision of greater access to health care. I continue with a review of critical changes to health care policy in the 1960s, including the Medicare and Medicaid provisions of the 1965 Social Security Act, the 1964 Civil Rights Act, and judicial activity of the era. Next, I explore health disparities and broader aspects of access to care, a critical issue that has dominated the discussion of health care and poverty since the 1960s.

I conclude with some suggestions for the future of health care and offer strategies for better ensuring access to care for all. Some of these strategies relate to issues that led to the passage of the 2010 Patient Protection and Affordable Care Act. This Act was passed to provide enhanced access to quality and affordable health insurance and reduce health care costs for families and businesses. It has set the stage for considerations of the intersections between health care and poverty as we move further into the twenty-first century.

ISSUES OF PUBLIC HEALTH AND HEALTH CARE ACCESS

Much of the current discussion around health care in the United States finds roots in the early twentieth century when the American Association of Labor, a group of Progressive Era advocates, argued for a form of national health insurance. This group of economists, political leaders, and social theorists drew upon the lessons of nationalized health care in Europe (particularly in England and Germany), to frame a possible American model for ensuring widespread health care access. Throughout the United States, efforts were introduced in various state assemblies, as well as through the national platforms, to develop strategies related to health care provisions.

However, after initial support from various political segments, this initiative began to lose momentum. Postwar animosities toward anything with perceived German association, such as some of the social insurance programs tied into health care provisions, were a source of the declining support. Many private insurance companies as well as the American Medical Association joined forces and launched campaigns against these initiatives. The ultimate result of these failed efforts was the early stage of a health system that was divided between communities with access to adequate care and those that lacked access to adequate care.

It was not until the New Deal Era and the presidency of Franklin Roosevelt that the need for widespread access to health care was perceived as an important social concern. As President Roosevelt explored various components of the social insurance programs that would emerge during the 1930s, he experimented with the idea of having a health insurance program as part of the broader Social Security efforts. However, Roosevelt faced opposition to his belief in widespread health coverage from the American Medical Association (AMA) and other organizations. Given political challenges that would surface with the passage of the income security measures of the 1935 Act, Roosevelt opted to forgo advancing any health care agendas as part of his New Deal legacy.

The issue of wide-scale health care would not reenter the central political spectrum for another ten years after the signing of the 1935 Social Security Act. In 1945, President Harry Truman asked Congress to create legislation for a national health insurance plan. A year later, the Truman administration's desires were encouraged by the work of Congressmen Robert Wagner, Reid Murray, and John Dingell, who introduced a bill that would have resulted in a national health insurance plan. While the efforts of the Wagner-Murray-Dingell bill ultimately did not succeed, the bill caught the attention of Senator Lister Hill of Alabama, who crafted a separate bill providing matching funds to states and local communities for assessing the needs of hospitals and assisting in their construction. In 1946, the resulting Hospital Survey and Construction Act—or the Hill-Burton Act—became law.

While Hill-Burton would ultimately be responsible for the construction of many of the nation's hospitals, it would also play a central role in the development of some of the disparities in care and access that would frequently strengthen the linkages between issues of poverty, race, and health care. Central to the act's widening of disparities was its Section 622(f), which noted:

> That the State plan shall provide for adequate hospital facilities for people residing in a State, without discrimination on account of race, creed or color, and shall provide for adequate hospital facilities for persons unable to pay therefore. Such regulation may require that before approval of any application for a hospital or addition to a hospital is recommended by a State agency, assurance shall be received by the State from the applicant that (1) such hospital or addition to a hospital will be made available to all persons residing in the territorial area of the applicant without discrimination on account of race, creed or color, but an exception shall be made in cases where separate hospital facilities are provided for separate population groups, if the plan makes equitable provisions on the basis of need for facilities and services of like quality for each such group; and (2) there will be made available to each such hospital or addition to a hospital a reasonable volume of hospital services to persons unable to pay therefor, but an exception shall be made if this requirement is not feasible from a financial standpoint. (Hospital Survey and Construction Act 1946, emphasis added)

The inclusion of what amounts to a *separate but equal* clause resulted in limited access to quality care for thousands of people throughout the country. Furthermore, clauses were inserted which specified that hospitals were private entities, whose operations could only be regulated at the state level and not by federal authorities. As a result, state entities were able to determine where hospitals were to be built, and the federal government could assume a minimal role in deciding who had access to the hospitals.

In the early 1950s, as hundreds of hospitals were being developed across the country with Hill-Burton funds, the nation experienced the transition to

Dwight Eisenhower's administration, which was not as engaged in the health care access debates as the Truman administration. While health care was not a major concern for Eisenhower, three dynamics began to emerge during his presidency that would impact health care debates. First was the civil rights movement of the 1950s and growing activity related to the desegregation of public facilities. Second was an increasing prevalence of private health insurance provision resulting from IRS regulations that permitted employers to provide insurance for employees with significant cost savings. Third was a growing concern related to the health care needs of the elderly that stemmed from a realization that the United States had acted on the general income security needs of the elderly through the 1935 Social Security Act, but had yet to adequately address some of the broad health care needs of this population.

HEALTH CARE AND THE POOR: 1960S

Underscoring many of the changes in the health care arena in the 1950s and 1960s were challenges related to access. People living in urban areas faced issues of general access; physicians were beginning to leave the cities and move to the suburbs. The shortage left hospital emergency rooms as a primary source of care for many urban citizens. In fact, emergency room visits increased by 175 percent between 1954 through 1964. The overload caused considerable issues with care quality. Many doctors complained that they were overworked and were reluctant to take weekend and evening shifts (Silver 1966).

While the differences in quality of health care assumed an urban-suburban divide by the early 1960s, formal racial segregation in the South continued to impact differences in health care access. One of the enablers of segregation in health care systems was the Hill-Burton Act, which—by limiting federal governmental interference in operational processes—permitted the maintenance of segregated floors and services. Between 1947 and 1974, the Hill Burton program disbursed \$3.7 billion to the states, contributing 30 percent of the funds for all hospital projects and generating an additional \$9.1 billion in local and state matching funds (Starr 1982). Federal funds supported 7,750 hospitals and clinics. At least 98 accepted no black patients; many others contained racially segregated wings and wards with basements and halls reserved for black patients. For example, Alabama used Hill-Burton funds to construct racially segregated or separate facilities in all but two of its sixty-seven counties (Smith 1998). Other southern states engaged in similar practices. As Knowles and Prewitt (1969) note, fourteen southern states constructed entire hospital systems based on the principle of "separate but equal." The problem was not confined to the South. In northern cities, too, many hospitals segregated black patients from white patients and discriminated against black health care workers (Smith 1998).

In 1963, the Federal Court of Appeals heard the case *Simkins v. Moses*, which determined that funding under Hill-Burton was unconstitutional—and ultimately voided any claim that the equal protection clause of the Fourteenth Amendment did not apply to private hospitals. This landmark decision led to the elimination of segregated health facilities. Within the six-month period between July and December in 1966, nearly every hospital in the country admitted patients regardless of race. Most racially segregated wards were dismantled, and hospitals began granting staff privileges to black physicians.

A year following the *Simpkins v. Moses* decision, the 1964 Civil Rights Act was passed by Congress. Central to the Act was Title VI, which placed a critical condition on organizations (including hospitals) that accepted federal funds; they would not be able to discriminate, lest they risk the forfeiture of funds. At the time the Act was signed, the majority of hospitals that received federal support did so as a result of Hill-Burton funding. A year later, with the passage of the 1965 Social Security Act, and its Medicare and Medicaid provisions, that would all change.

On July 30, 1965, Lyndon Johnson was joined by former President Harry Truman at the Truman Library in Independence, Missouri, for the signing of the 1965 Social Security Act. Two components of the Act that would be critical in shaping health care elements for the poor were Title XVIII, which established Medicare (focusing on the elderly, including the elderly poor) and Title XIX, which established Medicaid (focusing on the poor). At the signing, President Johnson declared:

> No longer will older Americans be denied the healing miracle of modern medicine. No longer will illness crush and destroy the savings they have so carefully put away over a lifetime so they might enjoy dignity in their later years. No longer will young families see their own incomes, and their own hopes, eaten away simply because they are carrying out their deep moral obligations to their parents, and to their uncles and aunts. . . . No longer will this Nation refuse the hand of justice to those who have given a lifetime of service and wisdom and labor to the progress of this progressive country. (Johnson 1965b)

Johnson's support of Medicaid provided indication of some of the optimism he and many of the people in his administration perceived of the ability of this new program to address the medical needs of the nation's elderly.

In March of 1966, several months prior to the official start of Medicare, the United States Surgeon General released a notification that no hospital would be enrolled in Medicare until it signed a certification guaranteeing that it did not discriminate or segregate on the basis of race, color, or national origin and that the facility was in compliance with Title VI guidelines. The financial incentives of receiving federal funding would ultimately entice hospitals to desegregate.

On June 30, 1966, the evening prior to the inauguration of the Medicare program, President Johnson noted the new program's goal to advance equity:

> Tomorrow, for the first time, nearly every older American will receive hospital care—not as an act of charity, but as the insured right of a senior citizen. Since I signed the historic Medicare act last summer, we have made more extensive preparation to launch this program than for any other peaceful undertaking in our Nation's history. . . . Now we need your help to make Medicare succeed. Medicare will succeed—if hospitals accept their responsibility under the law not to discriminate against any patient because of race. More than 92 percent of the beds in our Nation's general hospitals are already in compliance with the law. . . . This program is not just a blessing for older Americans. It is a test for all Americans—a test of our willingness to work together. (Johnson 1966)

The next day, on July 1, 1966, the startup date for Medicare, more than 6,500 hospitals were integrated and engaged in the initiative to provide widespread access to care.

CONTEMPORARY ISSUES

While the 1965 Social Security Act's Medicare title established a uniform approach for addressing the health care needs of the elderly, it demonstrated a lack of uniformity in addressing the health care needs of the poor. Medicaid provisions of the act, those dealing with health care for the poor, left much of the implementation of Medicaid to the discretion of the states. Ultimately, states did not have to participate in the program; they had wide discretion regarding eligibility and managing payment to providers. This ultimately established a system in which the health care needs of the poor were linked to the policies established by various state-level actors.

In 1967, amendments to the Social Security Act gave the states the option to cover poor children who were not supported by families with Aid to Dependent Children (AFDC). This enabled Medicaid's expansion to families based on income and not family reliance on welfare. Additionally, the amendment provided increased access to care for children such as the Early Periodic Screening Diagnosis and Treatment program within Medicaid (EPSDT) and expanded coverage to assure that children received comprehensive primary care and follow up for health problems.

Throughout the 1970s and 1980s, the financial situation linking health care and poverty was further exacerbated by white flight and urban decay. In the 1970s and 1980s, urban areas became increasingly poor and black. Inner-city hospitals that did not move to the suburbs risked losing their doctors and insured patients to hospitals that would. African Americans in the inner city became increasingly dependent on the few, crowded public hospitals that remained. With the shift in urban demographics, Title VI's implementing regulations prohibit not only intentional racial discrimination but also facially race-neutral policies and practices that had an adverse impact on minorities.

Also during the 1970s and 1980s, legislation was passed to require states participating in Medicaid to cover pregnant women and children under the age of six who were under 133 percent of the federal poverty level (FPL) and to cover children ages 6–18 who had incomes up to the FPL. As a result of these changes, the number of poor children on Medicaid grew exponentially during the 1980s and early 1990s. As the eligibility rules were changed to expand access to Medicaid for poor children, the costs began to rapidly increase. Because the states were allowed to manage their Medicaid programs as they chose, many states began to move their Medicaid beneficiaries into managed-care plans and away from fees-for-service plans. This shift in health care delivery caused a dramatic increase in the number of enrollees in the Medicaid program by the mid-1990s.

Thirty years after the development of Medicaid, the issue of health care access and poverty was again central to important policy discussions. The replacement of Aid for Families with Dependent Children (AFDC) with Temporary Assistance for Needy Families (TANF) as a result of the Personal Responsibility and Work Opportunity Act of 1996 separated the issues of cash payments related to welfare and health care access for the poor through Medicaid. This provided new Medicaid eligibility requirements for families with children based on income and resources and not their status as welfare recipients.

Despite expanded access from Medicaid, coverage of near-poor children remained limited in many states. This was due to the fact that the states had the option to expand Medicaid to families beyond the federal poverty line and still receive matching federal funds. Fewer than a third of states took advantage of this option. After advocates for poor families and policy makers lobbied for increased health care access for the poor, in 1997, Congress passed the State Children's Health Insurance Program (SCHIP) for poor uninsured children. This program marked the first effort to increase access to health care services for the poor since the creation of Medicare and Medicaid. The legislation allowed states to expand Medicaid eligibility to poor uninsured children aged eighteen and below, even if their family incomes exceeded Medicaid eligibility guidelines.

Under the provisions of SCHIP, the states were allowed to create programs that either covered all children eligible for Medicaid, create a new program for children who did not qualify for Medicaid, or use the Medicaid program to cover children who fell between a certain poverty level and establish a new program for children with higher household incomes (Swartz

2009). According to the Center for Medicare and Medicaid Services (CMS), sixteen states developed separate SCHIP programs with no expansion of Medicaid. Fifteen states and the District of Columbia expanded SCHIP through Medicaid expansion, and nineteen states used a hybrid approach. It is important to note that the SCHIP program is a block grant program that was authorized for ten years. Within three years of passage of SCHIP, Medicaid and SCHIP provided total coverage for 24 million children. Medicaid and SCHIP became the main source of health coverage for poor children from low income families.

While over 40 percent of poor children were covered by either SCHIP or Medicaid in 2000, thousands of other children remained uninsured and ineligible due to their immigration status (Hoffman and Pohl 2002). Many of the parents of these poor children continue to go uninsured. The factors related to the insurability of immigrant children and adults are complex and are often related to factors such as language, confusion about the Medicaid/SCHIP program rules and eligibility, and fear of the public welfare system. In addition, children of immigrants tend to receive lower quality services. Overall, most immigrant children were not eligible for Medicaid/SCHIP because of eligibility restrictions from the Welfare Reform Act of 1996.

SCHIP was reauthorized from 2009 until 2013. The current program allows states to increase the poverty limits from 200 to 300 percent and to cover legal immigrant children. Because SCHIP is not an entitlement program, funding is based on the number of children below 300 percent of poverty. Therefore, once states use their allotment of funds, they must rely on the current legislative revenue that comes from increased tobacco taxes (Swartz 2009).

ACCESS TO QUALITY HEALTH CARE AND HEALTH DISPARITIES

The issues of access to quality health care and health disparities are closely linked and guide much of the discussion related to health care today. When examining access to health care, it is necessary to focus on the extent to which individuals have health insurance and a regular source of care. Health insurance reduces out-of-pocket expenditures and has been shown to be the single most predictive indicator of utilization. Without coverage, many people find health care expensive and forgo care even when needed. Having a regular source of care reduces other barriers to care, facilitates access to health care services, and increases the likelihood of interacting with health care providers. In addition, having a regular source of care provides the entry point into the complex health care delivery system, particularly when specialty care is needed.

The rising costs of health care coupled with the mounting numbers of poor and uninsured has placed an increased burden on the health care system. The number of providers that accept Medicaid has decreased due to low rates of reimbursement and—in some parts of the country—a lack of primary care providers. In turn a rising number of poor people—who are often minorities or immigrants— are forced to access health care through hospital emergency rooms. This increases hospitals' responsibility to handle—but not be compensated for—the treatment of the nation's poor. Many of the challenges in health care today are linked to the ability of people obtain care from the health care system in a timely manner.

The quality of health care refers to the "degree to which health services for individuals and populations increase the likelihood of desired health outcomes and are consistent with current professional knowledge" (Institute of Medicine 1990, p. 21). Quality of health care can be evaluated for effectiveness, patient safety, timeliness, and patient centeredness. Effectiveness focuses on the outcomes or effect of care on a patient's health such as the reduction of symptoms, morbidity, or the probability of death. The measures for effectiveness look at treatment, management, and prevention of the disease.

Racial and ethnic health disparities are the result of differences in socioeconomic status, access to health care, education, environment, discrimination, stress, diet, cultural differences, and other factors. While a person's income is directly correlated to improved health outcomes, this is due not to wealth but to the environment in which they live.

Recognizing the challenges related to health care access and the quality of care along racial and ethnic categories, Congress requested in 1999 that the Institute of Medicine examine issues of access and quality of care as they impacted racial and ethnic minorities in the United States due to increasing awareness of the existing disparities. The report that resulted from the study, entitled *Unequal Treatment*, identified several findings related to racial and ethnic disparities in health care access. First is that such disparities in health care do exist. This finding allowed researchers engaged with the study to then both explore some of the reasons why such disparities might exist and some of the possible solutions for addressing them. Such explorations led to other findings on issues such as the existence of stereotyping and prejudice on the part of health care providers and the impact of such prejudice on the actions of providers. These disparities should be examined in a broader context of the historic inequalities that had existed before such groups. They should also be considered in the context of the structural issues, assumptions and prejudices of the providers, and receptiveness of the patients to care.

The report also provides some important recommendations regarding how some of these disparities might be addressed. Several strategies related to both legal and policy interventions were noted, including the application of civil rights law and applying the same degree of protections on plan consumers regardless of the level of their health care plan. Several of the strategies focused on developing effective interventions focused on the development of guidelines for care that were grounded in evidence-based systems as well as payment systems that would ensure a supply of services to minority groups. Others focused on ensuring patient empowerment and education. Other recommendations focused on ensuring adequate data availability and sufficient support for research on strategies for eliminating disparities.

A critical finding in the *Unequal Treatment* report was that racial and ethnic disparities in health are compounded by disproportionately reduced access to health care services. Although there are many factors that contribute to health status, ready access to health care services could reduce many of these disparities. The lack of insurance and other barriers to obtaining health services effectively diminish racial and ethnic minorities' utilization of preventive services and medical treatments that could reduce the burden of disease and contribute to improved health.

CONCLUSION: THE AFFORDABLE CARE ACT AND THE FUTURE OF HEALTH CARE FOR THE POOR

By the early part of the twenty-first century, two critical concerns were becoming central to the intersection of health care and poverty. First were factors related to health care costs. Second was an increasing gap in insurance coverage.

In 2010, President Barack Obama signed the Comprehensive Health Reform Patient Protection and Affordable Care Act (ACA) into law. The major provisions of the law focus on expanding coverage, controlling health care costs, and improving health care delivery—particularly for the poor and disadvantaged. The ACA requires most U.S. citizens and legal residents to have health insurance. The Act facilitates the creation of Health Benefit Exchanges to purchase insurance coverage with premium and cost-sharing credits to individuals and families between 133 percent and 400 percent of poverty, create small business exchanges, implement tax credits for employees who receive insurance through the exchanges, regulate the insurance marketplace, and expand Medicaid to 133 percent of poverty.

While many poor people without health insurance utilize subsidized health care services at community health centers and safety-net hospitals, until the passing of the ACA, there was not a nationally organized system of care for people who lack the means to pay for it (Collins et al. 2012). The ACA aimed to narrow the gap between the number of people who are insured and able to receive medical services by implementing a system of care that specifically addresses the health care needs of the poor.

The ACA also addressed various issues pertaining to health disparities. It requires enhanced reporting of data on race, ethnicity, sex, and primary language. In addition, the collection of access and treatment data for people with disabilities is required. The Secretary of Health and Human Services will provide an analysis of the data to monitor trends in disparities in the two years following the enactment of the law. As a result, the ACA is helping policymakers and others engaged in health care pertaining to the poor understand much of the data critical to making the policy-level changes that impact access to medical care.

In the last fifty years, since the onset of the War on Poverty, health care for the poor has been inconsistent and sporadic in its coverage of low income populations. We have experienced challenges to systems that limited access based on race and income. We have witnessed the expansion of those individuals covered under Medicare and Medicaid. We have experienced the rise of the recognition of challenges such as the affordability of care, quality of care, and a recognition of challenges related to health disparities. The implementation of Medicaid in 1965, and the more recent passage of the Affordable Care Act, creates a myriad of opportunities to learn from potential approaches for the United States.

While the ACA provides one set of tools for addressing the issues of health care needs, access, and broader issues of poverty, there are a number of challenges that still need to be addressed. Included among these are issues of addressing disparities in care, many of which have historically racist roots, and many of which have concerns stemming from broader issues of access to equitable care. Other approaches, relying on the creativity of various individuals in the public and private sectors, will be critical in helping to ensure that wide segments of the population—including those individuals who are most economically vulnerable—are able to access health care.

Chapter Eleven

The Educational Achievement Gap and Poverty

Lessons of the Elementary and Secondary Education Act and Head Start

Franklin Dickerson Turner

"I shall never forget the faces of the boys and the girls in that little Welhausen Mexican School," noted Lyndon Johnson in late 1965 as he reflected on his short-lived career almost forty years earlier as a teacher in Cotulla, Texas. "I remember even yet the pain of realizing and knowing then college was closed to practically every one of those children because they were too poor" (Johnson 1965). Johnson's career as a teacher in Cotulla was brief, but it had a significant impact on him. Coupled with some of his own experiences as a student in rural Texas, he was able to see firsthand poverty's impact on students' educational opportunities. Such experiences would later make Johnson cognizant during much of his political career of the educational needs of the poor; they would also make him an advocate for educational initiatives.

For most of the nation's history, the federal government played a limited role in education. The Supreme Court's decision in *Brown v. Board of Education* launched a discourse on the role of the federal government in ensuring equitable access to education. This interest carried into the Johnson era with relative ease, as both an interest in civil rights and poverty intersected and explored ways that the federal government could further engage in educational efforts, particularly as pertaining to the needs of the poor.

This chapter examines the intersection of education and poverty in the years leading to, during, and following The War on Poverty. I begin with an exploration of the linkages between education and poverty that developed during the 1950s and the early years of the Kennedy and Johnson administrations. Next, I discuss two of the education efforts launched during the era of Johnson's Great Society and the War on Poverty. First is Title I of the Elementary and Secondary Education Act (ESEA), which provided the foundation for educational efforts aimed at supporting low-income children in poor school districts across the country. Second is Head Start, which provided support for early childhood education. These efforts served as critical anchors for the development of initiatives aimed at supporting the education of children from economically marginalized backgrounds.

After reviewing the genesis of Title I and Head Start, I examine persisting challenges related to the educational achievement gap. I specifically consider some of the reasons why the achievement gap may persist in various parts of the nation. In examining these persistent challenges, I explore how poverty continues to inhibit some of these areas despite the impact of Title I and Head Start.

EDUCATION AND POVERTY INITIATIVES

"Today, education is perhaps the most important function of state and local governments," noted Chief Justice Earl Warren in the Supreme Court's 1954 ruling in *Brown v. Board of Education*, which declared state-imposed segregation based on race to be unconstitutional. The *Brown* decision changed education in the United States in two ways. First, by upholding that racially segregated schools violated the Equal Protection Clause of the Fourteenth Amendment, *Brown* shifted the nation from acceptance of the idea that children could be deprived of an adequate education because of their race. Second, it changed the framework for the role of the federal government in matters pertaining to education, by expanding the role of the federal government in shaping education policy.

During the early 1960s, social scientists and other researchers observed a wide set of educational inequities in student performance that often differed based on race, as well as socioeconomic status. A 1963 article in *The Nation* described a "two-year educational achievement gap" between the mostly black low-income students and the mostly white higher-income students in a New Jersey school district's elementary schools (Walker 1963). A year later, the city of Chicago, Board of Education Advisory Panel on the Integration of Public Schools report, known as the Hauser report, asserted that "intensified educational opportunities for Negro boys and girls would result in a major closing of the achievement gap between group performances of Negro students and other groups of students" (Hauser et al. 1964, 20–21).

For John Kennedy, education was an important part of his presidential initiatives. In an address to Congress in 1961, Kennedy presented an overview of the importance of education in the nation's agenda. He recognized increasing demands on schools and school systems. With a growing population of students, estimated at a gain of nearly one million pupils during each year of the 1960s, Kennedy saw the need for investing federal resources into schools. Through this endeavor he became increasingly aware of the fiscal limits that existed in many settings. "Too many state and local governments lack the resources to assure an adequate education for every child," he observed. "Too many classrooms are overcrowded. Too many teachers are underpaid" (Bernstein 1991, 229).

Despite Kennedy's desire to work on issues related to education, he was not able to pass legislation that addressed the intersection of education and poverty prior to his assassination in 1963. In the months following Kennedy's death, Lyndon Johnson found himself drawn to the issue of education, largely due to his view that education was a great equalizer in society as well as his view of education as what helped him to move beyond the poverty of rural Texas. As he once noted, "With education, instead of being condemned to poverty and idleness, young Americans can learn the skills to find a job and provide for a family" (Johnson 1965).

In the lead-up to the 1964 presidential election, the issue of equity in education remained a central concern of the federal government and, specifically, to President Johnson. Johnson's landslide victory in the election provided him an opportunity to implement several initiatives that advanced his antipoverty goals. Foremost among these was the ESEA, which served as the primary mechanism for Johnson to focus the War on Poverty on educational matters.

The ESEA was divided into six titles. Each had a significant role in providing resources or services directly to or in support of children in schools. Critical for addressing the needs of children in poverty was Title I, which provided formula-based funding to school-based services and interventions for children in low-income schools. Title I provided funding to schools with high populations of children from low-income families. Approximately one billion dollars was awarded annually throughout the 1960s to such schools in an effort to close the gap in educational funding and allocate resources for the neediest school districts.

EVALUATION AND KNOWLEDGE OF CHILDREN IN POOR SETTINGS

One of the early questions that arose in relation to Title I pertained to the effectiveness of these allocations in addressing the educational needs of the poor. A year following the passage of ESEA, Harold Howe, U.S. Commissioner of Education, commissioned Johns Hopkins University professor

James Coleman to conduct a national study on the education needs and access to educational resources for children across educational and racial boundaries. Released in 1966, the report, entitled Equality of Educational Opportunity (but commonly referred to as the "Coleman Report") showcased the availability of quality educational opportunities for children of different races, religions, and national origins. Over 600,000 students and 4,000 teachers were studied throughout the country.

Coleman found that most students attended schools where the students of their race made up the majority of the student body. He reported that academic success was directly correlated with the social composition of the schools, students' feeling that they had influence over their environment and future, the verbal ability of their teachers, and the background of the students' family, especially in the formative years of development. Coleman felt academic achievement was not correlated with the quality of a student's school as was believed prior to this research. In the report, it was noted that school structure and environment enforced the academic achievement gap between the blacks and whites.

According to Coleman, the sources of inequality between students were not in the school, but could first be found in the home, and connected largely to social influences. As he would note several years after the release of the 1960s report, the sources "lie in the schools' ineffectiveness to free achievement from the impact of the home, and in the schools' homogeneity which perpetuated the social influences of the home and its environments" (Coleman et al. 1976).

A year following the passage of the ESEA, President Johnson requested the U.S. Civil Rights Commission to investigate racial segregation in the schools and report their findings to him. Two years later, and a year after the publication of the Coleman report, the Commission report Racial Isolation in the Public Schools was released. The study's first finding emphasized that racial segregation in public schools was widespread and increasing. In a survey of seventy-five cities, for example, the report noted that 75 percent of black elementary school children went to schools that were 90 percent or more black. Of elementary school white children, 88 percent were in schools that were primarily white (U.S. Commission on Civil Rights 1967).

By the early 1970s, several of the Great Society programs were being scrutinized by both evaluators and individuals engaged in political processes. Richard Nixon was one critic, noting in 1970 that while Congress had been "extraordinarily generous in its support of education, particularly in its enthusiasm for trying to compensate through education for the environmental disadvantage of our least fortunate children," much of its actions had been based on faulty premises. The fault rested largely in the belief that simply adding additional resources for the education of children from low-income backgrounds would improve the educational performance of children from low-income backgrounds. "It is time to realize," he noted "that every time we invest a billion dollars in a compensatory program we raise the hopes of millions of our disadvantaged citizens, whose hopes are more than likely to be dashed" (Nixon 1970).

One area of controversy over the years has been around the impact of Title I programs on the academic achievement of low-income students. Research has been largely inconclusive with any conclusions regarding the program's impact on student academic achievement. Puma et al. (1993), for example, found that Title I programs do not decrease the achievement gap that exists between disadvantaged and advantaged students. Rotberg and Harvey (1993) found Title I achieved only modest short-term gains. Stringfield et al. (1997) reviewed urban and suburban/rural strategies for educating disadvantaged children and found that Title I tended to have a positive effect on student achievement.

One of the challenges with evaluating Title I rests on the fact that it is not a program with a prescribed plan of action for accomplishing the goal of improving schools and decreasing the achievement gap among students. Title I is a significant source of financial support from the federal government with numerous requirements that encompass areas such as teacher quality, comprehensive school reform, curriculum, and instruction.

How should Title I schools be considered in relation to the broader set of social issues many children in the Title I designated schools face? Often communities where there is a significant percentage of Title I funding in the schools confront a number of other social challenges—including high rates of homelessness, underemployment, mental health issues, and other issues that impact the target communities for Title I.

The rise of the assessment and standards movement of the 1980s and 1990s has had a dramatic influence on Title I schools. In the 1994 Improving America's School's Act, Congress asserted that all children could learn and most could master challenging material. The act called upon schools and school systems to meet these high levels of standards. This act pressed school districts to consider their roles in encouraging students to meet these levels of standards and achievement. Furthermore, in 2001, Congress reauthorized ESEA toward a more outcomes-based focus on address educational needs known as The No Child Left Behind Act (NCLB). Building upon many of the standards-based approaches that had been developing for several years, NCLB promoted standards-based educational reform established on the belief that creating high standards and developing measurable goals will improve the educational outcome of students. Under NCLB, states assess students at selected grade levels annually. Schools may only receive Title I funding if they achieve annual progress based on student performance on state standardized tests. Poor performance on standardized tests results in both disqualification from Title I funding and threatened schools to be subject to state governmental control. If a school does not meet AYP, NCLB provides parents the option to choose another school. Parents have several types of school options available, including several types of public schools, charter schools, magnet schools, private schools, and homeschooling.

Ultimately, the movement toward these standardized approaches has focused on achieving the progress of students and providing resources to schools based on such performance. The challenge that schools face is how such measurement might leverage resources for children in Title I settings.

HEAD START

While the educational needs of low-income children were much of the focus of ESEA, another Great Society initiative was emerging to address the educational needs of children in early childhood settings. This other effort, Head Start, was unlike ESEA. While ESEA was a law that impacted students from low-income backgrounds, Head Start was a specific program that grew out of the War on Poverty.

Much of Head Start's theoretical foundation can be traced to a perspective that emerged in the field of early childhood education. Much of this perspective was based on a belief that children's intelligence was not firmly established at birth and could be shaped through learning and experiences. A critical publication in framing this perspective was Joseph McVicker Hunt's *Intelligence and Experience* (1961), which argued that improved environmental impacts could significantly shape children's cognitive abilities. According to Hunt, this approach was essential for overcoming the cultural deprivation of economically disadvantaged children.

Three years after the publication of *Intelligence and Experience*, Charles Silberman, a noted author on racism and education, published an article in *Harper's* magazine entitled "Give Slum Children a Chance," in which he argued for early childhood educational opportunities for poor children. Silberman noted that reading deficiencies in the early grades is one of the reasons that students later drop out of school, and subsequently find themselves unemployed when they are adults (Silberman 1964).

In response to arguments on the importance of early childhood education, from Silberman and others, Lyndon Johnson's educational strategies increasingly focused on developing initiatives that focused on preschool efforts. In his January 1965 State of the Union address, Johnson presented a framework for a preschool program that would support growth in the areas of language and literacy, cognition and general knowledge, physical development and health, social and emotional development, and approaches to learning. Additionally, it would address such areas of child development by focusing on students, parents, and communities. He referred to the initiative as "Head Start."

Launched in the summer of 1965, the initial Head Start pilot provided over 560,000 disadvantaged children academic enrichment services, medical care, and food. The success of the initial summer program led to Johnson's reiterating his support for Head Start and announcing funding for year-round Head Start programs beginning the following fall. He also planned to continue summer sessions; moreover, he indicated that special "follow-through" programs were necessary for youngsters who attended the summer programs.

A year following the launch of Head Start, a White House Task Force on Early Childhood Development produced a comprehensive review of federally supported early childhood development initiatives. Throughout its report, the panel noted prior neglect of intellectual competence of children as a means of conceptualizing their growth. "This new emphasis on the value of [intellectual] competence is still in the process of being appreciated. It represents a substantial shift in emphasis from that on emotional and social adjustment which has dominated the past 30 or 40 years." Although agreeing that, in some of the pilot efforts, there was room for improvement, the task force nevertheless strongly endorsed the program.

The initial success of Head Start garnered even further support from within the Johnson administration. In his January 1967 State of the Union address, Johnson pledged to continue the expansion of the Head Start program. The following month, the president delivered a special message to Congress concerning children and youth in which he detailed plans for this expansion. He praised the program but acknowledged that its benefits could decline if not reinforced.

Through the next several decades, Head Start expanded to states throughout the nation and enrolled over 30 million, primarily low-income children in its programs. Later, variations of Head Start would appear that would greatly expand the program's reach to broader populations of low-income children. For example, the Early Head Start Program was launched in 1994 to serve children from birth to age three. Early Head Start programs work with families over the course of a full day and throughout the entire year. Furthermore, Early Head Start connects families to necessary medical, mental health, nutrition, and educational services.

While Early Head Start serves the youngest of children, Migrant and Seasonal Head Start programs specialize in servicing children of migrant families. The program provides preschool children of low-income migrant and seasonal farm workers with extensive resources beyond just educational programming, such as a comprehensive health program, parent involvement assistance, and social services. A key component of this program is the coordination of resources provided to these children and their families as they migrate from state to state.

Another example of how Head Start has adapted is in its provisions to assist children who are homeless or in foster care, which falls under one of three regulations given by the U.S. Department of Health and Human Services. First, Head Start agencies are charged with identifying children who are homeless and prioritizing their enrollment into a program. Second, the families of homeless children are allowed to apply, enroll in, and receive Head Start services while the needed documentation, such as financial eligibly information, is being acquired by the parents within a reasonable amount of time, depending of the uniqueness of each child's situation.

During this expansion, high-quality programs have positively impacted low-income children, preparing them for their later entry into primary and secondary schools (Ludwig and Phillips 2008). Current debates around expanding Head Start programs to children who may be from additional underserved populations has been critical in further addressing the needs of children from lower income backgrounds.

These examples provide overviews of Head Start's growth over the years and its expansion to wider segments of the population. In sum, over the five decades since it was launched, Head Start has served over 30 million children.

A PERSISTENT ACHIEVEMENT GAP

Head Start and Title I have been focused on providing for the educational needs of millions of children and youth at the economic margins over the past fifty years. One of the challenging realities of these educational efforts is that despite some of these initiatives, there are still persistent gaps in the educational achievement of children. Many of these gaps are correlated to the economic and racial differences of children. This section explores some of the issues that have risen related to the persistent educational gap and its challenges.

Over the years, emergent research in the area of socioeconomic status (SES) factors has framed much of the research related to the success and the challenges affiliated with students in Title I schools and Head Start. In this section, I explore some of these issues. Numerous experts declare that the achievement gap is a result of several factors such as educational resources at home and their community, accessing quality health care, nutrition, and a discrepancy in the resources available to poor versus wealthy children. Children from low socioeconomic status (SES) families tend to gain language skills more slowly, demonstrate delayed letter recognition and phonological awareness, and are at risk for reading difficulties (Aikens and Barbarin 2008). Children from low-SES homes are less likely to have the same exposure to oral and written vocabulary than their higher SES counterparts (Turner 2010). But, studies have found that low-SES children who are provided enriching learning environments by their parents in the home do begin kindergarten with the same school readiness gaps seen among their poor counterparts who were not exposed to a similar enriching environment (U.S. Department of Education 2000; Viadero 2000; Sparks 2011). The funds of knowledge research model states that within these diverse communities over generations strategies have emerged for developing skills, abilities, ideas, practices or bodies of knowledge, which are vital to a family's functioning and well-being (Veléz-Ibánez and Greenberg 1992).

Children who live in poverty are more likely to be absent from school all through their educational experiences, which greatly reduces their exposure to academic material, further adding to the learning gap between them and the more affluent peers (Zhang 2003). The high school dropout rate in the United States has consistently dropped (National Center for Education Statistics 2006), but the dropout rate for impoverished students has consistently increased. In 2007, the dropout rate of high school student between the ages of 16 and 24 years old was highest among low-income students (16.7 percent) as compared to high-SES students (3.2 percent) (National Center for Education Statistics 2008). Students who live in a low-SES household and are not able to read on or above grade level by third grade are three times as likely to drop out of high school than students who have never been poor (Hernandez 2011).

Parents who are able to maintain consistent employment should be able to provide stable housing and a healthy household (Coley and Baker 2010). A stable household is important to educational outcomes for student mobility, the movement of a student from one school to another. Students who frequently change schools tend to have lower academic outcomes than students who are more stationary (Rumberger 2003). Also, parents with stable income may be better able to afford to enroll their children in extracurricular and summer activities.

The poverty rate for a family that was headed by a single mother was 31 percent as compared to a family with a married couple had a poverty rate of 6 percent (Coley and Baker 2013). Children being raised in a single-parent household are more likely to encounter a range of negative outcomes in school and throughout their life (Sigle-Rushton and McLanahan 2002). Also, it may be difficult for a single mother to work, take care of household and transport, or pay for her children to receive tutoring and go to extracurricular activities.

The Education Trust reported that students living in poverty and members of racial minority groups are disproportionately concentrated in bottom-tier schools. For instance, black students in the state of California are six times as likely as White students to be enrolled in a school that is in the bottom third of schools in that state, and the probability of Latino and low-SES students of attending school in the bottom third of performance is almost four times that of their white counterparts.

These examples of issues illustrate some of the challenges that persist in current achievement gap issues. They also, and perhaps more importantly, provide some direction around how the strategies might be developed to continue to address the challenges over time.

CONCLUSION

Fifty years after the launch of the War on Poverty, a great deal can be learned regarding the achievement gap that endures today. The Johnson administration's comprehensive plan to end poverty sets the stage for including education as a part of a plan that also included economic development, health care, and other programs. Head Start and ESEA were two key components of the antipoverty strategies of the 1960s. While neither of these initiatives were able to fully eradicate poverty, they did provide a framework for considering some of the strategies that might be implemented from an educational perspective to address some of the pressing issues pertaining to poverty. Continued study of them raises questions regarding strategies for developing approaches to ensure that children in economically distressed circumstances can have a full range of educational opportunities that will ultimately help them succeed in life.

Chapter Twelve

Workforce Development in an Era of Diminishing Work

Michael Vorgetts

In late May of 1961, President Kennedy delivered a speech before a joint session of Congress on what were deemed "urgent national needs." Most famous for its declaration of a national goal to place a man on the moon by the end of the decade, the address also focused on some of the pressing economic needs that the nation confronted. "The task of abating unemployment and achieving a full use of our resources does remain a serious challenge for us all. Large-scale unemployment during a recession is bad enough, but large-scale unemployment during a period of prosperity would be intolerable" (John F. Kennedy Presidential Library and Museum n.d). At the time, the central issue driving the workforce discussions focused on the ability to adapt to the changing realities that automation was having on the workplace, most notably displacement of workers. The economic challenges were compounded by the effects of the "rolling adjustment" recession of 1960–61; high unemployment, high inflation, and low GDP. As the economic opportunities of the post–World War II period began to crest, the question of how to address some of the connections between economic and social realities with the workforce needs of the era framed many of the areas of concern.

Over the next several decades, the discourse and functions of workforce development shifted away from a conversation framed by workforce development linked to issues of labor force restructuring due to factors of automation to focusing workforce development initiatives linked to the job training and placement of low-income individuals. While much of this was evolving, the dialogue was shifting at the federal and state levels around workforce development. What was the best strategy to ensure practices that were effective? How did workforce development investments change at the federal and state levels? How has the shifting discourse around workforce development impacted the shifting realities of poverty in America?

This chapter examines the shifting discourse in the area of workforce development. It begins with an overview of the history of the field. Here, I trace the evolution of the discourse in the area of workforce development from the early 1960s discourse around the Manpower Development and Training Act of 1962 to the most recent statutory framework—The Workforce Investment Act of 1998 and its amendments.

Next, I examine some of the central issues related to workforce development. Over the years, several critical challenges have emerged related to the implementation of workforce development programs—particularly as they related to communities at the economic margins. I explore two of these in particular: the challenges of measuring impact and working with the workforce needs of unique populations facing high barriers to stable and gainful employment; specifically veterans, those reentering society from correctional facilities, and workers with disabilities. These populations offer workforce development initiatives and practitioners an opportunity to include workers into the workforce who do not have traditional routes via education and experience.

Next, I examine some of the issues related to workforce development in the state of Maryland, which, like other states, has been engaged in workforce development approaches increasingly in the past two decades as the appetite for addressing workforce development needs at the federal level has dissipated and states increasingly find themselves responsible for developing initiatives and programs to help alleviate changes and challenges for workers in a more complex and global economy. I conclude with a presentation of future challenges in the area of workforce development as related to matters of poverty alleviation.

A BRIEF HISTORY OF WORKFORCE DEVELOPMENT PROGRAMS

Workforce development has two distinct periods: from 1963 to 1970 and from 1971 to present. Wherein the first focused on "structural problems in the labor market—the intractable difficulties of the poor and disadvantaged who lacked the preparation, experience and skills to get and hold a job" (Mirengoff and Rindle 1976), the second period focuses on programs that were developed as a response to continuous unemployment levels. Increased awareness of the need for workforce development programs after World War II was primarily due to factors resulting from the experience of the depression: high unemployment and worker displacement. Additionally, the growth of technology which displaced manual workers and technical expertise needed in Cold War competition were particularly influential (Kremen

1974). As the improvements in technology became more cost-effective for companies and more sound at completing repetitive tasks such as assembly-line work, the growing threat of "automation" was seen as a death knell for jobs, especially in the manufacturing centers of the country.

Around this time the Department of Labor's U.S. Employment Service (USES) also began to more assertively counsel state employment agencies in employment planning (Kremen 1974). But it was the Vocational Retraining Act (VRA) of 1961 that became the first comprehensive federal workforce development program which had a funding mandate centered on cooperation with states in the delivery of training for unemployed workers. Its formula of training, transportation, and allowances for other expenses associated with training became the core of the first major program aimed at fixing structural employment and poverty: the Manpower Development and Training Act of 1962 (Kremen 1974).

MANPOWER DEVELOPMENT AND TRAINING ACT

The Manpower Development and Training Act (MDTA), signed into law by President Kennedy, would become a key plank of the War on Poverty under Lyndon Johnson. The MDTA arose out of an era of great anxiety over the effects that automation would have on the workforce. In addition to easing anxieties over automation, the MDTA strove to address growing distortions in economic growth among classes that were taking place during the 1960s while attempting to proactively address the country's "shifting employment needs" due to plant closures and relocation (Bachmura 1963, 61). Like the earlier VRA, it had three main components of funding: training and education, transportation for service users in need, and allowances for trainees. Additionally, it marked a sixty-fold increase in Department of Labor funding for workforce development to $3.7 billion and was a massive transition for federal efforts to tackle economically disadvantaged communities (Mirengoff and Rindle 1976; Bachmura 1963).

While initially aimed at the challenges of displacement and growing income inequality, it was the War on Poverty that shifted the focus of the MDTA from the dislocated to the poor and racial minorities. The initiatives and programs of this era confronted structural poverty and racial problems through training, education, and work experience for disenfranchised minorities and the economically disadvantaged (Holzer 2012). In the years immediately after the launch of the War on Poverty, the Work Incentives Program (WIN), and the Job Opportunities in the Business Sector (JOBS) programs were established in addition to the Employment Opportunity Act (1963–70). The former was a job program for people on welfare, while the latter supplemented salaries of low-income workers. Additionally, disadvantaged and low-income youth also became a critical component of workforce development with Jobs Corps, a residential work program which aims to take participants out of their home environment to relieve some of the strain from poor families while incorporating soft skills training such as "character building and teamwork" (Holzer 2012, 4).

The Comprehensive Employment and Training Act, 1974

As the 1960s unfolded into the 1970s, issues began to emerge around the lack of coordination between workforce development initiatives at the federal, state and local level; seventeen different federal programs existed with over 1,000 state and local projects overlapping across regions and industry sectors (Mirengoff and Rindle 1976). The emergence of these issues led to the Comprehensive Employment and Training Act of 1974 (CETA), which attempted to shift responsibility for workforce development programs to the state and local levels under more structured coordination efforts.

Philosophically, CETA was rooted in the belief that popular will could be more thoroughly expressed through a decentralized system, and that community involvement would increase. CETA's predecessor for the decentralization model was the Cooperative Area Manpower Planning System (CAMPS) from the mid-1960s, which had existed solely for information sharing between the federal government and localities but offered no structure of coordination to maximize program implementation effectiveness (Mirengoff and Rindle 1976). Further, it was assumed that local governments have a more intimate understanding of their populations, and thus could best serve their needs (Mirengoff and Rindle 1976, 4). Battles ensued over the benefits of strict categorical programs versus expansive language that allowed local officials to determine who benefited.

While CETA's original national goals were aimed at low-income groups and those "most in need" of manpower services, the language was left vague enough that federal, state, and local implementers wielded wide discretion over the types of people who could receive CETA services. Eighty-seven percent of the CETA funding was shared by local authorities, who still applied for the funds from the Department of Labor (Mirengoff and Rindle 1976). By shifting responsibility to states, it was hoped that workforce programs would eventually decategorize the service pool so that localities had more power to determine targeted groups. However, federal stipulations under the various titles meant that this wasn't possible in practice, though the decentralization piece of the legislation was more successful (Mirengoff and Rindle 1976).

In addition to procuring better coordination between government entities for service delivery, CETA also targeted specific areas of unemployment and focused efforts on Native Americans, migratory workers, and other groups with unique challenges to better incorporate these individuals into the workforce. Additionally, parts of CETA included employment training (Title I), the annual youth training camp (Title III) and temporary public service employment service programs (Title VI). The range of programs recognized that different programs were needed for different demographic groups (Holzer 2012, 5).

Prior to CETA, workforce development clients were often economically disadvantaged, however, they were less a proportion of the participants after CETA was implemented. This was due to the broadening of eligibility requirements to the general unemployed who were victims of the recession, the role of suburban committees in seeking relief for their local constituents, and the "creaming"—a practice whereby preference in enrollment is given to those most likely to improve their measured performance—of the best training candidates at the local level driven by the centrally established performance evaluation component of funding streams (Barnow and King 2005). The share of the program for the truly economically disadvantaged went from 87 percent in 1974 to 77 percent in 1975 although formulas for funding weighted poor- and low-income clients less than the unemployed (Mirengoff and Rindle 1976, 14–38).

The shift to the formula approach of Title I in 1975 also decreased the level of funding to cities relative to counties in 1974 workforce development funds. The share for cities went from 41.9 percent to 36.1 percent in just one year. CETA did aim at the unemployed but it made no distinction between recipients of services who were skilled and temporarily unemployed, on the one hand, and those who were unskilled and long-term unemployed, on the other hand (Mirengoff and Rindle 1976). A study of benefit distribution at the national level under CETA demonstrated that under Title I, the poor received less service although they saw increased services under new Public Service Employment Programs. Service to nonwhites decreased in both programs. This is best explained by:

> poor economic conditions and people's perceptions of them; the increased decision making role of elected officials and their preference for spreading the benefits around; and the shift from large-city and urban-county-based employment and training programs to a broader distribution of resources in suburban and rural jurisdictions. (Baumer et al. 1979, 171–96)

Changes ensued at both the national and local level. Analysis of participant service patterns at the local level reveal that nonwhites were enrolled at rates exceeding their estimated need. A study of 1970 Census data indicates that more women and nonwhites were reliant on CETA programs, however, nonwhites were generally enrolled at levels equaling or exceeding their proportion of the estimated need, while "women were consistently underserved in relation to their estimated need" (Baumer et al. 1979). Although the government recognized the low enrollment of women in CETA programs, Congress did not seek legislative action to address the issue. This may be the result of CETA administrators' inaccurate belief that shifts in certain groups' enrollment was a direct result of local economic conditions that led to alterations in characteristics of the poor and unemployed (Baumer et al. 1979, 186).

Various factors contributed to the shift away from servicing those who were most in need. CETA functioned with the knowledge that jobs needed to be created, and that it wasn't merely about developing skills for individuals; programs needed to be matched to needs of the private sector. This created greater opportunities for incorporating local decision makers and elected officials in workforce development programs' development process (Mirengoff and Rindle 1976, 66). The ineffective influence of advisory councils and local program decisions, from choosing contractors to the selection process, had a great impact on who received services. Programs utilized a variety of selection processes, from strict criteria for entrance to first come, first served. The choice of contractors who provided employment and training programs was influential due to the reputations of contractors, as this attracted or deterred specific groups of people; this did not however necessarily have a large impact as, "on the whole, the same program operators were used" (Mirengoff and Rindle 1976, 4). Significant in swaying the demographic of beneficiaries of CETA were the attitudes of manpower actors. Their perception that "higher levels of unemployment reduced the proportion of low-income people in the applicant pool," and lack of commitment to servicing the poor resulted in declining services to the poor overall (Baumer et al. 1979, 190).

As the 1970s closed, the attitudes toward how workforce development should be funded and who should be funding it began to take a more conservative turn. The recession of the late 1970s and its ill effects, rampant inflation and high unemployment, gave federal policy makers pause in terms of how best to fund workforce development initiatives and what types of partnerships and requirements should be necessitated for individuals to continue to receive workforce development training and social services.

The Job Training Partnership Act and Workforce Investment Act

The peak of employment and training funding for the poor was in 1980 under CETA (Holzer 2012, 2). The 1980 presidential election saw a return to core conservative values of smaller government and states' rights regarding program implementation. This dealt a real blow for the federal workforce development programs aimed at the economically disadvantaged. Total WIA funding today is $5 billion including the Job Corps and other parts of Title I. In 1979 total Workforce Development funding was about $20 billion in today's dollars (Holzer 2012). It wasn't just the reduction in the funding that made such a big different under President Reagan. Both the Job Training Partnership Act (JTPA) and its successor, the Workforce Investment Act (WIA), heralded an ideological shift to greater worker choice, focus on a wider pool of beneficiaries (the unemployed generally), decentralization, decreases in training programs, and overall decreases in federal funding (Holzer 2012, 9).

The programs of the JTPA included organizational and arrangement processes established under Title I, training for the economically disadvantaged, training for dislocated workers (a new feature in Workforce Development programs), and programs for migrant workers, Native Americans, and seasonal workers. There were some other fundamental shifts away from the precedents set by CETA however. JTPA aimed to boost the long-term earnings of workers and decrease their dependency on welfare. There were also shifts away from "income maintenance" to more stable and sustainable forms of employment support, and also toward more responsibility for states and more private sector involvement (Cook and Rawlins 1985).

Like workforce development efforts before it, the WIA tried to implement results of research showing that a developmental approach was best for youth. Comprehensive service delivery programs covering the soft and hard skills of interpersonal and professional skills through a wide community network was seen as vital in achieving this (Brown and Thakur 2006). By the 1990s, there was a specific concern on ensuring that as wide of a segment as possible was engaged in the general workforce. Much of this was the result of changes in many of the provisions of welfare laws. The passage of the 1996 Personal Responsibility and Work Opportunity Act framed many of the changes. Two years following the passage of PROWRA, the Workforce Investment Act of 1998[1] was passed.

As the primary vehicle for federal funding and coordination for workforce development in the United States, WIA was designed to reduce duplication of administrative and service delivery through a system based on informed consumer choice regarding career development, universal access to employment and training services, effective performance measurement, local governance, public-private partnerships, and state and local labor market responsiveness.

Key features of WIA programs are job support and education planning, a one-stop service center delivery model, the "work first" philosophy and service sequencing, systematic accountability, and application of market mechanisms in service delivery (O'Shea and King 2001). However, when it comes to education for youth, workforce development programs have become eclipsed in size and scale by grants for higher education. Today, funding for the poor is far higher in the Pell Grant program, and it appears that that is where the government believes it will have more impact on alleviating economic disadvantage (Holzer 2012, 2).

Finally, both the JTPA and the WIA made a move toward involvement of the private sector in use of some market forces and further emphasis on decentralization to make the programs more efficient. The State Job Training Coordinating Council (SJTCC) evolved from the Private Industry Council (PIC) of CETA. It stipulated that it must be made up of at least 30 percent of representatives from business (Cook and Rawlins 1985, 99). Seventy-eight percent of funds used by states in Title II A must use the same formula for funding as the federal funding to states. This has an effect of limiting state autonomy, one of its expressed aims (Cook and Rawlins 1985, 99). Services and definitions of dislocated workers are also left to the states. They are also responsible for carrying out the performance reporting and targeting of the populations (Cook and Rawlins 1985, 101).

In essence, the WIA replaced the JTPA since it was determined that the WIA model was designed to be flexible and responsive to the needs of the varying regions and peoples in need of service. The reality is that the WIA is a highly complex system that looks and functions differently in each state. The complexity of the model makes program design and redesign difficult and makes performance measurement exceptionally challenging. The WIA was scheduled for reauthorization in 2003 but currently has not been reauthorized, although provisions to the WIA were included in the 2009 American Recovery and Reinvestment Act. In 2013, Representatives John Tierney (D-MA), Ruben Hinojosa (D-TX), and George Miller (D-CA) introduced The Workforce Investment Act of 2013 but the legislation was referred to the Subcommittee on Higher Education and Workforce Training and no roll call vote was ever taken on the bill (H.R. 798—113th Congress 2013).

Assessing the Effectiveness of Workforce Development Programs

In assessing what has worked best in the history of workforce development since the Manpower Development and Training Act (MDTA) of 1962, researchers have been quick to note that each new federal effort has been strongly shaped by its predecessor. The service providers, institutional relationships, and organizational strategies tend to be reshaped but not replaced by the new system of funding, broadening of the target population, and participation incentives of new programs. The programs have provided significantly different delivery mechanisms and goals, but to the extent that they have been interlinked by shared characteristics, it is useful to evaluate them as one whole that has been evolving in new directions, all affected by similar challenges that have been difficult to overcome. This section is a discussion of the literature that evaluates workforce development programs over history and is subdivided into several central areas of discussion: (1) Geographic disparities; (2) The balance of supply and demand approaches to the labor market; (3) Strategies to reach the poor and chronically unemployed; (4) Devolution of responsibilities to the state and local levels; and (5) Performance measurement. First, however, we should look at what the programs have been credited with achieving overall.

Workforce development programs have been riddled with the problem of performance measurement. There has almost always been a lack of data on performance and a discrepancy between performance measures and program outcomes (Grubb 2001; Decker and Berk 2011, 906). Since 2009, the DOL has used a regression model to adjust performance to economic cycles, which has provided an enormous improvement. However, there has been little consensus on benchmarks and standards (Giloth 2000, 345). The GAO (2009) has said categorically that the WIA has limited evaluation abilities to even implement the performance measurement that it might wish to implement (Decker and Berk 2011). There are some more qualitative aspects of this problem. For example, maps of career advancement needed for both employees and employers have not been forthcoming under any of the programs (Giloth 2000, 347). On another qualitative level, there has also been a lack of "community or system level performance data," lack of understanding of whether and how local coordination takes place (Grubb and McDonnell 1996, 254).

Overall, national studies of workforce development programs have found a modest increase in earnings and employment among men and women. This has been calculated to be $2,681 and $2,698 respectively for individuals who used the training provided by the JTPA (Decker and Berk 2011). For short-term job training the increase in earnings is in the region of $200–500 (Grubb 2001, 33). The earnings gains reported here represent an increase in hourly wages as well as hours worked but slightly more the latter however, these benefits are known to decline altogether after four to five years (Holzer 2008, 12; Grubb 2001). Studies of the WIA have been fewer but some, such as that by Hollenbeck (2005), have found 10 percent improvement on employment rates and increases in average quarterly earnings of $800 (Decker and Berk 2011, 926). Heinrich (2009) found that the impact on dislocated workers is smaller because the opportunity cost of participation is greater due to their attachment to a specific labor market (Decker and Berk 2011).

Analyses of mandatory versus voluntary programs find that results for the two seem to work about the same in their effectiveness on earnings (Holzer 2008). This finding was reflected in the results for the difference between the three ITA approaches (counseling, guidance, or maximum choice), which was minimal. However, counseling increased earnings slightly more than the other two though the guided approach is least costly so offers greater value overall (Decker and Berk 2011, 16). The effectiveness of the JTPA and WIA in the long term probably means that they are cost-effective but don't really make a huge impact when it comes to a big issue such as poverty (Holzer 2012, 12). The JTPA, for example, more than paid for itself after five years of increased earnings for beneficiaries of the program (Holzer 2008, 13).

While we have a good idea of the empirical results of the programs in terms of the concrete impact on earnings, there is a shortage of data on more qualitative measures. New labor market complexity requires an integrated approach to measurement of performance that looks at administrative impacts, policy impacts, and systemic impacts (Giloth 2000).

Geographical Disparities

Writing a year after the establishment of the MDTA program and before its impact could be properly assessed, Frank Bachmura (1963) asked what its interaction would be with other programs and the other rural communities that it aimed to support (Bachmura 1963, 61). Subsequent scholars have asked similar questions and there seems to be a consensus in the literature now that, especially in the absence of federal funding increases, coordination between different program such as training and formal education programs has been lacking (Grubb 2001, 10). Later programs such as the JTPA and the WIA became more deliberate in their coordination goals, especially in coordination of the private and public sectors that would work together to create industry-relevant skills and identify the best candidates for training and support.

It had been recognized from as early as the MDTA that local regional development was a necessary ingredient of an antipoverty program, and policies have, with moderate success, tried to give priority to people living in a target labor market area so that the training efforts would have a positive effect on local industry. This impact would in turn boost future opportunities for employment in the area. The MDTA was indeed able to attract new industries to rural areas and improve employable skills in those industries (Bachmura 1963).

Strategies for the Hard to Reach

The MDTA aimed to address two kinds of people: those affected by technology and new entrants to the workforce needing skills to fit into the new economy (Bachmura 1963). It also aimed to target the "apprentice" fields, and it embraced formal schooling as well as vocational training in order to provide increased employment opportunities for individuals with different skills and interests (Bachmura 1963, 61). Later assessments of the effectiveness of workforce development programs, however, have observed that there has been a division between training based in community colleges, on the one hand, and training for welfare recipients geared toward low-wage jobs, on the other hand (King 1999, 71). But funding streams have had difficulty in reaching both populations within the same system. Many experts have argued that this points to the fundamental difficulty of reaching the most economically disadvantaged populations.

An overarching failure of many of the workforce development programs aimed specifically at the poor is that they have been seen as ineffective despite the fact that they actually often do work (Holzer 2008). According to Giloth, there remains an unanswered question of how to bring investment to poor neighborhoods and tie it to job growth (Giloth 2000, 349). The first step in meeting this challenge is to design programs that accurately identify target groups. It is a goal which may sound easy but which is seriously complicated by the lack of demographic information and data on the progress of program participants. This problem has been present since the time of the MDTA. In fact the MDTA came under fire at the time for neglecting women. Only heads of families and households were eligible, which excludes many women from receiving the training allowance (the allowance for expenses associated with the training, not the training itself) (Bachmura 1963).

But more than merely avoiding any problems of discrimination, there is clearly a need for different programs that are tailored specifically to meet the needs of different ages and genders (Holzer 2012). Youth unemployment is particularly concerning today when the high school graduation rate continues to be remarkably low. In 2004 it was 68 percent (Brown and Thakur 2006, 91). Other disadvantaged groups continue to slip through the net of the workforce development programs even today, despite the fact that since the MDTA priority has been given to low-income customers (Decker and Berk 2011). In 2004 minority groups had only a 50/50 chance of earning a high school diploma (Brown and Thakur 2006). Three quarters of Title I WIA funding doesn't go to the disadvantaged; rather it goes to adults, youth, dislocated workers, the Job Corps, and TANF, which targets the disabled as much as poor (Holzer 2008). On top of that participants only receive training after failing in "core" and "intensive" services (WIA) (King 1999, 65).

Another reason why individuals and communities living in poverty are missed is that the programs have historically been aimed at dislocated workers: those who were laid off without cause, unemployed formerly self-employed, and victims of facility closure. This population is easiest to reach and it has also been shown to demonstrate the most marked results for the workforce development programs. Finally, there is the problem that globalization and the hollowing out of middle-wage jobs are both to blame for decreases of interest in workforce development among the disadvantaged (Holzer 2008, 9).

Brown (2006) has offered a careful analysis of the key ways that programs can be more effective in reaching disadvantaged populations. He gives around twenty suggestions but just one theme specifically seems to emerge in other literature on the subject as being a priority area of focus. There is the need for a safe and structured environment, collaboration with other organizations, particularly focusing on engagement between the private and public sector, and finally, educational programs based on state standards and professional and industry standards (Brown and Thakur 2006). These areas all touch on a feature of best practices which are shared between diverse stakeholders in the process of matching beneficiaries to useful skills that will be anchored to industry needs.

Workforce Development Programs in Maryland

Maryland offers a unique example of a state that has successfully developed workforce development programming in the context of the Workforce Investment Act of 1998. As federal funds from the U.S. Department of Labor flowed into Maryland via WIA, Maryland's Department of Labor, Licensing and Regulation (DLLR) created twelve local Workforce Investment Areas (WIAs) across the state. For each WIA "there is a Local Workforce Investment Board (LWIB), which is comprised primarily of private sector representatives, policy makers, local administrative managers and business owners" (Maryland Department of Labor, Licensing, and Regulation 2014). The LWIBs are responsible for coordinating efforts to develop workforce plans based on the needs of their particular WIA including implementing programming that best supports the needs of the specific regions under each LWIB. DLLR houses the Office of Workforce development, which offers statewide programs for veterans, offenders reentering society, and dislocated workers.

Additionally, the Office of Workforce Development has also created the Rapid Response program, a DLLR initiative that coordinates intervention strategies for not only dislocated workers but for businesses faced with reducing their workforce (State of Maryland Department of Labor, Licensing and Regulation 2012). Designed to reduce the time between positions for dislocated workers, the Rapid Response program dispatches members of its Rapid Response team to meet discreetly with companies facing potential layoffs to assess the needs of those workers being displaced and how best to coordinate services to help reduce the time between positions for these workers. Furthermore, Rapid Response teams coordinate with other divisions within DLLR, such as Veterans Services and Rehabilitative Services, to formulate a specific and targeted plan for those individuals based on the assessment of need.

VETERANS' INITIATIVES

Veterans face a unique set of challenges when attempting to secure gainful and stable employment; thus the need for targeted, veteran-specific programmatic services is a vital component to reducing unemployment and underemployment among this population. According to the 2010 Maryland Workforce Indicators Report, Maryland has roughly 300,000 working-age veterans who are identified as unemployed, underemployed, or facing barriers to employment (Maryland: Governor's Workforce Investment Board 2010). In an effort to reduce these numbers, DLLR and the state of Maryland have taken some unique steps to match veterans with sustainable jobs and job growth. Utilizing the U.S. Department of Labor's noncompetitive Jobs for Veterans State Grants Program (JVSG), DLLR has created a veteran-specific component to its One Stop Career Center that specifically targets veterans with a series of training and placement services (State of Maryland Department of Labor, Licensing and Regulation 2012).

Through the One Stop Career Centers, veterans and their eligible spouses are provided Priority of Service, receiving precedence in resources for finding employment, training, and placement services under new or existing qualified job training programs (Maryland Department of Labor, Licensing and Regulation 2013). Additionally, those veterans are enrolled into the Maryland Workforce Exchange Virtual One Stop and are referred to staff who conduct assessments to determine what barriers to employment are present, if any, as well as provide referrals to other services if they are needed. If the assessment results show significant barriers to employment exist, intensive services such as case management are available to assist veterans in finding gainful employment. If no significant barriers are present, eligible veterans can utilize the services of the One Stop Shop such as resume assistance, labor market information, and referrals to other nontraining support services such as housing assistance and mental health services.

Legislatively, the workforce development needs of Maryland's veterans were addressed in 2013 with the passing of the Veterans Full Employment Act of 2013, which was created to ease the barriers for veterans to obtain occupational and professional licenses (State of Maryland Department of Labor, Licensing and Regulation 2012). For those eligible veterans and their spouses, the act expedites applications and waiting times for licensing procedures in Maryland as well as provides veterans with credit for military training, education, and experience with regards to occupational and professional licensing's educational and experience requirements. Furthermore, DLLR increased course offerings and training programs for staff members involved in veterans' workforce development. The trainings are designed to provide DLLR's veterans' representatives with the skills and training necessary to reduce veterans' workforce barriers.

PRISONER REENTRY INITIATIVES

Individuals returning from correctional institutions are another group identified by DLLR as having high barriers to sustainable employment. As many as 150,000 individuals are released annually from Maryland correctional institutes and county jails, many with significant barriers to sustainable and gainful employment (Maryland: Governor's Workforce Investment Board. 2010). In response to the need to better provide reentry services for ex-offenders, DLLR, in coordination with the Maryland Department of Public Safety and Corrections, has created programs such as the Maryland Re-Entry Initiative (MRI), which is aimed at "strengthening coordination between the prison systems, the One Stop System, and community resources to facilitate a smoother transition from incarceration to gainful and meaningful employment" (Maryland Department of Labor, Licensing, and Regulation 2013). Additionally, the MRI program focuses on correctional education and increasing employability, which have been identified as two of the largest barriers to sustainable employment for offenders reentering society.

Working internally with DLLR's Correctional Education Division and externally with DCPCS and nongovernmental reentry organizations such as the Center for Urban Families, MRI provides technical assistance to jobseekers with a criminal background including on-the-job and occupational skills training programs, access to the One Stop Career Center resources, and educational programming focused on expectations of employers and the realities of finding employment with a criminal record (State of Maryland Department of Labor, Licensing and Regulation 2012). Furthermore, MRI administers the Federal Bonding Program, a U.S. Department of Labor program that helps to subsidize and encourage employers to hire employees "at risk" or hard-to-place job seekers, through its Local Bonding Coordinators at each of DLLR's One Stop Career Centers (Federal Bonding Program n.d).

SKILLS2COMPETE AND THE MARYLAND WORKFORCE EXCHANGE

In addition to initiatives targeted to specific groups, Maryland's "Skills2Compete" program is the state's primary vehicle for increasing job growth and improving the state's position in the emerging global economy. The program is based on the belief that postsecondary education and/or training are essential to sustainable employment. Maryland has set a goal of increasing the number of Marylanders prepared for middle- and high-skilled jobs by increasing the number of Marylanders who receive skills training through the state's workforce system by 20 percent by 2018.

Skills2Compete was conceived by the National Skills Coalition, which is an organization that works with states to improve policies that expand education, training, and skills attainment options for workers and businesses. The National Skills Coalition's goal is to encourage coordination and improve performance measurement within state-run workforce development systems, as these have been long-standing weaknesses in the administration of workforce development. Moreover, the limited resources available for workforce development make the need for efficiency even more critical.

The state has determined that "middle skill" jobs make up the largest share of the labor market and are largely a product of the continuing growth of bioscience and health care industries in the state. Recent projections show that 37 percent of all job openings between 2010 and 2020 will be in middle-skill occupations and an additional 39 percent will be in high-skill occupations. Thus, three quarters of future job openings in the state will require some kind of postsecondary credential, certificate, or degree.

Through the coordination of various state and local backers as well as private and nonprofit stakeholders, Maryland's Skills2Compete initiative reflects the need for coordination in administration of workforce development programs and resources. Skills2Compete provides integration and coordination for the state's workforce system by (1) defining a single, measurable set of postsecondary goals for skills attainment; (2) establishing a platform for cross-agency alignment and accountability across the full range of the state's human capital programs; and (3) including a system of cross-agency data collection and reporting.

Skills2Compete's strategic plan includes seven elements designed to achieve the overall goal of increasing the number of citizens in the state who receive sophisticated job-skills training. Each strategy pertains to a partner group, such as community colleges, local workforce investment boards, or the state correctional department for issues related to prisoner reentry. The internal resources of the partner groups are then leveraged in specific action steps that are intended to maximize productivity toward creating a more efficient, coordinated system in the state.

Beyond simply encouraging individuals to participate in short-term workforce development efforts, a primary goal of Skills2Compete is to encourage workers to engage more significant new skills and knowledge training efforts to align the workforce with the needs of the current and future labor market. The ability to do this is enhanced through coordination of various state and local agencies and organizations, including the Governor's Workforce Investment Board, the Maryland Department of Labor, and local workforce boards and community colleges.

Although the Skills2Compete is still not considered to be on track to meet its primary goal, the StateStat program, in coordination with the various participating state agencies, will ensure that there is continued vigilance in this effort. This performance measurement and management process provides a structure for analysis and planning, implementation, and evaluation, which is essential for improving productivity and outcomes—especially in the highly complex and stratified area of workforce development.

CONCLUSION

Workforce development has played a critical role in moving individuals out of poverty. From the Kennedy administration's vision and investments in workforce development as a means to fix structural poverty to current initiatives aimed to offset deficits in skills and training, the concept of workforce development continues to develop amid the ever-growing challenges facing America's workforce. Workforce development, now more than ever, is facing considerable challenges from the technological gaps present in the workforce to cheaper, outsourced labor available in the globalized world of the twenty-first century.

The need for stronger investments is not just present in initial education and training but continued education and training in the fastest growing segments of employment. The race is on in the global economy and the countries that are winning, and keeping their citizens out of poverty, are those that are investing heavily in a highly skilled, highly educated workforce that is accessible in all sectors of employment. The vision behind such great workforce achievements as the Manpower and Development Training Act and Vocational Retraining Act needs to be rediscovered and revisited as the gap in skills and available jobs continues to grow. Our visions and expectations as a nation are only met when we have a highly developed, highly capable citizenry to meet those expectations and build on those visions. As we move deeper into a world of highly technical, highly efficient labor, the need to keep pace and adequately develop the workforce to meet these challenges is critical to not only keeping people out of poverty but to the security and prosperity of the nation as a whole.

NOTE

1. The Workforce Investment Act (WIA) was passed during the Clinton administration in 1998. It attempted to encourage businesses to participate in local delivery of Workforce Development Services.

Chapter Thirteen

Worker Cooperatives as Models for Economic Engagement

Daphne Berry

On December 3, 1861, roughly one hundred years before John Kennedy and Lyndon Johnson would begin their roles as president and vice president of the United States, President Abraham Lincoln delivered his first annual message on the state of the union. The long written document was delivered to Congress, read and entered into record by a clerk, without fanfare of a public presentation. Although it has since been overshadowed by the rhetorical grandeur of its successors, The Gettysburg Address and the Emancipation Proclamation, Lincoln's 1861 message is vital to our understanding of America's development as a capitalist democracy:

> Labor is prior to, and independent of, capital. Capital is only the fruit of labor, and could never have existed if labor had not first existed. Labor is the superior of capital, and deserves much the higher consideration. Capital has its rights, which are as worthy of protection as any other rights. Nor is it denied that there is, and probably always will be, a relation between labor and capital, producing mutual benefits. [1]

Just shy of 7,000 words, the speech offered members of the Senate and the House of Representatives an earnest view of the nation's financial state, troubled foreign relations with Great Britain, and the Union's enervated efforts to challenge the Confederacy. It also outlined principles of "higher calling," asking Americans to remember that they were fighting for a "vast future," the key to which rested in their ability to recognize the dignity of labor.

Early in the nineteenth century, cooperative (co-op) organizations were established to help alleviate the mass unemployment and poverty that came about in the wake of the Industrial Revolution (Schaars 1971). These organizations are still recognized as a means of engaging members—workers, producers, and consumers—in businesses that benefit them as well as other stakeholders. In some cases, they have been viewed as a means of encouraging economic engagement and building wealth in low-wealth communities (Jackall and Levin 1984; MCC 2014a; Nembhard 2002).

This chapter examines the role of co-ops in addressing strategies and issues related to social and economic exclusion. It suggests that these organizations might provide a means to involve people who are often marginalized and excluded from financial opportunities, including women and some minority groups, in the broader economic and civic fabric of their communities.

I begin with an overview of the cooperative movement in the United States, with a focus on a specific subset of co-ops: worker co-ops. These organizations, owned and democratically governed by their members, operate in numerous industries and focus on sustainable, quality jobs for their members, with the workers and the interests of the larger community of stakeholders in mind. I continue with an example of a worker co-op in an industry in which co-op members, customers, and the larger community could benefit from the successful operation of the business. I conclude with a discussion of lessons we can learn from the cooperative models discussed in this chapter. Ultimately, I suggest that with the development of appropriate policy, co-ops—in particular worker co-ops—might help to shape opportunities for economic engagement including for those populations at the economic margins.

THE COOPERATIVE MOVEMENT: AN OVERVIEW

A cooperative is a business owned and run by and for its members who, depending upon the type of cooperative organization, can be employees, consumers, producers, or a combination thereof. Participation in the government of the business is voluntary and democratic, and members seek collectively to meet their economic and other needs through joint management of their resources. Members share risks and rewards (ICA 2012).

History

While there are records of cooperative mutual fire insurance companies in Europe as early as the sixteenth century, the first highly successful cooperative on which there is definite information was in England in 1705. Modern business forms of industrial co-op enterprises in the United States and abroad can be traced to mid-eighteenth-century England, when co-ops, controlled primarily by consumers, were established for milling and baking. Purchasing cooperative enterprises also existed in Western European countries before

1800. However, Schaars (1971) attributes the beginning of the cooperative movement to Robert Owens, an industrialist and factory reformer who advocated for the establishment of co-ops to counter the negative effects of the Industrial Revolution on workers. Unemployment, poor working conditions, insufficient food and housing, and illness were among the problems faced by poor people. Owen conceptualized cooperative communities for sharing land, producing and purchasing commodities, and for housing. Although his early communities failed, Owen continued to preach organized cooperation as a way to solve societal problems.

In 1828, William King, another Englishman concerned about the welfare of working people, published a magazine called "The Cooperator" which provided information and instructions on cooperative business. King extended Owens's ideas, proposing that workers save money, operate democratically, publicize cooperatives, and reinvest profits to the benefit of the business. The Rochdale cooperatives, considered the source of modern cooperative values and principles, were likely influenced by William King's writings. The Rochdale vision was to establish a self-supporting community that would produce, distribute, educate, and govern to the benefit of its members. They would own homes and land, employ members who were unemployed or worked for very low wages, and limit dividends on equity capital. There were other movements elsewhere in Europe around the mid-1850s but none more influential in the development of a movement in the United States.

In Philadelphia in 1727, Benjamin Franklin formed a mutual aid association whose members included silversmiths, glaziers, cobblers, clerks, ironmasters, and joiners. The association was motivated by self-improvement, doing good for others in a way that would also benefit members, and profit (Canada 1997). Some years later (1752), Franklin founded a mutual insurance society which is thought to be the oldest cooperative in the United States. Between 1810 and 1870, cooperative dairies, processing plants, fruit, cotton, and wool marketing, a grain elevator, and buying clubs with capital and facilities became the sites of cooperative organization in Connecticut, Wisconsin, Michigan, and New York. Legislation relevant to co-ops appeared as early as 1857 (Schaars 1971).

Types of Cooperatives

The term "co-op" includes a range of institutional formations. The National Cooperative Business Association (NCBA) identifies five types (NCBA 2014). These different forms adhere to the same basic principles but their membership and goals vary. Members of consumer cooperatives purchase goods or use the cooperative's services. Consumer co-ops include credit unions, food cooperatives, health care cooperatives, housing cooperatives, and more. This type of co-op helps its members buy at prices and/or quality not available from other types of businesses. Producer cooperatives are owned by producers of farm commodities or crafts (such as artists). They cooperate to process or market their products in order to exert more influence over prices than they might have otherwise. Next, there are purchasing cooperatives and various hybrids. Purchasing co-ops are owned by independent businesses or municipalities and band together to enhance their purchasing power for goods and services from suppliers. An example is the Harris County, Texas, Department of Education which, through co-ops, purchases commodities, facilities, and food for schools (Harris County Department of Education 2014). Hybrid co-ops might include combinations of producer, consumer, and/or worker members in agricultural or retail operations.

Finally, there are worker co-ops. In these, members are owners and workers in the business. The United States Federation of Worker Cooperatives (USFWC) identifies two central characteristics of worker cooperative businesses: 1) workers invest in the business, and receive and determine how surplus is distributed and 2) workers govern themselves democratically and each member has one vote (USFWC 2014a). Being responsible for multiple roles—owners, managers, workers, and participants on the company board of directors—worker co-op members exercise ultimate control over the organization's products and services, income, wages, benefits, day-to-day operations, and so forth. Decisions regarding how profits from the business should be allocated are made with the best interests of workers, customers, the community, and other stakeholders in mind. Since membership is voluntary, not all of the workers in a worker co-op must be owners; some choose to be employees or if the business has operations in a different country from the home base, comparable ownership may not be possible for those workers. In general, worker co-ops encourage ownership and participation in democratic work processes as these are central to their values and mission.

Worker cooperatives operate in industries such as technology (communications, web design), retail (bakeries, restaurants, bicycles, copies, coffee), manufacturing (building), and services (home care, child care, cleaning, counseling, financial planning) (USFWC 2014b). Mondragon Corporation in northern Spain provides the most well-known example of what a co-op economy can achieve.

An Exemplar: Mondragon

The Mondragon Cooperative Corporation (MCC), a model for the world of cooperatives, is based in northern Spain. MCC is currently a €14 billion conglomerate of over 100 worker-owned and affiliated enterprises. Several types of cooperatives are represented in the organization. Mondragon's history begins with a priest, Father Maria Arizmendiarrieta, who began his work in a part of Spain where the people were poor and their culturally distinct communities were marginalized by the Spanish government. Father Arizmendiarrieta started a technical training school in 1943 which laid the foundations for the first cooperative business in the Corporation. In 1956, with five former students of his school, he started Ulgor, a name which combined the names of the founders, whose surnames were Usatorre, Larrañaga, Gorroñogoitia, Ormaechea, and Ortubay (MCC 2014a). The company was funded by people in the community and its first products were electrical and mechanical products for home use. Ulgor's constitution and bylaws (with some modifications) became models for cooperative governance. Among the functions specified were a general assembly in which all members (workers) have a responsibility to vote, a top policy-making/governing council (similar to a board of directors) whose members are elected by members of the cooperative, an audit committee, and a management council. Later they added a social council (Whyte and Whyte 1991). Two years later, excluded from the general social security system, he started a mutual benefit cooperative to provide protection for the cooperatives. Then, in 1959, the priest also founded Caja Laboral Popular, a cooperative bank made up of worker members and representatives from the associate cooperatives. This institution played an important role in the success of the Mondragon cooperatives because it served as a source of capital for them. For more than twenty years, with 25 percent of their share capital, the Mondragon cooperatives guaranteed all of Caja Laboral Popular's operations. As the organizations affiliated with Mondragon grew, they all affiliated themselves legally with the bank (Freundlich 1998; MCC 2014a).

In the first two decades of MCC's operations, La Caja Laboral was central to the support organizations that MCC developed to ensure its longevity. The bank provided financing for the MCC firms, other firms in the business community, and the general public through hundreds of branches in the Basque region of Spain. La Caja Laboral also developed a division to focus on management and consulting support for new or expanding ventures. Later, as needs changed and other support functions evolved with the Mondragon institutions, La Caja Laboral turned to more traditional consumer and business banking. Another institution within MCC, the Central Intercooperative Fund, along with affiliated companies, received 10 percent of the profits of the cooperative to provide patient venture capital (long term to allow companies time for maturity[2]) while organizations within MCC provided management and technical assistance. In addition to the financial support system, other Mondragon institutions that developed over the next decades included an engineering college in 1968, the precursor to their supermarket chain (Eroski), and a research and development center. Mondragon continued to expand, and while facing the same crises that other businesses in the industrialized world faced, remained successful (Freundlich 1998). Indeed, until the latter part of 2013, MCC companies had survived two recessions intact.

Wage reductions, reassignments, retraining, and financial support are part of MCC's action plans during business slowdowns within their ranks. At first, as Spain struggled through a double-dip recession, resulting in a 26 percent unemployment rate, Mondragon shed few jobs, and its workforce remained steady at around 84,000 people worldwide with about a sixth of them outside Spain. However, in November 2013, financial troubles amid the global financial crisis resulted in a bankruptcy filing for Fagor Electrodomésticos, an electrical appliance unit within MCC (Mondragon's General Council 2013). In an announcement regarding Fagor's failure, Mondragon said that the company was not viable, was no longer responding to market needs, and that additional financial resources would not ensure the future of the business (MCC 2013).

Cooperatives in the United States

From the nineteenth century to the present, cooperatives have blossomed in the United States. The NCBA estimates there are about 30,000 co-op businesses in the United States with over 100 million members. Of these, only a relatively small number are worker co-ops. The USFWC estimates (conservatively) that there are more than 350 worker cooperatives or similarly democratic workplaces in the United States with over 5,000 workers and over $500 million in annual revenues.

The plywood industry was once the locus of the largest and most durable worker-owned firms in U.S. manufacturing. Cooperative firms in the plywood industry developed as a result of cyclical swings in the construction industry and were a good example of cooperative organizations as a response to unemployment. Because of economic insecurity resulting from the cyclical nature of work in the industry, some workers formed new businesses; others purchased firms that were failing (Craig and Pencavel 1992; Greenberg 1984). When business slowed, the plywood co-ops focused on protecting jobs and compensated by lowering wages. Greenberg (1984) highlighted other differences between the worker-owned and conventional enterprises. In the latter, workers were closely watched and supervised in contrast to the autonomy and general support experienced by workers in the cooperatives. From the late 1940s to the early 1950s, nearly a quarter of the industry's output came from the co-ops; by the late 1950s, they produced nearly all of the industry's output. However, within the decade, production in other parts of the country reduced the contribution of the co-ops in the Pacific Northwest, and by the mid-1980s, only about 50 percent of the region's output was thought to be from the co-ops, down from the highs that began in the late 1950s. Over time, the number of member (owner) workers to nonmember workers in the plywood co-ops decreased, moving the businesses toward a form in which ownership was restricted to a few who hired labor. Such a move away from cooperative principles has been noted in other firms. "Unless there are substantial efficiency advantages from worker ownership or unless there is a strong commitment to the cooperative principle, worker owners are presented with strong incentives not to dilute their special status (and perhaps income) by sharing it with new members" (Craig and Pencavel 1992, 1092). While the issue of how new members are to be accommodated is a concern for worker co-ops, some organizations have identified methods that are considered fair and acceptable to all (e.g., Mondragon and others). Some of the most successful of the plywood co-ops were bought by larger companies while others went out of business. In most of them, workers were shareholders and vice versa (Craig and Pencavel 1992, 1084). As demonstrated by the Mondragon case, the plywood co-ops, and others, and as advocated by Robert Owen, William King, and the Rochdale pioneers, co-ops and co-op communities have the potential to address some of the societal problems associated with poverty, economic and social hardship, and unemployment.

THE CASE FOR WORKER COOPERATIVES IN REDUCING POVERTY AND UNEMPLOYMENT

As we have seen, as early as nineteenth-century England, cooperatives were formed to address poverty and unemployment by providing poor people with access to housing, production, distribution, and use. This focus on the alleviation of poor living conditions and poor quality of life has continued to the present. Nembhard (2002), distinguishing between income and wealth, goes beyond the case for poverty alleviation and argues that cooperatives, because of their focus on member well-being and member democratic control, possess the characteristics necessary for member wealth creation. The one member, one vote principle that provides member control of decision making and distribution of the surplus facilitates the ability to make specific decisions about return on investment to members. Nembhard provides anecdotal support for her assertions with examples from several U.S. cooperatives employing people whose incomes were poverty level before their affiliation with a cooperative. In these cases, once affiliated with the cooperative, the members received annual dividends or profit sharing, above-average wages, benefits, and access to career advancement. Worker cooperatives have also provided those in need of steady employment with jobs in organizations in which their jobs are a priority. As mentioned, the plywood cooperatives in the Pacific Northwest provided workers with control over their ability to work in an industry with cyclical needs and, in a conventional corporate environment, cyclical employment. Mondragon's worker cooperatives were also founded in a time of high unemployment. Birchall and Ketilson (2009) argue for the potential of co-ops to spur job creation and provide more examples in which the development of co-ops is deemed an effective response to economic crisis and high unemployment. One such example involves a response to a deep recession in Finland in the early 1990s. Unemployment, which had been around 3 percent prior to the deregulation of the markets, rose to over 20 percent. Numbers of employee-owned co-ops grew to around 1,400, of which over 1,200 were labor co-ops—a combination of training agencies, employment agencies, and job seekers. The employment agencies found jobs for members who were hired out temporarily. Birchall and Ketilson (2009) also highlight cooperative development agencies in Sweden that, since 1985, have supported the startup of between 200 and 400 new co-ops each year. Most of the member co-ops are worker co-ops.

Simmons and Birchall (2008) developed several arguments in exploring the potential for co-ops to reduce poverty. First, cooperative values and principles provide built-in advantages for poverty alleviation; capital is subordinate to labor and the needs of people. The fact that poor and less poor members have equal rights means that poor members share equally in surpluses. However, since one cooperative goal is to meet the needs of members, poverty reduction is not the primary focus but a by-product of equity and democracy within the organization. Second, the history of cooperatives in developed countries includes great achievements in poverty reduction. While the early co-op movement in Britain was not led by poor people, it is important to note that while self-help and autonomy are goals of cooperatives, the goals do not preclude outside efforts in support of successful co-ops. Third, even though there have been failures within cooperatives in developing countries, these do not indicate weaknesses in the cooperative model. The failures have been related to 1) the "top-down" nature of their management—they were not "autonomous associations" of people as directed in cooperative principles but organizations that were really state enterprises; 2) the government, civil service, and political parties all had vested interests different from those of the people they were supposed to be helping; and 3) resources for co-op development were often appropriated at the local level and so did not benefit the poor. Even with the aforementioned problems, there have been notable success stories among the failures (coffee co-ops in Kenya, dairy co-ops in India and Bangladesh, and credit co-ops everywhere).

Worker co-ops, as vehicles for sustainable employment with decent wages, may also be particularly effective vehicles to address economic disadvantages in contexts outside of development.[3] The success of this particular type of co-op in the United States in making a difference in poverty reduction is being put to the test in several industries. The home care industry includes several examples. Among these examples, Cooperative Home Care Associates is the largest, longest in operation, and most successful organization. The home care industry is one in which the worker who spends the most time with clients—the home care aide—also experiences low wages and often difficult working conditions. Researchers have found that in general, caring work pays less than other kinds of work even after adjustments for educational requirements, physical demands, union membership, and other job characteristics that usually affect pay (Dresser 2008; England and Folbre 1999). This results in a particularly stubborn problem in the home care industry. Research regarding the home care industry reveals that home health aide workers who are affiliated with worker co-ops experience more overall benefits than those working for other types of home care agencies. In particular, Birchall's (Simmons and Birchall 2008) argument for opportunity, empowerment, and security are borne out even in the less-than-favorable economic conditions and day-to-day work environments of these frontline home care workers.

Worker Cooperatives in the Home-Care Field: Setting the Stage

An overview of the home health care industry is important in understanding the opportunities for cooperative generation in this field. The home care industry is part of an industry of paraprofessionals known as "direct care" workers. Direct care workers are paraprofessionals in the long-term care industry who work with people who are elderly, injured, or disabled. These workers include certified nursing assistants, home health aides, personal care assistants, direct support professionals, and workers with other similar titles (Direct Care Alliance 2014). Home health aides assist clients with Activities of Daily Living (ADLs) such as eating, dressing, bathing, and toileting, and with Instrumental Activities of Daily Living (IADLs) such as using the telephone, doing laundry, shopping, preparing food, traveling, housekeeping, taking medicines, and handling finances. Depending upon state laws, and under supervision of a nurse or therapist, home health aides also perform clinical tasks such as taking blood pressure readings, administering oral medications, administering catheters, or changing surgical dressings. The work that direct care workers do is important to not only those for whom they provide services but also to the country's social system. A report profiling the United States direct care workforce indicates that these workers provide the majority of the paid hands-on care, supervision, and emotional support to the elderly and disabled in the United States. The majority of direct care workers work in long-term-care settings. The largest occupational group, at 40 percent of direct care workers, consists of home health aides (Smith and Baughman 2007, 20).

The growth of the home care industry is driven by several factors. First, the demographic reality of an aging population has framed a number of political and economic agendas over the years in terms of providing resources for this population. With this growing elderly population and an increase in the need for home and community-based care for them, a number of questions have arisen related to services for members of this demographic and how they might be provided. Stone (2004) highlights the importance of labor policy in the preparation, ongoing training, and compensation of the workforce. Changes in federal welfare laws over the last several decades may also have influenced the makeup of the workforce in this industry. The 1996 Personal Responsibility and Work Opportunity Act (PRWORA) required that welfare recipients become immediately employed. In some states, the occupations of ex-welfare recipients were listed as direct care workers, such as nurse's aide. In others, former recipients were documented as being in the health care sector in general. However, officials from states not providing detail at the occupational level provided anecdotal information that a substantial number of former welfare recipients were nurse's aides (Filinson, Cone, and Ray 2005, 167; Stone 2004).[4] Their demographics are also a factor in the economic and social environments of home care workers.

Ninety percent of home care workers are women. Approximately one-half are (non-Hispanic) white, one third are African American, and the remaining are Hispanic and other ethnicities (Scala 2008). Since non-Hispanic whites constitute about 75 percent of the overall United States population, the figures reveal the disproportionate number (in comparison to their representation in the population as a whole) of racial and ethnic minorities performing this work. Approximately 41 percent of home care workers have high school diplomas only, and 38 percent have attended college. While there is some variation in the educational backgrounds of direct-care workers, their pay and benefits are uniformly low, particularly for those not working for private pay clients. In the United States, home health aide jobs are characterized by poverty-level wages, part-time hours, and minimal benefits such as health insurance or paid earned leave time. These workers experience a high rate of occupational injury, hazards from exposure to communicable diseases, difficult patients, high emotional demands, limited opportunities for career advancement, and the effects of high turnover (Bureau of Labor Statistics 2013). In addition, home health aides rarely feel respected by their employers or supervisors, and despite a large amount of interaction with clients, are often excluded from decision making involving care support planning (Scala 2008, 9). Not surprisingly, turnover in the industry is high.

Although co-ops are a rare organizational form among home health care businesses, they have made some progress regarding some of the problems plaguing the industry. When examining worker-owned and governed companies, Rhodes and Steers (1981) found higher perceptions of participation in decision-making, pay equity, and performance-reward contingencies in workers in worker co-op environments as compared to those in conventional organizations. These perceptions led to higher commitment to the organization and lower turnover at the cooperative (although other outcomes such as absenteeism and tardiness were higher) (Rhodes and Steers 1981). Similarly, results from my own research indicate more positive outcomes (such as job satisfaction) at a home care worker cooperatives in comparison to two conventional types of home care organizations (Berry 2013). The case of Cooperatives Home Care Associates (CHCA), a home care agency in New York City, illustrates possibilities in addressing issues of poverty and economic marginalization through a worker cooperative-based effort. CHCA is a relatively large, seasoned organization upon which the few other worker co-op home care agencies that exist in the industry are modeled.

Cooperative Home Care Associates of New York City

Cooperative Home Care Associates (CHCA) was started in 1985 as part of a sectoral strategy for poverty alleviation. The worker cooperative structure, goals, and governance were identified as a good fit for addressing labor shortages in the home care industry while providing for the economic needs of urban poor women and their families. It was started with a focus on quality home health aide jobs. The focus expanded to becoming a model of workforce and compensation practices in the industry (Inserra, Conway, and Rodat 2002). While working toward this dual mission, CHCA has grown to be the largest worker cooperative in the United States, currently employing over 2,000 home care workers. It is distinguished from other efforts at job training or promoting transition from welfare to work because it has integrated a training program with a capacity to create and sustain employment opportunities, social goals, and business planning and management skills (Stone 2004). Between 75 and 90 percent of the home care workers are also owners, and each owner has one vote in the organization's affairs. CHCA's worker owners perform caregiving work, make some of the day-to-day decisions about their work environment, and participate in planning and decision making at the board of director level, which includes making decisions about how surplus revenues are allocated. The company allocates over 80 percent of annual revenues to the wages and benefits of workers. This includes dividends and contributions to 401(k) accounts (Berry and Schneider 2011).

One of the primary ways CHCA works toward quality jobs for caregivers and quality care for clients is through its training programs for home health aides. In 2009, one year before enrolling in the cooperative's home care training program, 66 percent of participants earned less than $5,000 per year, 53 percent lacked a high school or general equivalency degree, and 60 percent were immigrants to the United States (including those born in Puerto Rico). After new participant training is complete, CHCA employs most graduates in home health aide positions. Aides have access to and are schooled on the cooperative's finances, their own finances, and job mobility. The company also provides workers with retention support services such as a guaranteed hours program, a peer mentor program helping them transition successfully to employment, and coaching supervision to address problems in a nonpunitive environment while ensuring accountability (Berry and Schneider 2011). While earning home health aide certification in New York State requires only seventy-five hours of training, CHCA provides more in support of caregiver access to the many critical clinical and interpersonal skills involved in providing clients with quality services. CHCA worker owners also receive ongoing training and education in other areas toward the cooperative goal of full economic inclusion and participation. Indeed, because at one time at least, former welfare recipients comprised almost 85 percent of the workforce, CHCA's success is particularly extraordinary.

Home health aides at CHCA participate in workgroups focused on child care, health care, home care worker safety, and outward-looking matters such as service delivery and home care policy, developing a stance and preparing cooperative representatives to meet legislators. Speaking of two of their workgroups, one home care aide says:

> We [the Policy Action Group] advocate for ourselves and for our clients. We go to lobby in Albany every year and we're just about the only home care agency that goes all the time without the home care association. . . . On the Quality Improvement Group, we find ways to improve conditions and safety issues. . . . Some places [neighborhoods] are not that good. (from interview with CHCA home health aide, as cited in Berry and Schneider 2011)

This heavy focus on training and education is augmented by the efforts of the home care workers' union. Since 2003, CHCA's home care workers have also been represented by the 1199 SEIU United Healthcare Workers East, an affiliate of the Service Employees International Union (SEIU). The union advocates for higher wages and improved working conditions, educates and empowers workers to seek social and economic justice, and encourages members to acquire greater knowledge and skill in the health care sector (Berry and Schneider 2011). Despite the advocacy of the cooperative and the union, for the large majority of home care aides, pay and benefits are low. A recurring theme in discussions with home health aides is their need for better pay. A worker from another agency summed up the issue: "Taking care of patients is a hard job. I believe we should make $10 an hour for the work we have to do in patients' homes. We aides go through a lot with these patients" (Berry 2013). While Whitaker, Schneider, and Bau (2005) cite pay rates 20 percent higher for CHCA workers than other agencies in the city, at rates of less than $10/hour in New York City, being able to live without public assistance is still difficult for some.

Research regarding employee ownership along with participation in decision making in firms points to better productivity outcomes for those organizations (Kruse, Freeman, and Blasi 2010). In the case of research with

CHCA and other agencies at which neither participatory decision making nor ownership in the firm were present, workers at the cooperative indicated higher job-related attitudes such as job satisfaction than at the other agencies. Although sharing a common regulatory environment, pay scales, benefits, and access to unions, as workers at the other two agencies surveyed, the workers indicated that the cooperative workplace was significantly different in many productivity-related areas (Berry 2013). This outcome is also notable because in much of the direct care industry (albeit mostly in nursing home environments), as well as in other industries, studies of worker attitudes reveal different findings in nonprofit organizations and for-profit firms. In this research on the worker cooperative outcomes are different.

CHCA's support network includes a nonprofit agency, Paraprofessional Health Care Institute (PHI), which also advocates for quality home care jobs for direct care workers. PHI focuses its research, policy, and training expertise toward helping formerly unemployed women achieve economic independence. In keeping with their common mission with CHCA, PHI works with providers, consumers, labor advocates, and policymakers to strengthen home care jobs by developing recruitment, training, and supervision best practices and engaging federal policymakers on health care, aging, and workforce policy in the long-term-care sector (PHI 2014).

LESSONS OF HOME CARE AND THE WORKER COOPERATIVE MODEL

The example of CHCA provides several lessons for how worker cooperatives might be enlisted in efforts to address poverty reduction. History has shown that cooperatives, in general, have advantages in improving the economic conditions of people who are poor. The cooperative focus on labor as at least of equal importance to capital in enterprise is key in worker cooperative governance. This provides poorer members equal access, equal participation in decision making, and equal control of surplus.

Birchall and Ketilson (2009) have noted that where there have been failures of worker co-ops in developing countries, the co-ops were casualties of top down management and were state enterprises with interests directed elsewhere than toward members' welfare. In addition, they point out that resources were appropriated and not allowed to benefit the poor. In the case of the home care industry and CHCA, the organization was also begun by an affiliated nonprofit agency on behalf of unemployed people. That both those beginning and those subsequently participating in decisions made at the organization (including home health aides) kept cooperative principles of democratic member control—education, training, and information sharing—and concern for community in the forefront is clear. At CHCA, the results of ongoing training, active participation in organization life, and better compensation can be seen in increased skills, better worker attitudes, and increased tenure in the jobs. These are needed for a sustainable, autonomous, self-directed organization to succeed. But in the case of the home care industry, heavy affiliation with the state through regulatory and training controls and pay, past failures in enforcing equitable labor protections, and insufficiently high reimbursements for home care services to many clients is, perhaps, a cautionary tale. Since much of the funding for home care services and home health aide compensation comes from government sources, the long-standing exclusion of home health aides from the wage and overtime minimums specified by the Fair Labor Standards Act (FLSA) through an exemption provided to employers is a prime example of state interests not focused toward these workers (referencing Birchall's argument for co-ops in poverty reduction). These exclusions have been materially detrimental to the economic, social, and physical well-being of home health aides. However, the law has changed, and as of January 1, 2015, home health aides will be protected along with the millions of other workers covered by the FLSA. Nevertheless, the damage done to perceptions of the job and those who perform it lingers. Birchall and other have also noted (Birchall and Ketilson 2009; Jackall and Levin 1984a; Nembhard 2002) that cooperatives need networks of supporting institutions in order to maintain the autonomy that allows their focus on cooperative principles to survive and thrive. They need banking institutions to help supply capital, technical assistance for current and new co-ops, education and training systems, and a legal framework that supports collective ownership and operation. These support systems, found to be necessary at a minimum, were developed by a successful conglomerate such as the Mondragon cooperatives. Such a framework is even included in the cooperative principles: cooperatives are to serve members and strengthen the cooperative movement by working with local, national, regional, and international structures (toward realization of their principles and goals) (USFWC 2014c).

Research has shown that key characteristics of worker cooperatives such as ownership and participation in decision making are associated with the higher job satisfaction, higher organizational commitment, and lower turnover or intent to turnover (Berry 2013; Jackall and Levin 1984b; Rhodes 1981). CHCA reports better wages and benefits for their caregivers than other home care agencies in New York City (Whitaker et al. 2005). There is consensus that the focus of home care worker cooperatives on better jobs for caregivers, including steady hours, and an accompanying focused use of available resources, coalesce to result in (at least marginally) increased overall earnings for workers (Nembhard 2002; Whitaker et al. 2005). Low reimbursement rates from the federal government and the disproportionate numbers of conventional for-profit agencies in the United States that have dominated the industry, combined with no legal (or other) mandates for quality worker jobs or decent compensation have made sustaining a business with cooperative goals difficult in this industry. Nevertheless, what is notably different between home health aides at CHCA and those from other agencies is that worker co-op aides report respect from supervisors, trust in management, feelings that their voices are heard, and that they can work together with others who care about the work they do and about the clients they care for toward change for the better.

CONCLUSION

President Abraham Lincoln's exhortation that "Labor deserves higher consideration than capital" is telling given that it was part of his address to the nation regarding how people should perceive work, capital, and human labor. It was written as an exhortation to people of the United States to consider that those who labor should not be considered less human because of their lack of capital (neither those who were enslaved nor poor people who were not enslaved). More than 150 years later, we still find ourselves struggling with problems closely linked to subordination of labor to capital and a devaluation of certain types of labor, in particular that performed by certain groups of people. Worker cooperatives, by their very principles of autonomy, democracy, and control of the fruits of one's labor, work at the heart of these problems.

This chapter has presented some of the opportunities related to the worker co-op enterprises and examined them in the context of poverty alleviation. It has also illustrated some of the challenges related to a specific occupation in the direct care industry. CHCA is a success story with respect to providing sustainable jobs to people, many of whom were formerly unemployed, and providing them with job training and financial training related to the business, and therefore some level of upward mobility. In addition, these (mostly) women experience a sense of empowerment as owners and as workers who participate in decisions about many aspects of their work and how the business is run. By these measures, the worker co-ops have provided improved situations for this group of formerly unemployed workers. Given the high and increasing demand for well-trained, caring workers in this field, it is one in which the development of worker cooperatives might prove to be a strategy for creating jobs and building opportunities. However, if the extremely low wages and benefits for workers providing essential services to this large and growing segment of the nation's population continue to persist, there will continue to be problems from multiple perspectives: job tenure for workers and firms, quality care for those who need it, and the ills associated with poverty level wages for workers and communities. Many of the primarily women working in this industry, including some at the worker cooperative, must still be recipients of government assistance to be able to live. With much of the funding for home care services coming from government sources, this is a problem that federal and state governments should attend to.

CHCA, as a worker cooperative, seeks to maximize benefits to workers at whatever level the business is able to do so. In many other types of home care agencies, there are no such principles; indeed to the contrary, they capitalize on government exclusions to facilitate corporate retention of surplus and workers are disadvantaged in multiple ways. Cooperative principles are guidelines for organizations that seek to have labor and the people who labor occupy a central position in the relationship between labor and capital. For the home care industry to take full advantage of the benefits of the worker co-op form, attention must be paid to the interests of the women who do the work, not only providing job training and increasing their self-efficacy, but also compensating them fairly for their labors. CHCA is envisioned by stakeholders near and far as a sectoral strategy (home care) that is a model type of organization for addressing poverty because of its potential to address the needs of this workforce while also addressing the nation's need in this industry (Stone 2004; Conway et al. 2007).

Finally, there needs to be a national policy framework that not only encourages the development of cooperatives, and worker cooperatives in particular, but also supports the development of supporting networks for them. The Mondragon example provides a prime example of a committed and focused support network (see also Luviene's description of a civic infrastructure [2010]) for a cooperative community to thrive. Drawing from the example of Mondragon, we know that such infrastructure involves banks, continuously replenished venture capital-type funds for cooperative assistance, ideally an educational system such as a cooperative college, a legal framework that supports cooperative-type businesses, and not least, a network of cooperative businesses that have the support of not only their communities but also like-minded institutions. Some communities have begun to build efforts in these areas. The Evergreen Cooperatives provides one example. Their framework includes a worker cooperative laundry, a company focused on green energy such as solar panels, and a greenhouse growing several types of lettuce and herbs. In addition, "anchor institutions," nonprofit organizations that do not relocate and are committed to the economic development of local communities, are part of the support network. Finally, the overall national policy framework focused on cooperatives should include education for the U.S. population about what they are. As Jackall and Levin (1984) point out, as long as there is no civic literacy about cooperatives, their advantages can never be fully explored.

NOTES

1. http://www.presidency.ucsb.edu/ws/?pid=29502.
2. http://www.sba.gov/content/venture-capital.
3. Broadly related to poverty reduction.
4. Because available data did not sufficiently distinguish between the paraprofessional long-term care occupations, it is not possible to always distinguish here between nursing assistants/aides and home care aides.

Chapter Fourteen

Inclusive Capitalism and Poverty Alleviation

David Madland, Karla Walter, and Alex Ingrams

President Lyndon B. Johnson sparked the creation of the modern-day American safety net when he launched the War on Poverty in 1964. The War on Poverty and President Johnson's Great Society platform to address economic and racial inequalities created a federal assistance infrastructure that allowed millions of Americans to escape poverty; it remains foundational for fighting poverty today. As a result of these programs and a strong American economy, the number of Americans living in poverty fell by 42 percent in the first decade after the President's launch of the initiative (Ross et al. 1987). And today, federal safety net programs continue to reduce American poverty rates nearly by half. In fact, it is estimated that without War on Poverty policies, as well as innovations introduced after the Johnson era, such as the Earned Income Tax Credit, the portion of Americans living in poverty today would increase from 16 percent to 29 percent (Center on Budget and Policy Priorities 2014).[1] Yet, despite these improvements, nearly 50 million Americans remain stuck in poverty and dramatic changes in the American economy over the last half century have made it much more difficult for Americans to escape poverty.

In 1964, the year President Johnson announced the War on Poverty, the economy was booming. Additionally, historically low unemployment rates, strong labor market intermediaries such as unions, and long-standing government investments in infrastructure and education allowed workers to share in the benefits of this growing prosperity (Boteach et al. 2014). As a result, throughout the middle part of the twentieth century, workers were rewarded for their productivity increases with higher wages on roughly a one-to-one basis; as they become more productive, they received a corresponding increase in compensation.

Today, American workers at the very bottom confront vastly different labor market conditions. High unemployment rates, historically low unionization rates, and declining government investments in public goods make it harder for Americans at the middle and bottom to get ahead. Wages have decoupled from productivity, and low-wage workers are particularly disadvantaged. While in 1968, four years into the War on Poverty, the federal minimum wage reached an all-time high of $10.75 in real terms, since then, it has fallen 33 percent to $7.25 in 2014.[2]

At the same time, those at the very top of the income spectrum are doing the best they ever have; they are doing so, in part, because they are getting a bigger piece of the economic pie than ever before. According to a recent report from the Center on Budget and Policy Priorities, the share of national income going to the top one percent of households doubled between 1964 and 2012, from 11 percent to 22 percent (Parrott 2014). Today, the top 5 percent of the wealthiest Americans own two-thirds of household stock wealth (Stiglitz 2012).

And, despite the advances the War on Poverty made in ensuring a vital safety net to improve conditions for Americans living in poverty, we have made too little progress in ensuring that Americans can escape the cycle of poverty. A new study led by Raj Chetty, Professor of Economics at Harvard University, finds that a child born into a disadvantaged economic position today is just as likely to climb the economic ladder as a child born more than fifty years ago (Chetty et al. 2014).

Today, more than ever, Americans stuck at the bottom need government policies that don't just provide assistance to bring them just above the poverty threshold; they need more active labor market interventions designed to ensure that the private sector again supplies the sorts of good jobs that give workers a real shot at attaining middle-class status. From granting workers earned sick leave to raising the minimum wage to a livable wage to ensuring that workers are able to freely choose to join together in unions, there are many policy options to raise standards among private sector employers.

In addition, government should encourage companies to adopt programs that reward workers for a portion of the wealth they help create—a concept we call inclusive capitalism. From broad-based profit sharing and stock options to worker cooperatives and employee stock ownership plans, this kind of compensation goes well beyond simply paying wages or providing individual incentives; rather, it involves granting workers ownership stakes in the company or a share of its profits based on workers' collective performance.

Inclusive capitalism, when partnered with democratic workplace practices, has a proven record of helping workers and businesses alike in a myriad of ways. Moreover, if more widely adopted, it could help alleviate poverty, increase the wealth of low-wage workers, and reduce the income disparities between the very rich and the rest of working Americans. Despite this potential, policy to advance inclusive capitalism has not been part of the national dialogue for quite some time—and policymakers have never broadly embraced inclusive capitalism as a tool to reduce poverty.

Studies of inclusive capitalism have demonstrated its effectiveness in realizing a wide range of benefits. For workers, inclusive capitalism is associated with higher pay, expanded benefits and greater job security, participation in decision making, trust in the company and management, and better labor-management relations (Blasi et al. 2010; Buchele et al. 2010). For businesses, inclusive capitalism is often associated with increased productivity and profitability and a greater likelihood of corporate survival. In addition, companies benefit from greater worker loyalty and effort, lower turnover rates, and an increased willingness on the part of workers to suggest innovations (Buchele et al. 2010; Blasi and Kruse 1997; Park et al. 2004; Blair et al. 2000; Kruse 2002; Kaarsemaker 2006; Freeman 2007; Kruse et al. 2012). Finally, inclusive capitalism in the form of worker ownership is often thought to benefit democracy by giving workers a real, participatory role in their work life that can translate into their civic life (Smith 1985; Freeman 2007). Yet far too few workers enjoy the benefits of broad-based sharing programs. More than half of American workers do not have access or choose not to participate in inclusive capitalism programs and most participating workers receive only very modest amounts of income from these programs (Kruse, Blasi, and Park 2008).

What's more, sharing programs are sometimes implemented in ways that take advantage of workers. On occasion, companies have implemented sharing programs that expose workers to excessive risk, using the programs as a substitute for good wages and benefits or providing their workers little say on the job. Neither workers nor firms benefit from inclusive capitalism when workers are marginalized. Research suggests that the most successful broad-based sharing programs are those in which workers have a high level of trust of management, are paid wages at or above the market rate, and have a high level of job security and involvement in decision making over their work at the individual task level and at the department level. And for low-wage workers, ensuring that risk is mitigated and that the variable pay inherent in sharing programs does not jeopardize their financial well-being is particularly important.

The purpose of this chapter is to provide baseline knowledge that is essential to creating a broad discussion about inclusive capitalism policy as a tool to fight poverty. To help achieve this goal, the chapter describes the types of inclusive capitalism that firms currently practice and briefly reviews the history of federal policy in this area. Additionally, we highlight some key questions about how existing inclusive capitalism policy is working and the challenges to ensuring that inclusive capitalism helps all workers. Addressing these questions will be important for any future policy development. Lastly, we discuss the policies that could boost the use of inclusive capitalism programs in companies that employ low-wage workers.

We hope that it helps provide a path forward for academics interested in further investigating the capacity of these sorts of policies to alleviate poverty as well as advocates and policymakers to support broad-based and sustainable capital-sharing programs.

WHAT IS INCLUSIVE CAPITALISM?

The private sector has adopted a variety of programs to share capital ownership and capital-related income with their workers. These practices range from employee stock ownership plans and worker cooperatives (which allow workers an ownership stake in the company) to cash-based profit- and gain-sharing programs (which pay workers a portion of the capital-related income they helped generate but do not grant ownership).

The connection between all types of inclusive capitalism is that they compensate a broad base of workers—not just top executives—on the basis of group performance rather than individual performance. Some of these programs fundamentally change workers' relationships with their employers and provide significant capital payments, while others have fairly modest effects on workers. Here we describe the essential features of each type:

- *Worker cooperatives* are typically started by ideologically affiliated workers and are owned and democratically controlled by their member owners. Co-ops offer employees a purchase of equal-sized shares in the company. They are businesses that are majority or 100 percent owned by the employees, and each owner has voting rights in company decision making.
- *Employee Stock Option Plans (ESOPS)* are tax-qualified employee benefit plans that, with some exceptions, offer workers an ownership stake in their company without having to spend their own money to purchase stock. ESOP companies set up a trust fund into which they contribute new shares of its own stock or cash to purchase existing shares (Horwath 2008).[3] When workers retire or leave the company, they receive their stock, which the company must buy back at its fair market value unless the worker is able to sell it in the public market.
- *401(k)s in company stock* are retirement plans under which workers and companies make pretax contributions from their pay to buy company stock or the company gives employees company stock as a match to employee contributions. The government has increasingly scrutinized

401(k)s with investments in employer stock, as these plans have become the primary retirement vehicle for many workers. The government has made a number of changes to regulations in order to encourage investment diversity.

- *Stock options, restricted stock, phantom stock, and stock appreciation rights*[4] tie benefits to either the value of shares (as in restricted stock and phantom stock) or increases in stock prices (as with options and stock appreciation rights). Workers may or may not ever actually own shares except for during a very short period, when the awards are exercised.
- *Employee stock purchase plans (ESPPs)* subsidize the purchase of stocks outside of the retirement system, typically offering workers stock at a 10 percent to 15 percent price discount, usually at the lower price over a specified "offering period." Enrolled employees buy company shares with after-tax contributions deducted from their paychecks over the course of the offering period.
- *Profit sharing* payments can be either in cash (such as annual cash bonuses) or employer contributions of stock. Profit sharing becomes employee ownership when profits are received in the form of stock. There are two types of profit sharing: (1) cash profit sharing, and (2) deferred profit sharing that is paid out at retirement, death, disability, or sometimes at separation from service.
- *Gain sharing* plans give workers payments based on the performance of their unit rather than the entire company. Performance is typically measured as productivity or cost savings, and payments are typically made in cash.

This distinct repertoire of programs variously described as *shared capitalism*, *broad-based capitalism*, *partnership capitalism*, *universal capitalism*, or *inclusive capitalism* embraces about half of all employees in the economy—53.4 million workers in total (Madland and Walter 2013). According to the General Social Survey (2006 and 2010), 38 percent and 27 percent of workers participate in profit sharing and gain sharing, respectively, and 18 percent and 9 percent are stock owners or get stock options, respectively (Kruse et al. 2008).[5] Across the entire workforce, about 5 percent of workers are enrolled in ESOPs (Ibid.). Although thousands of large-, medium-, and small-sized businesses today use some form of inclusive capitalist programs, both the number of companies using inclusive capitalism, and the ways in which it is used, are very limited, given the urgency of today's wealth inequalities and inclusive capitalism's potential for poverty alleviation.

A BRIEF HISTORY OF INCLUSIVE CAPITALISM

In 1964 President Johnson declared a War on Poverty and established the Office of Economic Opportunity (OEO), the agency responsible for administering programs of the Economic Opportunity Act. Johnson promised to "strike away the barriers to full participation," and used the War on Poverty to create a federal assistance infrastructure that included programs such as the Supplemental Nutrition Assistance Program, formerly known as food stamps, Head Start, Medicaid, Pell Grants, Medicaid, and Medicare.

Though the effort was impressively broad, encompassing the "social, economic, legal, educational, and psychological" aspects of poverty, these programs focused on building the social safety net rather than on creating the kind of worker participation that would abate the inequalities of workplace pay and ownership (Cahn and Cahn 1964; Johnson 1964). Efforts to increase participation in broad-based sharing programs or other efforts to raise standards among private employers were not generally a part of the agenda.

Yet, as the program was debated, some advocates for the poor argued for more active interventions into the labor market to ensure that everyone could share the prosperity our nation was creating and that the private sector supplied good jobs throughout the economy that gave workers a real shot at the middle class. For example, while testifying before Congress in April 1964, Walter Reuther, President of the United Autoworkers, argued that "while [the proposals] are good, [they] are not adequate, nor will they be successful in achieving their purposes, excepting as we begin to look at the broader problems [of the United States' economy]. . . . Poverty, essentially, is a reflection of our failure to achieve a more rational, more responsible, more equitable distribution of the abundance that is now within our grasp" (House Committee on Education and Labor 1964). Moreover, the exclusion of inclusive capitalism programs represents a missed opportunity both in terms of raising the incomes and wealth of low-income workers and in generating bipartisan support.

Conservatives have attacked the War on Poverty virtually since the inception of the program. The lack of "buy-in" by significant political stakeholders has been viewed as a reason for the eventual defunding of a central plank of the War on Poverty, the Community Action Agencies, in 1968 (Melish 2010). And recent budget fights over fully funding SNAP demonstrate the ongoing partisan divide over safety net programs (Long et al. 2014).

Still, American policymakers of all political stripes have supported private sector–inclusive capitalism programs through both their words and policies since the founding of our nation (Coates 1991). Their ideas about how and why inclusive capitalism helps strengthen our nation have varied greatly, but policymakers have broadly agreed that our democracy and marketplace are stronger when workers can share in the capital their labor helps create.

In the decades following the War on Poverty, support for inclusive capitalism programs has crossed ideological and political divides and has been supported for a variety of reasons. Policymakers have argued that these programs boost profits and productivity, promote workplace participation, improve labor relations, bolster our capitalist system, ensure sustainable economic growth, deliver equitable compensation for workers, and even provide a bulwark against communism.

Former Vice President Hubert H. Humphrey Jr. argued that broad-based ownership was one of the pillars of our economy:

> capital and the question of who owns it and therefore reaps the benefit of its productiveness, is an extremely important issue that is complementary to the issue of full employment. . . . I see these as the twin pillars of our economy: Full employment of our labor resources and widespread ownership of our capital resources. Such twin pillars would go a long way in providing a firm underlying support for future economic growth that would be equitably shared. (Humphrey 1976)

And while President Ronald Reagan famously declared "poverty" the victor in the War on Poverty, he endorsed employee ownership as a form of "people's capitalism":

> The energy and vitality unleashed by this kind of People's Capitalism—free and open markets, robust competition, and broad-based ownership of the means of production—can serve this nation well. (Reagan 1987)

We highlight these two examples because they demonstrate the support of inclusive capitalism at various times by notable leaders at both ends of the political spectrum. Many others have endorsed policies encouraging employee ownership precisely because of the universal appeal of its numerous social and economic benefits.

Federal Policies to Promote Inclusive Capitalism

The current policy framework for inclusive capitalism started in the 1920s and has advanced episodically in a few infrequent waves of popularity. Policymakers have generally focused on supporting specific types of inclusive capitalism programs—especially deferred profit sharing and employee stock ownership plans—rather than promoting inclusive capitalism broadly. Moreover, both Republicans and Democrats have taken lead roles in advocating for policies to support inclusive capitalism.

This type of bipartisan support continues today among conservative leaders such as Rep. Dana Rohrabacher (R-CA) and Sen. Kelly Ayotte (R-NH) and progressives such as Sen. Bernie Sanders (I-VT) and Rep. Chaka Fattah

(D-PA), who all have sponsored legislation to expand government support for inclusive capitalism.[6]

Deferred Profit Sharing

The concept of profit sharing started in the private sector. Large companies such as Proctor & Gamble, Sears Roebuck and Co., Eastman Kodak Co., and S. C. Johnson & Son, Inc., began adopting profit sharing plans in the late nineteenth and early twentieth centuries in an attempt to combat labor unrest and unionization and to improve worker performance (Jacoby 1998). Profit sharing was first popularized in France in the nineteenth century and adopted in companies throughout Europe but, by the early twentieth century had become more pervasive in the United States than in other countries (Ibid., 13–14).

Initially, no government policies to encourage this type of sharing existed. However, in 1921 Congress passed the Revenue Act, which provided tax incentives to stock bonus and profit sharing plans.[7] Congress primarily intended the provisions as a way to motivate workers to be more productive but had the secondary goal of increasing savings among workers (Tax Policy 1987; Databook on Employee Benefits 2009). The new policy was intended to benefit companies and workers alike.

These tax incentives, however, did little to encourage the adoption of sharing programs at the time. Income tax rates on companies and individuals were so low, and so few workers paid income tax, that companies and workers gained little benefit from the favorable tax rules for sharing plans. Moreover, once the Great Depression hit, many employers terminated their sharing plans or failed to pay out the benefits (Moody 1938).

As the economy slowly began to recover, companies returned to profit sharing and federal policymakers looked to incent these practices further. In 1938 the Democratic-controlled U.S. Senate convened a "profit-sharing" committee, but it was the Republican representing Michigan, Arthur H. Vandenberg, who became the de facto leader of the committee (Ibid.).[8]

During the hearings, *The Milwaukee Journal* conjectured that profit sharing would be the "Republicans' New Deal," speculating that Republicans might try to use this private sector benefits program in the same way Democrats were setting up public sector social safety net programs (Ibid.; Jacoby 1998).[9] Vandenberg even toyed with the idea of providing broad tax incentives for profit sharing, but the final committee report recommended only that profit sharing contributions be exempt from payroll taxes, which Congress approved in 1939 (Ghilarducci 1992).

Profit sharing's real comeback took place during World War II, when companies adopted generous deferred profit sharing programs to attract scarce labor. Such benefits for workers were exempted from the wage and price controls the U.S. government instituted to protect against inflation. Furthermore, the War Labor Board gave employers even more encouragement by allowing them to transfer excess profits to deferred profit-sharing plans, thus avoiding government taxes designed to limit corporate profits to their prewar levels (Jacoby 1998). Half of all the profit-sharing plans in existence in 1947 were created during the war, according to labor historian Sanford Jacoby (1998). During the 1950s and 1960s, the number of profit-sharing plans continued to grow with federal government support (Jacoby 1998; Sharing The Profits 1954). Companies adopted these programs to serve as a supplement to other retirement programs and were further encouraged, because government allowed income from deferred profit sharing plans to be taxed at lower rates for capital income (Kruse, Blasi, and Park 2008).[10]

Subsequently, policymakers have taken less of an interest in encouraging the use of profit sharing. But employers still take advantage of the tax incentives available for deferred profit sharing programs, and today, about 20 to 30 percent of workers participate in deferred profit-sharing plans, according surveys from the Bureau of Labor Statistics (Moody 1938; Jacoby 1998).[11]

Employee Stock Ownership Plans

Employee stock ownership plans are the other type of inclusive capitalism that have a long and enduring history of government support. Today, these plans are one of the most prevalent forms of employee ownership, and their growth could not have happened without government interventions.

San Francisco lawyer and investment banker Louis Kelso started the first leveraged employee stock ownership plan, which enabled the employees of Peninsula Newspapers in Palo Alto, California, to buy the company from its founders in 1956. Kelso's idea—to use financial leverage to allow employees to purchase the company they worked for without having to spend any of their own money—had never been done before. Peninsula Newspapers needed a special exemption from the Internal Revenue Service in order to do so since the 1954 tax code prohibited borrowing by a tax-qualified plan from the plan sponsor or related entities.[12]

The IRS exemption allowed a limited number of companies to institute employee stock ownership plans, but Kelso was a true evangelist for these plans and supported more widespread employee ownership. He believed that by allowing workers to "sell" their labor in exchange for capital, policymakers could ensure stable income for workers—even as technological change exerted downward pressure on wages. Owning part of the firm, Kelso argued, would allow workers to receive compensation for their labor as well as their capital. Kelso said these types of arrangements would help stabilize the economy and promote democracy (Adler and Kelso 1958; Buxton and Menke 2010).[13]

Kelso won over a crucial supporter in Sen. Russell Long (D-LA). Long, like his father Huey Long, the populist Louisiana governor, was concerned about inequality and economic justice. Long held a front seat in the crafting of tax policy as chair of the Senate Finance Committee with (or for) whom he oversaw the design and reconciliation of the Employee Retirement Income Security Act of 1974; in turn, Long was eventually able to insert the ESOP definition and an exemption to the rule in the final version of the act (Buxton and Menke 2010).[14]

To date, federal policymakers have continued to support the expansion of employee stock ownership plans and have remained focused on using tax incentives to do so. Indeed, American policymakers from across the ideological spectrum continue to support specific types of sharing for the same reasons supporters have championed them throughout history: inclusive capitalism can be good for businesses and workers; it can be a boon to capitalism; and it can ensure sustainable economic growth.

Unfortunately, even though employers frequently adopt multiple types of sharing programs within the workplace, policymakers and activists also continue a siloed approach to the promotion of sharing policies.[15] Policy advocates lobby solely for their specific brand of inclusive capitalism rather than offering broader support for all types of sharing programs. Likewise, only a small minority of academic research studies the effects of more than one type of sharing,[16] and niche industries have developed to support private sector development of single types of sharing.

As a result, sharing policies tend to be viewed as serving niche communities rather than as a means by which to promote broader economic goals, such as alleviating poverty, rebuilding the middle class, or boosting high road standards across private employers. What's more, government policies to support sharing are very uneven across the various types of programs, and policy makers have not tackled some tough questions about how to ensure government policies that encourage inclusive capitalism also protect workers' interests.

FUNDAMENTAL QUESTIONS ABOUT INCLUSIVE CAPITALISM POLICIES

Governments have implemented a variety of policy mechanisms to support inclusive capitalism and in the decades following the War on Poverty, companies steadily increased their use of inclusive capitalism programs. These practices hold the potential to both improve business performance and provide workers with higher levels of compensation.

However, policymaker support for inclusive capitalism policies is relatively narrow.[17] Policymakers who support expanded use of inclusive capitalism policies often do so, because they have personal experience with it—as is the case with Indiana's state treasurer, who created a program to increase lending to employee stock ownership plans (ESOP Linked 2010)—or are focused on serving a specific constituency that lobby on one particular form of inclusive capitalism. Most telling, even during the current economic downturn—a time when elected officials are especially hungry for economic policy ideas to reduce inequality and support low-income and middle-class workers—inclusive capitalism policies are not a part of the larger national conversation.

Federal lawmakers introduced nine bills and resolutions that would have expanded government support for inclusive capitalism during the 112th session of Congress.[18] Yet, only the most modest piece of inclusive capitalism legislation received a vote: Senate Resolution 87 designating 2012 as the International Year of Cooperatives was passed by unanimous consent. None of the other bills have even had a committee hearing or received broad public recognition.

This lack of legislative action is due in part to the fact that there are several challenging questions that researchers and supporters of inclusive capitalism will need to address in order to build a broader dialogue around the potential for inclusive capitalism policies to address some of the fundamental challenges within our economy. One of the most prevalent questions includes,

> How do you ensure all workers—including low-wage workers, workers of color, and women—are able to access inclusive capitalism programs?

Inclusive capitalism's associated benefits of higher pay, expanded benefits, and greater job security; participation in decision making; trust in the company and management; and better labor-management relations do not occur equally for all kinds of workers (Blasi et al. 2010; Buchele et al. 2010). Research by Edward Carberry, at the University of Massachusetts Boston, indicates that workers of color and women are both less likely to participate in inclusive capitalism programs than white male workers and, when they do, they receive a smaller financial reward for participating in these programs. Carberry finds that these inequities are caused by occupational segregation; lower levels of educational attainment and fixed pay; and the ways in which companies structure and operate the plans. In addition, African American workers are less likely to participate in inclusive capitalism programs when they are able to choose to do so. As a result, Carberry concludes that employees with higher incomes are more likely to participate in sharing programs than low-income workers (Carberry 2010).

Moreover, since sharing programs are more likely to include higher income workers, in practice, they are not helping to fulfill their promise of reducing earnings and wealth inequality in the United States. Other scholars, such as Joan Meyers of Rutgers University, have noted that IC companies still tend to replicate the existing occupational segregation in the workforce rather than address it (Meyers 2005). Some unique characteristics of IC companies, such as their emotional and social appeal, have been found to favor elite workers. Low-wage workers can sometimes be crowded out (Sirianni 1993).

Advocates are looking for new ways to ensure that low-income workers both participate in, and benefit from, sharing programs. For example, the Evergreen Cooperatives of Cleveland, Ohio, are a loose-knit association of worker cooperatives that include a commercial laundry, a newspaper company, a solar panel and energy efficiency installation company, and a hydroponic urban greenhouse (Schor 2011, 4). They provide living wages for low- to medium- to high-skilled jobs in companies that are jointly owned by every person who works there. Every year, 10 percent of the profits of the cooperative are put back into the local community, so that more local cooperatives can be created. In order to ensure that the workers share in the growth, member businesses cannot be sold outside of the area. The founders of the cooperative calculate that they will give every participating worker an equity stake worth $85,000 after eight years, generate 5,000 new jobs within fifteen years, and rejuvenate a region that has recently experienced unemployment at 30 percent (Howard et al. 2010).

Researchers, advocates and policymakers should consider how to eliminate barriers to full participation in sharing programs among low-wage workers, workers of color, and women, and consider how to specifically target greater use of sharing programs in companies and industries that include low-income workers.

How Much of Worker Pay Should Be Variable?

Workers accept an additional measure of risk—with the promise of a potentially larger reward—by participating in inclusive capitalism policies and accepting that a portion of their pay will be variable. But just how much risk workers should take on through variable pay is open to debate, and current policy provides few guidelines. Workers, especially those at the bottom or middle of the wage scale, must be able to count on a reasonable level of consistent pay.

Academic research has found that the financial incentive programs that provide an increase over adequate levels of pay and pensions are more successful than those that put a large portion of pay or retirement income at risk (Blasi et al. 2010). Workers who feel financially insecure experience fewer of the positive outcomes associated with inclusive capitalism and are less interested in increasing their participation in such policies. Indeed, excessive economic insecurity, research finds, has the capability of reversing every positive individual and workplace outcome of inclusive capitalism (Ibid.).

Furthermore, evidence shows that most companies currently providing inclusive capitalism programs are doing so in addition to providing competitive wages. Several studies have found that average pay of workers in employee-owned firms is just as high as (or higher than) worker pay in non-employee-owned firms (Blasi et al. 1996; Kardas et al. 1998; Kim and Ouimet 2009). A General Social Survey analysis suggests that a majority of workers participating in inclusive capitalism programs have fixed pay that is either the same as or higher than market rates (Blasi 2006).[19]

Researchers, advocates, and policymakers should consider how to ensure that variable pay supplements good wages. Effective supplementation can encourage more companies to adopt sharing programs. Variable pay must be of a significant amount to encourage greater investment by workers in the success of their company but, at the same time, variable pay should be looked at as an addition to—and never a substitution for—a living wage.

What Is the Relationship between Inclusive Capitalism Policy and Worker Decision-Making Ability?

Inclusive capitalism programs at their best can imbue workplaces with a collective entrepreneurial spirit, where all workers feel invested and empowered to make decisions in their company's best interests. Numerous studies have confirmed this link between the success of inclusive capitalism programs and worker participation. As early as 1987, the General Accounting Office—now the Government Accountability Office—found that employee stock ownership plans are associated with improved corporate performance only when they are combined with participative decision-making structures (General Accounting Office 1987).

More recently, academics Richard Freeman, Joseph Blasi, and Douglas Kruse examined a set of studies based on the General Social Survey and a sample of more than 40,000 employees in companies with inclusive capitalism. The result of their investigation found that worker productivity "works best when it combines monetary incentives with employee decision-making and personnel and labor policies that empower and encourage employees" (Freeman et al. 2010, 23). Further, an even more expansive 2012 study by the same authors—that which reviews 780 companies employing more than 300,000 workers—confirms that the best results happen when broad-based inclusive capitalism is combined with a supportive company culture (Kruse et al. 2012). Research on inclusive capitalism programs consistently finds that companies and workers do best when they have more autonomy on the job, greater job security, and are allowed to participate in decision making (Kruse et al. 2010). This decision making can occur through unions, employee involvement committees, or team production arrangements that allow workers more say over how they achieve work tasks. Workers need to have job security in order to recommend labor-saving improvements that could potentially jeopardize their current position. In addition, they need a measure of autonomy over their individual work along with input into broader workplace systems in order to effectively recommend and implement changes (Appelbaum et al. 2000).

In short, when workers have a high level of job security and involvement in decision making over their everyday assignments and at the department level, they are best able to take advantage of the incentives of inclusive capitalism. But despite this, government policies do little to ensure that companies adopt participatory structures along with financial incentive programs or to even educate companies about the benefits of increased worker participation. And in cases where companies are not adopting these structures, government may well be rewarding practices that provide little public benefit.

Researchers, advocates, and policymakers should consider how to encourage more participation by workers in the daily operations of companies with inclusive capitalism programs.

Is Retirement Policy the Best Way to Promote Inclusive Capitalism?

Government policies to support inclusive capitalism tend to favor programs that are structured as retirement savings, such as employee stock ownership plans, deferred profit sharing, and employer contributions to 401(k)s. This structure allows workers to enjoy the benefits of ownership while encouraging savings for retirement, which is particularly valuable for many Americans who face severe deficits in their retirement savings.

But delivering the benefits of inclusive capitalism through retirement can potentially represent a significant risk to workers since company failure could cause workers to lose their jobs and wipe out their retirement savings.[20] Fortunately these sorts of horror stories are rare. Research shows that both public and private companies with employee stock ownership plans are less likely than their counterparts without employee ownership to go bankrupt or disappear for another reason (Park et al. 2004; Blair et al. 2000). Moreover, most ESOP retirement benefits are awarded in addition to—rather than as a substitute for—other retirement benefits, so company failure would not typically wipe out a worker's entire retirement savings. Employee stock ownership plans are four times more likely to have defined benefit pension plans and more than five times more likely to have 401(k) plans than workers in comparable companies without sharing programs (Blasi and Kruse 2001; Largest Study 2002).

The risk associated with an overconcentration of employer stock in a company 401(k), however, is more common. On average, workers hold 14 percent of their net wealth in employer stock, and almost 16 percent of workers hold twice that amount—28 percent of their net wealth (Blasi et al. 2010). Most often workers own this stock as part of their 401(k) plan (Blasi et al. 2010).[21] In comparison, a pension fund generally may not hold more than 10 percent of its assets in employer stock.

When workers are exposed to excessive risk—based on a worker's level of economic security—all the positive benefits of inclusive capitalism to both workers and the company can be reversed, according to researchers Blasi and Kruse from Rutgers University and Harry Markowitz from the University of California, San Diego (Blasi, Kruse, and Markowitz 2010).

Conversely, there are significant benefits in allowing workers to receive their benefits immediately, rather than waiting until retirement. Immediate sharing can serve as strong motivation for workers to improve performance and gives them the flexibility to use their capital in the way they see fit—just as other owners would. More flexibility can improve the ability of workers to make their wealth work for long-term financial growth. Many companies provide both deferred and immediate-sharing benefits for exactly these reasons. But many immediate-sharing programs, such as gain sharing and cash profit sharing, enjoy little government support. Researchers, advocates, and policymakers should consider how to limit the risks of participation in retirement-based inclusive capitalism programs and how to promote different timelines for when workers receive rewards other than primarily upon retirement.

POLICIES TO PROMOTE BROAD-BASED SHARING PROGRAMS

Today the inclusive capitalism advocacy movement spans government, not-for-profit, and business sectors. Yet, more than half of American workers do not have access or choose not to participate in inclusive capitalism programs. Specifically, those who could benefit the most from these types of sharing programs are low-income workers who participate less frequently than higher income workers.

Moreover, new proposals to promote broad-based sharing programs often fail to be enacted. This is in part due to the challenging questions discussed above that supporters of inclusive capitalism will need to address in order to build a broader base of support for inclusive capitalism policies. However, as advocates move forward in addressing these questions, they can also advance policies to promote broad-based sharing programs at all levels of government.

The policies below will not overcome all barriers that prevent businesses from more widely adopting broad-based sharing programs, but they will help ensure that sharing policies are sufficiently broad-based to include low- and middle-income workers; increase awareness of these programs among business and community leaders; and ensure that companies receive the support and assistance they need to adopt and operate sharing programs.

Ensure That Only Companies with Broad-Based Sharing Programs Receive Tax Advantages

Currently, companies can deduct incentive compensation costs from their corporate taxes no matter how narrowly they are shared among their workforce and no matter how large the compensation. As a result, companies often adopt performance pay programs for only top executives, rather than broad-based inclusive capitalism programs that also benefit low- and middle-income workers.

The federal government should reform tax incentives for performance pay linked to company-wide performance so that only companies with broad-based sharing plans are rewarded. Companies adopting these sorts of broad-based sharing plans include industry leaders such as Google Inc., Cisco Systems, and Wegmans Food Markets, Inc. Specifically, the government should adopt a proposal by academics Richard Freeman, Joseph Blasi, and Douglas Kruse, which would only give favorable treatment to performance-based compensation systems if all of the company's full-time employees participated in them and if the value expended on the top 5 percent of employees by salary was also expended on the bottom 80 percent of employees by salary (Freeman et al. 2011).

Promote Awareness and Provide Technical Assistance to Private Sector Businesses

Inclusive capitalism programs are not always well understood by the business community. Companies are often unaware of the benefits of empowering their workforce by sharing capital income and ownership broadly and lack the technical knowledge to evaluate whether to adopt these programs or even how to do so.

Inclusive capitalism can provide important benefits to many small and medium-sized privately held businesses. Many business owners of the baby boom generation, for example, must soon decide what do with their businesses when they retire. Selling to employees rather than to a competitor who may ship the company's equipment and jobs overseas is one way for these owners to preserve good local jobs, yet few of these business owners know that employee ownership is an option.

For instance, the Evergreen Cooperatives of Cleveland, Ohio, already mentioned, is pioneering an innovative model that could be replicated in communities across the United States. The cooperatives leverage the purchasing power of major local government and community institutions to create jobs and build wealth for low-income residents. The economic and technical strength of the Cooperatives derives from its support from local "anchor" institutions such as universities and hospitals. These institutions provide the much-needed capital for spending on promotion of the enterprise network and on the financial and technical infrastructure needed to get new businesses up and running.

State and federal governments should promote inclusive capitalism and democratic workplace culture by establishing centers that providing education and outreach, technical assistance, and training to private businesses and community institutions; and encouraging business schools to include information about these programs in their research and curricula.[22] This approach builds on a successful model for increasing one type of sharing: the Employee Ownership Center. Both Vermont and Ohio have launched Employee Ownership Centers that have been successful in increasing awareness throughout the state and facilitating the conversion of small and medium-sized businesses to employee ownership structure.

Use Government Purchasing to Support Inclusive Capitalism

State and federal governments spend hundreds of billions of dollars each year to purchase goods and services and they use this spending to support various types of businesses—often by creating contracting set-aside programs. But the unique structure of employee-owned companies can preclude them from qualifying for some of these programs.

At the federal level, the Historically Underutilized Business Zone, or HUB Zone, program—a contracting set-aside program that benefits economically disadvantaged areas—includes regulations to allow ESOP participation. Yet, the government frequently falls below its goals for contracting with companies included in this program.

State and federal governments should ensure that employee-owned companies are eligible for their various contracting set-aside programs and ensure that they are meeting program goals for contracting with these types of companies.

Designate a Privileged Company Structure

Traditional business structures can inhibit companies from adopting inclusive capitalism policies. In theory, stockholders could sue chief executive officers if profit making is not their sole objective. State governments have enacted laws to allow businesses to more easily adopt sharing policies without fear of shareholder reprisal and leverage capital for startups.

To date, seventeen states have passed legislation recognizing the establishment of the *benefit corporation,* which offers legal protection to owners to look beyond short-term financial gains.[23] By law, these companies must create a material positive impact on society; consider how decisions affect employees, community, and the environment; and publicly report their social and environmental performance. Companies applying for this status must complete a third-party assessment that may evaluate—among other things—whether firms have an employee ownership structure or offer broad-based stock, stock equivalents, or stock options to employees.[24] This does not guarantee that every benefit corporation will offer inclusive capitalism programs, but it can provide a significant legal protection to companies with broad-based sharing programs.

CONCLUSION

Today the American economy is in crisis. As a nation, we face weak economic growth, excessive speculative economic activities that don't build societal wealth, high unemployment, stagnant worker compensation, and dramatic differences in income and wealth between struggling low- and middle-income workers and the very rich. Inclusive capitalism, when implemented correctly, can begin to address these fundamental problems with our economy while simultaneously improving workers' well-being and the performance of businesses. Despite this potential, however, government policies to promote inclusive capitalism have never been used broadly as a tool to fight poverty and raise standards among private employers. In order to raise inclusive capitalism as a viable solution to alleviate many of the problems plaguing our economy, researchers, advocates, and policymakers must address several challenging questions around how to ensure that these programs benefit the workers that need them the most. Now it is time to bring these concepts into the center of the debate about economic disparity and how government can rebuild our economy to work for all of us.

NOTES

1. See detail of benefits and transfers in Short 2013.
2. Calculated using the *CPI Inflation Calculator*. Historical federal minimum wage figures from *History of Federal Minimum Wage Rates Under the Fair Labor Standards Act, 1938–2009,* Bureau of Labor Statistics (Last accessed on 22 February 2014 from http://www.dol.gov/whd/minwage/chart.htm).
3. Shares in the account are allocated to workers' individual accounts based on relative pay or some more equitable formula.

4. Note that Kruse, Freeman, and Blasi, "Shared Capitalism at Work," (2010) did not include restricted stock, phantom stock, or stock appreciation rights in their categorizations. We have grouped these programs with stock options based on our own analysis of the programs.

5. General Social Survey (Last accessed on 17 March 2014 from http://www3.norc.org/GSS+Website/).

6. Sen. Bernie Sanders proposed two pieces of legislation in 2012 to support employee ownership: The Worker Ownership, Readiness and Knowledge Act, Senate Bill 3421, 112th Cong. (2012); To Provide for the Establishment of the United States Employee Ownership Bank, Senate Bill 3419, 112th Cong. (2012). Rep. Fattah, Sen. Ayotte, and Rep. Rohrabacher have also introduced inclusive capitalism legislation. They are respectively the authors of The National Cooperative Development Act, House Resolution 3677, 112th Cong. (2011); A Bill to Modify the Definition of Fiduciary Under the Employee Retirement Income Security Act of 1974 to Exclude Appraisers of Employee Stock Ownership Plans Senate Bill 1232, 112th Cong. (2011); To Amend the Internal Revenue Code of 1986 to Exclude From Gross Income Compensation Received by Employees Consisting of Qualified Distributions of Employer Stock, House Resolution 786, 112th Cong. (2012).

7. Many employers began awarding workers stock bonuses in lieu of profit sharing during the stock market boom of the 1920s, but the stock market crash of 1929 and ensuing depression made these plans worthless. See: Coates 1991.

8. Vandenberg insisted in one interview that he was not promoting profit sharing to stabilize the national economy but rather to stabilize labor management relations. Vandenberg argued, however, that profit sharing could "preserve the profit system of capitalism," indicating that he had a broader vision for how profit sharing would affect the economy. See Jacoby 1998; Ibid.

9. Ibid.

10. Bureau of Labor Statistics, "National Compensation Survey" (2003 and 2005).

11. Ibid.; Ibid.

12. See Menke and Buxton (2010). Early employee stock ownership plans were eligible to apply for an exemption based on a 1953 IRS ruling allowing corporations to use profit sharing or stock bonus plans to borrow money for investment in company stock.

13. Ibid.

14. Ibid.

15. See Blasi, Kruse, and Park (2008). According to authors' analysis of the 2006 General Social Survey, 14 percent of American workers reporting they participate in a combination of share capitalism programs.

16. A pioneering group of academics and practitioners have identified inclusive capitalism programs as a cohort and a small body of research is being developed on the effects of these programs on workers and businesses. See, for example, Kruse, Freeman, and Blasi (2010).

17. According to a 1975 Peter Hart poll, two-thirds of respondents reported that developing "a program in which employees own a majority of the company's stock" would do more good than harm for the economy and 56 percent said that they would definitely or probably support a presidential candidate that favored allowing people who worked in companies to select management, set policies, and share the profits. See: Kruse and Blasi 1999.

18. This includes: The Promotion and Expansion of Private Employee Ownership Act of 2011, Senate Bill 1512, 112th Cong. (2011), and its companion bill, House Resolution 1244; the Employee Stock Ownership Plan Promotion and Improvement Act of 2011, Senate Bill 101, 112th Cong. (2011); A Bill to Modify the Definition of Fiduciary Under the Employee Retirement Income Security Act of 1974 to Exclude Appraisers of Employee Stock Ownership Plans, Senate Bill 1232; The National Cooperative Development Act, House Resolution 3677; To Amend the Internal Revenue Code of 1986 to Exclude From Gross Income Compensation Received by Employees Consisting of Qualified Distributions of Employer Stock, House Resolution 786; A resolution designating the year of 2012 as the "International Year of Cooperatives" Senate Resolution 87, 112th Congress; The Worker Ownership, Readiness and Knowledge Act, Senate Bill 3421, 112th Congress; To Provide for the Establishment of the United States Employee Ownership Bank, Senate Bill 3419, 112th Congress. Four of these bills supported employee stock ownership plans by increasing company tax advantages, expanding

access to government contracts, and reducing regulatory requirements for ESOP companies; two bills focused on cooperatives aiming to increase awareness of cooperatives and provide loans and grants to support their development; two bills were aimed at boosting employee ownership through both ESOPs and cooperatives by providing education, outreach, and technical assistance and increasing lending to employee owned firms; and one bill provided valuable tax incentives for workers and employers participating in stock grant programs.

19. Analysis on file with the authors.

20. In recognition of these risks, the Pension Protection Act of 2006 included provisions requiring employee stock ownership plans and defined contribution plans that hold publicly traded employer stocks to allow workers to diversify their holdings after three to six years. But privately held employee stock ownership plans are not subject to the changes and workers are not offered the option to diversify a portion of their holdings until they approach retirement. In privately held employee stock ownership plans, participants who are at least fifty-five years of age and complete at least ten years of participation in the plan may diversify the investment of a portion of their accounts in assets other than employer securities. See: Katten Muchin Rosenman LLP, Pension Protection Act of 2006 Impacts ESOPs (2006).

21. According to the National Bureau of Economic Research Company Survey (2001–2006), 33.5 percent of workers own employer stock through a 401(k) compared to 17.6 percent who do so through an employee stock purchase plan; 8.1 percent through an employee stock ownership plan; 7.3 percent through open market purchase and 5 percent through exercising options and keeping stock.

22. At the federal level, Sen. Bernie Sanders (I-VT) introduced the Worker Ownership, Readiness, and Knowledge Act, which would create a program to encourage worker participation in business decision making and—more narrowly—encouraged firms to adopt employee ownership structures. Sanders introduced the WORK Act in the 112th Congress; WORK Act, S. 3421, 112 Cong. 2 Sess. (2012).

23. States have passed other types of laws that create a privileged corporate status for companies that pursue a public purpose as well as financial profitability. This includes California's Flexible Purpose Corporation and Low-Profit Limited Liability Corporations, or L3Cs, enacted in eight states. These laws could potentially allow companies to adopt inclusive capitalism policies, but companies are not evaluated on whether they do so.

24. B Corporation, "Sample Benefit Corporation Impact Assessment" (2010). State benefit corporation laws require companies receiving the status to be assessed by a third party. B Lab, a third-party assessor providing the B Corporation certification, evaluates companies on their participation in inclusive capitalism programs.

Conclusion

Kyle Farmbry

"In the richest nation on Earth," observed Barack Obama on the fiftieth anniversary of Lyndon Johnson's declaration of the War on Poverty "far too many children are still born into poverty, far too few have a fair shot to escape it, and Americans of all races and backgrounds experience wages and incomes that aren't rising, making it harder to share in the opportunities a growing economy provides" (Obama 2014).

The half century between Lyndon Johnson's 1964 State of the Union address declaring the War on Poverty and Barack Obama's 2014 speech acknowledging its anniversary, provided numerous lessons on how poverty might be understood, and strategies for addressing its impact. Some of what has been learned has been presented in this book. The authors have explored poverty as it has impacted various groups of people in the 1960s as well as today. The rural poor in Appalachia, youth under the care of the juvenile justice systems, the immigrant poor, the mothers and children who comprise a significant percentage of the people below the poverty line, and others represent many of the groups at the center of the concerns of the authors in this book.

Often overlooked in poverty discourse is that poverty's impact is not solely upon individuals below a certain income threshold and their immediate communities. We are all affected when a large percentage of the nation's citizens are struggling to achieve their basic economic needs. Less than a year before Lyndon Johnson's 1964 address, Martin Luther King, Jr. wrote in his Letter from Birmingham City Jail, "We are all caught in an inescapable network of mutuality, tied in a single garment of destiny. What affects one directly, affects all indirectly" (King 1963). King's notion of an intertwined destiny, particularly between those with basic means and those struggling to meet their core needs, provides a core tenet that has guided this book.

Today's discourse on poverty increasingly recognizes the widening economic disparities between groups of people. Fifty years of lessons since Johnson's 1964 State of the Union speech launching the War on Poverty have provided opportunities to learn what works and what does not work in addressing some of the challenges of inequity and economic divide. However, despite a half a century of accumulated knowledge since the launch of the antipoverty efforts of the 1960s, we clearly still have wide gaps between segments of our population.

For many of the areas examined in these pages, investments in areas of education, job creation, and social infrastructure will help address the challenges of poverty. Whether such investments should be made at the state, local, or federal level has been an evolving debate for decades. More recent debate has introduced questions of the roles of the private for-profit and the private nonprofit sectors in working to address societal needs related to poverty. We have learned that each sphere—the public, private, and nonprofit—brings a set of opportunities for addressing poverty. Each also brings its own set of unique challenges.

This book will hopefully be part of a dialogue as we confront issues of poverty, inequality, and the social needs shaped by our growing economic divisions. A central hope that I believe I share with the authors is that the outcome of the dialogue will bring us closer to being able to reverse trends toward greater economic division and marginalization. I would suggest framing some of the thought and action that might result along three interrelated themes: *encouraging innovation for poverty alleviation*; *addressing the issue of the wealth gap*; and *building ongoing learning systems around poverty knowledge.*

INNOVATION FOR POVERTY ALLEVIATION

Over the past several decades the emergence of various social entrepreneurs has helped to shape many of the innovations that have helped to bring thousands of people from below the poverty threshold. Many of the social entrepreneurs that emerged from the War on Poverty who were involved with developing some of the strategies of the 1960s and 1970s provided some of the models for further addressing the challenges of the time. Their work led to the development of Head Start programs, various community-based organizations, low-income housing initiatives, and service providers for the needs of the economically marginalized.

The realm of the social entrepreneurs today has expanded beyond the public sector. Indeed, we can have innovation focused on addressing some of the broader social needs coming from the nonprofit and public sectors in ways likely never conceived by those involved in the efforts of the War on

Poverty fifty years ago. Numerous education initiatives have emerged over the past decades, driven by recognition of continued educational challenges in many of our economically marginalized communities. New initiatives in areas of health care, housing, and social service delivery are emerging—and being driven by the ideas of the innovators and social entrepreneurs who are identifying strategies for advancing their ideas for institutions to respond to critical community needs.

The experiences of the individuals behind the innovative initiatives that emerged from the War on Poverty, as well as the experiences engaged in more recent strategies for addressing poverty and its resulting challenges, are worth further study and extrapolation of lessons. Such lessons will help us frame a better understanding of the infrastructure needed to build further institutional frameworks to assist with antipoverty strategies emerging from the public, private, and nonprofit sectors in the future.

ADDRESSING THE WEALTH GAP

The growing wealth gap is, and likely will continue to be, a concern of policy makers involved in the broad poverty discourse. Developing ways that individuals can better engage in the economic opportunities that exist should be a component of the efforts that evolve as we look for ways to address poverty in our society. Much of the poverty discourse has been focused on issues of poverty alleviation. However, one proposition to consider: might we focus instead on questions of wealth generation?

The chapters by Berry and Madland et al. in this book discuss the notion of democratic capitalism as a means of engaging people in the broad economic fabric. For Berry, it is a matter of expanding the use of worker cooperatives as a tool for engagement. As she points out, worker cooperatives not only provide a means for workers to own their place of employment, but they also provide a means for employers to gain an understanding of sets of democratic processes that can assist with such ownership.

Madland et al. point to some of the complex structures that have evolved to support the growth of inclusive capitalism and employee ownership infrastructure. Ten years following the passage of the Economic Opportunity Act and the initiatives created by the War on Poverty, Congress passed the Employee Retirement Income Security Act (ERISA), which facilitated the development of instruments that enabled an increased rate of employee ownership, and ultimately wealth creation for a wide range of employees of firms. Interests in asset-driven development that emerged in the late 1980s and early 1990s also provided examples of how the concept of wealth generation—particularly for individuals not always at the center of the asset development discourse—was critical. These approaches permit us to examine the dynamics of poverty and explore ways that ownership might be further explored as a strategy for addressing poverty and growing asset divisions.

DATA, MEASUREMENT, AND ONGOING LEARNING

In the mid-1960s, as policy makers were developing what would be the core initiatives of the War on Poverty, questions began to arise around how to measure the impact of such initiatives. Molly Orshansky's development in 1963 and 1964 of poverty thresholds adopted by the federal government helped to provide some of the measures that would be used over the next several decades. Other measures being developed as the social sciences and public policy arenas increasingly intersected provided decision makers in the various agencies engaged with the War on Poverty a growing set of tools for measuring changes and developments in the communities where various antipoverty initiatives were being piloted. Today, in an era when notions of big data continue our reliance on quantitative means for much of our decision making, we find ourselves conceptualizing some of the processes for the design and implementation of various programs with evaluation and measurement as a core component of our antipoverty initiative development processes.

We have amassed a half century of data related to poverty in the years since the War on Poverty. Ensuring that we have adequate means for making sense of and processing the lessons we have learned will help identify strategies for moving forward with solutions effectively. One of the challenges in thinking about what we have learned in the various fields that intersect with our attempts to confront poverty relates to the question of how we ensure that we don't lose the potential for learning more. Many of the people who were engaged in the development of programs during the War on Poverty have retired from the institutions where they worked. Many of the valuable lessons of what worked and, more importantly, what didn't work, are at risk of being lost in institutional transitions. Some of the answers we seek in today's struggles with poverty in our nation may rest in the lessons of those individuals who were at the front lines of the War on Poverty several decades ago.

Thus, to prevent ourselves from repeating past errors, we need the development of learning systems that will enable us to effectively capture and build upon lessons from the past as well as ensure that we continue learning about the many facets of poverty and strategies for dealing with them in the future.

CONCLUSION

We would be naive to assume that anything we have directly or indirectly proposed will lead to immediate and direct solutions for solving the challenges wrought by poverty in our society. However, I would suggest that all of the authors whose work has been gathered here would agree that building a strategic dialogue with the perspectives of public, private, and nonprofit sectors actors begins to shape a starting point for action related to poverty. I would also argue that we would be cynics to deny ourselves of any belief in the ability of the basic human spirit to be compassionate and innovative as we weigh our options for moving forward in continuing to address some of the challenges of poverty in our nation. I think the authors of the chapters included in this book would agree with me, that while a nation that is absent the poverty that currently exists will not be realized in our lifetimes, we can still aim to build such a nation for future generations.

Bibliography

Adams, Jane, and D. Gorton. 2006. "Confederate Lane: Class, Race, and Ethnicity in the Mississippi Delta." *American Ethnologist 33* no. 2: 288–309

Adler, Margot. 2007. "Gault Case Changed Juvenile Law." *Gault Case Changed Juvenile Law*. Podcast audio. May 19.

Adler, Mortimer, and Louis Kelso. 1958. *The Capitalist Manifesto*. New York: Random House.

AFP. 2014. "Mondragon boss quits after Fagor failure." The Local. Last modified January 18. http://www.thelocal.es/20140118/mondragon-president-resigns-after-fagor-failure .

Agency for Healthcare Research and Quality, *2005 National Healthcare Quality Report*, U.S. Department of Health and Human Services (Rockville, Md., 2005).

Ahmed, Syed M., Jeanne P. Lemkau, Nichol Nealeigh, and Barbara Mann. 2001. "Barriers to Healthcare Access in a Non-Elderly Urban Poor American Population." *Health & Social Care in the Community* 9, no. 6: 445–453.

Aikens, Nikki L., and Oscar Barbarin. 2008. "Socioeconomic Differences in Reading Trajectories: The Contribution of Family, Neighborhood, and School Contexts." *Journal of Educational Psychology* 100, no. 2: 235–251.

Aizer, Anna, and Joseph J. Doyle Jr. 2013. *Juvenile Incarceration, Human Capital and Future Crime: Evidence from Randomly-Assigned Judges*. Working Paper 19102. National Bureau of Economic Research.

Alexander, Michelle. 2010. *The New Jim Crow: Mass Incarceration in the Age of Colorblindness*. New York: The New Press.

Alfred, Mary V., and Dominque T. Chlup. 2009. "Neoliberalism, Illiteracy, and Poverty: Framing the Rise of Black Women's Incarceration." *The Western Journal of Black Studies* 33, no. 4: 240–249.

Alkadry, Mohamad G., and Brandi Blessett. 2010. "Aloofness or Dirty Hands: Administrative Culpability in the Making of the 2nd Ghetto." *Administrative Theory and Praxis* 32, no. 4: 552–576.

Allard, Scott W., and Benjamin Roth. 2010. "Strained Suburbs: The Social Service Challenges of Rising Suburban Poverty." *Metropolitan Opportunity Series*. Washington, DC: Brookings Institution.

Amendment to the Juvenile Courts Act of 1987, H.R. HB 0083 § Section 5–750 (2011).

American Civil Liberties Union. "School-to-Prison Pipeline." Accessed February 11, 2014. https://www.aclu.org/school-prison-pipeline .

Anacker, Katrin B. 2012. "Shaky Palaces? Analyzing Property Values and their Appreciation in Minority First Suburbs." *International Journal of Urban and Regional Research*. 36, no. 4: 791–816.

Andersen, Ronald M., Thomas H. Rice, and Gerald F. Kominski. 2007. *Changing the U.S. Health Care System: Key Issues in Health Services Policy and Management.* 3d. edition. *San Francisco: Jossey-Bass*, pp. 3–31.

Anderson, Elijah. 1999. *Code of the Street*. New York: W. W. Norton.

Anderson, Gerard, and Jane Horvath. 2004. "The Growing Burden of Chronic Disease in America." *Public Health Reports* 119, no. 3: 263–270.

Anderson, Jenny, and Vikas Bajaj. 2007. "Calm Returns to Market, but Worries Persist Over Subprime Loans." *New York Times*, March 1, 2007. C1, C4.

———. 2008. "Reviewer of Subprime Loans to Aid Inquiry." *New York Times,* January 27.

Anderson, Martin. 1964. *The Federal Bulldozer: A Critical Analysis of Urban Renewal, 1949–1962*. Cambridge, MA: MIT Press, 1964.

Andrews, Edmund L. 2007a. "Bernanke Not Worried About Market Drops." *New York Times.* March 1, 2007. C5.

———. 2007b. "Ex-Fed Chief Gone, but Not Forgotten." *New York Times*, March 2, 2007. C1.

Annie E. Casey Foundation. 2012. *Kids Count Data Snapshot on High Poverty Communities.* Baltimore, MD: Annie E. Casey Foundation, 2012.

Appalachian Higher Education Network. "About the Network," last visited March 25, 2014, http://iel.org/ahecenters/about.html .

Appalachian Regional Commission. *Appalachia*. A report by the President's Appalachian Regional Commission (Washington, DC, 1964), available at http://www.arc.gov/about/ARCAppalachiaAReportbythePresidentsAppalachianRegionalCommission1964.asp (last visited March 25, 2014).

———. *Appalachian Capital Policy Initiative Project Summary* (Washington, DC, 2012).

———. "The Appalachian Region," last visited March 25, 2014, http://www.arc.gov/appalachian_region/TheAppalachianRegion.asp .

———. "ARC History," last visited March 25, 2014, http://www.arc.gov/about/ARCHistory.asp .

———. *ARC Launches Appalachian Community Capital Initiative to Build Access to Credit in Region* (Washington, DC, 2013).

———. "Community Infrastructure," last visited March 25, 2014, http://www.arc.gov/infrastructure .

———. "County Economic Status in Appalachia, FY 2014," last visited March 24, 2014, http://www.arc.gov/research/MapsofAppalachia.asp?MAP_ID=71 .

———. *Economic Overview of Appalachia—2011* (Washington, DC, 2011).

———. "Entrepreneurship and Business Development," last visited March 25, 2014, http://www.arc.gov/entrepreneurship .

———. *Moving Appalachia Forward: Appalachian Regional Commission Strategic Plan 2011–2016* (Washington, DC, 2010).

———. "Poverty Rates, 2007–2011," last visited March 25, 2014, http://www.arc.gov/reports/custom_report.asp?REPORT_ID=47 .

———. "Transportation and Highways (ADHS)," last visited March 25, 2014, http://www.arc.gov/program_areas/index.asp?PROGRAM_AREA_ID=19 .

Appalachian Regional Development Act of 1965, H.R. 4, 89th Cong (1965).

Appelbaum, Eileen, Thomas Bailey, Peter Berg, and Arne L. Kalleberg. 2000. *Manufacturing Advantage: Why High Performance Work Systems Pay Off.* Ithaca, NY: Cornell University Press.

Auerhahn, Kathleen. 1999. "Selective Incapacitation and the Problem of Prediction Criminology." *Criminology* 37, no. 4: 703–734.

Bachmura, Frank T. 1963. "The Manpower Development and Training Act of 1962—Its Significance for Rural Areas." *Journal of Farm Economics*, 45, no. 1: 61–72.

Bane, Mary Jo., and David T. Ellwood. 1994. *Welfare Realities: From Rhetoric to Reform.* Cambridge: Harvard University Press.

Banerjee, Mahasweta M. 2003. "Realities of Life Before and After Welfare Reform: Perspectives of Women of Color." *Qualitative Social Work* 2, no. 4: 411–433.

Barnosky, Jason. 2006. "The Violent Years: Responses to Juvenile Crime in the 1950s." *Polity* 38, no. 3: 314–344.

Barnow, Burt S., and Christopher T. King. 2005. *The Workforce Investment Act in Eight States*, a report prepared at the request of the United States Department of Labor, Employment and Training Administration. Washington: U.S. Department of Labor.

Baumer, Donald C., Carl E. Van Horn, and Mary Marvel. 1979. "Explaining benefit distribution in CETA programs." *Journal of Human Resources* 14, no. 2: 171–196.

Beatty, Barbara. 2012. "Rethinking Compensatory Education: Historical Perspectives on Race, Class, Culture, Language, and the Discourse of the Disadvantaged Child." *Teachers College Record* 114, no. 6: 1–11.

Bechard, Stephanie, Connie Ireland, Bruce Berg, and Brenda Vogel. 2011. "Arbitrary Arbitration: Diverting Juveniles in the Justice System—A Reexamination after 22 years." *International Journal of Offender Therapy and Comparative Criminology* 55, no. 4: 606–625.

Becker, Gary S. 1962. "Investment in Human Capital: A Theoretical Analysis." *Journal of Political Economy* 70, no. 5: 9–49.

———. *Human Capital*. 1975. New York: Columbia University Press.

Berkovec, James A., Glenn B. Canner, Stuart A. Gabriel, and Timothy H. Hanman. 1994. "Race, Redlining, and Mortgage Loan Performance." *Journal of Real Estate Finance and Economics* 9 no. 3: 263–294.

Bernake, Ben S., 2007. "The Recent Turmoil and its Economic and Policy Consequences," speech, New York Economic Club, New York, October 15.

Bernard, A. B., J. Bradford, and P. K. Schott. 2005. *Assessing the Impact of Trade Liberalization on Import-Competing Industries in the Appalachian Region*. Appalachian Regional Commission.

Bernstein, Irving. 1991. *Promises Kept: John F. Kennedy's New Frontier*. Oxford: Oxford University Press.

Berry, Daphne P. 2013. "Effects of Cooperative Membership and Participation in Decision Making on Job Satisfaction of Home Health Aides." *Advances in the Economic Analysis of Participatory & Labor-Managed Firms* 14: 3–25.

Berry, Daphne P., and Stu Schneider. 2011. "Improving the Quality of Home Health Aide Jobs: A Collaboration Between Organized Labor and a Worker Cooperative." In *Employee Ownership and Shared Capitalism: New Directions in Research*, ed. Edward J. Carberry. Ithaca: Cornell University Press. 59–89.

Berube, Alan, and Elizabeth Kneebone. 2008. *Reversal of Fortune: A New Look at Concentrated Poverty in the 2000s*. Washington: Brookings Institution.

Best, Rachel. 2010 "Situation or Social Problem: The Influence of Events on Media Coverage of Homelessness." *Social Problems* 57, no. 1: 74–91.

Bianchi, Suzanne M., and John Robinson. 1997. "What Did You Do Today? Children's Use of Time, Family Composition, and the Acquisition of Social Capital." *Journal of Marriage and the Family*. 59: 332–344.

Bifulco, Robert. 2005. "District-Level Black-White Funding Disparities in the United States, 1987–2002." *Journal of Education Finance* 31 no. 2: 172–194.

Binder, Arnold, and Susan L. Polan. 1992. "The Kennedy-Johnson Years, Social Theory, and Federal Policy in the Control of Juvenile Delinquency." *Crime & Delinquency* 37, no. 2: 242–262.

Birchall, Johnston, and Lou Hammond Ketilson. 2009. *Resilience of the Cooperative Business Model in Times of Crisis*. Geneva: International Labour Organization.

Black, Dan A., Mark Mather, and Seth G. Sanders. 2007. *Standards of Living in Appalachia, 1960–2000*, report prepared at the request of the Appalachian Regional Commission, Washington: Population Reference Bureau.

Blair, Margaret, Douglas Kruse, and Joseph Blasi. 2000. "Is Employee Ownership an Unstable Form? Or a Stabilizing Force?" In Thomas Kochan and Margaret Blair, eds., *New Relationship: Human Capital and the American Corporation*. Washington: The Brookings Institution.

Blasi, Joseph. Analysis of the 2006 General Social Survey "Pay and HR Measures, by Type of Shared Capitalism." Analysis on file with the authors (Madland et al.).

Blasi, Joseph, and Douglas Kruse. 1997. "Employee Ownership, Employee Attitudes and Firm Performance: A Review of the Evidence." In Daniel Mitchell, David Lewin, and Mahmood Zaidi, eds., *Handbook of Human Resources Management*. Greenwich: JAI Press: 113–151.

Blasi, Joseph, Richard Freeman, and Douglas Kruse. 2010. "Do Workers Gain by Sharing? Employee Outcomes Under Employee Ownership, Profit Sharing and Broad Based Stock Options." In Douglas L. Kruse, Richard B. Freeman, and Joseph R. Blasi, eds. *Shared Capitalism at Work: Employee Ownership, Profit and Gain Sharing, and Broad-Based Stock Options*. Chicago: University of Chicago Press, pp. 257–289.

Blasi, Joseph, Richard Freeman, and Harry Markowitz. 2010. "Risk and Lack of Diversification Under Employee Ownership and Shared Capitalism." In Douglas L. Kruse, Richard B. Freeman, and Joseph R. Blasi, eds. *Shared capitalism at work: Employee ownership, profit and gain sharing, and broad-based stock options*. Chicago: University of Chicago Press, pp. 105–138.

Blasi, Joseph R., Douglas L. Kruse, and Harry M. Markowitz. 2010. "Risk and lack of diversification under employee ownership and shared capitalism." In *Shared Capitalism at Work: Employee Ownership, Profit and Gain Sharing, and Broad-based Stock Options*. Chicago: University of Chicago Press, pp. 105–136.

Bluestone, Barry, and Bennett Harrison. 1982. *The Deindustrialization of America*. New York: Basic Books.

Blumer, Herbert. 1958. "Race Prejudice as a Sense of Group Position." *The Pacific Sociological Review* 1:3–7.

Bonnie, Richard J., Robert L. Johnson, Betty M. Chemers, and Julie A. Schuck. 2013. "Reforming Juvenile Justice: A Developmental Approach." Washington: National Research Council.

Boteach, Melissa, Erik Stegman, Sarah Baron, Tracey Ross, and Katie Wright. 2014. "The War on Poverty: Then and Now. Applying Lessons Learned to the Challenges and Opportunities Facing a 21st-Century America." Washington: The Center for American Progress.

Bradford, Spike. 2013. "Common Ground: Lessons Learned From Five States That Reduced Juvenile Confinement by More Than Half." Washington: Justice Policy Institute.

Brauer, Carl M. 1982. "Kennedy, Johnson, and the War on Poverty." *The Journal of American History* 69 no. 1: 98–119.

Braunstein, Sandra F. 2007. "Statement of Sandra F. Braunstein, Federal Reserve Division of Consumer Affairs." Congressional Testimony, 25 July. Washington: Federal Reserve Board.

Bravo, Rosa. 2003. "Medición de la pobreza desde un enfoque de género," document presented at the Expert Meeting on Poverty and Gender, Economic Commission for Latin America and the Caribbean (ECLAC)/International Labor Organization (ILO), Santiago, Chile, August 12–13.

Bridge, Gary. 2001. "Bourdieu, Rational Action and the Time-Space Strategy of Gentrification." *Transactions of the Institute of British Geographers* 26 no. 2: 205–216.

Brock, Nailah R. 2009. "African Americans and Welfare Term Limits: Comparative Analysis of State Term Limit Politics Under the Personal Responsibility and Work Opportunity and Reconciliation Act of 1996." *Journal of Black Studies* 39, no. 6: 962–973.

Brooks, David. 2008. "Two Cheers for Wall Street." *New York Times*, January 25, 2008. A27.

Brooks, Rick, and Constance Mitchell Ford. 2007. "The United States of Subprime: Data Show Bad Loans Permeate the Nation; Pain Could Last Years." *Wall Street Journal*, October 11, 2007. A1.

Brooks-Gunn, Jeanne, and Greg J. Duncan. 1997. "The Effects of Poverty on Children." *The Future of Children* 7, no. 2: 55–71.

Brown, David E., and Mala B. Thakur. 2006. "Workforce Development for Older Youth." *New Directions for Youth Development* 111: 91–104.

Brown, Hana. 2013. "The New Racial Politics of Welfare: Ethno-Racial Diversity, Immigration and Welfare Discourse Variation." *Social Science Review* 87, no. 3: 586–612.

Brown, Richard E., Victoria D. Ojeda, Roberta Wyn, and Rebecka Levan. 2000. "Racial and Ethnic Disparities in Access to Health Insurance and Health Care." Los Angeles: UCLA Center for Health Policy Research.

Brown-Saracino, Japonica, and Cesraea Rumpf. 2011. "Diverse Imageries of Gentrification: Evidence from Newspaper Coverage in Seven U.S. Cities, 1986–2006." *Journal of Urban Affairs* 33 no. 3: 289–315.

Browning, Lynnley. 2008. "Small Law Firm at Center of Loan Universe." *New York Times*, February 1, 2008. C6

Brownstein, Henry H. 1996. *The Rise and Fall of a Violent Crime Wave—Crack Cocaine and the Social Construction of a Crime Problem*. Albany, NY: Harrow and Heston.

Bruegmann, Robert. 2005. *Sprawl: A Compact History*. Chicago: University of Chicago Press.

Buchele, Robert, Douglas L. Kruse, Loren Rodgers, and Adria Scharf. 2010. "Show Me the Money, Does Shared Capitalism Share the Wealth?" In *Shared Capitalism at Work: Employee Ownership, Profit and Gain Sharing, and Broad-based Stock Options*. Chicago: University of Chicago Press: 351–376.

Budig, Michelle J., and Paula England. 2001. "The Wage Penalty for Motherhood." *American Sociological Review* 66: 204–225.

Bureau of Labor Statistics, "Nursing Aides, Orderlies, and Attendants: Similar Occupations." Bureau of Labor Statistics (Jan. 8, 2014), available at http://www.bls.gov/ooh/healthcare/nursing-assistants.htm#tab-7 (last accessed October 27, 2013).

Bush, George. 1990, November 29. "Statement on Signing the Immigration Act of 1990." Online by Gerhard Peters and John T. Woolley, The American Presidency Project. Accessed http://www.presidency.ucsb.edu/ws/?pid=19117 .

———. 2002. Remarks on Homeownership. June 17.

Buxton, Dickson, and John Menke. 2010. "The Origin and History of the ESOP and its Future Role as a Business Succession Tool." *Journal of Financial Service Professionals*. Accessed March 5, 2014. http://www.menke.com/archives_articles/origin-history-of-esops.pdf

Cahn, Edgar S., and Jean C. Cahn. 1964. "The War on Poverty: A Civilian Perspective." *The Yale Law Journal*, 73 no. 8: 1317–1352.

Canada, Mark. 1997. "Benjamin Franklin." The University of North Carolina at Pembroke. Accessed January 8, 2013. http://www2.uncp.edu/home/canada/work/canam/franklin.htm .

Carberry, Edward. 2010. "Who Benefits from Shared Capitalism?" In *Shared Capitalism at Work: Employee Ownership, Profit and Gain Sharing, and Broad-based Stock Options*. Chicago: University of Chicago Press: 317–350.

Cardoso, Fernando H., and Ernesto Zedillo. 2009. "The War on Drugs is a Failure: We Should Focus Instead on Reducing Harm to Users and on Tackling Organized Crime." *The Wall Street Journal*, February 23. Accessed 2014. http://online.wsj.com/article/SB123535114271444981.html .

Carey, Corinne A. 2005. "No Second Chance: People with Criminal Records Denied Access to Public Housing." *University of Toledo Law Review* 36, no. 3: 545–594.

Caudill, Harold M. 1963. *Night Comes to the Cumberlands: A Biography of a Depressed Era*. Boston, MA: Little, Brown, and Co, 1963.

Center for the Advancement of Health. 2003. "The Forgotten Population: Health Disparities and Minority Men." *Facts of Life: Issue Briefings for Health Reporters* 8, no. 5.

Center for Immigration Studies. 1995. "Three Decades of Mass Immigration: The Legacy of the 1965 Immigration Act." Accessed May 2, 2007. http://www.cis.org/articles/1995/back395.html .

Chambliss, William J. 2001. *Power, Politics, and Crime*. Boulder: Westview Press.

Chaplin, Duncan, and Jeffrey Capizzano. 2006. "Impacts of a Summer Learning Program: A Random Assignment Study of Building Educated Leaders for Life (BELL)." Washington, DC: The Urban Institute.

Charles, Suzanne Layni. 2011. *Suburban Gentrification: Understanding the Determinants of Single-Family Residential Redevelopment, A Case Study of the Inner-Ring Suburbs of Chicago, IL, 2000–2010*. Cambridge: Harvard University Joint Center for Housing Studies.

Chetty, R., N. Hendren, P. Kline, E. Saez, and N. Turner. 2014. The Equality of Opportunity Project. Harvard University. Accessed February 26, 2014. http://www.equality-of-opportunity.org .

Chin, Gabriel. 2002. "Race, the War on Drugs, and the Collateral Consequences of Criminal Conviction." *Journal of Gender, Race & Justice* 6: 253–296.

Chin, Gabriel J., and Richard W. Holmes. 2002. "Effective Assistance of Counsel and the Consequences of Guilty Pleas." *Cornell Law Review* 87, no. 3: 697–742.

Claire, William H., 1959. "Urban Renewal and Transportation" *Traffic Quarterly*, 13, no. 3: 414–422.

Clampet-Lundquist, Susan, Kathryn Edin, Andrew S. London, Ellen Scott, and Vicki Hunter. 2003. "'Making a Way of No Way': How Mothers Meet Basic Family Needs While Moving from Welfare to Work." *MDRC*. Working Paper Series No. 14.

Clear, Todd R. 2009. *Imprisoning Communities: How Mass Incarceration Makes Disadvantaged Neighborhoods Worse*. New York: Oxford University Press.

Closing the Gap: Solutions to Race–Based Health Disparities. 2005. Oakland: Applied Research Center

Coates, Edward M., III, 1991. "Profit Sharing Today: Plans and Provisions." *Monthly Labor Review*. Washington, DC: Bureau of Labor Statistics, 1991.

Coley, Richard J., and Bruce Baker. 2010. Poverty and Education: Finding the Way Forward. *The College Record*, 112 no. 3: 579–620.

Collett, Merrill. 1989. *The Cocaine Connection: Drug Trafficking, and Inter-American Relations*. New York: Foreign Policy Association. New York.

Collins, Sara R., Ruth Robertson, Tracy Garber, and Michelle M. Doty. 2012. *Young, Uninsured, and in Debt: Why Young Adults Lack Health Insurance and How the Affordable Care Act is Helping*. Washington: Commonwealth Fund.

Commins, John. 2013. "State Health Disparities Trace Medicaid Expansion." Health Leaders Media. Last modified December 16, 2013. Accessed January 14, 2014. http://www.healthleadersmedia.com/content/HEP-299309/State-Health-Disparities-Trace-Medicaid-Expansion .

Congressionally Mandated Study of Educational Growth and Opportunity, Interim Report. Bethesda, MD: Abt Associates, 1993.

Conway, Maureen, Amy Blair, Steven L. Dawson, and Linda Dworak-Munoz. 2007. "Sectoral Strategies for Low-Income Workers: Lessons from the Field." New York: Aspen Institute. Accessed October 26, 2013. http://www.aspeninstitute.org/sites/default/files/content/docs/07–014.PDF/ .

Cook, Robert F., and V. Lane Rawlins. 1985. "The Job Training Partnership Act: New Federalism in Transition." *Publius: The Journal of Federalism*, 15, no. 3 (1985): 97–110.

Cooke, Thomas, and Sarah Marchant. 2006. The Changing Intrametropolitan Location of High-Poverty Neighborhoods in the US, 1990–2000. *Urban Studies*, 23 (11): 1971–1989.

Cose, Ellis. 2002. *The Envy of the World: On Being a Black Man in America*. New York: Washington Square Press.

Coverage Matters: Insurance and Health Care. Committee on the Consequences of Uninsurance. Board on Health Care Services. Institute of Medicine. National Academies Press. Washington. 2001.

Coyle, Michael. 2003. "Race and Class Penalties in Crack Cocaine Sentencing." In *Race and Class Penalties in Crack Cocaine Sentencing*. Washington, DC: n.p. Accessed 2014. http://www.hawaii.edu/hivandaids/Race%20and%20Class%20Penalties%20in%20Crack%20Cocaine%20Sentencing.pdf .

CPI Inflation Calculator, Bureau of Labor Statistics. Accessed February 22, 2014. http://www.bls.gov/data/inflation_calculator.htm .

Craig, Ben, and John Pencavel. 1992. "The Behavior of Worker Cooperatives: The Plywood Companies of the Pacific Northwest." *American Economic Review* (19): 1083–1105.

Cronkite, Walter. 2006. "Telling the Truth about the War on Drugs." *The Huffington Post*, March 1. Accessed 2014. http://www.huffingtonpost.com/walter-cronkite/telling-the-truth-about-t_b_16605.html .

Crump, Jeff, Kathe Newman, Eric S. Belsky, Phil Aston, David H. Kaplan, Daniel J. Hammel, Elvin Wyly. 2008. "Cities Destroyed (Again) For Cash: Forum on the U.S. Foreclosure Crisis." *Urban Geography* 29, no. 8: 745–784.

Cullen, Francis T. 1994. "Social Support as an Organizing Concept for Criminology: Presidential Address to the Academy of Criminal Justice Sciences." *Justice Quarterly* 11, no. 4: 527–559.

Currie, Elliott. 1998. *Crime and Punishment in America*. New York: Macmillan.

Dawson, Robert O. 1990. "The Future of Juvenile Justice: Is It Time to Abolish the System?" *Journal of Criminal Law and Criminology* 81, no. 1: 136–155.

Decker, Paul T., and Jillian A. Berk. 2011. "Ten Years of the Workforce Investment Act (WIA): Interpreting the Research on WIA and Related Programs." *Journal of Policy Analysis and Management* 30, no. 4: 906–926.

Demleitner, Nora V. 2000. "Continuing Payment on One's Debt to Society: The German Model of Felon Disenfranchisement as an Alternative." *Minnesota Law Review* 84, no. 4: 753–804.

de Rugy, V. 2004. "President Reagan, Champion Budget-Cutter." American Enterprise Institute. Last modified June 9. Accessed 2014. http://www.aei.org/papers/economics/fiscal-policy/ president-reagan-champion-budget-cutter/ .

Deutsche, Rosalyn, and Cara Gendel Ryan. 1984. "The Fine Art of Gentrification." *October* 31: 91–111.

Dhillon, Conley H. 1963. "Area Redevelopment Act—What Has It Accomplished?" *Challenge*, April, 21–24.

Dinnerstein, Leonard. 1985. "The Supreme Court and the Rights of Aliens." *This Constitution* 8: 24–35.

Division of Manpower Development and Training, Bureau of Adult Vocational Education. 1966. *The Manpower Development and Training Act; Programs and Procedures*. Washington, DC: U.S. Department of Health, Education, and Welfare.

Division of Workforce Development and Adult Learning. 2012. *Maryland Annual Report: Workforce Investment Act Title 1 – B Program Year 2012*, Maryland Department of Labor, Licensing and Regulation. Baltimore: Maryland Department of Labor.

Dovidio, John F., and Samuel. L. Gaertner. 2002. "Aversive Racism." *Advances in Social Psychology* 36: 1–46.

Dresser, Laura. 2008. "Cleaning and Caring in the Home: Shared Problems? Shared Possibilities." *The Gloves-Off Economy: Workplace Standards at the Bottom of Americ a ' s Labor Market*. Champaign, IL: Labor and Employment Relations Association: 111–135.

Duncan, Greg J., Pamela A. Morris, and Chris Rodrigues. 2011. "Does Money Really Matter? Estimating Impacts of Family Income on Young Children's Achievement With Data From Random-Assignment Experiments." *Development Psychology* 47, no. 5: 1263–1279.

Dymski, Gary A. 2007. "From Financial Exploitation to Global Banking Instability: Two Overlooked Roots of the Subprime Crisis." Accessed February 21, 2014: http://www.soas.ac.uk/economics/events/crisis/43938.pdf (2007).

Economic Opportunity Act of 1964. Title II. Part 1. Sec 202(a)(3). Public Law 88–452.

Edelman, Peter B. 2012. *So Rich, So Poor: Why It's So Hard to End Poverty in America*. The New Press.

Edin, Kathryn, and Laura Lein. 1997. "Work, Welfare, and Single Mothers' Economic Survival Strategies." *American Sociological Review* 62, no. 2: 253.

Edson, Charles. L. 2011. "Affordable Housing—An Intimate History: Legal Guide to Affordable Housing Development," *Journal of Affordable Housing & Community Development Law*, 20: 193–214.

Edwards, Grace Toney, and JoAnn Aust Asbury. 2006. *A Handbook to Appalachia: An Introduction to the Region*. Edited by Ricky L. Cox. Knoxville: University of Tennessee Press.

Eller, Ronald D. 2008. *Uneven Ground: Appalachia since 1945*. Lexington: University Press of Kentucky.

Enchautegui, Maria E. 2013. "A Comparison of Family and Employment Immigrants and Possible Implications of a Shift toward Skilled Immigration."

Engel, Kathleen C., and Patricia A. McCoy. 2007. "Turning a Blind Eye: Wall Street Finance of Predatory Lending." *Fordham Law Review* 75, no. 4: 2039–2103.

Engel, Kathy, and Patricia McCoy. 2002. "A Tale of Three Markets: The Law and Economics of Predatory Lending." *Texas Law Review* 80, no. 6: 1255–1381.

England, Paula, and Nancy Folbre. 1999. "The Cost of Caring." *The Annals of the American Academy of Political and Social Science* 561, no. 1: 39–51.

Episcopal Community Development. "About Us." Last modified 2011. http://ecdonline.org/?page_id=5 .
Espenshade, Thomas J., Michael Fix, Wendy Zimmerman, and Thomas Corbett. 1996. "Immigration and Social Policy: New Interest in an Old Issue." *Focus* 18, no. 2: 11–13.
"ESOP Linked-Deposit Program," In.gov, http://www.in.gov/tos/2360.htm (last accessed February 26, 2014).
Evans, Benjamin F., Carrie E. Thompson, Emily Zimmerman, Steven H. Woolf, and Amber D. Haley. 2012. *Access to Food Providers and Recreational Facilities in South Delta, Mississippi and its Relationship to Health*. Virginia Commonwealth University Center on Human Needs.
Evans, Tim. 2003. *"Realistic Opportunity?" The Distribution of Affordable Housing and Jobs in New Jersey*. New Jersey Future.
Federal Reserve Board, "Proposed Rule, Revisions to Regulation Z. Draft Federal Register Notice and Request for Comment." Washington, DC: Board of Governors of the Federal Reserve, 2007.
Feld, Barry C. 1993. "Criminalizing the American Juvenile Court." *Crime and Justice* 17: 197–280.
Feldman, Lisa, Vincent Schiradi, and Jason Ziendenberg. "Too Little Too Late: President Clinton's Prison Legacy." Justice Policy Institute. Last modified February 1, 2001. http://www.justicepolicy.org/research/2061 .
Fessler, Kathryn Bondy. 2008. "Reclaiming a Spoiled Maternal Identity: Young mothers' Experiences and Rejection of Stigma." PhD dissertation—The University of Michigan.
Filinson, Rachel, Donna Cone, and Eileen Ray. 2005. "Welfare Reform and the Long-Term Care Workforce." *Educational Gerontology* 31, no. 2: 161–179.
Financial Post. 2007. "Miami Condominium Appears to be at Ground Zero in Blizzard of Fraud. Reuters." *Financial Post*, November 14, 2007.
Fisher, Stephen L., ed. 1993. *Fighting Back in Appalachia: Traditions of Resistance and Change*. Philadelphia: Temple University Press.
Fite, Paula J., Porche Wynn, and Dustin A. Pardini. 2009. "Explaining Discrepancies in Arrest Rates between Black and White Male Juveniles." *Journal of Consulting and Clinical Psychology* 77, no. 5: 916–927.
Fix, Michael E. 1997 "Restore Benefits to Legal Immigrants or Face a Poverty Dead-End." Commentary. *Los Angeles Times*. October 15.
Fix, Michael E., and Randy Capps. 2011. Immigrants and Welfare: An Overview to. In *Immigrants and Welfare: The Impact of Welfare Reform on America's Newcomers*, edited by Michael E. Fix, 1–36. New York: Russell Sage Foundation.
Foley v. Connelie, 435 U.S. 291 (1978).
Foucault, Michael. 1977. *Discipline and Punish: The Birth of the Prison*. New York: Pantheon Books.
Fox, Rachel. 1987. "Selling Out of Mount Laurel: Regional Contribution Agreements in New Jersey's Fair Housing Act, The." *Fordham Urb. LJ* 16: 535–572.
Fox, Robert A., Donald L. Platz, and Kathleen S. Bentley. 1995. "Maternal Factors Related to Parenting Practices, Development Expectations, and Perceptions of Child Behavior Problems." *The Journal of Genetic Psychology* 156, no. 4: 431–441.
Fox, Sanford J. 1970. "Juvenile Justice Reform: An Historical Perspective." *Stanford Law Review* 22, no. 6: 1187–1239.
Fraser, Nancy, and Linda Gordon. 1994. "A Genealogy of Dependency: Tracing a Keyword of the U.S. Welfare State." *Signs* 19, no. 2: 309–336.
Fredrickson, H. George. 2010. *Social Equity and Public Administration: Origins, Developments, and Applications*. Armonk: M. E. Sharpe.
Freeman, Lance. 2005. "Displacement or Succession? Residential Mobility in Gentrifying Neighborhoods." *Urban Affairs Review* 40, no. 4: 463–491.
Freeman, Richard B., Joseph Blasi, and Douglas L. Kruse, eds., 2010. "Introduction," In *Shared Capitalism at Work: Employee Ownership, Profit and Gain Sharing, and Broad-based Stock Options*. Chicago: University of Chicago Press

———. 2011. *Inclusive Capitalism for the American Workforce: Reaping the Rewards of Economic Growth through Broad-based Employee Ownership and Profit Sharing*. Washington: Center for American Progress.

Freeman, Steven F. 2007. *Effects of ESOP Adoption and Employee Ownership: Thirty Years of Research and Experience*. Philadelphia: University of Pennsylvania Scholarly Commons.

Freundlich, Fred. 1998. "The Mondragón Cooperative Corporation (MCC): An Introduction." Ownership Associates, Inc. Accessed February 2014. http://www.ownershipassociates.com/mcc-intro.shtm .

Frost, William Goodell. 1976. "Our Contemporary Ancestors in the Southern Mountains." *Appalachian Heritage* 4, no. 4: 70–80.

Gabbidon, Shaun L. 2010. *Race, Ethnicity, Crime, and Justice: An International Dilemma*. Thousand Oaks: Sage.

Gahlinger, Paul G. 2001. *Illegal Drugs: A Complete Guide to Their History, Chemistry, Use and Abuse*. Salt Lake City: Sagebrush Press.

Galbraith, John Kenneth. 1998 (1958). *The Affluent Society*. New York: Houghton Mifflin.

Garrett, Katherine E. 2006. *Living in America: Challenges Facing New Immigrants and Refugees*. Princeton: Robert Wood Johnson Foundation.

Ghilarducci, Teresa. 1992. *Labor's Capital: The Economics and Politics of Private Pensions*. Cambridge: Massachusetts Institute of Technology.

Gilbert, J. A. 1986. *Cycle of Outrage: America's Reaction to the Juvenile Delinquent in the 1950s*. New York: Oxford University Press.

Gilens, Martin. 1996. "Race and Poverty in America: Public Misperceptions and the American News Media." *Public Opinion Quarterly*, 60, no. 4: 515–541.

———. 1999. *Why Americans Hate Welfare: Race, Media and the Politics of Anti-Poverty Policy*. Chicago: University of Chicago Press.

Gilligan, Healther Tirado. "Food Deserts Aren't the Problem." Slate. Last modified February 10, 2014. Last accessed February 10, 2014. http://www.slate.com/articles/life/food/2014/02/food_deserts_and_fresh_food_access_aren_t_the_problem_poverty_not_obesity.html

Giloth, Robert P. 2000. "Learning from the Field: Economic Growth and Workforce Development in the 1990s." *Economic Development Quarterly* 14, no. 4: 340–359.

Gimbert, Belinda, Linda Bol, and Denelle Wallace. 2007. "The Influence of Teacher Preparation on Student Achievement and the Application of National Standards by Teachers of Mathematics in Urban Secondary Schools." *Education and Urban Society* 40, no. 1: 91–117.

Glick, Jonathan. 2008. "Gentrification and the Racialized Geography of Home Equity." *Urban Affairs Review* (44) 2: 280–295.

Goetz, Edward. 2011. Gentrification in Black and White: The Racial Impact of Public Housing Demolition in American Cities. *Urban Studies* 48(8): 1581–1604.

Gordon, Linda. 1990. *Women, the State, and Welfare*. Madison: University of Wisconsin Press.

Gottschalk, Marie. 2006. *The Prison and the Gallows: The Politics of Mass Incarceration in America*. New York: Cambridge University Press.

Governor's Workforce Investment Board. *2010 Maryland's Workforce Indicators*. Baltimore, Md., 2010.

Gradin, Carlos. 2008. "Poverty Among Minorities in the United States: Explaining the Racial Poverty Gap for Blacks and Latinos," Working Paper No. 2008–96. Retrieved from The Society for the Study of Economic Inequality website: .

Graham v. Richardson, 403 U.S. 365 (1971).

Greenberg, Edward S. 1984. "Producer Cooperatives and Democratic Theory: The Case of the Plywood Firms." In *Worker Cooperatives in America*, edited by Robert Jackall and Henry M. Levin. Berkeley: University of California Press.

Greenspan, Alan. 2007. "U.S. Moving Closer to Recession: Appearance on ABC News This Week." Accessed December 16. http://www.abcnews.com .

Greenwald, Bruce C., and Joseph E. Stiglitz. 1991. "Information, Finance, and Markets: The Architecture of Allocative Mechanisms." Working Paper 3652. Cambridge, MA: National Bureau of Economic Research.

Grist, Peter. 2010. “Housing and GDP.” National Association of Home Builders. Last modified April 10. Accessed March 2014. http://www.nahb.org/generic.aspx?sectionID=734&genericContentID=136170 .

Grogger, Jeffrey. 2003. “The Effects Of Time Limits, The EITC, and Other Policy Changes on Welfare Use, Work, and Income Among Female-Headed Families.” *Review of Economics and Statistics* 85, no. 2: 394–408.

Grubb, W. Norton. 2001. “From Isolation to Integration: Postsecondary Vocational Education and Emerging Systems of Workforce Development.” *New Directions for Community Colleges*, pp. 27–37.

Grubb, W. Norton, and Lorraine M. McDonnell. 1996. “Combating Program Fragmentation: Local Systems of Vocational Education and Job Training.” *Journal of Policy Analysis and Management* 15: 252–270.

Gutfreund, Owen D. 2004. *Twentieth–Century Sprawl: Highways and the Reshaping of the American Landscape*. New York: Oxford University Press, 2004.

Haaga, John. 2004. *Educational Attainment in Appalachia*. Washington, DC: Population Reference Bureau.

Hagan, John, John D. Hewitt, and Duane F. Alwin. 1979. “Ceremonial Justice: Crime and Punishment in a Loosely Coupled System.” *Social Forces* 58, no. 2: 506–527.

Haines, David W. 2007. Refugees. In Mary C. Waters, and Reed Ueda (eds.), The *New Americans. A Guide to Immigration since 1965*. Cambridge: Harvard University Press, pp.56–69.

Hainmueller, Jens, and Michael J. Hiscox. 2010. “Attitudes toward Highly Skilled and Low-skilled Immigration: Evidence from a Survey Experiment.” *American Political Science Review* 104, no. 1: 61–84.

Hancock, Ange-Marie. 2004. *The Politics of Disgust: The Public Identity of the “Welfare Queen.”* New York: New York University Press.

Handler, Joel. 1965. “The Juvenile Court and the Adversary System: Problems of Function and Form.” *Wisconsin Law Review* 7: 10–11.

Hanson, Gordon, Kenneth Schev, Matthew Slaughter, and Antonio Spilimbergo. 2002. “Fiscal Impacts of Immigration.” In *Immigration Policy and the Welfare System,* edited by Tito Boeri, Gordon Hanson, and Barry McCormick. New York: Oxford University Press, pp. 232–249.

Hanson, S., and Pratt, G. 1995. *Gender, Work, and Space*. New York: Routledge.

Harbison, A. 2013. The Surprising Ways Globalization is Changing One of the Most Remote Parts of the U.S. Retrieved from http://www.policymic.com/articles/55571/the-surprising-ways-globalization-is-changing-one-of-the-most-remote-parts-of-the-u-s .

Harrington, Michael. 1986 (1962). *The Other America: Poverty in the United States*. New York: Penguin.

Harris County Department of Education. 2014. Cooperative. Retrieved on Jan. 25, 2014 from http://www.hcde-texas.org/default.aspx?name=PurchCoopHCDE .

Hasen, Suzy. 2012. “What Can Mississippi Learn From Iran?” *New York Times*. Last modified July 27. Accessed January 18, 2014. http://www.nytimes.com/2012/07/29/magazine/what-can-mississippis-health-care-system-learn-from-iran.html?pagewanted=all&_r=1& .

Hatsukami, Dorothy K., and Marian W. Fischman. 1996. “Crack Cocaine and Cocaine Hydrochloride: Are the Differences Myth or Reality?” *Journal of the American Medical Association* 276, no. 19: 1580–1588.

Hatton, Timothy J., and Jeffrey G. Williamson. 2002. “What Fundamentals Drive World Migration?” National Bureau of Economic Research. http://www.nber.org/papers/w9159 .

Hauser, Philip M., S. M. McMurrin, J. M. Nabritjr, L. W. Nelson, and William R. Odell. 1964. “Report to the Board of Education of the City of Chicago by the Advisory Panel on Integration of the Public Schools.” Chicago: Board of Education.

Hays, Sharon. 2003. *Flat Broke with Children: Women in the Age of Welfare Reform*. Oxford: Oxford University Press.

Hedges, Chris. 2013. “Criminalizing Poverty Keeps 2.2 Million in U.S. Prisons.” *CCPA Monitor*, 34–35.

Hellegers, Adam P. 1999. "Reforming HUD's 'One Strike' Public Housing Evictions Through Tenant Participation." *Journal of Criminal Law and Criminology* 90: 323–361.

Hernandez, Donald J. 2011. "Double Jeopardy: How Third-Grade Reading Skills and Poverty Influence High School Graduation." Annie E. Casey Foundation.

Hersh, Matthew Brian. 2010. "Taking Foreclosures to Task." *Shelterforce, Journal of Affordable Housing and Community Building.* Last accessed March 20, 2014 http://www.shelterforce.org/article/2013/taking_foreclosures_to_task/P1/ .

Hochschild, Jennifer L. 1996. *Facing Up to the American Dream: Race, Class, and the Soul of the Nation.* Princeton University Press.

Hofferth, Sandra L., and John F. Sandberg. 2001. *Journal of Marriage and Family*, 63: 295–308.

Hoffman, Catherine, and Mary Pohl. 2002. *Health Insurance Coverage in America: 2002 Data Update.* Pub. No. 4007. Washington: Kaiser Commission on Medicaid and the Uninsured.

Holden, Gwen A., and Robert A. Kapler. 1995. *Juvenile Justice: Deinstitutionalizing Status Offenders.* Bethesda: ABT Associates.

Holliday, A. L., and R. E. Dwyer. 2000. Suburban Neighborhood Poverty in U.S. Metropolitan Areas in 2000. *City & Community*, 8, no. 2, 155–176.

Holman, B., and J. Ziedenberg. 2006. *Dangers of Detention: The Impact of Incarcerating Youth in Detention and Other Secure Facilities.* Washington, DC: Justice Policy Institute.

Holzer, Harry J. 2008. "Workforce Development as an Antipoverty Strategy: What Do We Know? What Should We Do?" http://www.urban.org/publications/411782.html .

———. 2012. "Going, Going . . . Gone? The Evolution of Workforce Development Programs for the Poor since the War on Poverty." Paper presented at War on Poverty Conference, Ann Arbor, MI, June 12–13.

Hopkins, Daniel J. 2010. "Politicized Places: Explaining Where and When Immigrants Provoke Local Opposition." *American Political Science Review* 104, no. 1: 40–60.

Horwath, Crowe. "A Comprehensive Guide to ESOPs." (2008) Accessed June 2012. https://www.croweesopadvantage.com/pdfs/Comprehensive%20Guide%20to%20ESOPs.pdf .

Hospital Survey and Construction Act of 1946 , U.S. Code, vol. 42, sec 291e.

Houck, Max M., and Jay A. Siegel. 2010. *Fundamentals of Forensic Science*, 2nd Edition. Burlington: Academic Press.

House Committee on Education and Labor, Hearings, 88th Congress, 2nd sess, 1964. Washington, DC: Government Printing Office, 1964, 422–469.

House, James S., and David R. Williams. 2003. "Understanding and Reducing Socioeconomic and Racial/Ethnic Disparities in Health." In Richard Hofrichter, ed. *Health and Social Justice: Politics, Ideology, and Inequity in the Distribution of Disease.* San Francisco: Jossey-Bass.

Howard, T., L. Kuri, and I. P. Lee. 2010. The Evergreen Cooperative Initiative of Cleveland, Ohio. A Sense of Place: Place-Based Grantmaking in Practice. White Paper Prepared for The Neighborhood Funders Group Annual Conference. Minneapolis, MN.

Howell, James C. 2009. *Preventing and Reducing Juvenile Delinquency: A Comprehensive Framework.* 2nd ed. Los Angeles: Sage.

Hughes, Dana C., and Sandy Ng. "Reducing Health Disparities Among Children." *JSTOR.* N.p., n.d. Web. 07 Dec. 2013.

Humphrey, Hubert Jr., "Letter to the Editor," *Washington Post*, July 20, 1976.

Hungerford, T., and Solon, G., 1987 "Sheepskin Effects in the Return to Education," *Review of Economics and Statistics*, 69: 175–177.

Hunt, Joseph McVicker. 1961. *Intelligence and Experience.* New York: Ronald Press Co.

Iceland, J. *Poverty in America.* 2006. Berkeley: University of California Press.

Immigration Act of 1990, P.L. No. 101–649, 104 Stat. 4978 (1990).

Immigration Control and Reform Act of 1986, P.L. No. 99–603, 100 Stat. 3445 (1986).

In re Gault, 407 P.2d 760 (Ariz. Sup. Ct. 1965).

In re Gault, 387 U.S. 1 (1967).

Ingebretsen, Edward J. 1998. "Staking the Monster: A Politics of Remonstrance." *Religion and American Culture: A Journal of Interpretation* 8, no. 1: 91–116.

Inserra, Anne, Maureen Conway, and John Rodat. 2002. *The Cooperative Home Care Associates: A Case Study of a Sectoral Employment Development Approach*. Queenstown, MD: Aspen Institute.

Institute of Children, Poverty and Homelessness. 2013. "The American Almanac of Family Homelessness 2013." http://www.icphusa.org/Publications/AmericanAlmanac/ .

Institute of Medicine. 1990. *Medicare: A Strategy for Quality Assurance*. K. N. Lohr, ed. Washington: National Academy Press.

———. 1993. *Committee on Monitoring Access to Personal Health Care Services* Michael Millman, ed. Washington, DC: National Academy Press.

International Cooperative Alliance (ICA). 2012. "Cooperative Identity, Values, and Principles." Accessed October 26, 2013. http://ica.coop/en/what-coop/cooperative-identity-values-principles .

Ives, Richard, and Preeti Ghelani. 2006. "Polydrug Use (the Use of Drugs in Combination): A Brief Review." *Drugs: Education, Prevention & Policy* 13 no. 3: 225–232.

Jackall, Robert, and Henry M. Levin. 1984a. "Introduction." In *Worker Cooperatives in America*, edited by Robert Jackall and Henry M. Levin. Berkeley: University of California Press.

———. 1984b. "Conclusion." In *Worker Cooperatives in America*, edited by Robert Jackall and Henry M. Levin. Berkeley: University of California Press.

Jackson, Kenneth J. 1985. *Crabgrass Frontier: The Suburbanization of the United States*. New York: Oxford University Press.

Jacobs, Jane. 1993 (Original 1961). *The Death and Life of Great American Cities*. New York: The Modern Library.

Jacobson, Michael. 2005. *Downsizing Prisons: How to Reduce Crime and End Mass Incarceration*. New York: New York University Press.

Jacoby, Sanford M. 1998. *Modern Manors: Welfare Capitalism since the New Deal*. Princeton: Princeton University Press.

Jeffrey, Julie Roy. 1978. *Education For Children of the Poor: A Study of the Origins and Implementation of the Elementary and Secondary Education Act of 1965*. Columbus: The Ohio State University Press.

Johnson, Christopher. 2007. "A Re-Count of Poverty in US Central Cities: Just Who and Where are the Urban Poor?" *Urban Studies* 44, no. 12: 2283–2303.

Johnson, Lyndon B. "Annual Message to Congress on the State of the Union" (speech, Washington, DC, January 8, 1964).

———. "Annual Message to Congress on the State of the Union" (speech, Washington, DC, January 4, 1965).

———. "Annual Message to the Congress on the State of the Union" (speech, Washington, DC, January 10, 1967).

———. "156–The President's News Conference" (interview, Washington, DC, April 1, 1965).

———. "Remarks at Southwest Texas State College Upon Signing the Higher Education Act of 1965" (speech, Southwest Texas State College, San Marcos, TX, November 8, 1965).

———. 1965b. Statement of the President on the Signing of the Medicare Bill—July 30.

———. 1966. Statement by the President on the Inauguration of the Medicare Program. June 30.

Joseph, Mark L., Robert J. Chaskin, and Henry S. Webber. 2007. "The Theoretical Basis for Addressing Poverty Through Mixed-Income Development." *Urban Affairs Review* 42 no. 3: 369–409.

Kaarsemaker, Eric. 2006. "Employee Ownership and Human Resources Management: A Theoretical and Empirical Treatise with a Digression on the Dutch Context," PhD dissertation, Radbound University.

Kain, John. F. 1992. "The Spatial Mismatch Hypothesis: Three Decades Later." *Housing Policy* 3, no. 2: 371–460.

Kandel, William A. 2011. *The U.S. Foreign-Born Population: Trends and Selected Characteristics*. Washington: Library of Congress Congressional Research Service

Kardas, Peter, Jim Keogh, and Adria Scharf, 1998. "Wealth and Income Consequences of ESOPs and Employee Ownership: A Comparative Study from Washington State." *Journal of Employee Ownership Law and Finance* 10, no. 4: 3–52.

Kasarda, John D. 1993. "Inner-City Concentrated Poverty and Neighborhood Distress: 1970 to 1990." *Housing Policy Debate* 4, no. 3: 253–302.

Keely, Charles B. 1971. "Effects of the Immigration Act of 1965 on Selected Population Characteristics of Immigrants to the United States." *Demography* 8, no. 2: 157–169.

Keiffer, Chris. 2014. "Game Changer? Advocates Hail Common Core as Pivotal for Mississippi Students." *DJournal*. January 5. Accessed February 11, 2014. https://djournal.com/news/game-changer-advocates-hail-common-core-pivotal-mississippi-students .

Kennedy, Edward M. 1981. "Refugee Act of 1980." *International Migration Review* 15, nos. 1/2: 141–156.

Kennedy, John F. 1960. Address to the Greater Houston Ministerial Association, September 12.

Kiffmeyer, Thomas. 2008. *Reformers to Radicals: The Appalachian Volunteers and the War on Poverty*. Lexington: University Press of Kentucky.

Kim, Han E., and Paige Parker Ouimet. 2009 "Employee Capitalism or Corporate Socialism? Broad-based Employee Stock Ownership." U.S. Census Bureau Center for Economic Studies Paper No. CES-WP- 09–44.

King, Martin Luther. 1963. *Why We Can't Wait*. Boston: Beacon Press.

King, Ryan S. 2008. "Disparity By Geography: The War on Drugs in America's Cities." Washington, DC: The Sentence Project.

King v. Smith, 392 U.S. 309 (1968).

King's Dream Remains an Exclusive Goal; Many Americans See Racial Disparities. 2013. Washington, DC: Pew Research Center.

Kneebone, Elizabeth., and Alan Berube. 2013. *Confronting Suburban Poverty in America*. Washington, DC: Brookings Institution.

Knowles, Louis L., and Kenneth Prewitt. 1969. *Institutional Racism in America*. Englewood Cliffs, NJ: Prentice-Hall.

Kohler-Hausmann, Julilly. 2007. "The Crime of Survival: Fraud Prosecutions, Community Surveillance, and the Original 'Welfare Queen.'" *Journal of Social History* 41, no. 2: 329–354.

Kothari, Monika. 2011. "The Hart-Cellar Act. A Demographic Revolution." The Center for the Study of the Presidency & Congress: Presidential Fellows Blog. http://presidentialfellows.wordpress.com/2011/09/21/the-hart-cellar-act-a-demographic-revolution/ .

Koyama, Jill. 2014. "In the War on Poverty, Don't Forget Refugees." *The Huffington Post*, January 23.

Kramer, Ronald. C. 2000 "Poverty, Inequality and Youth Violence." *The Annals of the American Academy of Political Science* 567, no. 123: 123–138.

Krause, D. D., M. L. Warren, L. M. Nancy, J. S. Cossman, and T. Konrad. 2012. "An Analysis of Oral Health Disparities and Access to Services in the Appalachian Region." Raleigh, NC: PDA, Inc.

Kremen, Gladys Roth. 2013. "MDTA: The Origins of the Manpower Development and Training Act of 1962." United States Department of Labor. N.p., n.d. Web. December 19.

Kruse, Douglas. 2002. "Research Evidence on the Prevalence and Effects of Employee Ownership," Testimony before the Subcommittee on Employer-Employee Relations, House Committee on Education and the Workforce, U.S. House of Representatives. February 13.

Kruse, Douglas, and Joseph Blasi. 1999. "Public Opinion Polls on Employee Ownership and Profit Sharing." *The Journal of Employee Ownership Law and Finance* 11, no. 3: 3–25.

Kruse, Douglas, Joseph Blasi, and Richard Freeman. 2012. "Does Linking Worker Pay to Firm Performance Help the Best Firms Do Even Better?" Working Paper 17745. National Bureau for Economic Research.

Kruse, Douglas L., Joseph R. Blasi, and Rhokeun Park. 2008. "Shared capitalism in the US economy? Prevalence, characteristics, and employee views of financial participation in enterprises." No. w14225. National Bureau of Economic Research.

———. 2010. "Shared Capitalism in the US Economy." *In Shared Capitalism at Work: Employee Ownership, Profit and Gain Sharing, and Broad-based Stock Options*. University of Chicago Press, p. 41

Kruse, Douglas L., Richard B. Freeman, and Joseph R. Blasi. 2010. *Shared Capitalism at Work: Employee Ownership, Profit and Gain Sharing, and Broad-based Stock Options*. Chicago: University of Chicago Press.

Ku, Leighton, and Brian Bruen. 2013. "Poor Immigrants Use Public Benefits at a Lower Rate than Poor Native-Born Citizens." *Cato Institute* 17: 1–8.

Lefstein, Norman. 1967. "In re Gault, Juvenile Courts and Lawyers." *American Bar Association Journal* 53, no. 9: 811–814.

Leger, Donna Leinwand. 2013. "OxyContin a Gateway to Heroin for Upper-Income Addicts." *USA Today*, June 28. Accessed 2014. http://www.usatoday.com/story/news/nation/2013/04/15/heroin-crackdown-oxycodone-hydrocodone/1963123/ .

Lens, Vicki, and Collene Cary. 2010. "Negotiating the Disco Discourse of Race within the United States Welfare System." *Ethnic and Racial Studies* 33, no. 6: 1032–1048.

Levin, Josh. 2013. "The Real Story of Linda Taylor, America's Original Welfare Queen." *Slate Magazine*, December 19, 2013. Accessed 2013.

Levitt, Steven D. 2004 "Understanding Why Crime Fell in the 1990s: Four Factors That Explain the Decline and Six That Do Not." *The Journal of Economic Perspectives* 18, no. 1: 163–190.

Lewis, Oscar. 1966. "The Culture of Poverty." *Scientific American* 215 no. 4: 19–25.

———. 1968. *La Vida: A Puerto Rican Family in the Culture of Poverty*. New York: Random House

Lieberman, Robert C. 1998 *Shifting the Color Line: Race and the American Welfare State*. Cambridge, MA: Harvard University Press.

Life. (n.d). *Life in Appalachia: Photos from a Valley of Poverty, 1964*. Retrieved from http://life.time.com/history/life-in-appalachia-photos-from-a-valley-of-poverty-1964/#1 .

Lillie-Blanton, Marsha, and Caya B. Lewis. 2005. "Policy Challenges and Opportunities in Closing the Racial/Ethnic Divide in Health Care. Race, Ethnicity, and Health Care." Washington: The Henry J. Kaiser Family Foundation, Washington.

Lindsey, Ben B., and Harvey J. O'Higgins. 1970. *The Beast*. Seattle: University of Washington Press.

Lipsey, Mark W. 2009. "The Primary Factors that Characterize Effective Interventions with Juvenile Offenders: A Meta-Analytic Overview." *Victims and Offenders* 4, no. 2: 124–147.

Lloyd, Robert. 2014. "Review: 'Spies of Mississippi': Espionage in the Heart of Dixie." *Los Angeles Times*. February 10.

Loewen, James W. 2005. *Sundown Towns: Hidden Dimensions of American Racism*. New York: The New Press.

Long, Michael W., Cindy W. Leung, W. Y. Lilian, Cheung, Susan J. Blumenthal, and Walter C. Willett. 2014. "Public Support for Policies to Improve the Nutritional Impact of the Supplemental Nutrition Assistance Program (SNAP)." *Public Health Nutrition* 17 no. 1: 219–224.

Ludwig, Jens, and Deborah A. Phillips. 2008. "Long-term Effects of Head Start on Low-income Children." *Annals of the New York Academy of Sciences* 1136, no. 1: 257–268.

Luviene, Nicholas. 2010. "Building a Platform For Economic Democracy: A Cooperative Development Strategy for the Bronx." Master's thesis. Massachusetts Institute of Technology.

MacLanahan, Sara. 2007. "Single Mothers, Fragile Families." *In Ending Poverty in America*, edited by J. Edwards, M. Crain, and A. L. Kalleberg. New York: The New Press, pp. 77–87.

Mader, Jackie. 2013. "New standards bring big changes for Mississippi students" *The Hechinger Report*, December 22, 2013. http://hechingerreport.org/content/new-standards-bring-big-changes-for-mississippi-students_14210/ .

———. 2013. "A Shorter School Year and Mandatory Homework: What Mississippi's Lawmakers Are Proposing for Education This Year." Hechinger Ed Blog. Last modified January 23. Accessed February 2014. http://hechingered.org/content/a-shorter-school-year-and-mandatory-homework-what-mississippis-lawmakers-are-proposing-for-education-this-year_6529/ .

Madland, David, and Karla Walter. 2013. *Growing the Wealth: How Government Encourages Broad-Based Inclusive Capitalism*. Washington, DC: Center for American Progress.

Males, Mike A., Christina Stahlkopf, and Dan Macallair. 2007. *Crime Rates and Youth Incarceration in Texas and California Compared: Public Safety or Public Waste?* San Francisco: Center on Juvenile and Criminal Justice.
Mann, Coramae Richey. 1994. "A Minority View of Juvenile 'Justice.'" *Washington and Lee Law Review* 51, no. 2: 465–478.
Mansfield, Cathy Lesser. 1999. "The Road to Subprime HEL Was Paved with Good Congressional Intentions: Usury Deregulation and the Subprime Home Equity Market." *South Carolina Law Review* 51: 473–588.
Marcus, Norman. 1970. Exclusionary Zoning: The Need for a Regional Planning Context. *New York Law Forum*, 732–740.
Martin, Daniel C., and James E. Yankay 2012. "Refugees and Asylees: 2011." *Annual Flow Report.* Washington, DC: U.S. Department of Homeland Security, Office of Immigration Statistics.
Martin, Lori L. 2011. "Debt to Society: Asset Poverty and Prisoner Reentry." *Review of Black Political Economy* 38: 131–143.
Martinson, Robert. 1974. "What Works? Questions and Answers about Prison Reform." *The Public Interest* 35: 22–55.
Maryland Department of Labor, Licensing and Regulation. 2013. *Maryland's One Stop Career Centers: Workforce Investment Act System*. Baltimore: Maryland Department of Labor.
———. 2013. *State of Maryland Integrated Workforce Plan Section II: State Operational Plan*. Baltimore: Maryland Department of Labor.
Massey, Douglas S. 1995. "The New Immigration and Ethnicity in the United States." *Population and Development Review* 21, no. 3: 631–652.
Matsunaga and Yamauchi. 2004. "Is the Government Failure Theory Still Relevant? A Panel Analysis Using US Data." *Annals of Public and Cooperative Economics* 75 no. 2, 227–263.
Mauer, Marc. 2009. *The Changing Racial Dynamics of the War on Drugs*. Washington: The Sentencing Project.
Mayor of Baltimore v. Wells Fargo Bank, N.A., 677 F. Supp. 2d 847 (D. Md. 2010).
McCord, Charles William, John Howard, Bernard Friedberg, and Edwin Harwood. 1969. *Life Styles in the Black Ghetto*. New York: W. W. Norton & Co.
McGraw, Jake. 2014. "Three New Year's Resolutions for Mississippi." *The Hechinger Report*. http://hechingerreport.org/content/three-new-years-resolutions-for-mississippi_14358/ .
McLoyd, Vonnie. C., Nikki Aikens, and Linda Burton. 2006. "Childhood Poverty, Policy, and Practice." In W. Damon, R. Lerner, A. Renninger, and I. Sigel, eds. *Handbook of Child Psychology*: Vol. 4. Child Psychology in Practice (6th ed., pp. 700–775). New York: Wiley.
McWilliams, John C. 1990. The Protectors: *Harry J. Anslinger and the Federal Bureau of Narcotics, 1930–1962*. Newark, DE: University of Delaware.
Melish, T. J. Maximum. 2010. "Feasible Participation of the Poor: New Governance, New Accountability, and a 21st Century War on the Sources of Poverty." *Yale Human Rights & Development Law Journal* 13: 1–133.
Mendel, Richard A. 2011. "No Place for Kids: The Case for Reducing Juvenile Incarceration." Baltimore: Annie E. Casey Foundation.
Mendelberg, Tali. 2001. *The Race Card: Campaign Strategy, Implicit Messages, and the Norm of Equality*. Princeton: Princeton University Press.
Mennel, Robert. M. 1983. "Attitudes and Policies Toward Juvenile Delinquency in the United States: A Historiographical Review." *Crime and Justice* 4: 191–224.
Meyers, Joan S. 2005. "Workplace Democracy Comes of Age: Economic Stability, Growth, and Workforce Diversity." *Research in the Sociology of Work* 16: 205–237.
Middlemass, Keesha M. 2007. "The Carceral States of America." In *Racializing Justice, Disenfranchising Lives: The Racism, Criminal Justice, and Law Reader*, edited by Manning Marable, Ian Steinberg, and Keesha M. Middlemass. New York: Palgrave Macmillan.
Middlemass, Keesha M. Forthcoming. *The Mark of Cain: Socially Disabled by a Felony Conviction*. New York: New York University Press.
Miller, Kathleen K., and Bruce A. Weber. 2003. *Persistent Poverty Across the Rural-Urban Continuum*. Columbia, MO: Rural Poverty Research Center.

Miller-Adams, Michelle. 2002. *Owning Up: Poverty, Assets, and the American Dream*. Washington, DC: Brookings Institution.

Minor, Kevin I. 1993. "Juvenile Delinquency and the Transition to Monopoly Capitalism." *Journal of Sociology and Social Welfare* 20: 59–80.

Mirengoff, William, and Lester Rindle. 1976. The Comprehensive Employment and Training Act: Impact on People, Places, Programs: An Interim Report, prepared at the request of the Committee on Evaluation of Employment and Training Programs, Assembly of Behavioral and Social Sciences, National Research Council. Washington, DC: National Academy Press.

Mississippi Economic Council—The State Chamber of Commerce. "Governor Outlines Health Care Development Strategy at Summit." MEC The State Chamber of Commerce Mississippi Economic Council. http://www.msmec.com/home-page-featured-article/governor-certifies-health-care-zone-master-plans-for-12–mississippi-communities .

Mississippi Health Advocacy Program. "Medicaid Expansion." Expand Health Care Mississippi Health Care Access. http://www.accessms.org/wp-content/uploads/2013/01/MHAP-Medicaid-Expansion-Brochure-Web3–copy.pdf .

Mittelstadt, Jennifer. 2005. *From Welfare to Workfare: the Unintended Consequences of Liberal Reform, 1945–1965*. Chapel Hill: University of North Carolina Press, 2005.

Mohl, Raymond A. 1995. "Making the Second Ghetto in Metropolitan Miami, 1940–1960," *Journal of Urban History*, 21: 395–427.

———. 2002. The Interstates and the Cities: Highways, Housing, and the Freeway Revolt. Research Report. Poverty and Race Research Action Council.

Mondragon Cooperative Corporation. 2013. "Mondragon General Council reaches unanimous agreement on the future of Fagor Electrodomésticos, Mondragon's General Council. http://www.mondragon-corporation.com/eng/mondragons-general-council-reaches-unanimous-agreement-on-the-future-of-fagor-electrodomesticos/ .

———. 2014. "Mondragon Corporation, Co-operative Experience, History." http://www.mondragon-corporation.com/eng/co-operative-experience/history/ .

Mood, Frederic D. Weinfield, and Robert L. York. 1967. "Equality of Educational Opportunity." *American Journal of Sociology* 32, no. 3: 354–356.

Moody, Blair. 1938. "Republican Party's New Deal is Seen as Based on Profit Sharing: Senate Group Gathers Facts." *Milwaukee Journal*, November 27. Accessed March 5, 2014. http://news.google.com/newspapers?nid=1499&dat=19381127&id=hXYxAAAAIBAJ&sjid=HCIEAAAAIBAJ&pg=6672,2818580 .

Moretti, Enrico. 2012. *The New Geography of Jobs*. New York: Houghton Mifflin Harcourt Publishing Co.

Morgenson, Gretchen. 2008. "Baltimore is Suing Bank Over Foreclosure Crisis." *New York Times*, January 8, 2008. http://www.nytimes.com/2008/01/08/us/08baltimore.html .

———. 2008. "Lender Tells Judge it 'Recreated' Letters." *New York Times*, January 8. http://www.nytimes.com/2008/01/08/business/08lend.html?pagewanted=print .

Moss, Phillip, and Christ Tilly. 1991 *Why Black Men are Doing Worse in the Labor Market: A Review of Supply-Side and Demand-Side Explanations*. New York: Social Science Research Council.

Moynihan, Daniel Patrick. 1969. *Maximum Feasible Misunderstanding: Community Action in the War on Poverty*. New York: The Free Press.

———. 1969. *On Understanding Poverty: Perspectives from the Social Sciences*. New York: Basic Books.

———. 1973. *The Politics of A Guaranteed Income: The Nixon Administration and the Family Assistance Plan*. New York: Random House.

Mulchaly, Richard P. 2000. *A Social Contract for the Coal Fields: The Rise and Fall of the United Mine Workers of America Welfare and Retirement Fund*. Knoxville: University of Tennessee Press.

Murphy, Alexandra K. 2007. "The Suburban Ghetto: The Legacy of Herbert Gans in Understanding the Experience of Poverty in Recently Impoverished American Suburbs." *City & Community* 6, no. 1: 21–37.

———. 2010. The Symbolic Dilemmas of Suburban Poverty: Challenges and Opportunities Posed by Variations in the Contours of Suburban Poverty. *Sociological Forum* 25, no. 3: 541–569.

Murray, Charles. 1984. *Losing Ground: American Social Policy, 1950–1980*. New York: Basic Books.

Musto, David F. 1991. "Opium, Cocaine and Marijuana in American History." *Scientific American*, July, 1991.

———. 1999. *The American Disease: Origins of Narcotic Control,* 3rd Edition. New York: Oxford University Press.

Nadasen, Premilla. 2007. "From Widow to 'Welfare Queen': Welfare and the Politics of Race." *Black Women, Gender & Families* 1, no. 2.

NCEO. "ESOP Vesting, Distribution, and Diversification Rules." The National Center for Employee Ownership. Accessed March 5, 2014. http://www.nceo.org/articles/esop-vesting-distribution-diversification .

———. "How an Employee Stock Ownership Plan (ESOP) Works." Accessed March 5, 2014. http://www.nceo.org/main/article.php/id/8/ .

———. "Largest Study Yet Shows ESOPs Improve Performance and Employee Benefits." Accessed March 5, 2014. http://www.nceo.org/articles/esops-improve-performance-employee-benefits .

National Center for Educational Statistics. 2000. *From the Early Childhood Longitudinal Study, Kindergarten Class of 1998–99, Fall 1998,* NCES 2000–070. Washington: United States Department of Education.

———. 2006. *The Condition of Education*, Washington, DC: United States Department of Education.

———. 2008. *Digest of Education Statistics*, Washington, DC: United States Department of Education.

National Center for Health Statistics, 2005. *Health United States, 2005: With Chartbook on Trends in the Health of Americans*. Hyattsville: National Center for Health Statistics.

National Community Reinvestment Coalition 2007. *Access to Capital and Credit for Small Businesses in Appalachia.* Washington, DC: National Community Reinvestment Coalition.

National Cooperative Business Association. nd. "Types of Cooperatives." Accessed January 20, 2014. http://usa2012.coop/about-co-ops/types .

National Education Association. 2014. "Rankings of the States 2012 and Estimates of School Statistics 2013." Accessed February 24. http://www.nea.org/home/54597.html .

National Juvenile Justice Network. 2007 *Advances in Juvenile Justice Reform 2006–2007.* Washington: National Juvenile Justice Network.

National Juvenile Justice Network and Texas Public Policy Foundation. 2013. *The Comeback States: Reducing Youth Incarceration in the United States*. Washington: National Juvenile Justice Network.

National Research Council. 2000. *Promoting Health: Strategies from Social and Behavioral Research*. Washington: National Academy Press.

NCRC. (n.d). *NCRC Releases Report on Capital and Credit Access for Small Businesses in the Appalachian Region.* Retrieved from http://www.ncrc.org/media-center/press-releases/item/903–ncrc-releases-report-on-capital-and-credit-access-for-small-businesses-in-the-appalachian-region .

Neill, M., L. Guisbond, and B. Schaeffer. 2004. *Summary Report: Failing Our Children, How "No Child Left Behind" Undermines Quality and Equity in Education*. Jamaica Plain, MA: The National Center for Fair and Open Testing.

Nembhard, Jessica Gordon. 2002. "Cooperatives and Wealth Accumulation: Preliminary Analysis." *American Economic Review* 92, no. 2: 325–329.

Neubeck, Kenneth J., and Noel A. Cazenave. 2002 *Welfare Racism: Playing the Race Card Against America's Poor*. New York: Routledge.

New York Times. "F.B.I. Chief Opposed Use of 'Delinquent,'" *New York Times*, December 30, 1960, 2:3.

Newman, Kathe. 2009. "Post-Industrial Widgets: Capital Flows and the Production of the Urban," *International Journal of Urban and Regional Research* 33, no. 2: pp. 314–331.

Niedt, Christopher. 2006. Gentrification and the Grassroots: Popular Support in the Revanchist Suburb. *Journal of Urban Affairs* 28, no. 2: 99–120.

Nixon, Richard. 1970. "Special Message to the Congress on the Administration's Legislative Program," speech, The White House, Washington, DC, September 11.

No Child Left Behind. "Mississippi Report Card." Mississippi Report Card. Last modified 2012. Accessed February 2014. http://www.gsd.k12.ms.us/testing/NCLBsta11–12.pdf.

Norris, Pippa, and Ronald Inglehart. 2004. *Sacred and Secular: Religion and Politics Worldwide*. New York: Cambridge University Press.

NPR. (n.d). *Transcript: JFK's Speech on His Religion*. Retrieved December 16, 2013, http://www.npr.org/templates/story/story.php?storyId=16920600.

Nwokocha, Paschal O. 2008. "American Employment-Based Immigration Program in a Competitive Global Marketplace: Need for Reform." *William Mitchell Law Review* 35, no. 1: 38–67.

Nyhan, Ronald C., and Mohammad G. Alkadry. 1999. "The Impact of School Resources on Student Achievement test scores," *Journal of Education Finance* 25: 211–228.

Obama, Barack H. 2014. "Statement by the President on the 50th Anniversary of the War on Poverty," speech, The White House, Washington, DC, January 8.

Office of Juvenile Justice and Delinquency Prevention. 2012. *OJJDP Statistical Briefing Book* Washington: Office of Juvenile Justice and Delinquency Prevention.

Office of Public Affairs. 2012. "Website provides information on state health care infrastructure." Mississippi State University. Last modified October 01. http://www.msstate.edu/web/media/detail.php?id=5715.

Office of Refugee Resettlement, U.S. Dept. of Health and Human Services, "Fiscal Year 2012 Refugee Arrivals" (Jan. 24, 2013), available at http://www.acf.hhs.gov/programs/orr/resource/fiscal-year-2012–refugee-arrivals.

———. "History: Annual Refugee Arrival Data by Resettlement State and Country of Origin," available at http://www.acf.hhs.gov/programs/orr/about/history (last accessed March 25, 2014).

Ogbu, John U. 2003. *Black American Students in an Affluent Suburb: A Study of Academic Disengagement*. New York: Routledge.

O'Shea, Dan, and Christopher T. King. 2001. "The Workforce Investment Act of 1998: Restructuring Workforce Development Initiatives in States and Localities."http://www.utexas.edu/research/cshr/pubs/pdf/wia_final_2001.pdf.

Pager, Devah. 2007. *Marked: Race, Crime and Finding Work in an Era of Mass Incarceration*. Chicago: University of Chicago Press.

Parikh, Rahul. 2006. "Obesity in Kids?—See Poverty Line / Solution is Lifting People Out of the Class of Poor." *San Francisco Chronicle*. August 13, 2006. Accessed January 19, 2014.

Park, Rhokeun, Douglas Kruse, and James Sesil. 2004. "Does Employee Ownership Enhance Firm Survival?." *Advances in the Economic Analysis of Participatory & Labor-Managed Firms* 8: 3–33.

Parrott, Sharon. 2014. "War on Poverty: Large Positive Impact, But More Work Remains." Washington: Center on Budget and Policy Priorities.

Passel, Jeffrey S. 2011. "Demography of Immigrant Youth: Past, Present, and Future." *The Future of Children* 21, no. 1: 19–41.

PDA. 2012. *Health Care Costs and Access Disparities in Appalachia*. Raleigh: PDA, Inc.

Pearce, Diana, Barbara E. Wall, and William Werpehowski. 1990. "The Feminization of Poverty." *Journal for Peace and Justice Studies* 2, no. 1: 1–20.

Pearlstein, Steven. 2007. "No Money Down Falls Flat." *Washington Post,* March 14, D1.

Pence, Karen M. 2003. "Foreclosing on Opportunity: State Laws and Mortgage Credit." *The Review of Economics and Statistics* 88, no. 1:177–182.

Peri, Giovanni. n.d. "Immigrant Workers, Native Poverty and Labor Market Competition." *Center for Poverty Research* 1, no. 3. http://poverty.ucdavis.edu/sites/main/files/file-attachments/policy_brief_peri_immigration_print.pdf.

Peterson, Christopher. 2007. *Predatory Structured Finance.* Gainesville, FL: Levin College of Law, University of Florida.

PHI. 2014. Nursing and Residential Care Workers Suffer Highest Occupational Injury Rates. Retrieved on Jan. 2, 2013 from http://phinational.org/blogs/nursing-and-residential-care-workers-suffer-highest-occupational-injury-rates .
Piven, Frances Fox, and Richard Cloward. 1993. *Regulating the Poor: The Functions of Public Welfare*. New York: Vintage.
Pollard, Kelvin, and Linda A. Jacobsen. 2014. *The Appalachian Region: A Data Overview From the 2007–2011 American Community Survey Chartbook*. Accessed March 26, 2014. http://www.prb.org/pdf13/appalachia-census-chartbook-2012.pdf .
Private School Review. "Mississippi Private Schools." Private School Review. Accessed 2014. http://www.privateschoolreview.com/state_private_schools/stateid/MS .
Profitt, N. J. 1999. "Book Review: Battered Women, Children, and Welfare Reform: The Ties That Bind." *Affilia* 14, no. 4: 491–493.
Plyler v. Doe, 457 U.S. 202 (1982).
Racial and Ethnic Disparities in Access to Health Insurance and Healthcare. 2000. Los Angeles: UCLA Center for Health Policy Research.
Raley, Gordon A. 1995. "JDDP Act: A Second Look." *Juvenile Justice* 2, no. 2: 11–18.
Reagan, Ronald. 1987. "Project Economic Justice," speech, the White House, Washington, DC
Rector, Robert. 2006. "Importing Poverty: Immigration and Poverty in the United States. A Book of Charts." Washington: The Heritage Foundation.
Refugee Act of 1980, 8 U.S.C.S. §§ 1521 et seq.
Relman, John P. 2003. "Taking it to the Courts: Litigation and the Reform of Financial Institutions" in Gregory D. Squires, ed., *Organizing Access to Capital: Advocacy and the Democratization of Financial Institutions*. Philadelphia: Temple University Press, 55–71.
Relman, John P., Fred Rivera, Meera Trehan, and S. Sphilpa. Satoskar. 2004. "Designing Federal Legislation That Works: Legal Remedies for Predatory Lending." In *Why the Poor Pay More: How to Stop Predatory Lending*, edited by Gregory D. Squires. Westport, CT: Praeger, pp. 153–184.
Renuart, Elizabeth. 2004. "An Overview of the Predatory Lending Process." *Housing Policy Debate* 15, no. 3: 467–502.
Renzetti, Claire M. 2001. "One Strike and You're Out: Implications of a Federal Crime Control Policy for Battered Women." *Violence Against Women* 7, no. 6: 685–698.
Report of the National Advisory Commission on Civil Disorders. 1968. New York: Bantam Books.
Reynolds, David, Charles Teddlie, Sam Stringfield, and Bert Creemers. 2002. *Class Schools: International Perspectives on School Effectiveness*. London: Routledge/Falmer.
Rhodes, Susan R., and Richard M. Steers. 1981. "Conventional vs. Worker-Owned Organizations." *Human Relations* 34, no. 12: 1013–1035.
Richie, Beth. 2012. *Arrested Justice: Black Women, Violence and America's Prison Nation*. New York: New York University Press.
Rivera, Amaad, Brenda Cotto-Escalera, Anisha Desai, Jeannette Huezo, and Dedrick Muhammad. 2008. "Foreclosed: State of the Dream 2008." Boston: United for a Fair Economy.
Roback, Jennifer. 1982. "Wages, Rents and the Quality of Life." *Journal of Political Economy* 90: 1257–1278.
Roberts, Ashley. 2010. "Stanley Furniture Laying Off 530 Employees." *WSLS10*, May 12. .
Rodgers, Harrell R. 2005. *American Poverty in a New Era of Reform*. Armonk: M.E. Sharpe.
Rosenberger, Leif R. 1996. *America's Drug War Debacle*. Brookfield: Ashgate Publishing Co.
Ross, Christine, Sheldon Danzinger, and Eugene Smolensky. 1987. "The Level and Trend of Poverty in the United States, 1939–1979." *Demography* 24, no. 4: 587–600.
Rotberg, Iris, and James Harvey. 1993. "Federal Policy Options for Improving the Education of Low-Income Students: Volume I, Findings and Recommendations." *Rand*. Santa Monica: Institute on Education and Training.
Rothstein, Richard. 2004. *Class and Schools: Using Social, Economic and Educational Reform to Close the Black-White Achievement Gap*. Washington DC: Economic Policy Institute.
Rubinowitz, Leonard S., and James E. Rosenbaum. 2000. *Crossing the Class and Color Lines: From Public Housing to White Suburbia*. Chicago: University of Chicago Press.

Rumberger, Russell W. 2003. "The Causes and Consequences of Student Mobility." *Journal of Negro Education* 72, no. 1: 6–21.

Ruth, Henry, and Kevin R. Reitz. 2003. *The Challenges of Crime: Rethinking Our Response*. Cambridge: Harvard University Press.

Ryan, William. 1976. *Blaming the Victim*. New York: Pantheon Books.

Sadovnik, Alan R., Peter W. Cookson, and Susan F. Semel. 2006. *Exploring Education: An Introduction to the Foundations of Education*. Needham Heights: Allyn and Bacon.

Salamon, Lester, and Alan Abrahamson. 1986. "The Nonprofit Sector and the Federal Budget." Washington, DC: The Urban Institute.

Salsich, Peter W. 1999. "Thinking About Affordable Housing and Neighborhood Development." *Stetson Law Review* 28: 577–605.

Sampson, Robert J. 2012. *Great American City: Chicago and the Enduring Neighborhood Effect*. Chicago: University of Chicago Press.

Sassen, Saskia. 1991. *The Global City: New York, London, Tokyo*. Princeton: Princeton University Press.

Satter, Beryl. 2010. *Family Properties: Race, Real Estate, and the Exploitation of Black Urban America*. New York: Metropolitan Books.

Scala, Elise. 2008. *Home and Community Based Services Workforce and Quality Outcomes*. In E. Scala, L. Hendrickson, and C. Ryan, ed. A Compendium of Three Discussion Papers: Strategies for Promoting and Improving and Improving the Direct Service Workforce. New Brunswick: Rutgers Center for State Health Policy.

Schaars, Marvin A. 1971. *Cooperatives, Principles and Practices*. Madison: University of Wisconsin.

Schmidt, Dana Adams. 1971. "President Orders Wider Drug Fight; Asks $155 Million." *New York Times,* June 18, 1971.

Schor, Juliet B. 2011. *True Wealth: How and Why Millions of Americans are Creating a Time-Rich, Ecologically Light, Small-Scale, High-Satisfaction Economy*. New York: Penguin.

Scott, Charles L., and Joan B. Gerbasi. 2005. *Handbook of Correctional Mental Health*. Arlington: American Psychiatric Publishers.

Scott, Ellen K., Kathryn Edin, Andrew S. London, and Rebecca Joyce Kissane. 2004. "Unstable Work, Unstable Income: Implications for Family Well-Being in the Era of Time-Limited Welfare." *Journal of Poverty* 8, no. 1: 61–88.

Shappley, Jessica. 2012. New State Level Census Data Findings Emphasize Urgency for State to Fully Implement Health Care Reform. *Policy Matters Blog*. Mississippi Economic Policy Council. September 13. Accessed March 28, 2014. http://mepconline.org/new-state-level-census-data-findings-emphasize-urgency-for-state-to-fully-implement-health-care-reform .

"Sharing the Profits: Businessmen Get a New Religion." 1954. *Time*. December 6, 1954.

Sherman, Arloc, Sharron Parrott, and Danilo Trisi. 2014. *Chart Book: The War on Poverty at 50, Section 3*, January 7. Last accessed March 25, 2014, http://www.cbpp.org/cms/index.cfm?fa=view&id=4073 .

Shields, John. 2004. "No Safe Haven: Work, Welfare, and the Growth of Immigrant Exclusion." In *Immigrants, Welfare Reform, and the Poverty of Policy*, Philip Kretsedemas and Ana Aparicio, eds. Westport: Praeger, pp. 35–62.

Short, Kathleen. 2013. *The Research Supplemental Poverty Measure: 2012*, U.S Bureau of the Census. Washington: Bureau of the Census.

Shriver, Maria, and the Center for American Progress. 2009. "The Shriver Report: A Woman's Nation Changes Everything."

———. 2014. "The Shriver Report: A Woman's Nation Pushed Back from the Brink."

Sigle-Rushton, Wendy, and Sara McLanahan. 2002. "Father Absence and Child Well-Being: A Critical Review." Princeton: Robert Wood Johnson Foundation.

Silberman, Charles E. 1964. "Give Slum Children a Chance." *Harper's magazine*, May.

Silver, Michael. 1966. "The Emergency Department Problem." *Journal of the American Medical Association* 198: 146.

Silverglate, Harvey A. 2011. *Three Felonies a Day: How the Feds Target the Innocent*. New York: Encounter Books.

Simkins v. Moses, 323 F.2d 959 (1963).

Simmons, Richard, and Johnston Birchall. 2008. "The Role of Co-operatives in Poverty Reduction: Network Perspectives." NGPA Working Paper No. 10. Accessed February 1, 2014. http://www.lse.ac.uk/internationalDevelopment/research/NGPA/publications/WP10_RoleofCoops_web.pdf.

Singer, Audrey. 2004. "Welfare Reform and Immigrants: A Policy Review." In *Immigrants, Welfare Reform, and the Poverty of Policy*, Philip Kretsedem and Ana Aparicio, eds. Westport: Praeger, pp. 21–34.

Sirianni, Carmen. 1995. "Learning Pluralism: Democracy and Diversity in Feminist Organizations." In *Democratic Community: NOMOS XXXV*, edited by John W. Chapman and Ian Shapiro. New York: New York University Press, pp. 283–312.

Sirin, Cigdem V. 2011. "From Nixon's War on Drugs to Obama's Drug Policies Today: Presidential Progress in Addressing Racial Injustices and Disparities." *Race, Gender & Class* 18, no. 3–4: 82–99.

Smith, Anna Marie. 2007. *Welfare Reform and Sexual Regulation*. New York: Cambridge University Press.

Smith, David Barton. 1998. "Addressing Racial Inequities in Health Care: Civil Rights Monitoring and Report Cards." *Journal of Health Politics, Policy and Law* 23, no. 1: 75–105.

Smith, Kristen, and Reagan Baughman. 2007. "Caring for America's Aging Population: A Profile of the Direct-Care Workforce." *Monthly Labor Review* 130, no. 9: 20–26.

Smith, Richard. 1997. "The future of healthcare systems." *BMJ: British Medical Journal* 314: 1495.

Smith, Stephen. 1985. "Political Behavior as an Economic Externality: Econometric Evidence on the Relationship between Ownership and Decision Making Participation in U.S. Firms and Participation in Community Affairs." In *Advances in the Economic Analysis of Participatory and Labor-Managed Firms*, Derek C. Jones and Jan Svejnar, eds. Greenwich: JAI Press.

Snow, Catherine, and Patton Tabors. "Intergenerational Transfer of Literacy." *In Family Literacy: Directions in Research and Implications for Practice*, Benjamin L. Ann and Jerome E. Lord, eds. Washington, DC: U.S. Department of Education, pp. 73–79.

Snyder, Howard N., and Melissa Sickmund. 1995. *Juvenile Offenders and Victims: A National Report*. Washington: Office of Juvenile Justice and Delinquency Prevention.

Soss, Joe, Richard C. Fording, and Sanford F. Schram. 2011. *Disciplining the Poor: Neoliberal Paternalism and the Persistent Power of Race*. Chicago: University of Chicago Press.

Soss, Joe, Sanford F. Schram, Thomas P. Vartanian, and Erin O'Brien. 2001. "Setting the Terms of Relief: Explaining State Policy Choices in the Devolution Revolution." *American Journal of Political Science* 45, no. 2: 378–395.

Southern Education Foundation. 2013. "A New Majority: Low Income Students in the South and Nation." http://www.southerneducation.org/Programs/P-12–Program/Early-Ed/NewMajority-by-location-within-states.aspx#.UwF-6P0p-MM.

Sponsored Enterprises, GAO/T-AFMD-89-16 (statement of James L. Kirkman before the Subcommittee on Oversight, House Ways and Means Committee, U.S. House of Representatives, September 28, 1989).

Stansby, Janet Friedman. 1967. "In Re Gault: Children are People." *California Law Review* 55, no. 4: 1204–1218.

Starr, Paul. 1982. *The Social Transformation of American Medicine*. New York: Basic Books.

State and County Estimates for 1993, U.S. Bureau of the Census (Washington, DC, 1993).

SteelFisher, Gillian K. 2004. "Addressing Unequal Treatment: Disparities in Healthcare." New York: The Commonwealth Fund.

Stein, Sam. 2011. "Barbour On Mississippi's 18 Percent Uninsured: No One Lacks Access To Health Care." *Huff Post Politics*, April 20. Accessed January 6, 2014. http://www.huffingtonpost.com/2011/04/20/barbour-on-mississippis-1_n_851690.html 1–6–14.

Steinbeck, John. 1939. *The Grapes of Wrath*. New York: Viking Press.

Steven, Raphael, and Eugene Smolensky. 2009. "Immigration and Poverty in the United States." *Focus* 26, no. 2: 27–31.

Stiglitz, Joseph E. 2012. *The Price of Inequality: How Today's Divided Society Endangers Our Future*. New York: W. W. Norton & Company.

Stone, Robyn I. 2004. "The Direct Care Worker: The Third Rail of Home Care Policy." *Annual Review of Public Health* 25: 521–537.

Strauss, Valerie. 2013. "Mississippi Governor: Educational Troubles Began when 'Mom Is in the Workplace." *The Answer Sheet*, June 4. Accessed February 2014. http://www.washingtonpost.com/blogs/answer-sheet/wp/2013/06/04/mississippi-governor-educational-troubles-began-when-mom-got-in-the-workplace/ .

Stringfield, Sam, Mary Ann Millsap, and Rebecca Herman. 1997. "Urban and Suburban/Rural Special Strategies for Educating Disadvantaged Children: Final Report." Washington, DC: U.S. Department of Education.

Stuntz, William J. 2001. "The Pathological Politics of Criminal Law." *Michigan Law Review* 100: 505–600.

Sugrue, Thomas J. 2005. *The Origins of the Urban Crisis: Race and Inequality in Postwar Detroit*. Princeton: Princeton University Press.

———. 2008. *Sweet Land of Liberty: The Forgotten Struggle for Civil Rights in the North*. New York: Random House.

Sundquist, James L. 1968. *Politics and Policy: The Eisenhower, Kennedy and Johnson Years*. Washington, DC: Brookings Institution Press.

Suro, Roberto, Jill H. Wilson, and Audrey Singer. 2011. "Immigration and Poverty in America's Suburbs." Brookings Institution. http://www.brookings.edu/research/papers/2011/08/04–immigration-suro-wilson-singer .

Sutter, John D. 2013 "The Most Unequal Place in America." CNN, October 30. Accessed February, 2014. http://www.cnn.com/2013/10/29/opinion/sutter-lake-providence-income-inequality/ .

Swartz, Katherine. 2009. *Health Care for the Poor: For Whom, What Care, and Whose Responsibility?* in *Changing Poverty, Changing Policies*, M. Cancian and S. Danziger, eds. New York: Russell Sage Foundation Press.

Teitz, Michael B., and Karen Chapple. 1998. "The Causes of Inner-City Poverty: Eight Hypotheses in Search of Reality." *Cityscape: A Journal of Policy Development and Research* 3: 33–70.

Thompson, Anthony C. 2008. *Releasing Prisoners, Redeeming Communities: Reentry, Race and Politics*. New York: New York University Press.

Tilak, Jandhyala B. G. 2002. "Education and Poverty." *Journal of Human Development* 3: 191–207.

Timmer Ashley S., and Jeffrey G. Williamson. 1998. "Immigration Policy Prior to the 1930s: Labor Markets, Policy Interactions, and Globalization Backlash." *Population and Development Review* 24, no. 4: 739–771.

Toft, Jessica. 2010. "The Political Act of Public Talk: How Legislators Justified Welfare Reform." *Social Service Review* 84, no. 4: 563–596.

Transportation Research Board's National Cooperative Highway Research Program (NCHRP). 2006. *Task -1: The Interstate and National Highway System: A Brief History and Lessons Learned*. Washington: The National Academies.

Travis, Jeremy. 2005. *But They All Come Back: Facing the Challenges of Prisoner Reentry*. Washington, DC: The Urban Institute.

Turner, Franklin Dickerson. 2010. "Evaluating the Effectiveness of Fluency Oriented Reading Instruction with Increasing Black and Latino, As Compared to Asian and White Second-Grade Students' Reading Fluency." *Journal of Negro Education* 79 no. 2: 112–124.

U.S. Bureau of the Census, *S0501 Selected Social Characteristics of the Native-Born and Foreign-Born Populations [Data], 2010 American Community Survey 5–Year Estimates* (Washington, DC).

U.S. Commission on Civil Rights, *Racial Isolation in the Public Schools*, Research report no. 7, CCR Clearinghouse Publication (Washington, DC, 1967).

U.S. Department of Agriculture. 2013. Rural America at a Glance.

U.S. Department of Health and Human Services, *Report of the Secretary's Task Force on Black and Minority Health*, 8 vols. (Washington, DC: U.S. Government Printing Office, 1985).

U.S. Department of Homeland Security, *Yearbook of Immigration Statistics: 2011* (Washington, DC: U.S. Dept. of Homeland Security, Office of Immigration Statistics, 2012).

U.S. Department of Labor, Office of Policy Planning and Research. 1965. The Negro Family: The Case for National Action. Washington, DC: U.S. Department of Labor.

U.S. Federation of Worker Cooperatives. nd. "Frequently Asked Questions About Worker Cooperatives," *US Federation of Worker Cooperatives*, last visited January 18, 2014, http://www.usworker.coop/about/what-is-a-worker-coop .

———. nd. "Resources," *US Federation of Worker Cooperatives*, last visited January 18, 2014, http://www.usworker.coop/usfwc-resources .

———. 2014c. "What is a Worker Coop?" *US Federation of Worker Cooperatives*, last visited January 18, 2014, http://www.usworker.coop/about/what-is-a-worker-coop .

U.S. General Accounting Office. 1987. *Employee Stock Ownership Plans: Little Evidence of Effects on Corporate Performance* Washington: Government Printing Office.

———. *Health Care: Approaches to Address Racial and Ethnic Disparities*, briefing prepared for Congressional Staff of Senator Bill Frist, GAO-03–862R (Washington, DC, 2003).

———. *Elementary School Children: Many Change Schools Frequently, Harming their Education*, report to Marcy Kaptur, U.S. House of Representatives, GAO/HEHS-94–45 (Washington, DC, 1994).

U.S. Government Accountability Office, *Financial Markets and Institutions: Government.*

U.S. Housing Act of 1937, 75 U.S.C. § 50 Stat. 888 et seq. (1937).

U.S. Housing Act of 1949, 81 U.S.C, § 63 Stat 578 et seq. (1949).

U.S. Sentencing Commission. *1995 Annual Report* (Washington, DC, 1995).

Velasquez-Manoff, Moises. 2014. "What Happens When the Poor Receive a Stipend?" *New York Times*. Last modified January 18.

Velez-Ibanez, Carlos G., and James B. Greenberg. 1992. "Schooling Processes Among U.S. Mexicans, Puerto Ricans, and Cubans: A Comparative, Distributive, and Case Study Approach." In T. Weaver, ed. *Hispanics in the United States*. Houston, Texas: Arte Publico Press.

Von Hoffman, Alexander. 2009. "A Study in Contradictions: The Origins and Legacy of the Housing Act of 1949." *Housing Policy Debate* 11: 299–326.

Wacquant, Loïc. 2009. "The New Peculiar Institution: On the Prison as Surrogate Ghetto." *Theoretical Criminology* 4, no. 3: 377–89.

———. 2009. *Prisons of poverty*. Vol. 23. Minneapolis: University of Minnesota Press.

Wacquant, Loïc J., and William Julius Wilson. 1989. "The Cost of Racial and Class Exclusion in the Inner City," *Annals of the American Academy of Political and Social Sciences*, 501: 8–25.

Walker, Gerald. 1963. "Englewood and the Northern Dilemma." *The Nation*, July 6, 1963: 7–10.

Waters, Mary C., and Reed Ueda. 2007. *The New Americans. A Guide to Immigration since 1965*. Cambridge: Harvard University Press.

Werner, Emmy E., and Ruth S. Smith. 1992. *Overcoming the Odds: High Risk Children from Birth to Adulthood.* Ithaca, NY: Cornell University Press.

Westerm, Bruce, and Becky Pettit. 2010. "Incarceration and Social Inequality." *Dædalus* 139, no. 3: 8–19.

Whitaker, Julie, Stu Schneider, and Margaret Bau. 2005. "Home Care Cooperatives: Worker Ownership in Focus." Accessed January 2, 2013. h ttp://www.uwcc.wisc.edu/info/health/homecare.pdf .

White, Lawrence J. 2002. "The Credit Reporting Industry: An Industrial Organization Analysis." NYU Center for Law Research Paper No. 01-001. http://papers.ssrn.com/sol3/papers.cfm?abstract_id=267083 .

White House: Office of the Press Secretary, "Presidential Memorandum—Refugee Admissions for Fiscal Year 2014," WhiteHouse.gov (Oct. 2, 2013), available at http://www.whitehouse.gov/the-press-office/2013/10/02/presidential-memorandum-refugee-admissions-fiscal-year-2014 .

Whitehouse, Mark. 2007. "Day of Reckoning: 'Subprime' Aftermath: Losing the Family Home." *Wall Street Journal*. May 30, 2007.

Whyte, William Foote, and Kathleen King Whyte. 1991. *Making Mondragon: The Growth Dynamics of the Worker Cooperative Complex*. Ithaca: Cornell University Press.

Willen, Liz. 2012. "Mississippi Learning: Why the State's Students Start Behind—and Stay Behind. *Mississippi Learning: Why the State's Students Start Behind—and Stay Behind.*" *Time,* July 27, 2012.

Williamson, Kevin D. 2014. "The White Ghetto: In Appalachia the Country is Beautiful and the Society Is Broken." *National Review Online*, January 9. Accessed March 29, 2014. http://www.nationalreview.com/article/367903/white-ghetto-kevin-d-williamson .

Wilson, James Q. 1966. *Urban Renewal: The Record and the Controversy*. Cambridge: MIT Press.

Wilson, William Julius. 1980. *The Declining Significance of Race: Blacks and the Changing American Institutions*. Chicago: The University of Chicago Press.

———. 1987. *The Truly Disadvantaged: The Inner City, The Underclass, and Public Policy*. Chicago: The University of Chicago Press.

———. 1996. *When Work Disappears: The World of the New Urban Poor*. Princeton, NJ: Princeton University Press.

Wodak, Alex, Craig Reinarman, Peter Cohen, and Colin Drummond. 2002. "For and Against Cannabis Control: Costs Outweigh the Benefits." *British Medical Journal* 324: 105–108.

World Population Statistics. "Mississippi Population 2013." World Population Statistics. http://www.worldpopulationstatistics.com/mississippi-population-2013/ (accessed February 24, 2014).

Workforce Investment Act of 2013, H.R. 798, 113th Cong (2013).

Wyly, E. K., and D. J. Hammel. 2004. "Gentrification, Segregation, and Discrimination in the American Urban System." *Environmental & Planning Association*, 36 (7): 1215–1241.

Wyly, Elvin K., Mona Atia, Holly Foxcroft, Daniel J. Hamme, Kelly Phillps-Watts. 2006. "American Home: Predatory Mortgage Capital and Neighborhood Spaces of Race and Class Exploitation in the United States." *Geografiska Annaler: Series B, Human Geography*, 88 B, no. 1: 105–132.

Wyly, Elvin K., Markus Moos, Holly Foxcroft, and Emmanuel Kabahizi. 2008. "Subprime Mortgage Segmentation in the American Urban System." *Tijdschrift voor Economische en Sociale Geografie* 99, no. 1: 3–23.

Yarrow, Andrew L. 2011. "A History of Federal Child Antipoverty and Health Policy in the United States Since 1900." *Child Development Perspectives* 5, no. 1: 66–72.

Zhang, Ming. 2003. "Links Between School Absenteeism and Child Poverty." *Pastoral Care in Education* 21, no. 1: 10–17.

Zigler, Edward F., and Susan Muenchow. 1992. *Head Start: The Inside Story of America's Most Successful Educational Experiment*. New York: Basic Books.

Zimring, F. E. 1998. "The Youth Violence Epidemic: Myth or Reality?" 33 *Wake Forest Law Review* 727.

Zolberg, Aristide R. 2007. "Immigration Policy Control: Law and Implementation." In *The New Americans. A Guide to Immigration since 1965,* Mary C. Waters, Reed Ueda and Helen B. Marrow, eds. Cambridge: Harvard University Press, pp. 29–42.

Index

About the Editor

Kyle Farmbry is Acting Dean of The Graduate School and an Associate Professor in The School of Public Affairs and Administration (SPAA) at Rutgers University–Newark. Prior to joining the faculty of Rutgers, Farmbry taught at The University of Texas at San Antonio in San Antonio, Texas, San Diego State University in San Diego, California, and Grand Valley State University in Grand Rapids, Michigan. In February of 2009, Dr. Farmbry was selected as one of thirty-five people from around the world to serve as a Fulbright New Century Scholar. In this role, he was engaged in research examining factors of youth entrepreneurial and civic engagement in South Africa. In 2005, he was awarded a grant from the Japan Foundation's Center for Global Partnerships for a project entitled U.S.-Japanese NGO Network Development in the HIV/AIDS Crisis for exploratory work on nongovernmental organizations working in Japan on HIV/AIDS. In February of 2009, Dr. Farmbry's book *Administration and The Other: Explorations of Diversity and Marginalization in the Political Administrative State* was published by Rowman & Littlefield. In August 2012, his book *Crisis, Disaster, and Risk: Institutional Response and Emergence* was published by M. E. Sharpe. Dr. Farmbry received his BA, MPA, and PhD degrees from The George Washington University. He completed his JD degree at the Rutgers University School of Law.

About the Contributors

Mohamad G. Alkadry serves as Associate Professor and Director of the Florida International University (FIU) Master of Public Administration Program. He also serves as an affiliate faculty member of the FIU Women's Center. He received his PhD from Florida Atlantic University (2000) and his Master's of Public Policy and Public Administration from Concordia University in Quebec (1996). His undergraduate work was done at Carlton University in Canada (2002, 2004) and the American University of Beirut in Lebanon. Alkadry has over thirty peer-reviewed publications and one edited book (with Hugh Miller): *These Things Happen: Stories from the Public Sector*. His work appears in *Review of Public Personnel Administration*, *International Journal of Organizational Theory and Behavior*, *Public Administration Review*, *Administration and Society*, *Public Integrity*, *Journal of Education Finance*, *Social Work in Health Care*, *Public Productivity and Management Review*, *Public Administration and Management*, *Administrative Theory and Praxis*, among other journals. He recently published a book (with Leslie E. Tower) entitled: *Women and Public Service: Barriers, Challenges and Opportunities*. M. E. Sharpe).

Portia Allen-Kyle is a dedicated social justice researcher and advocate. She is the co-founder of Why.Race.Still.Matters, a social commentary blog and social media endeavor dedicated to highlighting the salience of race in the twenty-first century and sparking conversations on progress toward racial equality. Allen-Kyle earned a bachelor's degree in Economics and Africana Studies from Wellesley College, and a master's degree in African-American Studies from Columbia University. Her research focuses on race, social control, neighborhood change, and experiences of law; she has taught courses on the intersections of race and ethnicity, law, and criminal justice at both St. Thomas Aquinas College and Rutgers University.

Daphne Berry is an Assistant Professor of Management at the University of Hartford. Her research is on employee ownership, and diversity and social issues in organizations. Her past research has examined outcomes associated with various organizational forms including conventionally owned and managed for-profit, nonprofit, and worker cooperative businesses. She is also on the editorial board of a new journal on cooperative organizations, the *Journal of Co-operative Organization and Management.* Berry has bachelor's and master's degrees in Electrical Engineering from the University of Notre Dame and Rice University respectively and a PhD in Management with a concentration in Organization Studies from the University of Massachusetts at Amherst.

Sebawit G. Bishu, is currently a PhD student of Public Affairs at Florida International University. Ms. Bishu has a master's degree in urban planning from Addis Ababa University in Ethiopia and a second master's degree in public administration from Old Dominion University in Virginia. In her academic and professional work experience Bishu has engaged in teaching at Addis Ababa University in Ethiopia and has also worked with the physical design and planning workforce in Ethiopia in the fields of architecture and urban planning. She has also worked in the social and economic development policy areas with the Economic and Social Council (UN-ECOSOC) of the United Nations in New York. Bishu's current research areas are focused on gender issues in the public sector and the intersection of gender and poverty in urban development.

Franklin Dickerson Turner is an Assistant Professor of Educational Psychology at Queens College, The City University of New York. He received his B.S. in African American History from Florida A&M University, M.A. in Educational Psychology from Rutgers University–New Brunswick, and PhD in Urban Systems with a Concentration in Educational Psychology from Rutgers University-Newark. Prior to starting graduate school Turner was a middle school teacher in the Philadelphia School District, and he worked extensively in the nonprofit and public service fields. His research focuses on the achievement gap, mentoring, popular culture, fatherhood, and race and social class, especially in educational settings. He has published and presented in the areas of the racial and socioeconomic achievement gap, literacy acquisition, student stress, the importance of mentoring, fathers' involvement in child rearing, and coping skills.

Portia Diñoso Campos is a postdoctoral research associate and adjunct professor at the Askew School of Public Administration and Policy at Florida State University in Tallahassee, Florida. She is also assistant managing editor of *Public Administration Review*. She earned her PhD from Rutgers University in Newark, New Jersey, and her research interests include social capital, civic engagement, and immigration policy. A native of Jacksonville, Florida, Campos is an advocate for increasing cultural awareness and is dedicated to celebrating the diverse cultures of the Asian and the Pacific regions.

Rachel Dolezal holds a Master of Fine Arts degree from Howard University and has over ten years of experience teaching Black Studies and Art History at Eastern Washington University and North Idaho College. She has raised two sons as a single mother, sometimes holding together as many as five part-time jobs to pay the bills. Her scholarly research focuses on the intersection of race, class, and gender with an emphasis on how visualizations of black women affect life chances and outcomes in American culture. Dolezal is an award-winning artist, columnist, TV producer, professor, and community activist in the Inland Northwest.

Susan M. Glisson has served as the Executive Director of the William Winter Institute for Racial Reconciliation since 2002. She is a native of Evans, Georgia, and earned bachelor's degrees in Religion and in History from Mercer University, a master's degree in Southern Studies from the University of Mississippi, and a PhD in American Studies from the College of William and Mary. Glisson specializes in the history of race and religion in the United States, especially in the black struggle for freedom. She has numerous publications, has been quoted widely in the media and has supported community projects throughout the state for the Institute since its inception.

Alex Ingrams is a doctoral student in the School of Public Affairs and Administration, Rutgers University–Newark. He previously worked in government relations for a nonprofit and in the private sector in Washington, D.C., and London. He has published on the topic of international development and entrepreneurship education and has presented and led public policy workshops in the United States, the U.K., and as far afield as the Republic of Yemen. Ingrams has an MPP from American University and a BA from Cambridge University.

David Madland is the Director of the American Worker Project and the Managing Director of the Economic Policy team at the Center for American Progress. He has written extensively about the economy and American politics on a range of topics including retirement policy, labor unions, and workplace standards such as the minimum wage. His current work focuses on the importance of the middle class to the economy and democracy, as well as policies to restore the strength of the middle class. Madland has appeared frequently on television shows, including the PBS *News Hour* and CNN's *Crossfire*, been cited in such publications as the *New York Times*, the *Wall Street Journal*, the *Washington Post, and* the *New Yorker*, and been a guest on dozens of radio talk shows across the United States. He has testified before Congress on a number of occasions, as well as several state legislatures. Madland has a doctorate in government from Georgetown University and received his bachelor of science from the University of California, Berkeley. Dr. Madland is the co-author of *Interest Groups in Elections*, a book about the role and influence of interest groups in American democracy, and is the author of many academic articles.

Regina Malveaux, JD, is a nonprofit executive with a fifteen-year career in organizations serving poor women, children, and families. Malveaux began her career as a student organizer for the Children's Defense Fund and raised two young children while completing her undergraduate and law degrees. She holds an undergraduate degree in Social Policy from San Diego State University and a law degree from Howard University School of Law. Ms. Malveaux was 1 of 10 competitively selected Head Start Fellows in the Administration for Children & Families during the Clinton Administration and also worked in both Congress and the White House. She is honored to have the opportunity to serve families in her current role as Executive Director of a local YWCA.

Joanna Maulbeck is an education activist and a scholar of education, with much of her research focusing on the intersection of education and poverty. She has taught elementary school and college students—both undergraduate and graduate—in Mali, South Africa, Thailand, and the United States. Maulbeck earned a bachelor's degree in Elementary Education/Psychology from The College of New Jersey (TCNJ) and a master's degree in Global Affairs from Rutgers University. She is currently completing her PhD studies at Rutgers University; serves as an associate at the Center for the Study of Genocide and Human Rights, as well as Carnegie Council's Ethics Fellow for the Future; and teaches Child Development at TCNJ

Keesha M. Middlemass, PhD, is an Assistant Professor of American Politics, Urban Politics and Public Policy at Trinity University in San Antonio, Texas. Her research examines issues at the intersection of race, institutions and public policy. Her scholarship is published in *Aggressive Behavior*, *Criminal Justice & Behavior* and *Social Science Quarterly*. Her co-edited book, *Racializing Justice, Disenfranchising Lives*, explores the systemic crisis of mass imprisonment and mass disenfranchisement. Middlemass's single-authored book manuscript is under contract with New York University Press; utilizing an ethnographic research model, she links public policies, community factors and individual experiences to demonstrate how a felony conviction is socially disabling. Middlemass is a former Andrew Mellon Post-Doctoral Fellow on Race, Crime and Justice at the Vera Institute of Justice and a former American Political Science Association Congressional Fellow. She earned her PhD and MA from the School of International & Public Affairs at the University of Georgia.

Al Passarella is the Research Coordinator at Advocates for Children and Youth; a Baltimore, Maryland, based youth advocacy firm that evaluates the effectiveness of programs and policies for the state's children and youth. Previously, he worked as the Senior Research Associate at Education Law Center in Newark, New Jersey, specializing in equitable education funding for low-income school districts, and as a research consultant, where he provided expert analysis for firms working on issues related to urban community and economic development. Currently, his research interests are in the areas of Family Economic Security, Juvenile Justice, and Racial Equity Issues. Passarella is a graduate of William Paterson University of New Jersey (BA: Political Science) and the School of Public Affairs and Administration (SPAA) at Rutgers University–Newark (MPA: Public Administration).

Venessa Perry is the President/CEO of Health Resource Solutions (HRS), a company dedicated to developing solutions to health care issues that affect the underserved. During her twenty-year career she has worked in many organizations domestically and internationally: hospitals, non-profits and government educating and developing the capacity of the organizations to provide quality services to the underserved. Venessa is a leading expert in minority health, health disparities, HIV/AIDS, access to care and other issues that affect minorities. She is a veteran of the U.S. Army where she served as a nurse for ten years, holds a bachelor's degree in Biology from Trinity College, a master's in Public Health from the George Washington University School of Public Health, and was a W.K. Kellogg Foundation Emerging Leaders in Public Health Fellow. Currently, she is completing her doctorate in Counseling Psychology at Walden University.

Jennifer A. Stollman is an American historian who received her training at both Michigan State University and the University of Michigan. After teaching undergraduate and graduate students for eighteen years, Stollman decided to commit herself full time as an educator and activist. Currently, she is the Academic Director for the William Winter Institute for Racial Reconciliation housed at the University of Mississippi. Focusing on the institutional mission "ending all oppression based on difference," she creates and executes professional and student development and workshops on diversity issues, cultural humility programming, anti-oppression activism, focuses on creating systemic and institutional change and campus crisis management as it relates to oppression incidents. She has shared her strategies, techniques and programs with several other campuses across the United States. She also researches and publishes on American history, college campus anti-oppression strategies, curriculum, programming, and crisis management.

Rosie Jayde Uyola is an activist documentary filmmaker and American Studies digital humanities scholar. She is currently serving as a fellow at The Institute on Ethnicity, Culture, and the Modern Experience at Rutgers University. Uyola's recent project, Newark Remembers: Commemoration and Memory in America's 21st Century City, explores the links between public commemoration, civic engagement, and urban development.

Michael Vorgetts serves as the Acting Commissioner of the Maryland Department of Labor, Licensing and Regulation—Division of Occupational and Professional Licensing. The Division is charged with protecting consumers and ensuring a fair competitive environment for individuals who work in twenty-five regulated industries in the state. The Division licenses more than 225,000 individuals and businesses, and coordinates with the various other divisions of the state's labor department to facilitate workforce development, fair labor standards, and economic development activities in Maryland.

Karla Walter is Associate Director of the American Worker Project at The Center for American Progress. Karla focuses primarily on improving the economic security of American workers by increasing workers' wages and benefits, promoting workplace protections, and advancing workers' rights at work. Prior to joining American Progress, Walter was a research analyst at Good Jobs First, providing support to officials, policy research organizations, and grassroots advocacy groups striving to make state and local economic development subsidies more accountable and effective. She has co-authored several studies that promote economic development policies that meet workers' needs and advocate for greater corporate accountability. Previously, she worked as a legislative aide for Wisconsin State Rep. Jennifer Shilling. Her work has been referenced in the *New York Times* and other newspapers. Walter earned a master's degree in urban planning and policy from the University of Illinois at Chicago.

Lightning Source UK Ltd.
Milton Keynes UK
UKOW04n0621161217
314508UK00012B/1059/P

9 780739 190784